普通高等教育"十一五"国家级规划教材

21 世纪高等学校精品规划教材

电子商务专业英语
（第二版）

主　编　孙建忠　　白凤仙

副主编　岳　鹤　宋　敏　王社伟

中国水利水电出版社
www.waterpub.com.cn

内 容 提 要

本书是普通高等教育"十一五"国家级规划教材。

本书第一版于 2004 年出版，第二版在延续第一版编写风格的基础上，为更好地适应教学改革需求，考虑电子商务技术的发展，根据广大读者使用的反馈和作者多年讲授该课程的教学经验，在保持第一版教材编写风格的基础上，对各章节的内容、结构等进行了修订、调整、完善和补充。全书共 14 章，主要内容包括：电子商务的基本概念、电子商务的技术基础、电子商务模式、B2B 电子商务、电子支付系统、电子商务安全、电子商务定价、网络营销、电子商务法律问题、电子物流、建设成功的网上企业、建立电子商务应用以及案例分析等。本书内容覆盖了当今电子商务技术的各个方面，并力求体现电子商务的最新发展。

本书所有内容均取材于最近几年国外出版的原版教材和互联网，内容新颖，系统性强。每一章都围绕一个主题，配有学习指导、详细注释和参考译文以及精心安排的练习，可以使学生很快掌握课文要点。每章还介绍一个专业英语学习专题，帮助读者掌握专业英语的阅读、翻译和写作技巧。

本书既可作为高等院校电子商务及相关专业电子商务专业英语教材，也可用作管理与技术人员了解并学习电子商务知识的参考书。

本书课后练习的参考答案、课文的参考译文以及电子教案，均可从中国水利水电出版社以 及 万 水 书 苑 网 站 下 载 ， 网 址 为 ： http://www.waterpub.com.cn/softdown/ 和 http://www.wsbookshow.com。

图书在版编目（CIP）数据

电子商务专业英语 / 孙建忠，白凤仙主编. -- 2版
. -- 北京：中国水利水电出版社，2009.10

普通高等教育"十一五"国家级规划教材. 21世纪高
等学校精品规划教材

ISBN 978-7-5084-6934-8

Ⅰ. ①电… Ⅱ. ①孙… ②白… Ⅲ. ①电子商务－英
语－高等学校－教材 Ⅳ. ①H31

中国版本图书馆CIP数据核字(2009)第195560号

策划编辑：雷顺加　责任编辑：庞永江　加工编辑：谢琛　封面设计：李佳

书　　名	普通高等教育"十一五"国家级规划教材 21世纪高等学校精品规划教材 电子商务专业英语（第二版）
作　　者	主编 孙建忠　白凤仙　副主编 岳鹤　宋敏　王社伟
出版发行	中国水利水电出版社 （北京市海淀区玉渊潭南路 1 号 D 座　100038） 网址：www.waterpub.com.cn E-mail: mchannel@263.net（万水） 　　　　sales@waterpub.com.cn 电话：(010) 68367658（营销中心）、82562819（万水）
经　　售	全国各地新华书店和相关出版物销售网点
排　　版	北京万水电子信息有限公司
印　　刷	北京蓝空印刷厂
规　　格	184mm×260mm　16 开本　17 印张　424 千字
版　　次	2004 年 1 月第 1 版 2009 年 10 月第 2 版　2009 年 10 月第 3 次印刷
印　　数	10001—14000 册
定　　价	28.00 元

序

　　自 20 世纪 90 年代中后期以来，随着互联网的飞速发展，电子商务无疑已成为最热门的课题之一。世界各地都非常重视电子商务的应用与研究，高等院校更是如此。近两三年来，为了促进我国电子商务的发展，我国以高等院校为主体出版了大量的电子商务方面的教材和著作，这对于我国开展电子商务、培养电子商务方面的专业人才大有益处。但大多数教材还主要集中于中文翻译或中文改编版本的层面上。随着我国高等教育国际化的发展，越来越多的高校开始重视中英文双语教学，为此一些高校引进了部分英文原版或影印版教材，这些教材在受到师生欢迎的同时也面临着一些新的问题，如与我国实际结合不紧、内容选择单一、难度不易掌握、教学量难于控制、过多的专业词汇不利于学生自学等。为此，一些从事双语教学的高校教师根据形势的需要，结合自身的教学实践，编写出了新一代的专业英语教材，以更好地满足新时期高校双语教学，这些都是很有意义的尝试。由孙建忠、王斌主编，白凤仙、鲍玉昆副主编的《电子商务专业英语》（本科版）就是其中之一。其实，由孙建忠、王斌、白凤仙等合编的《电子商务专业英语》（高职高专版）已于 2003 年元月出版，并且受到了读者的好评。本科版教材吸取了原高职高专版的编写经验，参阅了大量最新出版的电子商务著作与文献资料，结合在武汉部分高校开展的双语教学实践，突出了如下特点：

- 注重教材的可读性与知识性的统一，所选课文不仅有一定的趣味性，而且专业性强、难度适中。
- 注重教材的知识面与内容新颖性的统一，所选课文既覆盖了电子商务领域的各个方面，又反映了电子商务的最新发展、难度适中。
- 本书增加了科技论文英文写作、商务英文信函写作、构词法、阅读难点分析等四个专题，有助于学生熟悉和掌握电子商务英语的必要技能，扩大知识面。

　　本教科书主要适合普通高等院校电子商务方向的本科生，也可供研究生和电子商务专业人士参考。

华中科技大学管理学院院长　张金隆教授（博导）
2003 年 10 月

第二版前言

本书是普通高等教育"十一五"国家级规划教材，是用英语编写的电子商务技术教材。本书第一版于 2004 年出版后得到了广大读者的热心支持，为了更好地适应教学改革的需求，考虑电子商务技术的发展，根据广大读者使用的反馈和作者多年讲授该课程的教学经验，在保持第一版教材编写风格的基础上，进行了改版，对各章节的内容、结构等进行了修订、调整、完善和补充。

改版后主要突出以下特点：

- 注重专业知识的系统性，贯彻知识面与内容新颖性统一的原则，所选课文既覆盖了电子商务领域的各个方面，又力求反映电子商务的最新发展，以满足新时期高校双语教学的需要；
- 注重教材的可读性与知识性的统一，所选课文既有一定的趣味性，又专业性强、难度适中；
- 紧密结合我国实际，增加了有关国内电子商务发展和典型案例等内容；
- 针对中国学生的特点，增加了科技论文英文写作、商务英文信函写作、构词法、阅读难点分析等专题，有助于学生切实掌握电子商务英语的必要技能。
- 注重专业技能培养，每章练习题除覆盖相应知识点外，还有一定的创新性实践作业，引导学生查阅最新的文献资料，掌握学科前沿；鼓励学生正确运用专业知识，进行分析案例、设计电子商务策略等。

本书的编写目的首先是让学生掌握电子商务的基本定义和术语，了解电子商务的专业基础知识，学会电子商务英语基本的表达与翻译；其次是介绍电子商务领域的一些最新发展。全书共 14 章，主要内容包括：电子商务的基本概念、电子商务的技术基础、电子商务模式、B2B 电子商务、电子支付系统、电子商务安全、电子商务定价、网络营销、电子商务法律问题、电子物流、建设成功的网上企业、建立电子商务应用以及案例分析等。

本书所有内容均取材于最近几年国外出版的原版教材和互联网，内容新颖，系统性强。每一章都围绕一个主题，配有学习指导、详细注释和参考译文以及精心安排的练习，可以使学生很快掌握课文要点。每章还介绍一个专业英语学习专题，帮助读者掌握专业英语的阅读、翻译和写作技巧。

本书既可作为高等院校电子商务及相关专业电子商务专业英语教材，也可用作管理与技术人员了解并学习电子商务知识的参考书。

本书由大连理工大学孙建忠教授和白凤仙副教授主编，河南工业大学岳鹤老师、宋敏老师、王社伟老师任副主编。主要编写人员具体分工为：第 1、5 章由宋敏编写，第 2、3、4 章由白凤仙编写，第 6、13 章由王社伟编写，第 7、9、12、14 章由岳鹤编写，第 8、10、11 章与各章专题由孙建忠编写，孙建忠还负责全书的统稿工作，并对各章内容进行了修订。华中科技大学鲍玉昆副教授（博士）、大连理工大学姚卫红副教授参加了部分内容编写和讨论。此外，研究生刘然、刘博强、许伟、罗雅琴、李默竹、王博等同学参与了本书部分文字录入和绘图等工作。

本书第一版承蒙华中科技大学张金隆教授和蔡淑琴教授对教材大纲提出了建设性的意见，对第二版编写仍有很高的指导意义，在此表示由衷的感谢！北京市、上海市、大连市、广州市、武汉市、郑州市等部分高校的学生参加了本书的教学改革工作，在此一并致谢。

由于作者水平有限，加之编写时间仓促，本书在编写过程中难免出现疏漏，恳请读者不吝赐教。联系地址：sjzbfx@163.com

编者
2009 年 10 月

第一版前言

随着 21 世纪的到来和中国加入 WTO，电子商务在我国必将迅速发展。电子商务不仅为我们带来了全新的商业和经营理念，带来了无限商机，也为我们带来了巨大的挑战。电子商务打破了国界的限制，它不仅对信息基础设施、法律体系提出了更高的要求，也需要人们更新观念与意识，提高人力资源能力，而语言能力就是一个重要的方面。由于诸多原因，国际上最通用的语言还是英语。而因特网的普及，更巩固了英语作为跨文化交往通用语言的地位。为了更好地迎接电子商务的挑战，必须具备较高的英语水平。

本书是 21 世纪高等院校电子商务专业英语教材，本书的编写目的，首先是让学生掌握电子商务专业英语的基本定义和术语，了解电子商务的专业基础知识，学会电子商务英语基本的表达与翻译；其次是介绍了电子商务领域的一些最新发展。

本书根据现阶段我国电子商务学科的教学特点，精心组织，合理选材。本书内容全部取自国外电子商务教材、专著、报告以及权威网站资料，并由编者进行了必要的改编。本书主要内容包括：电子商务起源与模型、因特网与环球网基础、EDI、在线支付、移动电子商务、电子商务安全、法律与税收问题、电子客户关系管理、电子商务各种模式、电子商务策略、电子物流、网络营销、动态定价、电子政务、案例分析等内容。考虑到读者的需要，我们还系统而扼要地介绍了电子商务词汇构成规律、电子商务专业英语的阅读翻译技巧、学术论文的英文写作和商务信函的英文写作等四个专题。本书的练习答案、课文的参考译文以及专题内容均可从中国水利水电出版社网站（www.waterpub.com.cn）下载。

在本书的编写过程中，华中科技大学管理学院院长、电子商务方向的博士生导师张金隆教授对教材大纲提出了建设性的意见，并欣然为本书作序。张金隆教授与华中科技大学蔡淑琴教授（电子商务方向博士生导师）在百忙之中为本书进行主审，编者在此向两位教授表示衷心的感谢。武汉市部分院校的同学参与了本书的部分教学实践工作，在此一并致谢。

本书第 1、2、3、5、6、7、9、10、11 章由大连理工大学白凤仙老师编写，第 4、12、15、16 章及专题 4 由王斌博士编写，第 8、13、14、18 章由华中科技大学鲍玉昆副教授（博士）编写，第 17 章与专题 1、2、3 由大连理工大学孙建忠教授（博士）编写，孙建忠还负责全书的统稿工作，并对各章内容进行了修订。

由于作者水平有限，加之编写时间仓促，本书在编写过程中难免出现疏漏，恳请读者不吝赐教。联系地址：sjzbfx@163.com 或 icekingp@yahoo.com.cn

编 者

2003 年 10 月

目　　录

Chapter 1　Introduction to E-Commerce

当今，电子商务正在以前所未有的力量冲击着人们千百年来形成的商务观念与模式，是企业实现跨越式发展的必然选择。通过本章的学习，读者应该掌握以下内容：

学习指导

- 什么是电子商务，以及它在成长过程中所经历的二次浪潮。
- 企业在实施电子商务时，为何专注于盈利模式和业务流程的分析，而不是商业模式。
- 经济因素如何产生了培育电子商务第二次浪潮的商业环境？
- 企业如何使用价值链和 SWOT 分析来发现电子商务的机遇。
- 电子商务的国际化性质以及在全球范围内开展电子商务时企业所面临的挑战。
- 掌握有关专用术语及缩略语。

1.1　Introduction

Very few people in the United States truly enjoy their hunt for a new or used car. Although many auto dealers have worked to improve their customers' experiences by introducing fixed pricing and "no-haggle" policies, a number of auto dealers continue to use aggressive sales approaches that can leave buyers exhausted, confused, or even worried that they might have been cheated in the transaction. In 1995, Autobytel (Autobytel's URL is http://www.autobytel.com) launched an online car-buying service that promised purchasers a haggle-free experience and offered car dealers a way to increase new vehicle sales volumes and reduce selling costs.

Buying a car with the assistance of Autobytel requires that the buyer register with an Autobytel Website and specify the desired auto in detail, usually after researching the vehicle's options and features on the Internet or by visiting local dealers. More than 95 percent of car buyers today do research on the Internet before buying their cars. Autobytel provides the buyer with a firm price quote for the selected car, then forwards the buyer's contact information to a local participating dealer. Dealers pay Autobytel a subscription fee to receive exclusive rights to referrals from a particular geographic area for the brands of vehicles that they sell. The dealer contacts the buyer, who then completes the purchase transaction at the dealer's location.

The buyer benefits from a speedy, hassle-free, straight forward, and predictable buying process. The dealer benefits by selling more automobiles and not paying a commission to a salesperson. Autobytel receives a monthly subscription fee from each dealer that it has under contract and sells advertising to insurance and finance companies on its Web site. Autobytel currently has contracts with more than 20,000 auto dealers. Autobytel's revenue from fees paid by auto dealers on these transactions is more than $70 million per year (the company earns another $20 million each year by selling advertising on its Web site and marketing services to car dealers). Internet sales referrals to dealers from Autobytel and companies like it accounted for about 30 percent of all U.S. new vehicle sales in 2007.

Autobytel experienced rapid growth in sales from its inception in 1995 through 2002, when sales growth flattened. Like many other companies launched during the early boom years of electronic commerce, Autobytel had to change its focus. Instead of pursuing a strategy of revenue growth at all costs, it began to examine its costs carefully. The company also took steps to improve the quality of its service by ending relationships with a number of dealers who were generating significant numbers of customer complaints. Since 2004, Autobytel has expanded by buying other companies and offering sales management services and software to auto dealers. Autobytel has emerged from the difficult years of 2001 through 2003 and today is a growing and generally profitable participant in the second wave of electronic commerce that you will learn about in this chapter.

New Words & Phrases

dealer   n. 商人，经销商

exhausted   adj. 耗尽的，疲惫的

sales volume   销售量

brand   n. 商标

subscription fee 入网费，加盟费

inception   n. 开始，开端

electronic commerce 电子商务

boom   n. 繁荣

no-haggle 不砍价

transaction   n. 交易，事务

exclusive right 专有权，专营权利

benefits from 通过……获益

revenue   n. 收入，收益

flatten   v. 变平

pursue   vt. 追求

emerged from 露出，浮现

Notes

1. Dealers pay Autobytel a subscription fee to receive exclusive rights to referrals from a particular geographic area for the brands of vehicles that they sell. 译为 "经销商付费给 Autobytel 以便获得 Autobytel 只把自己推荐给特定区域顾客的权利。"

2. Internet sales referrals to dealers from Autobytel and companies like it accounted for about 30 percent of all U.S. new vehicle sales in 2007. 译为 "Autobytel 公司和类似于 Autobytel 的公司在网上的汽车销量已占全美新车销量的 30%。"

1.2   Electronic Commerce: The Second Wave

The business phenomenon that we now call electronic commerce has had an interesting history. From humble beginnings in the mid-1990s, electronic commerce grew rapidly until 2000, when a major downturn occurred. Many people have seen news stories about the "dot-com boom" followed by the "dot-com bust" or the "dot-bomb". In the period from 2000 to 2003, many industry observers were writing obituaries for electronic commerce. Just as the unreasonable expectations for immediate success fueled the high expectations during the boom years, overly gloomy news reports colored perceptions during this time. Beginning in 2003, with the general economy still in the doldrums, electronic commerce began to show signs of new life. Companies that had survived the downturn were not only seeing growth in sales again, but many of them were showing profits. Although the rapid expansion and high levels of investment of the boom years are not likely to be repeated, the second wave of electronic commerce is well under way. This section defines electronic commerce and describes how it is growing once again in its second wave.

1.2.1　Electronic Commerce and Electronic Business

To many people, the term "electronic commerce" means shopping on the part of the Internet called the World Wide Web (the Web). However, electronic commerce (or e-commerce) also includes many other activities, such as businesses trading with other businesses and internal processes that companies use to support their buying, selling, hiring, planning, and other activities. Some people use the term electronic business (or e-business) when they are talking about electronic commerce in this broader sense. For example, IBM defines electronic business as "the transformation of key business processes through the use of Internet technologies". Most people use the terms "electronic commerce" and "electronic business" interchangeably. In this book, the term electronic commerce (or e-commerce) is used in its broadest sense and includes all business activities that use Internet technologies. Internet technologies include the Internet, the World Wide Web, and other technologies such as wireless transmissions on mobile telephones or **personal digital assistants** (**PDA**s). Companies that operate only online are often called dot-com or pure dot-com businesses to distinguish them from companies that operate in physical locations (solely or together with online operations).

1.2.2　Categories of Electronic Commerce

Some people find it useful to categorize electronic commerce by the types of entities participating in the transactions or business processes. The five general electronic commerce categories are **business-to-consumer**, **business-to-business**, **business processes**, **consumer-to-consumer**, and **business-to-government**. The three categories that are most commonly used are:
　　• Consumer shopping on the Web, often called business-to-consumer (or **B2C**).
　　• Transactions conducted between businesses on the Web, often called business-to-business (or B2B).
　　• Transactions and business processes in which companies, governments, and other organizations use Internet technologies to support selling and purchasing activities.
　　Some researchers define a fourth category of electronic commerce, called **consumer-to-consumer** (or **C2C**), which includes individuals who buy and sell items among themselves. For example, C2C electronic commerce occurs when a person sells an item through a Web auction site to

another person. In some books, C2C sales are included in the B2C category because the person selling the item acts much as a business would for purposes of the transaction.

Finally, some researchers also define a category of electronic commerce called **business-to-government** (or **B2G**); this category includes business transactions with government agencies, such as paying taxes and filing required reports. An increasing number of states have Web sites that help companies do business with state government agencies. For example, the CA.gov Procurement site makes it easy for businesses to conduct online transactions with the state of California. In some books, B2G transactions are included in our discussions of B2B electronic commerce. Table 1-1 summarizes these five categories of electronic commerce.

Table 1-1　Electronic commerce categories

Category	Description	Example
Business-to-consumer (B2C)	Businesses sell products or services to individual consumers	Walmart.com sells merchandise to consumers through its Web site
Business-to-business (B2B)	Businesses sell products or services to other businesses	Grainger.com sells industrial supplies to large and small businesses through its Web site
Business processes that support buying and selling activities	Businesses and other organizations maintain and use information to identify and evaluate customers, suppliers, and employees. Increasingly, businesses share this information in carefully managed ways with their customers, suppliers, employees, and business partners	Dell Computer uses secure Internet connections to share current sales and sales forecast information with suppliers. The suppliers can use this information to plan their own production and deliver component parts to Dell in the right quantities at the right time
Consumer-to-consumer (C2C)	Participants in an online marketplace can buy and sell goods to each other.	Consumers and businesses trade with each other in the eBay.com online marketplace
Business-to-government (B2G)	Businesses sell goods or services to governments and government agencies	CA.Gov procurement site allows businesses to sell online to the state of California

1.2.3　The Second Wave of Electronic Commerce

Economists Chris Freeman and Francisco Louçã describe four waves that occurred in the Industrial Revolution in their book *As Time Goes By*. Many researchers predict that electronic commerce and the information revolution brought about by the Internet will go through similar waves. Those researchers agree that the second wave of electronic commerce has begun. This section outlines the defining characteristics of the first wave of electronic commerce and describes how the second wave is different.

The first wave of electronic commerce was predominantly a U.S. phenomenon. Web pages were primarily in English, particularly on commerce sites. The second wave is characterized by its international scope, with sellers doing business in many countries and in many languages. Language translation and currency conversion are two impediments to the efficient conduct of global business in the second wave.

In the first wave, easy access to start-up capital led to an overemphasis on creating new large enterprises to exploit electronic commerce opportunities. Investors were excited about electronic commerce and wanted to participate, no matter how much it cost or how weak the underlying ideas were. In the second wave, established companies are using their own internal funds to finance gradual expansion of electronic commerce opportunities. These measured and carefully considered investments are helping electronic commerce grow more steadily, though more slowly.

The Internet technologies used in the first wave, especially in B2C commerce, were slow and inexpensive. Most consumers connected the Internet using dial-up modems. The increase in broadband connections in homes is a key element in the B2C component of the second wave. In 2004, the number of U.S. homes with broadband connections began to increase rapidly. Most industry estimates showed that about 12 percent of U.S. homes had broadband connections in early 2004. By late 2007, those estimates were ranging between 40 and 50 percent. Other countries, such as South Korea, subsidize their citizens' Internet access and have an even higher rate of broadband usage. Although these connections are more expensive, they are more than 10 times faster than dial-up. This increased speed not only makes Internet use more efficient, it can alter the way people use the Web. For example, a broadband connection allows a user to watch movies and television programs online—something that is impossible to do with a dial-up connection.

In the first wave, Internet technologies were integrated into B2B transactions and internal business processes by using bar codes and scanners to track parts, assemblies, inventories, and production status. These tracking technologies were not well integrated. Also, companies sent transaction information to each other using a patchwork of communication methods, including **fax**, **e-mail**, and **EDI**. In the second wave, **Radio Frequency Identification** (**RFID**) devices and smart cards are being combined with biometric technologies, such as fingerprint readers and retina scanners, to control more items and people in a wider variety of situations. These technologies are increasingly integrated with each other and with communication systems that allow companies to communicate with each other and share transaction, inventory level, and customer demand information effectively.

The use of electronic mail (or e-mail) in the first wave was as a tool for relatively unstructured communication. In the second wave, sellers are using e-mail as an integral part of their marketing and customer contact strategies.

Online advertising was the main intended revenue source of many failed dot-com businesses in the first wave. After a two-year dip in online advertising activity and revenues, companies began the second wave with a renewed interest in making the Internet work as an effective advertising medium. Some categories of online advertising, such as employment services (job wanted ads) are growing rapidly and are replacing traditional advertising outlets. Companies such as Google have devised ways of delivering specific ads to Internet users who are most likely to be interested in the products or services offered by those ads.

The sale of digital products was fraught with difficulties during the first wave of electronic commerce. The music recording industry was unable (or, some would say, unwilling) to devise a way to distribute digital music on the Web. This created an environment in which digital piracy—the theft of musical artists' intellectual property—became rampant. The promise of electronic books was also unfulfilled. The second wave is fulfilling the promise of available technology by supporting the legal distribution of music, video, and other digital products on the Web. Apple Computer's iTunes Web site is an example of a second wave digital product distribution business that is meeting the needs of consumers and its industry.

Not all of the future of electronic commerce is based in its second wave. Some of the most successful first-wave companies, such as Amazon.com, eBay, and Yahoo! continue to thrive by offering increasingly innovative products and services. The second wave of electronic commerce will provide new opportunities for these businesses, too.

New Words & Phrases

phenomenon   n. 现象

downturn   n. （价格或活动）开始下降

bomb   v. 轰炸，失败

gloomy   adj. 黑暗的，令人沮丧的

in the doldrums 意气消沉，无精打采

transformation   n. 转型，转变

wireless transmissions 无线传输

characteristics   n. 特性，特征

currency conversion 外汇汇兑

start-up   n. 启动

overemphasis   n. 过分的强调

underlying   adj. 根本的，潜在的

be integrated into 统一到……中

assembly   n. 装配，组装

patchwork   n. 拼凑物

fingerprint reader 指纹读取器

dip   n. 凹陷处

devise   vt. 想出；计划；设计；发明

music recording industry 唱片业

intellectual property 知识产权

thrive   vi. 兴盛，兴隆

humble   adj. 谦逊的，卑微的

bust   v. 打破，打碎

obituary   n. 讣告，讣闻

perception   n. 感知，观念

under way 已经开始并进行着

interchangeably   adv. 可交地，可替交地

business processes 业务流程

predominantly   adv. 主要地，显著地，突出地

impediment   n. 妨碍、阻碍某事物进展的人或物

capital   n. 资金，资本

exploit   vt. 开发，开采

subsidize vt. 给……津贴或补贴，资助或补助……

bar codes   n. 条形码

inventory   n. 详细目录，存货清单

biometric technology   生物技术，生物辨识技术

retina   n. 视网膜

renewed   adj. 复兴的，重申的

fraught   adj. 充满着不愉快的事情的

piracy   n. 盗版，非法翻印

rampant   adj. 猖獗的

innovative   adj. 新发明的，新引进的，革新的

Abbreviations

e-commerce(electronic commerce) 电子商务

PDA (personal digital assistants) 掌上电脑

B2C(business-to-consumer) 企业与消费者间电子商务

B2B(business-to-business) 企业间电子商务

C2C(consumer-to-consumer) 消费者间的电子商务

B2G(business-to-government) 企业与政府间的电子商务

EDI(Electronic Data Interchange) 电子数据交换，无纸贸易

RFID(Radio Frequency Identification) 射频识别

e-mail(electronic mail) 电子邮件

Notes

1. Just as the unreasonable expectations for immediate success fueled the high expectations during the boom years, overly gloomy news reports colored perceptions during this time. "就好像在泡沫年代突然地成功激起了不切实际的期望一样，此时媒体报道的色彩又过分灰暗。"

2. An increasing number of states have Web sites that help companies do business with state government agencies.本句中的 that 引导定语从句，用来修饰 Web sites。译为"美国有越来越多的州建立了网站来帮助企业和政府机构进行交易。"

3. This created an environment in which digital piracy—the theft of musical artists' intellectual property—became rampant. 本句中"the theft of musical artists' intellectual property"是对"digital piracy"的进一步说明。译为"这就产生了数字盗版——侵犯音乐家知识产权——十分猖獗的环境。"

1.3   Business Models, Revenue Models, and Business Processes

A business model is a set of processes that combine to achieve a company's goal, which is to yield a profit. In the first wave of electronic commerce, many investors sought out start-up companies with appealing business models. A good business model was expected to lead to rapid sales growth and market dominance. The idea that the key to success was simply to copy the business model of a successful dot-com business led the way to many business failures, some of them quite dramatic.

Copying or adapting someone else's business model is neither an easy nor wise road map to success. Instead, companies should examine the elements of their business; that is, they should identify business processes that they can streamline, enhance, or replace with processes driven by Internet technologies.

Companies and investors do still use the idea of a revenue model, which is a specific collection of business processes used to identify customers, market to those customers, and generate sales to those customers. The revenue model idea is helpful for classifying revenue- generating activities for communication and analysis purposes.

1.3.1   Focus on Specific Business Processes

In addition to the revenue model grouping of business processes, companies think of the rest of their operations as specific business processes. Those processes include purchasing raw materials or goods for resale, converting materials and labor into finished goods, managing transportation and logistics, hiring and training employees, managing the finances of the business, and many other activities.

In some cases, business processes use traditional commerce activities very effectively, and technology cannot improve them. Products that buyers prefer to touch, smell, or examine closely can be difficult to sell using electronic commerce. For example, customers might be reluctant to buy items that have an important element of tactile feel or condition such as high-fashion clothing (you cannot touch it online and subtle color variations that are hard to distinguish on a computer monitor can make a large difference) or antique jewelry (for which elements of condition that require close inspection can be critical to value) if they cannot closely examine the products before agreeing to purchase them.

1.3.2　Product/Process Suitability to Electronic Commerce

One business process that is especially well suited to electronic commerce is the selling of commodity items. A commodity item is a product or service that is hard to distinguish from the same products or services provided by other sellers; its features have become standardized and well known. Gasoline, office supplies, soap, computers, and airline transportation are all examples of commodity products or services, as are the books and CDs sold by Amazon.com.

Another key factor that can make an item well suited to electronic commerce is the product's shipping profile. A product's shipping profile is the collection of attributes that affect how easily that product can be packaged and delivered. A high value-to-weight ratio can help by making the overall shipping cost a small fraction of the selling price. An airline ticket is an excellent example of an item that has a high value-to-weight ratio. Products that are consistent in size, shape, and weight can make warehousing and shipping much simpler and less costly. The shipping profile is only one factor, however. Expensive jewelry has a high value-to-weight ratio, but many people are reluctant to buy it without examining it in person unless the jewelry is sold under a well-known brand name and with a generous return policy.

A combination of electronic and traditional commerce strategies works best when the business process includes both commodity and personal inspection elements.

New Words & Phrases

business model　商业模型
dominance　n. 优势；支配地位；控制力
streamline　vt. 简化使效率更高
logistics　n. 物流
antique　n. 古董

yield　v. 生产，出产，带来
dramatic　adj. 戏剧性的
revenue model　盈利模式
tactile　adj. 触觉的，触觉感知的
profile　n. 轮廓，外形

Notes

1. The idea that the key to success was simply to copy the business model of a successful dot-com business led

the way to many business failures, some of them quite dramatic. 句子的主干是 "The idea……led the way to……", 句中的 "that" 引导定语从句, 修饰 "idea"。本句译为 "认为成功的关键就是简单地模仿成功的.com 公司的想法导致了许多企业的失败, 其中有些公司十分具有戏剧性。"

2. Companies and investors do still use the idea of a revenue model, which is a specific collection of business processes used to identify customers, market to those customers, and generate sales to those customers.句中的 "do" 起强调作用, "which" 引导非限定性定语从句, 用来修饰 "revenue model"。本句译为 "企业和投资者当前依然在使用盈利模式的思想, 即用于识别客户、向其推销并从中获取收益的业务流程的集合。"

3. A commodity item is a product or service that is hard to distinguish from the same products or services provided by other sellers. 句中"that"引导定语从句, 用来修饰"a product or service", "provided by other sellers" 是过去分词做定语, 修饰 "products or services"。本句译为 "这里的商品是指不同商家提供的同类产品或服务很难加以区分。"

1.4   Economic Forces and Electronic Commerce

Economics is the study of how people allocate scarce resources. One important way that people allocate resources is through commerce (the other major way is through government actions, such as taxes or subsidies). Many economists are interested in how people organize their commerce activities. One way people do this is to participate in markets. Economists use a formal definition of **market** that includes two conditions: first, that the potential sellers of a good come into contact with potential buyers, and second, that a medium of exchange is available. This medium of exchange can be currency or barter. Most economists agree that markets are strong and effective mechanisms for allocating scarce resources. Thus, one would expect most business transactions to occur within markets. However, much business activity today occurs within large hierarchical business organizations, which economists generally refer to as **firms**, or **companies**.

These large firms often conduct many different business activities entirely within the organizational structure of the firm and participate in markets only for purchasing raw materials and selling finished products. If markets are indeed highly effective mechanisms for allocating scarce resources, these large corporations should participate in markets at every stage of their production and value-generation processes. Nobel laureate Ronald Coase wrote an essay in 1937 in which he questioned why individuals who engaged in commerce often created firms to organize their activities. He was particularly interested in the hierarchical structure of these business organizations. Coase concluded that transaction costs were the main motivation for moving economic activity from markets to hierarchically structured firms.

1.4.1   Transaction Costs

Transaction costs are the total of all costs that a buyer and seller incur as they gather information and negotiate a purchase-and-sale transaction. Although brokerage fees and sales commissions can be a part of transaction costs, the cost of information search and acquisition is

often far larger. Another significant component of transaction costs can be the investment a seller makes in equipment or in the hiring of skilled employees to supply the product or service to the buyer.

1.4.2 Markets and Hierarchies

Coase reasoned that when transaction costs were high, businesspeople would form organizations to replace market-negotiated transactions. These organizations would be hierarchical and would include strong supervision and worker-monitoring elements.

<u>The practice of an existing firm replacing one or more of its supplier markets with its own hierarchical structure for creating the supplied product is called **vertical integration**.</u>

1.4.3 Using Electronic Commerce to Reduce Transaction Costs

Businesses and individuals can use electronic commerce to reduce transaction costs by improving the flow of information and increasing the coordination of actions. By reducing the cost of searching for potential buyers and sellers and increasing the number of potential market participants, electronic commerce can change the attractiveness of vertical integration for many firms.

To see how electronic commerce can change the level and nature of transaction costs, consider an employment transaction. The agreement to employ a person has high transaction costs for the seller—the employee who sells his or her services. These transaction costs include a commitment to forego other employment and career development opportunities. Individuals make a high investment in learning and adapting to the culture of their employers. If accepting the job involves a move, the employee can incur very high costs, including actual costs of the move and related costs, such as the loss of a spouse's job. Much of the employee's investment is specific to a particular job and location; the employee cannot transfer the investment to a new job.

If a sufficient number of employees throughout the world can telecommute, then many of these transaction costs could be reduced or eliminated. Instead of uprooting a spouse and family to move, a worker could accept a new job by simply logging on to a different company server!

1.4.4 Network Effects

Economists have found that most activities yield less value as the amount of consumption increases. For example, a person who consumes one hamburger obtains a certain amount of value from that consumption. As the person consumes more hamburgers, the value provided by each hamburger decreases. Few people find the fifth hamburger as enjoyable as the first. This characteristic of economic activity is called the law of diminishing returns. In networks, an interesting exception to the law of diminishing returns occurs. As more people or organizations participate in a network, the value of the network to each participant increases. This increase in value is called a network effect.

1.4.5 Using Electronic Commerce to Create Network Effects

Your e-mail account, which gives you access to a network of other people with e-mail accounts, is an example of a network effect. If your e-mail account were part of a small network, it would be less valuable than it is. Most people today have e-mail accounts that are part of the Internet. In the early days of e-mail, most e-mail accounts only connected people in the same company or organization to each other. Internet e-mail accounts are far more valuable than single-organization e-mail accounts because of the network effect.

New Words & Phrases

scarce	adj. 缺乏的，罕见的	barter	n. 物物交换，易货
firm	n. 公司	mechanism	n. 机制
motivation	n. 动机，诱因	incur	vt. 遭受；招致，引起
brokerage	n. 经纪业，佣金，经纪费	coordination	n. 协调，和谐
forego	vt. 走在…之前，居先	telecommute	vi. 远程办公
uprooting	n. 倒根，挖除伐根	network effect	网络效应
diminishing returns	收益递减		

Notes

1. The practice of an existing firm replacing one or more of its supplier markets with its own hierarchical structure for creating the supplied product is called vertical integration. 译为"现有的公司建立等级制的结构来生产自己所需要的产品以代替供应商市场的做法称为垂直一体化。"

1.5　Identifying Electronic Commerce Opportunities

Internet technologies can be used to improve so many business processes that it can be difficult for managers to decide where and how to use them. One way to focus on specific business processes as candidates for electronic commerce is to break the business down into a series of value-adding activities that combine to generate profits and meet other goals of the firm.

Commerce is conducted by firms of all sizes. Smaller firms can focus on one product, distribution channel, or type of customer. Larger firms often sell many different products and services through a variety of distribution channels to several types of customers. In these larger firms, managers organize their work around the activities of strategic business units. Multiple business units owned by a common set of shareholders make up a firm, or company, and multiple firms that sell similar products to similar customers make up an **industry**.

1.5.1 Strategic Business Unit Value Chains

In his 1985 book, *Competitive Advantage*, Michael Porter introduced the idea of **value chains**. A value chain is a way of organizing the activities that each strategic business unit undertakes to design, produce, promote, market, deliver, and support the products or services it sells. In addition to these **primary activities**, Porter also includes **supporting activities**, such as human resource management and purchasing, in the value chain model.

1.5.2 Industry Value Chains

Porter's book also identifies the importance of examining where the strategic business unit fits within its industry. Porter uses the term **value system** to describe the larger stream of activities into which a particular business unit's value chain is embedded. However, many subsequent researchers and business consultants have used the term **industry value chain** when referring to value systems. When a business unit delivers a product to its customer, that customer may, for example, use the product as purchased materials in its value chain. By becoming aware of how other business units in the industry value chain conduct their activities, managers can identify new opportunities for cost reduction, product improvement, or channel reconfiguration.

As they examine their industry value chains, many managers are finding that they can use electronic commerce and Internet technologies to reduce costs, improve product quality, reach new customers or suppliers, and create new ways of selling existing products. For example, a software developer who releases annual updates to programs might consider removing the software retailer from the distribution channel for software updates by offering to send the updates through the Internet directly to the consumer. This change would modify the software developer's industry value chain and would provide an opportunity for increasing sales revenue (the software developer could retain the margin a retailer would have added to the price of the update), but it would not appear as part of the software developer business unit value chain. By examining elements of the value chain outside the individual business unit, managers can identify many business opportunities, including those that can be exploited using electronic commerce.

The value chain concept is a useful way to think about business strategy in general. When firms are considering electronic commerce, the value chain can be an excellent way to organize the examination of business processes within their business units and in other parts of the product's life cycle. Using the value chain reinforces the idea that electronic commerce should be a business solution, not a technology implemented for its own sake.

1.5.3 SWOT Analysis: Evaluating Business Unit Opportunities

Now that you have learned how to identify industry value chains and break each value chain down into strategic business units, you can learn one popular technique for analyzing and evaluating business opportunities. Most electronic commerce initiatives add value by either reducing transaction costs, creating some type of network effect, or a combination of both. In SWOT analysis (the acronym is short for strengths, weaknesses, opportunities, and threats), the analyst first looks into the business unit to identify its strengths and weaknesses. The analyst then reviews the environment in which the business unit operates and identifies opportunities presented by that environment and the threats posed by that environment. Figure1-1 shows questions that an analyst would ask in conducting a SWOT analysis.

Strengths	Weaknesses
• What does the company do well ? • Is the company strong in its market ? • Does the company have a strong sense of purpose and the culture to support that purpose ?	• What does the company do poorly ? • What problems could be avoided ? • Does the company have serious financial liabilities ?
Opportunities	**Threats**
• Are industry trends moving upward ? • Do new markets exist for the company's products/services ? • Are there new technologies that the company can exploit ?	• What are competitors doing well? • What obstacles does the company face ? • Are there troubling changes in the company's business environment(technologies, laws, and regulations) ?

Figure 1-1　SWOT analysis questions

By considering all of the issues that it faces in a systematic way, a business unit can formulate strategies to take advantage of its opportunities by building on its strengths, avoiding any threats, and compensating for its weaknesses. In the mid-1990s, Dell Computer used a SWOT analysis to create a business strategy that helped it become a strong competitor in its industry value chain. Dell identified its strengths in selling directly to customers and in designing its computers and other products to reduce manufacturing costs. It acknowledged the weakness of having no relationships with local computer dealers. Dell faced threats from competitors such as Compaq (now a part of Hewlett-Packard) and IBM, both of which had much stronger brand names and reputations for quality at that time. Dell identified an opportunity by noting that its customers were becoming more knowledgeable about computers and could specify exactly what they wanted without having Dell salespeople answer questions or develop configurations for them. It also saw the Internet as a potential marketing tool. The results of Dell's SWOT analysis appear in Figure 1-2.

The strategy that Dell followed after doing the analysis took all four of the SWOT elements into consideration. Dell decided to offer customized computers built to order and sold over the phone, and eventually, over the Internet. Dell's strategy capitalized on its strengths and avoided relying on a dealer network. The brand and quality threats posed by Compaq and IBM were lessened by Dell's ability to deliver higher perceived quality because each computer was custom made for each buyer. Ten years later, Dell observed that the environment of personal computer sales had changed and did start selling computers through dealers.

New Words & Phrases

shareholder　n. 股东　　　　　　　　　　industry　n. 行业
value chains　价值链　　　　　　　　　　primary activities 基本活动

Strengths	Weaknesses
• Sell directly to consumers • Keep costs below competitors' costs	• No strong relationships with computer retailers
Opportunities	**Threats**
• Consumer desire for one-stop shopping • Consumer know what they want to buy • Internet could be a powerful marketing tool	• Competitors have stronger brand names • Competitors have strong relationships with computer retailers

Figure 1-2　Results of Dell's SWOT analysis

supporting activities 辅助活动　　　　　　consultants　n. 顾问

life cycle 生命周期　　　　　　　　　　　formulate　vt. 构想出，规划

capitalized on 充分利用某事物

Abbreviations

SWOT(strengths, weaknesses, opportunities, and threats)　态势分析法（优势、劣势、机会、威胁）

Notes

1. A value chain is a way of organizing the activities that each strategic business unit undertakes to design, produce, promote, market, deliver, and support the products or services it sells. 句中"it sells"为定语从句，此处省略了"which"。本句译为"价值链是一种组织活动的方法，这些活动是策略性业务单位承担他所销售的产品或服务的设计、生产、促销、销售、运输和售后服务的活动。"

2. Porter uses the term value system to describe the larger stream of activities into which a particular business unit's value chain is embedded. 译为"波特使用术语价值系统来描述某个业务单位的价值链所嵌入的更大的业务活动流。"

3. For example, a software developer who releases annual updates to programs might consider removing the software retailer from the distribution channel for software updates by offering to send the updates through the Internet directly to the consumer. 句子的主干为"a software developer…might consider…"，"who"引导定语从句，修饰"developer"。本句译为"例如，每年都升级程序的软件开发商可能会考虑从分销渠道中去除软件零售商，转向通过互联网直接向用户提供软件升级。"

1.6　International Nature of Electronic Commerce

Because the Internet connects computers all over the world, any business that engages in electronic commerce instantly becomes an international business. When companies use the Web to improve a business process, they are automatically operating in a global environment. The key issues that any company faces when it conducts international commerce include trust and culture, language, and infrastructure. The related issues of international law and currency are covered in subsequent chapters.

1.6.1 Trust Issues on the Web

It is important for all businesses to establish trusting relationships with their customers. Companies with established reputations in the physical world often create trust by ensuring that customers know who they are. These businesses can rely on their established brand names to create trust on the Web. New companies that want to establish online businesses face a more difficult challenge because a kind of anonymity exists for companies trying to establish a Web presence.

Customers' inherent lack of trust in "strangers" on the Web is logical and to be expected; after all, people have been doing business with their neighbors—not strangers—for thousands of years. When a company grows to become a large corporation with multinational operations, its reputation grows commensurately. Before a company can do business in dozens of countries, it must prove its trustworthiness by satisfying customers for many years as it grows. Businesses on the Web must find ways to overcome this well-founded tradition of distrusting strangers, because today a company can incorporate one day and, through the Web, be doing business the next day with people all over the world. For businesses to succeed on the Web, they must find ways to quickly generate the trust that traditional businesses take years to develop.

1.6.2 Language Issues

Most companies realize that the only way to do business effectively in other cultures is to adapt to those cultures. The phrase "think globally, act locally" is often used to describe this approach. The first step that a Web business usually takes to reach potential customers in other countries, and thus in other cultures, is to provide local language versions of its Web site. This may mean translating the Web site into another language or regional dialect. Researchers have found that customers are far more likely to buy products and services from Web sites in their own language, even if they can read English well. Only about 400 million of the world's 6 billion people learned English as their native language.

The translation services and software manufacturers that work with electronic commerce sites do not generally use the term "translation" to describe what they do. They prefer the term "localization", which means a translation that considers multiple elements of the local environment, such as business and cultural practices, in addition to local dialect variations in the language. The cultural element is very important because it can affect—and sometimes completely change—the user's interpretation of text.

1.6.3 Cultural Issues

An important element of business trust is anticipating how the other party to a transaction will act in specific circumstances. A company's brand conveys expectations about how the company will behave, therefore companies with established brands can build online businesses more quickly and easily than a new company without a reputation. For example, a potential buyer might like to know how the seller would react to a claim by the buyer that the seller misrepresented the quality of the goods sold. Part of this knowledge derives from the buyer and seller sharing a common language and common customs. Business partners ideally have a common legal structure for resolving disputes. The combination of language and customs is often called culture. Most researchers agree that culture varies across national boundaries and, in many cases, varies across regions within nations. All companies must be aware of the differences in language and customs that make up the culture of any region in which they intend to do business.

Some errors stemming from subtle language and cultural standards have become classic examples that are regularly cited in international business courses and training sessions. For example, General Motors' choice of name for its Chevrolet Nova automobile amused people in Latin America—no va means "it will not go" in Spanish. Pepsi's "Come Alive" advertising campaign fizzled in China because its message came across as "Pepsi brings your ancestors back from their graves."

1.6.4 Culture and Government

Some parts of the world have cultural environments that are extremely inhospitable to the type of online discussion that occurs on the Internet. These cultural conditions, in some cases, lead to government controls that can limit electronic commerce development. The Internet is a very open form of communication. This type of unfettered communication is not desired or even considered acceptable in some cultures. For example, a Human Rights Watch report stated that many countries in the Middle East and North Africa do not allow their citizens unrestricted access to the Internet. The report notes that many governments in this part of the world regularly prevent free expression by their citizens and have taken specific steps to prevent the exchange of information outside of state controls. For instance, Saudi Arabia, Yemen, and the United Arab Emirates all filter the Web content that is available in their countries.

In most North African and Middle Eastern countries, officials have publicly denounced the Internet for carrying materials that are sexually explicit, anti-Islam, or that cast doubts on the traditional role of women in their societies. In many of these countries, uncontrolled use of Internet technologies is so at odds with existing traditions, cultures, and laws that electronic commerce is unlikely to exist locally at any significant level in the near future. In contrast, other Islamic countries in that part of the world, including Algeria, Morocco, and the Palestinian Authority, do not limit online access or content.

1.6.5 Infrastructure Issues

Businesses that successfully meet the challenges posed by trust, language, and culture issues still face the challenges posed by variations and inadequacies in the infrastructure that supports the

Internet throughout the world. Internet infrastructure includes the computers and software connected to the Internet and the communications networks over which the message packets travel. In many countries other than the United States, the telecommunication industry is either government owned or heavily regulated by the government. In many cases, regulations in these countries have inhibited the development of the telecommunication infrastructure or limited the expansion of that infrastructure to a size that cannot reliably support Internet data packet traffic.

Local connection costs through the existing telephone networks in many developing countries are very high compared to U.S. costs for similar access. This can have a profound effect on the behavior of electronic commerce participants. For example, in countries where Internet connection costs are high, few businesspeople would spend time surfing the Web to shop for a product. They would use a Web browser only to navigate to a specific site that they know offers the product they want to buy. Thus, to be successful in selling to businesses in such countries, a company would need to advertise its Web presence in traditional media instead of relying on Web search engines to deliver customers to their Web sites.

Until the late 1990s, most Europeans paid for the amount of time they used the telephone line, including time for local calls. In the United States, telecommunication companies have long sold local telephone service as a flat-rate access system, in which the consumer or business pays one monthly fee for unlimited telephone line usage. Activists in European countries argued that flat-rate access was a key to the success of electronic commerce in the United States. Although many factors contributed to the rapid rise of U.S. electronic commerce, many industry analysts agree that flat-rate access was one of the most important. As more European telecommunication providers began to offer flat-rate access, electronic commerce in those countries increased dramatically.

New Words & Phrases

anonymity   n. 匿名，作者不明（或不详）

commensurate   adj. 相称的，相当的

dispute   n. 辩论，争端，争执

unfettered   adj. 无拘无束的

flat-rate access   固定费率访问

multinational   adj. 多国的，跨国的

anticipate   vt. 预感，期望

stem from   来自，起源于，由...造成

at odds with   与...不和，与...争吵

Notes

1. For businesses to succeed on the Web, they must find ways to quickly generate the trust that traditional businesses take years to develop. 句中"that"引导定语从句，修饰"trust"。本句译为"为了在网络上成功，企业必须想办法快速获取传统企业花费多年才能建立起来的信任。"

2. A company's brand conveys expectations about how the company will behave, therefore companies with established brands can build online businesses more quickly and easily than a new company without a reputation. 译为"品牌传达了对公司行为的期望，因而有知名度品牌的公司比无名的新公司可以更快、更容易地在网上开展业务。"

Reading Material——Benefits of EC

Benefits to Organizations

EC's benefits to organizations are as follows.

Global Reach. EC expands the marketplace to national and international markets. With minimal capital outlay, a company can easily and quickly locate the best suppliers, more customers, and the most suitable business partners worldwide. Expanding the base of customers and suppliers enables organizations to buy cheaper and sell more.

Cost Reduction. EC decreases the cost of creating, processing, distributing, storing, and retrieving paper-based information. High printing and mailing costs are lowered or eliminated.

Supply Chain Improvements. Supply chain inefficiencies, such as excessive inventories and delivery delays, can be minimized with EC. For example, by building autos to order instead of for dealers' showrooms, the automotive industry is expecting to save tens of billions of dollars annually just from inventory reduction.

Extended Hours: 24/7/365. The business is always open on the Web, with no overtime or other extra costs.

Customization. Pull-type production (build-to-order) allows for inexpensive customization of products and services and provides a competitive advantage for companies that implement this strategy.

New Business Models. EC allows for many innovative business models that provide strategic advantages and/or increase profits. Combining group purchasing with reverse auctions is one example of an innovative business model.

Vendors' Specialization. EC allows for a high degree of specialization that is not economically feasible in the physical world. For example, a store that sells only dog toys (*dogtoys.com*) can operate in cyberspace, but in the physical world such a store would not have enough customers.

Rapid Time-to-Market. EC reduces the time between the inception of an idea and its commercialization due to improved communication and collaboration.

Lower Communication Costs. EC lowers telecommunication costs—the Internet is much cheaper than VANs.

Efficient Procurement. EC enables efficient e-procurement that can reduce administrative costs by 80 percent or more, reduce purchase prices by 5 to 15 percent, and reduce cycle time by more than 50 percent.

Improved Customer Relations. EC enables companies to interact more closely with customers, even if through intermediaries. This allows for personalization of communication, products, and services, which promotes better CRM and increases customer loyalty.

Up-to-Date Company Material. Any material on the Web, such as prices in catalogs, can be correct up to the minute. Company information can always be current.

No City Business Permits and Fees. Online companies that are not registered businesses with employees do not need any permits to operate nor do they pay license fees. If the business is registered, city fees and licenses apply.

Other Benefits. Other benefits include improved corporate image, improved customer service, ease in finding new business partners, simplified processes, increased productivity, reduced paperwork, increased access to information, reduced transportation costs, and increased operation and trading flexibility.

Benefits to Individuals (Consumers)

The benefits of EC to individuals are as follows.

Ubiquity. EC allows consumers to shop or perform other transactions year-round, 24 hours a day, from almost any location.

More Products and Services. EC provides consumers with more choices; they can select from many vendors and from more products.

Customized Products and Services. Dell customizes computers and sells them at competitive prices. Customers can get an increased number of products (from shoes to dolls to cars) and services just the way they want them.

Cheaper Products and Services. EC frequently provides consumers with less-expensive products and services by allowing them to shop in many places and conduct quick comparisons.

Instant Delivery. In the cases of digitized products, EC allows for almost instant delivery.

Information Availability. Consumers can locate relevant and detailed product information in seconds, rather than days or weeks. Also, multimedia support is cheaper and better.

Participation in Auctions. EC makes it possible for consumers to participate in virtual auctions. These allow sellers to sell things quickly and buyers can locate collectors' items and bargains.

Electronic Communities. EC allows customers to interact with other customers in electronic communities and exchange ideas as well as compare experiences.

No Sales Tax. In many countries, online business is exempt from sales taxes.

Benefits to Society

The benefits of EC to society are as follows.

Telecommuting. More individuals can work at home and do less traveling for work or shopping, resulting in less traffic on the roads and reduced air pollution.

Higher Standard of Living. Some merchandise can be sold at lower prices, allowing less-affluent people to buy more and increase their standard of living.

Homeland Security. EC technologies facilitate homeland security by improving communication, coordination, information interpretation, and so on.

Hope for the Poor. Because of EC, people in Third World countries and rural areas are now able to enjoy products and services that were unavailable in the past. These include opportunities to learn a skilled profession or earn a college degree.

Availability of Public Services. Public services, such as health care, education, and distribution of government social services, can be done at a reduced cost and/or improved quality. For example, EC provides rural doctors and nurses access to information and technologies with which they can better treat their patients.

New Words & Phrases

outlay   n. 支出；费用

ubiquity   n. 到处存在，（同时的）普遍存在

科技英语的特点

比起非科技英语来，科技英语有四多，即复杂长句多、被动语态多、非谓语动词多、词性转换多。

一、复杂长句多

科技文章要求叙述准确，推理谨严，因此一句话里包含三四个甚至五六个分句的，并非少见。译成汉语时，必须按照汉语习惯破成适当数目的分句，才能条理清楚，避免洋腔洋调。这种复杂长句居科技英语难点之首，读者要学会运用语法分析方法来加以解剖，以便以短代长，化难为易。例如：

Factories will not buy machines unless they believe that the machine will produce goods that they are able to sell to consumers at a price that will cover all cost.

这是由一个主句和四个从句组成的复杂长句，只有进行必要的语法分析，才能正确理解和翻译。现试译如下：

除非相信那些机器造出的产品卖给消费者的价格足够支付所有成本，否则厂家是不会买那些机器的。

也可节译如下：

要不相信那些机器造出的产品售价够本，厂家是不会买的。

后一句只用了 24 个字，比前句 40 个字节约用字 40%，而对原句的基本内容无损。可见，只要吃透原文的结构和内涵，翻译时再在汉语上反复推敲提炼，复杂的英语长句，也是容易驾驭的。又如：

There is an increasing belief in the idea that the "problem solving attitude" of the engineer must be buttressed not only by technical knowledge and "scientific analysis" but that the engineer must also be aware of economics and psychology and, perhaps even more important, that he must understand the world around him.

这个长句由一个主句带三个并列定语从句构成，试译如下：

越来越令人信服的想法是：工程师不仅必须用技术知识和科学分析来加强解决问题的意向，而且也一定要了解经济学和心理学，而可能更为重要的是：必须懂得周围世界。

这两个例句初步说明了英语复杂长句的结构和译法。

二、被动语态多

英语使用被动语态大大多于汉语，如莎士比亚传世名剧《罗密欧与朱丽叶》中的一句就两次用了被动语态：

Juliet was torn between desire to keep Romeo near her and fear for his life, should his presence be detected.

朱丽叶精神上受到折磨，既渴望和罗密欧形影不离，又担心罗密欧万一让人发现，难免有性命之忧。

科技英语更是如此，有三分之一以上用被动语态。例如：

(a) No work can be done without energy.

译文：没有能量决不能做功。

(b) All business decisions must now be made in the light of the market.

译文：所有企业现在必须根据市场来作出决策。

(c) Automobiles may be manufactured with computer-driven robots or put together almost totally by hand.

译文：汽车可以由计算机操纵的机器人来制造，或者几乎全部用手工装配。

以上三例都用被动语态。但译成汉语时都没有用被动语态，以便合乎汉语传统规范。例(c)的并列后句，其谓语本应是 may be put together。put 是三种变化形式一样的不规则动词，在这里是过去分词，由于修辞学上避免用词重复出现的要求，略去了 may be 两词，所以并非现在时，而是被动语态。

科技英语之所以多用被动语态，为的是要强调所论述的客观事物（四例中的 work, necessaries, business decisions, automobiles），因此放在句首，作为句子的主语，以突出其重要性。

三、非谓语动词多

英语每个简单句中，只能用一个谓语动词，如果读到几个动作，就必须选出主要动作当谓语，而将其余动作用非谓语动词形式，才能符合英语语法要求。

非谓语动词有三种：动名词、分词（包括现在分词和过去分词）和不定式。例如：

(a) 要成为一个名符其实的内行，需要学到老。

这句中，有"成为"、"需要"和"学"三个表示动作的词，译成英语后为：

To be a true professional requires lifelong learning.

可以看出，选好"需要"（require）作为谓语，其余两个动作："成为"用不定式形式 to be，而"学"用动名词形式 learning，这样才能符合英语语法要求。

(b) 任何具有重量并占有空间的东西都是物质。

这句包含"是"（在英语中属于存在动词）、"具有"和"占有"三个动作，译成英语为：

Matter is anything having weight and occupying space.

将"是"（is）当谓语（系动词），而"具有"（having）和"占有"（occupying）处理为现在分词，连同它们的宾语 weight 和 space 分别构成现在分词短语作为修饰名词 anything 的定语。

(c) 这门学科为人所知的两大分支是无机化学和有机化学。

这句有"为人所知"和"是"两个动词，译成英语后为：

The tow great divisions of this science known are inorganic chemistry and organic chemistry.

这里将"是"(are) 作为谓语系动词，而将"为人所知"(known) 处理为过去分词。

上述三例分别列举了三种非谓语动词的使用情况。其必要性都是为了英语语法上这条铁定的要求：每个简单句只允许有一个谓语动词。这就是英语为什么不同于其它语言，有非谓语动词，而且用得十分频繁的原因。

四、词性转换多

英语单词有不少是多性词，即既是名词，又可用作动词、形容词、介词或副词，字形无殊，功能各异，含义也各不相同，如不仔细观察，必致谬误。例如：

(a) above

介词：above all (things) 首先，最重要的是　　　　形容词：for the above reason 由于上述理由

副词：As (has been) indicated above 如上所指出

(b) light

名词：（启发）in (the)light of 由于，根据；（光）high light(s) 强光，精华；（灯）safety light 安全指示灯

形容词：（轻）light industry 轻工业；（明亮）light room 明亮的房间；（淡）light blue 淡蓝色；（薄）light coating 薄涂层

动词：　（点燃）light up the lamp 点灯

副词：　（轻快）travel light 轻装旅行　　　　　　（容易）light come, light go 来得容易去得快

诸如此类的词性转换，在德、俄等西方语言中是少有的，而科技英语中却屡见不鲜，几乎每个技术名词都可转换为同义的形容词。词性转换增加了英语的灵活性和表现力，读者必须从上下文判明用词在句中是何

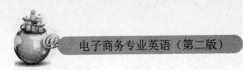

种词性，而且含义如何，才能对全句得到正确无误的理解。

我们在科技翻译实践中，要充分体现以上各个特点，重视信息传递，注意调整句式、篇章，以使译文叙述条理、逻辑连贯，同时还要注意准确使用科技术语。

Exercises

I. Answer the following questions

1. List the five general electronic commerce categories.

2. What's a business model? Was the key to success simply to copy the business model of a successful dot-com business?

3. What's a revenue model?

4. List some products suitability to Electronic Commerce.

5. What are transaction costs?

6. What's a network effect?

7. Relate the key issues that any company faces when it conducts international commerce.

8. Explain the difference between language translation and language localization.

II. Fill in the blanks in each of the following

1. The term electronic commerce (or e-commerce) is used in its broadest sense and includes all business activities that use _____ technologies.

2. Companies that operate only online are often called _____ or _____ businesses to distinguish them from companies that operate in physical locations (solely or together with online operations).

3. The second wave is characterized by its _____ scope, with sellers doing business in many countries and in many languages.

4. A _____ item is a product or service that is hard to distinguish from the same products or services provided by other sellers; its features have become standardized and well known.

5. A combination of _____ and _____ commerce strategies works best when the business process includes both commodity and personal inspection elements.

6. The practice of an existing firm replacing one or more of its supplier markets with its own hierarchical structure for creating the supplied product is called_____.

7. Businesses and individuals can use electronic commerce to reduce transaction costs by improving the flow of _____ and increasing the _____ of actions.

8. A _____ is a way of organizing the activities that each strategic business unit undertakes to design, produce, promote, market, deliver, and support the products or services it sells.

III. Questions and Discussion

1. Can you give more benefits of EC? If yes, please list them.

2. Discuss what changes EC makes in your life.

Chapter 2 The Internet and World Wide Web: E-Commerce Infrastructure

本章主要分析 Internet 和万维网(WWW)的现在与将来，它们如何工作、如何进化以及如何支持电子商务。通过学习，读者应该掌握以下内容：

学习指导

- 了解 Internet 的起源。
- 能够确定 Internet 的关键技术概念。
- 能够描述 Internet 协议与应用程序的作用。
- 能够解释当前 Internet 的结构。
- 理解当前 Internet 的局限。
- 能描述 Internet II 的潜在作用。
- 理解万维网(World Wide Web)的工作原理。
- 能够描述 Internet 和万维网的特征及其服务如何支持电子商务。

Most people love the Web, but hate the wait. Studies have shown that most people won't stay on a site if the page and its contents take more than eight seconds to load. That's bad news for anyone seeking to use the Web for e-commerce.

Slow-loading Web pages sometimes result from poor design, but more often than not, the problem stems from the underlying infrastructure of the Internet. As you'll learn in this chapter, the Internet was originally developed to carry text-based e-mail messages among a relatively small group of researchers, not bandwidth hogging graphics, sound, and video files to millions of people.

This chapter examines the Internet and World Wide Web of today and tomorrow, how it evolved, how it works, and how the present and future infrastructure of the Internet and the Web enables e-commerce.

2.1 The Internet: Technology Background

What is the Internet? Where did it come from, and how did it support the growth of the World Wide Web? What are the Internet's most important operating principles? As noted in Chapter 1, the **Internet** is an interconnected network of thousands of networks and millions of computers (sometimes called *host computers* or just *hosts*) linking businesses, educational institutions, government agencies, and individuals together. The Internet provides around 400 million people around the world (and over 170 million people in the United States) with services such as e-mail, newsgroups, shopping, research, instant messaging, music, videos, and news. No one organization controls the Internet or how it functions, nor is it owned by anybody, yet it has provided the infrastructure for a transformation in commerce, scientific research, and culture. The word *Internet* is derived from the word *internetwork* or the connecting together of two or more computer networks. The **World Wide Web**, or **Web** for short, is one of the Internet's most popular services, providing access to over one billion Web pages, which are documents created in a programming language called HTML and which can contain text, graphics, audio, video, and other objects, as well as "hyperlinks" that permit a user to jump easily from one page to another[1].

2.1.1　The Evolution of The Internet 1961—2000

Internet I—today's Internet—has evolved over the last forty years. In this sense, the Internet is not "new"; it did not happen yesterday. Although journalists and pundits talk glibly about "Internet" time—suggesting a fast-paced, nearly instant, worldwide global change mechanism, in fact, it has taken forty years of hard work to arrive at today's Internet.

The history of the Internet can be segmented into three phases. In the first phase, the *Innovation Phase*, from 1961 to 1974, the fundamental building blocks of the Internet were conceptualized and then realized in actual hardware and software. The basic building blocks are: packet-switching hardware, client/server computing, and a communications protocol called TCP/IP (all described more fully below). The original purpose of the Internet, when it was conceived in the late 1960s, was to link together large mainframe computers on college campuses. This kind of one-to-one communication between campuses was previously only possible through the telephone system or postal mail.

In the second phase, the *Institutional Phase*, from 1975 to 1995, large institutions such as the Department of Defense and the National Science Foundation provided funding and legitimization for the fledging invention called the *Internet*. Once the concept of the Internet had been proven in several government-supported demonstration projects, the Department of Defense contributed a million dollars to develop the concepts and demonstration projects into a robust military communication system that could withstand nuclear war. This effort created what was then called ARPANET (Advanced Research Projects Agency Network). In 1986, the National Science Foundation assumed responsibility for the development of a civilian Internet (then called NSFNet) and began a ten-year-long $200 million expansion program.

In the third phase, the *Commercialization Phase*, from 1995 to 2001, government agencies encouraged private corporations to take over and expand both the Internet backbone and local service to ordinary citizens—families and individuals across America and the world who were not students on campuses. By 2000, the Internet's use had expanded well beyond military installations and research universities. The E-commerce I period begins—arguably—in 1994 with the first effort to advertise and market on the Web.

2.1.2　The Internet: Key Technology Concepts

In 1995, the Federal Networking Council (FNC) took the step of passing a resolution formally defining the term *Internet*.

"Internet" refers to the global information system that—

(*i*)   *is logically linked together by a globally unique address space based on the Internet Protocol (IP) or its subsequent extensions/follow-ons;*

(*ii*)   *is able to support communications using the Transmission Control Protocol/Internet Protocol (TCP/IP) suite or its subsequent extensions/follow-ons, and/or other IP-compatible protocols; and*

(*iii*)   *provides, uses or makes accessible, either publicly or privately, high level services layered on the communications and related infrastructure described herein.*

Based on the definition, the Internet means a network that uses the IP addressing scheme, supports the Transmission Control Protocol (TCP), and makes services available to users much like a telephone system makes voice and data services available to the public[2].

Behind this formal definition are three extremely important concepts that are the basis for understanding the Internet: packet switching, the TCP/IP communication protocol, and client/server computing[3]. Although the Internet has evolved and changed dramatically in the last 30 years, these three concepts are at the core of how the Internet functions today and are the foundation for Internet II.

Packet Switching. Packet switching is a method of slicing digital messages into parcels called "**packets**," sending the packets along different communication paths as they become available, and then reassembling the packets once they arrive at their destination. Prior to the development of packet switching, early computer networks used leased, dedicated telephone circuits to communicate with terminals and other computers. In circuit-switched networks such as the telephone system, a complete point-to-point circuit is put together, and then communication can proceed. However, these "dedicated" circuit-switching techniques were expensive and wasted available communications capacity—the circuit would be maintained regardless of whether any data was being sent. For nearly 70% of the time, a dedicated voice circuit is not being fully used because of pauses between words and delays in assembling the circuit segments, both of which increased the length of time required to find and connect circuits. A better technology was needed.

The first book on packet switching was written by Leonard Kleinrock in 1964, and the technique was further developed by others in the defense research labs of both the United States and England. With packet switching, the communication capacity of a network can be increased by a factor of 100 or more. The communication capacity of a digital network is measured in terms of bits per second. Imagine if the gas mileage of your car went from 15 miles per gallon to 1,500 miles per gallon—all without changing too much of the car!

In packet-switched networks, messages are first broken down into packets. Appended to each packet are digital codes that indicate a source address (the origination point) and a destination address, as well as sequencing information and error control information for the packet. Rather than being sent directly to the destination address, in a packet network, the packets travel from computer to computer until they reach their destination. These computers are called routers. **Routers** are special purpose computers that interconnect the thousands of different computer networks that make up the Internet and route packets along to their ultimate destination as they travel[4]. To ensure that packets take the best available path toward their destination, the routers use computer programs

called **routing algorithms.**

Packet switching does not require a dedicated circuit but can make use of any spare capacity that is available on any of several hundred circuits. Packet switching makes nearly full use of almost all available communication lines and capacity. Moreover, if some lines are disabled or too busy, the packets can be sent on any available line that eventually leads to the destination point.

TCP/IP. While packet switching was an enormous advance in communication capacity, there was no universally agreed upon method for breaking up digital messages into packets, routing them to the proper address, and then reassembling them into a coherent message. This was like having a system for producing stamps, but no postal system (a series of post offices and a set of addresses).

TCP/IP answered the problem of what to do with packets on the Internet and how to handle them. **TCP** refers to the Transmission Control Protocol (TCP). **IP** refers to the Internet Protocol (IP). A **protocol** is a set of rules for formatting, ordering, compressing, and error-checking messages. It may also specify the speed of transmission and means by which devices on the network will indicate they have stopped sending and/or receiving messages. Protocols can be implemented in either hardware or software. TCP/IP is implemented in Web software called *server software* (described below). TCP is the agreed upon protocol for transmitting data packets over the Web. TCP establishes the connections among sending and receiving Web computers, handles the assembly of packets at the point of transmission, and their reassembly at the receiving end.

TCP/IP is divided into four separate layers, with each layer handling a different aspect of the communication problem. The Network Interface Layer is responsible for placing packets on and receiving them from the network medium, which could be a Local Area Network (Ethernet) or Token Ring Network, or other network technology. TCP/IP is independent from any local network technology and can adapt to changes in the local level. The Internet Layer is responsible for addressing, packaging, and routing messages on the Internet. The Transport Layer is responsible for providing communication with the application by acknowledging and sequencing the packets to and from the application. The Application Layer provides a wide variety of applications with the ability to access the services of the lower layers. Some of the best known applications are Hyper Text Transfer Protocol (HTTP), File Transfer Protocol (FTP), and Simple Mail Transfer Protocol (SMTP), all of which we will discuss later in this chapter.

IP Addresses. TCP handles the packetizing and routing of Internet messages. IP provides the Internet's addressing scheme. Every computer connected to the Internet must be assigned an address —otherwise it cannot send or receive TCP packets. For instance, when you sign onto the Internet using a dial-up telephone modem, your computer is assigned a temporary address by your Internet Service Provider.

Internet addresses, known as **IP addresses**, are 32-bit numbers that appear as a series of four separate numbers marked off by periods, such as 201.61.186.227. Each of the four numbers can range from 0 to 255. This "dotted quad" addressing scheme contains up to 4 billion addresses (2^{32}). The leftmost number typically indicates the network address of the computer, while remaining numbers help to identify the specific computer within the group that is sending (or receiving) a message.

The current version of IP is called Version 4, or IPv4. Because many large corporate and government domains have been given millions of IP addresses each (to accommodate their current and future work forces), and with all the new networks and new Internet-enabled devices requiring unique IP addresses being attached to the Internet, a new version of the IP protocol, called IPv6 is being adopted. This scheme contains 128-bit addresses, or about one quadrillion (10^{15}).

Figure 2-1 illustrates how TCP/IP and packet switching work together to send data over the Internet.

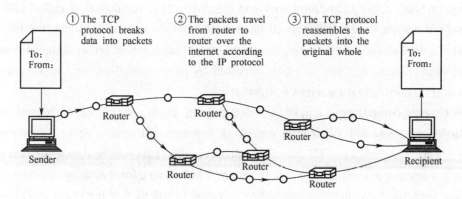

Figure 2-1   Routing Internet messages: TCP/IP and packet switching

Domain Names and URLs. Most people cannot remember 32-bit numbers. IP addresses can be represented by a natural language convention called **domain names. The domain name system (DNS)** allows expressions such as cnet.com to stand for numeric IP addresses (cnet.com's numeric IP is 216.200.247.134). **Uniform resource locators (URLs),** which are the addresses used by Web browsers to identify the location of content on the Web, also use domain names as part of the URL. A typical URL contains the protocol to be used when accessing the address, followed by its location. For instance, the URL htttp://www.azimuth-interactive.com/flash_test refers to the IP address 208.148.84.1 with the domain name "azimuth-interactive.com" and the protocol being used to access the address, Hypertext Transfer Protocol (HTTP). A resource called "flash_test" is located on the server directory path /flash_test. A URL can have from two to four parts, for example name1.name2. name3.org. We discuss domain names and URLs further in Section 3.4. Table 2-1 summarizes the important components of the Internet addressing scheme.

Table 2-1   Pieces of the Internet puzzle: names and addresses

IP addresses	Every computer connected to the Internet must have a unique address number called an *Internet Protocol address*. Even computers using a modem are assigned a temporary IP address
Domain names	The DNS (domain name system) allows expressions such as aw.com (Addison Wesley's Web site) to stand for numeric IP locations
DNS servers	DNS servers are databases that keep track of IP addresses and domain names on the Internet

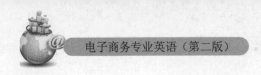

cont.

Root servers	Root servers are central directories that list all domain names currently in use. DNS servers consult root servers to look up unfamiliar domain names when routing traffic
ICANN	The Internet Corporation for Assigned Numbers and Names (ICANN) was established in 1998 to set the rules for domain names and IP addresses and also to coordinate the operation of root servers. It took over from private firms such as NetSolutions.com

Client/Server Computing. While packet switching exploded the available communication capacity and TCP/IP provided the communication rules and regulations, it took a revolution in computing to bring about today's Internet and the Web. That revolution is called *client/server computing* and without it, the Web—in all its richness—would not exist. In fact, the Internet is a giant example of client/server computing in which over 70 million host server computers store Web pages and other content that can be easily accessed by nearly a million local area networks and hundreds of millions of client machines worldwide[5].

Client/server computing is a model of computing in which very powerful personal computers called **clients** are connected together in a network together with one or more server computers. These clients are sufficiently powerful to accomplish complex tasks such as displaying rich graphics, storing large files, and processing graphics and sound files, all on a local desktop or handheld device. **Servers** are networked computers dedicated to common functions that the client machines on the network need, such as storing files, software applications, utility programs such as Web connections, and printers (See Figure 2-2).

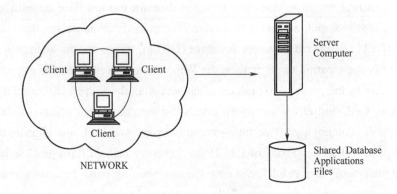

Figure 2-2　the client/server computing model

To appreciate what client/server computing makes possible, you must understand what preceded it. In the mainframe computing environment of the 1960s and 1970s, computing power was very expensive and limited. For instance, the largest commercial mainframes of the late 1960s had 128k of RAM and 10 megabyte disk drives, and occupied hundreds of square feet. There was insufficient computing capacity to support graphics or color in text documents, let alone sound files or hyper linked documents and databases.

With the development of personal computers and local area networks during the late 1970s and early 1980s, client/server computing became possible. Client/server computing has many advantages over centralized mainframe computing. For instance, it is easy to expand capacity by adding servers and clients. Also, client/ server networks are less vulnerable than centralized computing architectures. If one server goes down, backup or mirror servers can pick up the slack; if a client machine is inoperable, the rest of the network continues operating. Moreover, processing load is balanced over many powerful smaller machines rather than being concentrated in a single huge machine that performs processing for everyone. Both software and hardware in client/server environments can be built more simply and economically.

Today there are about 450 million PCs in existence worldwide. Most of these PCs can display and process graphics, sound files, and colored text. They have memories up to 512MB, 20 gigabyte hard drives, and occupy about two square feet. These personal "supercomputers", when tied together in local area networks or into large wide area networks such as the Web, make it possible for millions of people to enjoy "rich" Web documents and experiences. Soon these capabilities will move to handheld devices such as the Palms and HP Jornada, and wireless cell phones (much "thinner clients")[6]. In the process, more computer processing will be performed by central servers (reminiscent of mainframe computers of the past).

2.1.3   Other Internet Protocols and Utility Programs

There are many other Internet protocols that provide services to users in the form of Internet applications that run on Internet clients and servers. These Internet services are based on universally accepted protocols—or standards—that are available to everyone who uses the Internet. They are not owned by any one organization but are services that were developed over many years and given to all Internet users.

HTTP: Hypertext Documents. HTTP (short for **Hyper Text Transfer Protocol**) is the Internet protocol used for transferring Web pages (described in the following section). The HTTP protocol runs in the Application Layer of the TCP/IP model. An HTTP session begins when a client's browser requests a Web page from a remote Internet server. When the server responds by sending the page requested, the HTTP session for that object ends. Because Web pages may have many objects on them—graphics, sound or video files, frames, and so forth—each object must be requested by a separate HTTP message.

SMTP, POP, and IMAP: Sending E-mail. E-mail is one of the oldest, most important, and frequently used Internet services. **SMTP (Simple Mail Transfer Protocol)** is the Internet protocol used to send mail to a server. **POP (Post Office Protocol)** is used by the client to retrieve mail from an Internet server. You can see how your browser handles SMTP and POP by looking in your browser's Preferences or Tools section, where the mail settings are defined. You can set POP to retrieve e-mail messages from the server and then delete the messages on the server, or retain them on the server. **IMAP (Internet Message Access Protocol)** is a more current e-mail protocol supported by many servers and all browsers. IMAP allows users to search, organize, and filter their mail prior to downloading it from the server.

FTP: Transferring Files. FTP (File Transfer Protocol) is one of the original Internet services.

It is a part of the TCP/IP protocol and permits users to transfer files from the server to their client machine, and vice versa. The files can be documents, programs, or large database files. FTP is the fastest and most convenient way to transfer files larger than 1 megabyte, which many mail servers will not accept.

SSL: Security. SSL (Secure Sockets Layer) is a protocol that operates between the Transport and Application Layers of TCP/IP and secures communications between the client and the server. SSL helps secure e-commerce communications and payments through a variety of techniques such as message encryption and digital signatures.

Telnet: Running Remote. Telnet is a terminal emulation program that runs in TCP/IP. You can run Telnet from your client machine. When you do so, your client emulates a mainframe computer terminal. (The industry standard terminals defined in the days of mainframe computing are VT-52, VT-100, and IBM 3250.) You can then attach yourself to a computer on the Internet that supports Telnet and run programs or download files from that computer. Telnet was the first "remote work" program that permitted users to work on a computer from a remote location.

Finger: Finding People. You can find out who is logged onto a remote network by using Telnet to connect to a server, and then typing "finger" at the prompt. **Finger** is a utility program supported by UNIX computers. When supported by remote computers, finger can tell you who is logged in, how long they have been attached, and their user name. Obviously there are security issues involved with supporting finger, and most Internet host computers do not support finger today.

Ping: Testing the Address. You can "**ping**" a host computer to check the connection between your client and the server. The ping (**Packet InterNet Groper**) program will also tell you the time it takes for the server to respond, giving you some idea about the speed of the server and the Internet at that moment. You can run ping from the DOS prompt on a personal computer with a Windows operating system by typing: Ping <domain name>.

Tracert: Checking Routes. Tracert is one of several route-tracing utilities that allow you to follow the path of a message you send from your client to a remote computer on the Internet.

New Words & Phrases

underlying adj. 基础的，根本的	video n. 电视，录像，视频
bandwidth n. 带宽	hog vt. 贪心攫取；独占
hyperlink n. [计]超链接	pundit n. 空谈家，权威性的评论者
glibly adv. 流利地，流畅地	conceptualize v. 使有概念
legitimization n. 合法化，认为正当	institutional adj. 制度上的，机构上的
fledging n. 刚会飞的幼鸟，无经验的人	follow-on 继续
slice vt. 把...切成薄片；把...分成部分	break down 破坏；拆散细分；分类
disabled n. 禁止使用的	quad n. 四元组
mainframe n. [计]主机，大型机	vulnerable adj. 易受攻击的，易受……的攻击
gigabyte n. 十亿字节（giga-为字首，"十亿"）	supercomputer n. [计] 超型计算机
reminiscent adj. 怀旧的；回忆的	Domain Name 域名

host computer (host)　主机

packet-switching　分组交换技术

circuit switching　线路转接

Router　[计]路由器

Ethernet　n. 以太网

Telnet　远程登录

Ping　测试 IP 地址的程序

UNIX　美国 AT&T 公司的操作系统

instant messaging　即时信息服务

client/server　客户机/服务器

bit　n. [计]位，比特

routing algorithm　路径算法

token ring networks　令牌环形网

Finger　查找器（查找因特网用户的程序）

Tracert　检查路由器程序

let alone　更不用说…

Abbreviations

TCP (Transfer Control Protocol)　传输控制协议

FTP (File Transfer Protocol)　文件传输协议

HTTP(Hypertext Transfer Protocol)超文本传输协议

URL (Uniform Resource Locator)　统一资源定位

SSL (Security Socket Layer)　加密套接字协议层

RAM (random access memory)　随机存储器

IP(Internet Protocol)　网际协议

POP (Post Office Protocol)邮局协议

IP address　IP 地址

DNS (domain name system)　域名系统

ARPANET (Advanced Research Projects Agency Network)　美国国防部高级研究计划局建立的阿帕网

ICANN (Internet Corporation for Assigned Names and Numbers)　因特网域名与地址管理组织

SMTP (Simple Message Transfer Protocol)简单邮件传输协议，用于电子邮件的传输

IMAP (Internet Message Access Protocol) Internet 消息访问协议

Notes

1. The **World Wide Web**, or **Web** for short, is …, providing access to over one billion Web pages, which are … and which can contain … as well as "hyperlinks" that… another. "全球信息网,或简称万维网,是英特网上最流行的服务之一,提供对超过 10 亿网页的访问,这些网页是由一种叫做 HTML(超文本链接标示语言)的编程语言生成的文件,它可以包含本文、图形、声频、视频和其他的对象、以及允许用户容易地跳跃到其他网页的"超链接"。"

2. Based on the definition, the Internet means a network that uses …, supports …, and makes …. 本句 that 引起一个由三个并列句组成的定语从句,译为:"基于这个定义,因特网表示这样一个网络——使用 IP 地址分配方案、支持传输控制协议,而且非常类似于电话系统使公众能够使用声音和数据服务它使用户可以使用多种服务。"

3. Behind this formal definition are three extremely important concepts that are the basis for understanding the Internet: packet switching, the TCP/IP communications protocol, and client/server computing.本句是倒状句,译为:"在这个正式的定义背后,隐含着三个极端重要的概念: 分组交换、TCP/IP(传输控制协议/网际协议)通信协议和客户/服务器计算技术,它们乃是理解因特网的基础。"

4. **Routers** are special purpose computers that interconnect the thousands of different computer networks that make up the Internet and route packets along to their ultimate destination as they travel. 本句中第一个 that 引起的定语从句是并列句,interconnect，and route 为两个动词。译为:"路由器是一种特殊用途的计算机,它将组成因特网的成千上万个不同计算机网络互相联接起来,并在信息包旅行时将它们的向终

极目的地发送。"

5. In fact, the Internet is a giant example of client/server computing in which over 70 million host server computers store Web pages and other content that can be easily accessed by nearly a million local area networks and hundreds of millions of client machines worldwide. " 事实上，因特网是客户机/服务器计算技术的一个巨大实例，其中，超过 7000 万部主机服务器计算机储存网页和其他内容，这些网页和内容能被全世界接近一百万个局域网和数亿台客户机容易地访问。"

6. Soon these …such as the Palms and HP Jornada, and …(much "thinner clients").其中，Palms 指是 Palm 公司生产的掌上电脑，HP Jornada 为惠普公司生产的手持和掌上型电脑，thinner clients 译为瘦客户。

2.2　The Internet Today

Roughly 1.4 billion people use the Internet on a regular basis in 2008. This number is expected to surpass 1.9 billion unique users, or 30% of the world's population, in 2012, according to IDC. One would think that with such incredible growth, the Internet would be overloaded. However, this has not been true for several reasons. First, client/server computing is highly extensible: By simply adding servers and clients, the population of Internet users can grow indefinitely. Second, the Internet architecture is built in layers so that each layer can change without disturbing developments in other layers. For instance, the technology used to move messages through the Internet can go through radical changes to make service faster without being disruptive to your desktop applications running on the Internet.

The Internet can be viewed conceptually as having four layers: the network technology substrate, transport services and representation standards, middleware services, and applications. The network technology substrate is composed of telecommunication networks and protocols. The transport layer houses the TCP/IP protocol. The application layer contains client applications such as the World Wide Web, e-mail, and audio or video playback. **Middleware** is the glue that ties the applications to the communication networks, and includes such services as security, authentication, addresses, and storage repositories. Users work with applications (such as e-mail) and rarely become aware of middleware that operates in the background. Because all layers use TCP/IP and other common standards linking all four layers, it is possible for there to be significant changes in the network layer without forcing changes in the application layer. The network layer is described below.

2.2.1　The Internet Backbone

Figure 2-3 illustrates the main physical elements of today's Internet. The Internet's **backbone** is formed by **Network Service Providers (NSPs)**, which own and control the major networks. The backbone has been likened to a giant pipeline that transports data around the world in milliseconds. In the United States, the backbone is composed entirely of fiber-optic cable (described more fully below), with bandwidths ranging from 155 Mbps to 2.5 Gbps. **Bandwidth** measures how much data can be transferred over a communication medium within a fixed period of time, and is usually expressed in bits per second (bps), kilobits (thousands of bits) per second (Kbps), megabits (millions of bits) per second (Mbps), or gigabits (billions of bits) per second (Gbps).

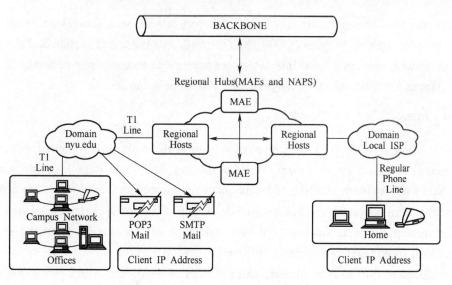

Figure 2-3   Internet I network architecture

Connections to other continents are made via a combination of undersea fiber optic cable and satellite links. The backbones in foreign countries typically are operated by a mixture of private and public owners. The U.S. backbone is one of the most developed because the Internet's infrastructure was developed here. The backbone has built-in redundancy so that if one part breaks down, data can be rerouted to another part of the backbone. **Redundancy** refers to multiple duplicate devices and paths in a network.

2.2.2   Network Access Points and Metropolitan Area Exchanges

In the United States there are a number of hubs where the backbone intersects with regional and local networks, and where the backbone owners connect with one another[1]. These hubs are called **Network Access Points (NAPs)** or **Metropolitan Area Exchanges (MAEs),** and use high-speed switching computers to connect the backbone to regional and local networks, and exchange messages with one another. The regional and local networks are owned by local Bell operating companies (RBOCs—pronounced "ree-bocks"), and private telecommunication firms such as MFS Corporation; they generally are fiber optic networks operating at over 100 Mbps. The regional networks lease access to Internet Service Providers, private companies, and government institutions.

The Internet backbone connects regional networks, which in turn provide access to the Internet to Internet Service Providers, large firms, and government agencies.

2.2.3   Campus Networks

Campus networks are generally local area networks operating with a single organization—such as New York University or Microsoft Corporation. In fact, most large organizations have hundreds of such local area networks. These organizations (representing about 60 million workers) are sufficiently large that they lease access to the Web directly from regional and national carriers.

These local area networks generally are running Ethernet (a local area network protocol) and have operating systems such as Windows 2000 (NT), Novell, or others that permit desktop clients to connect the Internet through a local Internet server attached to their campus networks. Connection speeds in campus networks are in the range of 10—100 Mbps to the desktop.

2.2.4   Internet Service Providers

The firms that provide the lowest level of service in the multi-tiered Internet architecture by leasing Internet access to home owners, small businesses, and some large institutions are called **Internet Service Providers (ISPs)**[2]. ISPs are retail providers—they deal with "the last mile of service" to the curb, the home, the business office. About 45 million American households connect the Internet through either national or local ISPs. ISPs typically connect the Internet and MAEs or NAPs with high-speed telephone or cable lines (up to 45 Mbps).

There are major ISPs such as America Online, MSN Network, and AT&T World-Net and about 5,000 local ISPs in the United States, ranging from local telephone companies offering dial-up and DSL telephone access, to cable companies offering cable modem service, to small "mom and pop" Internet shops that service a small town, city, or even county with mostly dial-up phone access (Boardwatch, 2001). If you have home or small business Internet access, an ISP will be providing you the service.

There are two types of ISP service: narrowband and broadband. **Narrowband** service is the traditional telephone modem connection now operating at 56.6 Kbps (although the actual throughput hovers around 30 Kbps due to line noise that causes extensive resending of packets). This is the most common form of connection worldwide. **Broadband** service is based on DSL, cable modem, telephone (T1 and T3 lines), and satellite technologies. Broadband—in the context of Internet service —refers to any communication technology that permits clients to play streaming audio and video files at acceptable speeds—generally anything above 100 Kbps.

The term **DSL** refers to **digital subscriber line** service, which is a telephone technology for delivering high-speed access through ordinary telephone lines found in your home or business. Service levels range from about 150 Kbps all the way up to 1 Mbps. DSL service requires that customers live within two miles (about 4,000 meters) of a neighborhood telephone switching center.

Cable modem refers to a cable television technology that piggybacks digital access to the Internet on top of the analog video cable providing television signals to a home[3]. Cable modem services ranges from 350 Kbps up to 1 Mbps. Cable service may degrade if many people in a neighborhood log on and demand high-speed service all at once.

T1 and **T3** are international telephone standards for digital communication. T1 lines offer guaranteed delivery at 1.54 Mbps, while T3 lines offer delivery at 43 Mbps. T1 lines cost about $1,000—$2,000 per month, and T3 lines between $10,000 and $30,000 per month. These are leased, dedicated, guaranteed lines suitable for corporations, government agencies, and businesses such as ISPs requiring high-speed guaranteed service levels.

Some satellite companies are offering broadband high-speed digital downloading of Internet content to homes and offices that deploy $18''$ satellite antennas. Service is available beginning at 256 Kbps up to 1 Mbps. In general, satellite connections are not viable for homes and small businesses because they are only one-way—you can download from the Internet at high speed, but cannot upload to the Internet at all. Instead, users require a phone or cable connection for their uploading.

2.2.5　Intranets and Extranets

The very same Internet technologies that make it possible to operate a worldwide public network can also be used by private and government organizations as internal networks. An **intranet** is a TCP/IP network located within a single organization for purposes of communication and information processing. Many corporations are moving away from proprietary local area networks such as Windows 2000 and Novell, and toward a single internal intranet to handle the firm's information processing and communication needs. Internet technologies are generally far less expensive than proprietary networks, and there is a global source of new applications that can run on intranets. In fact, all the applications available on the public Internet can be used in private intranets.

Extranets are formed when firms permit outsiders to access their internal TCP/IP networks. For instance, General Motors permits parts suppliers to gain access to GM's intranet that contains GM's production schedules[4]. In this way, parts suppliers know exactly when GM needs parts, and where and when to deliver the parts.

Intranets and extranets generally do not involve commercial transactions in a marketplace, and they are mostly beyond the scope of this text. Extranets will receive some attention as a type of B2B exchange.

2.2.6　Who Governs the Internet?

Aficionados and promoters of the Internet often claim that the Internet is governed by no one, and indeed cannot be governed, and that it is inherently above and beyond the law. In fact, the Internet is tied into a complex web of governing bodies, national legislatures, and international professional societies. There is no one governing body that controls activity on the Internet. Instead, there are several organizations that influence the system and monitor its operations. Among the governing bodies of the Internet are:

- The *Internet Architecture Board (IAB)*, which helps define the overall structure of the Internet.
- The *Internet Corporation for Assigned Names and Numbers (ICANN)*, which assigns IP addresses, and the *Internet Network Information Center (InterNIC)*, which assigns domain names.
- The *Internet Engineering Steering Group (IESG)*, which oversees standard setting with respect to the Internet.
- The *Internet Engineering Task Force (IETF)*, which forecasts the next step in the growth of the Internet, keeping watch over its evolution and operation.

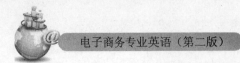
- The *Internet Society (ISOC)*, which is a consortium of corporations, government agencies, and nonprofit organizations that monitors Internet policies and practices.
- The *World Wide Web Consortium (W3C)*, which sets HTML and other programming standards for the Web.

While none of these organizations has actual control over the Internet and how it functions, they can and do influence government agencies, major network owners, ISPs, corporations, and software developers with the goal of keeping the Internet operating as efficiently as possible.

In addition to these professional bodies, the Internet must also conform to the laws of the sovereign nation-states in which it operates, as well as the technical infrastructures that exist within the nation-state[5]. Although in the early years of the Internet and the Web there was very little legislative or executive interference, this situation will change in the near future as the Internet plays a growing role in the distribution of information and knowledge, including content that some find objectionable[6].

New Words & Phrases

substrate   n. 衬底，基底

authentication   n. 证明，鉴定

backbone   n. 主干，干线

Mbps   n. 兆比特每秒

redundancy   n. 冗余

tier   n. 一层，一排

mom and pop shop   n. 小零售铺，夫妻店

narrowband   n. 窄带

throughput   n. 吞吐量，生产能力

modem   n. 调制解调器

aficionado   n. <西班牙>狂热爱好者，迷

Intranet   企业内部互联网

piggyback   n. 机载；v. 搭载

middleware   n. 中间设备，中间件

repository   n. 储存库，资料档案库

pipeline   n. 流水线，管线

Gbps   n. 千兆比特每秒

built-in   adj. 内置的，嵌入的 n.内置

curb   n. 路边

dial-up   拨号上网

broadband   n. 宽带

objectionable   adj. 该反对的，不能采用的

delay   n. 延迟

sovereign   adj. 统治的；n.统治者

Extranets   企业外部互联网

Abbreviations

NAP (Network Access Point) 网络访问节点

DSL (digital subscriber line) 数字用户线

Metropolitan Area Exchange (MAE) 城域交换站

W3C (World Wide Web Consortium) 万维网联合会

ISP (Internet Service Provider) Internet 服务提供者

ISOC (Internet Society) Internet 协会

IAB (Internet Architectrue Board) Internet 架构委员会

IETF (Internet Engineering Task Force) Internet 工程任务组

IESG (Internet Engineering Steering Group) Internet 工程指导组

Notes

1. In the United States there are a number of hubs where …, and where …. 句中 hubs 有两个 where 引起的并列定语，译为："在美国，有许多网络中心——此处因特网主干与区域性和地方性网络交叉，主干拥有者也此处彼此连接。"

2. The firms that provide the lowest level of service in the multi-tiered Internet architecture by leasing Internet access to home owners, small businesses, and some large institutions are called Internet Service Providers (ISPs). "在多层次因特网体系中通过向家庭出租因特网访问通道提供最低水平服务的公司、小型企业和一些大机构叫做因特网服务提供商(ISP)。"

3. Cable modem refers to a cable television technology that piggybacks digital access to the Internet on top of the analog video cable providing television signals to a home. "电缆调制解调器是一种在向家庭提供电视信号的视频电缆上搭载对因特网进行数字式访问的有线电视技术。"

4. For instance, General Motors permits parts suppliers to gain access to GM's intranet that contains GM's production schedules.本句在翻译时易引起歧义，应引起注意。如译为："举例来说，通用汽车公司允许零部件供应商访问包含公司生产进度的内联网。"会引起歧义，好像还有不包含生产进度的内联网。故应译为："举例来说，通用汽车公司允许零部件供应商访问公司的内联网，它的内联网包含生产进度。"

5. In addition to these professional bodies, the Internet must also conform to the laws of the sovereign nation-states in which it operates, as well as the technical infrastructures that exist within the nation-state.其中，nation-state 指民族国家，译为："除了这些专业团体，因特网还必须符合所在的主权民族国家的法律,以及这个民族国家现有的技术基础。"

6. this situation will change in the near future as the Internet plays a growing role in the distribution of information and knowledge, including content that some find objectionable. 句中 as 意为："由于、因为"，全句译为："这种情形在不久的将来就会改变，因为因特网在传播信息和知识方面扮演越来越重要的角色，包括传播一些有人反对的内容。"

2.3   Internet II: The Future Infrastructure

To appreciate the benefits of Internet II, you must first understand the limitations of the Internet's current infrastructure.

2.3.1   Limitations of Internet I

Much of the Internet's current infrastructure is several decades old (equivalent to a century in Internet time). It suffers from a number of limitations, including:

- *Bandwidth limitations.* There is insufficient capacity throughout the backbone, the metropolitan switching centers, and most importantly, to the "last mile" to the house and small business. The result is slow service (congestion) and a very limited ability to handle video and voice traffic.

- *Quality of service limitations.* Today's information packets take a circuitous route to get to their final destinations. This creates the phenomenon of **latency**— delays in messages caused by the uneven flow of information packets through the network. In the case of e-mail, latency is not noticeable. However, with streaming video and synchronous communication, such as a telephone call, latency is noticeable to the user and perceived as "jerkiness" in movies or delays in voice communication. Today's Internet uses "best efforts" quality of service, (QOS), which makes no guarantees about when or whether data will be delivered, and provides each packet with the same level of service, no matter who the user is or what type of data is contained in the packet. A higher level of service quality is required if the Internet is to keep expanding into new services (such as video on demand or telephony).

- *Network architecture limitations*. Today, a thousand requests for a single music track from a central server will result in a thousand efforts by the server to download the music to each requesting client. This slows down network performance as the same music track is sent out a thousand times to clients that might be located in the same metropolitan area. This is very different from television, where the program is broadcast once to millions of homes.
- *Language development limitations*. HTML, the language of Web pages, is fine for text and simple graphics, but poor at defining and communicating "rich documents" such as databases, business documents, or graphics. The tags used to define an HTML page are fixed and generic.

Now imagine an Internet at least 100 times as powerful as today's Internet, an Internet not subjected to the limitations of bandwidth, protocols, architecture, and language detailed above. Welcome to the world of Internet II, and the next generation of e-commerce services and products.

2.3.2 The Internet2® Project

Internet2® is a consortium of more than 180 universities, government agencies, and private businesses that are collaborating to find ways to make the Internet more efficient.

Their work together is a continuation of the kind of cooperation among government, private, and educational organizations that created the original Internet.

The idea behind Internet2 is to create a "giant test bed" where new technologies can be tested without impacting the existing Internet.

The three primary goals of Internet2 are to:

- Create a leading edge network capability for the national research community;
- Enable revolutionary Internet applications; and
- Ensure the rapid transfer of new network services and applications to the broader Internet community.

Some of the areas Internet2 participants are focusing on in this pursuit are advanced network infrastructure, new networking capabilities, middleware, and advanced applications.

2.3.3 The Larger Internet II Technology Environment

The Internet2 project is just the tip of the iceberg when it comes to near-term future enhancements to the Internet. In fact, we believe that a whole new era is about to begin that we call *Internet II*. For instance, **NGI (Next Generation Internet)** is another project initiated and sponsored by the federal government that is focused on developing advanced applications and networking capabilities needed by U.S. government agencies such as NASA and the Department of Energy. In addition, other groups—mostly private corporations and industries—are making extraordinary efforts to expand Internet capacity in order to support new services and products that they believe the public will demand in the near future.

The increased bandwidth and expanded network connections of the Internet II era will result in benefits beyond faster access and richer communications. Enhanced reliability and quality of Internet transmissions will create new business models and opportunities. Some of the major benefits of these technological advancements include IP multicasting, latency solutions, guaranteed service levels, lower error rates, and declining costs.

IP Multicasting. IP multicasting is a set of technologies that enables efficient delivery of data to many locations on a network. Rather than making multiple copies of a message intended to be distributed to multiple recipients at the point of origin of a message, multicasting initially sends just one message and does not copy it to the individual recipients until it reaches the closest common point on the network, thereby minimizing the bandwidth consumed. Network performance is significantly improved because it isn't bogged down with the processing and transmission of several large data files; each receiving computer doesn't have to query the transmitting server for the file. Multicasting technologies are already making their way into today's Internet through the use of Mbone (a special-purpose backbone for delivering video data).

Latency Solutions. One of the challenges of packet switching, where data is divided into chunks and then sent separately to meet again at the destination, is that the Internet does not differentiate between high-priority packets, such as video clips, and those of lower priority, such as self-contained e-mail messages. Because the packets cannot yet be simultaneously reassembled, the result is distorted audio and video streams.

Internet II, however, holds the promise of **diffserve**, or differentiated quality of service—a new technology that assigns levels of priority to packets based on the type of data being transmitted. Videoconference packets, for example, which need to reach their destination almost instantaneously, would receive much higher priority than e-mail messages. In the end, the quality of video and audio will skyrocket without undue stress on the network. Live and on-demand TV and video will be possible once Internet II is completed.

Guaranteed Service Levels. In today's Internet, there is no service-level guarantee and no way to purchase the right to move data through the Internet at a fixed pace. The Internet is democratic—it speeds or slows everyone's traffic alike. With Internet II, it will be possible to purchase the right to move data through the network at a guaranteed speed in return for higher fees.

Lower Error Rates. Improved capacity and packet switching will inevitably impact quality of data transmissions, reducing error rates and boosting customer satisfaction.

Declining Costs. As the Internet pipeline is upgraded, the availability of broadband service will

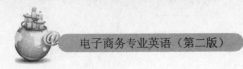
expand beyond major metropolitan areas, significantly reducing the costs of access. More users means lower cost, as products and technology catch on in the mass market. Higher volume usage enables providers to lower the cost of both access devices, or clients, and the service required to use such products. Both broadband and wireless service fees are expected to decline as geographic service areas increase, in part due to competition for that business.

New Words & Phrases

congestion　n. 阻塞	appreciate　vt. 领会，鉴赏，感激，察觉
circuitous　adj. 迂回线路的	latency　n. 等待时间
streaming　adj. 流型的；n. 流	synchronous　adj. 同时的，同步的
jerkiness　n. 不平稳，颠簸	tag　n. 标志，特征，标记[识]；标识符
multicasting　多信道广播（技术，方法）	multicasting　n. 多信道广播（技术，方法）
diffserve　区别质量的服务	videoconference　n. 视频会议

Abbreviations

AOL (American On-Line) 美国在线服务公司

NASA (National Aeronautics and Space Administration) (美国)国家航空航天局

Notes

1. Today's Internet uses "best efforts" quality of service, (QOS), which makes …, and provides … in the packet. 本句的结构是一个主语 Internet，两个谓语 uses, provides，而 which 引起的定语从句修饰 QOS。译文："今天的因特网使用"最大努力"的服务品质，对数据何时或是否被递送没有任何保证；而且无论使用者是谁或信息包中包含什么类型的数据，都为每个信息包提供相同水平的服务。"

2. Now imagine an Internet at least …, an Internet not subjected to … detailed above. 本句为祈使句，两个 an Internet 都是 imagine 的宾语。译文："现在想象一下因特网的功能至少是目前的 100 倍，想象一下一个不受上述带宽、协议、结构和语言限制的因特网。"

3. One of the challenges of packet switching, where data is …, is that the Internet does not differentiate between high-priority packets,… and those of lower priority, …译文："将数据分为多块、然后分开传送以便到达目的地后再集合的分组交换技术，面临的挑战之一是因特网不区别高优先权信息包如图像修剪，与低优先权信息包如自我包容的电子邮件信息。"

2.4　The World Wide Web

Without the World Wide Web, there would be no e-commerce. The invention of the Web brought an extraordinary expansion of digital services to millions of amateur computer users, including color text and pages, formatted text, pictures, animations, video, and sound. In short, the Web makes nearly all the rich elements of human expression needed to establish a commercial marketplace available to nontechnical computer users worldwide.

2.4.1   Hypertext

Web pages can be accessed through the Internet because the Web browser software operating your PC can request Web pages stored on an Internet host server using the HTTP protocol. **Hypertext** is a way of formatting pages with embedded links that connect documents to one another, and that also link pages to other objects such as sound, video, or animation files. When you click on a graphic and a video clip plays, you have clicked on a hyperlink. For example, when you type a Web address in your browser such as http://www.sec.gov, your browser sends an HTTP request to the sec.gov server requesting the homepage of sec.gov.

HTTP is the first set of letters at the start of every Web address, followed by the domain name. The domain name specifies the organization's server computer that is housing the document. Most companies have a domain name that is the same as or closely related to their official corporate name. The directory path and document name are two more pieces of information within the Web address that help the browser track down the requested page. Together, the address is called a Uniform Resource Locator, or URL. When typed into a browser, a URL tells it exactly where to look for the information. For example, in the following URL: http://www.megacorp.com/content/features/082602.html

http=the protocol used to display Web pages

www.megacorp.com: domain name

content/features: the directory path that identifies where on the domain Web server the page is stored

082602.html: document name and its format (an html page)

The most common domain extensions currently available and officially sanctioned by ICANN are shown in the list below. Countries also have domain names such as .uk, .au, and .fr (United Kingdom, Australia, and France). Also shown in the list below are recently approved top-level domains .biz and .info, as well as new domains under consideration. In the near future, this list will expand to include many more types of organizations and industries.

.com Commercial organizations/businesses

.edu Educational institutions

.gov U.S. government agencies

.mil U.S. military

.net Network computers

.org Nonprofit organizations and foundations

New Top-Level Domains approved May 15, 2001:

.biz business firms

.info information providers

New Top-Level Domains proposed:

.aero Air transport industry .

.coop Cooperatives

.museum Museums

.name Individuals

.pro Professionals

2.4.2　Markup Languages

Although the most common Web page formatting language is HTML, the concept behind document formatting actually had its roots in the 1960s with the development of Generalized Markup Language (GML).

SGML. In 1986, the International Standards Organization adopted a variation of GML called **Standard Generalized Markup Language**, or **SGML**. The purpose of SGML was to help very large organizations format and categorize large collections of documents. The advantage of SGML is that it can run independent of any software program but, unfortunately, it is extremely complicated and difficult to learn. Probably for this reason, it has not been widely adopted.

HTML. HTML (HyperText Markup Language) is a GML that is relatively easy to use. HTML provides Web page designers with a fixed set of markup "tags" that are used to format a Web page. When these tags are inserted into a Web page, they are read by the browser and interpreted into a page display. You can see the source HTML code for any Web page by simply clicking on the "Page Source" command found in all browsers.

HTML functions to define the structure and style of a document, including the headings, graphic positioning, tables, and text formatting. Since its introduction, the two major browsers—Netscape's Navigator and Microsoft's Internet Explorer—have continuously added features to HTML to enable programmers to further refine their page layouts. Unfortunately, many of the enhancements only work in one company's browser, and this development threatens the attainment of a universal computing platform. Worse, building browsers with proprietary functionality adds to the costs of building e-commerce sites. Whenever you build an e-commerce site, special care must be taken to ensure the pages can be viewed by major browsers, even outdated versions of browsers.

HTML Web pages can be created with any text editor, such as Notepad or Wordpad, using Microsoft Word (simply save the Word document as a Web page) or any one of several Web page editors.

XML. Extensible Markup Language (XML) takes Web document formatting a giant leap forward. **XML** is a new markup language specification developed by the W3C (the World Wide Web Consortium). XML is a markup language like HTML, but it has very different purposes. Whereas the purpose of HTML is to control the "look and feel" and display of data on the Web page, XML is designed to describe data and information.

For instance, if you want to send a patient's medical record—including diagnosis, personal identity, medical history information, and any doctor's notes—from a database in Boston to a hospital in New York over the Web, it would be impossible using HTML. However, with XML, these rich documents (database records) for patients could be easily sent over the Web and displayed.

XML is "extensible," which means the tags used to describe and display data are defined by the user, whereas in HTML the tags are limited and predefined. XML can also transform information into new formats, such as by importing information from a database and displaying it as a table. With XML, information can be analyzed and displayed selectively, making it a more powerful alternative to HTML. This means that business firms, or entire industries, can describe all of their invoices, accounts payable, payroll records, and financial information using a Web-compatible markup language. Once described, these business documents can be stored on intranet Web servers and shared throughout the corporation.

XML is not yet a replacement for HTML. Currently, XML is fully supported only by Microsoft's Internet Explorer 5, and is not supported by Netscape (although this may change). Whether XML eventually supplants HTML as the standard Web formatting specification depends a lot on whether it is supported by future Web browsers. Currently, XML and HTML work side by side on the same Web pages. HTML is used to define how information should be formatted, and XML is being used to describe the data itself.

2.4.3   Web Servers and Clients

We have already described client/server computing and the revolution in computing architecture brought about by client/server computing. You already know that a server is a computer attached to a network that stores files, controls peripheral devices, interfaces with the outside world —including the Internet—and does some processing for other computers on the network.

But what is a Web server? **Web server software** refers to the software that enables a computer to deliver Web pages written in HTML to client machines on a network that request this service by sending an HTTP request. The two leading brands of Web server software are Apache, which is free Web server shareware that accounts for about 60% of the market, and Microsoft's NT Server software, which accounts for about 20% of the market.

Aside from responding to requests for Web pages, all Web servers provide some additional basic capabilities such as the following:

- *Security services*—These consist mainly of authentication services that verify that the person trying to access the site is authorized to do so. For Web sites that process payment transactions, the Web server also supports Secure Sockets Layer (SSL), the Internet protocol for transmitting and receiving information securely over the Internet. When private information such as names, phone numbers, addresses, and credit card data need to be provided to a Web site, the Web server uses SSL to ensure that the data passing back and forth from the browser to the server is not compromised.

- *File Transfer Protocol (FTP)*—This protocol allows users to transfer files to and from the server. Some sites limit file uploads to the Web server, while others restrict downloads, depending on the user's identity.

- *Search engine*—Just as search engine sites enable users to search the entire Web for particular documents, search engine modules within the basic Web server software package enable indexing of the site's Web pages and content, and permit easy keyword searching of the site's content. When conducting a search, a search engine makes use of an *index*, which is a list of all the documents on the server. The search term is compared to the index to identify likely matches.

- ***Data capture*** — Web servers are also helpful at monitoring site traffic, capturing information on who has visited a site, how long the user stayed there, the date and time of each visit, and which specific pages on the server were accessed. This information is compiled and saved in a log file, which can then be analyzed by a user log file. By analyzing a log file, a site manager can find out the total number of visitors, average length of each visit, and the most popular destinations, or Web pages.

The term *Web server* is sometimes also used to refer to the physical computer that runs Web server software. Leading manufacturers of Web server computers are IBM, Compaq, Dell, and Hewlett Packard. Although any personal computer can run Web server software, it is best to use a computer that has been optimized for this purpose. To be a Web server, a computer must have the Web server software described above installed and be connected to the Internet. Every Web server machine has an IP address. For example, if you type *http://www.aw.com/laudon*, in your browser, the browser software sends a request for HTTP service to the Web server whose domain name is *aw.com*. The server then locates the page named "laudon" on its hard drive, sends the page back to your browser, and displays it on your screen.

Aside from the generic Web server software packages, there are actually many types of specialized servers on the Web, from **database servers** that access specific information with a database, to **ad servers** that deliver targeted banner ads, to **mail servers** that provide mail messages, and **video servers** that provide video clips. At a small e-commerce site, all of these software packages might be running on a single machine, with a single processor. At a large corporate site, there may be hundreds of discrete machines, many with multiple processors, running specialized Web server functions described above.

A **Web client**, on the other hand, is any computing device attached to the Internet that is capable of making HTTP requests and displaying HTML pages. The most common client is a Windows PC or Macintosh, with various flavors of UNIX machines a distant third. However, the fastest growing category of Web clients are not computers at all, but personal digital assistants (PDAs) such as the Palm and HP Jornada, and cellular phones outfitted with wireless Web access software. In general, Web clients can be any device—including a refrigerator, stove, home lighting system, or automobile instrument panel—capable of sending and receiving information from Web servers.

2.4.4　Web Browsers

The primary purpose of Web browsers is to display Web pages, but browsers also have added features, such as e-mail and newsgroups (an online discussion group or forum).

Currently 94% of Web users use either Internet Explorer or Netscape Navigator, but recently some new browsers have been developed that are beginning to attract attention. The browser Opera is becoming very popular because of its speed—it is currently the world's fastest browser—and because it is much smaller than existing browsers (it can almost fit on a single diskette). It can also remember the last Web page you visited, so the next time you surf, you can start where you left off. And like the big two, you can get it for free; the catch is that you have to watch blinking ads in one corner, or pay $40 for the ad-free version of Opera.

The browser NeoPlanet is also gaining new fans, primarily because of the 500+ *skins*, or design schemes, that come with it. Using skins, you can design the browser to look and sound just the way you'd like it to, rather than being limited to the standard look provided by Navigator and Internet Explorer. However, NeoPlanet requires Internet Explorer's technology in order to operate, so you must also have IE installed on your computer.

New Words & Phrases

animation　n. 动画	browse　v. n.浏览
Mosaic　最早出现的 WEB 浏览器	Hypertext　n. 超文本
extension　n. 扩展名	supplant　vt. 排挤掉，代替
browser　n 浏览器	surf　vi. 作冲浪运动，vt.在……冲浪
Macintosh　n. Apple 公司于 1984 年推出的一种系列微机，麦金托什机	
Netscape　美国 Netscape 公司，以开发 Internet 浏览器闻名	

Abbreviations

SGML (Standard Generalized Markup Language) 标准通用置标语言

GUI (graphical user interfaces) 图形用户接口(软件)

XML (Extensible Markup Language) 可扩展链接标示语言

Reading Material——The Internet and The Web: Features

The Internet and the Web have spawned a number of powerful new software applications upon which the foundations of e-commerce are built.

1　E-Mail

Since its earliest days, **electronic mail**, or e-mail, has been the most-used application of the Internet. Over 210 billion emails were sent every single day in 2008, according to recent research by the Web site performance business firm Pingdom. **E-mail** uses a series of protocols to enable messages containing text, images, sound, and video clips to be transferred from one Internet user to another. Because of its flexibility and speed, it is now the most popular form of business communication—more popular than the phone, fax, or snail mail (the U.S. Postal Service).

In addition to text typed within the message, e-mail also allows **attachments**, which are files inserted within the e-mail message. The files can be documents, images, or sound or video clips.

Although e-mail was designed to be used for interpersonal messages, it can also be a very effective marketing tool. E-commerce sites purchase e-mail lists from list providers and send mail to prospective customers, as well as existing customers. The response rate from targeted e-mail campaigns can be as high as 20%, extraordinary when compared to banner ad response rates of less than 1%. Most e-commerce sites also have a "Contact Us" section that

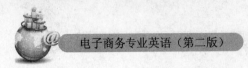
includes an e-mail contact, to make requests and comments easier for customers.

However, in addition to this acceptable practice of communicating with people who have requested such contact, some companies also use e-mail as a mass mailing technique, also known as **spam,** or unsolicited e-mail. There are a number of state laws against spamming, but it is still the bane of the Web.

2　Search Engines

Search engines can be Web sites themselves, such as Google and AltaVista, or a service within a site that allows users to ask for information about various topics. A **search engine** identifies Web pages that appear to match keywords, also called *queries*, typed by the user and provides a list of the best matches. A query can be a question, a series of words, or a single word for the search engine to look for.

How exactly individual search engines work is a proprietary secret, and at times defies explanation. Some search engines—among them AltaVista—seek to visit every Web page in existence, read the contents of the home page, identify the most common words or keywords, and create a huge database of domain names with keywords. Sometimes the search engines will just read the meta tags and other keyword sections of the home page. This is faster, but Web designers often stuff an extraordinary number of keywords into their meta tags. The program that search engines unleash on the Web to perform this indexing function is called a *spider* or *crawler*. Unfortunately, as the number of Web pages climbs to over two billion, more and more pages are missed by the search engines. Google, perhaps the most complete search engine, contains references to only about half (one billion) of all Web pages. And the engines do not always overlap, which means you may miss a page on one engine, but pick it up on another. It's best therefore to use multiple search engines.

Other search engines use different strategies. Google uses a collaborative filtering technique: It indexes and ranks sites based on the number of users who request and land at a site. This method is biased by volume: You see the Web pages others have asked to see. Yahoo, on the other hand, uses a staff of human indexers to organize as many pages as they can. It is very difficult to get your site registered on Yahoo because of the limitations of their method, which is biased toward sites that somehow come to the attention of Yahoo staff. Once again, the best advice is to use several different search engines.

One of the newest trends in search engines is focus; instead of trying to cover every possible information need that users have, some search engines are electing to specialize in one particular area. By limiting their coverage to such topics as sports, news, medicine, or finance, niche search engines are hoping to differentiate themselves from the crowd and provide better quality results for users. FindLaw.com, a search engine and directory of legal information, has seen its searches rising steadily. The same is true of Moreover.com, a search engine that specializes in collecting and reporting news headlines from more than 1,800 news sites.

Although the major search engines are used for tracking down general information of interest to users, such as a site for buying beer-making supplies, or statistics on Internet usage in Barbados, they have also become a crucial tool within e-commerce sites. Customers can more easily search for the exact item they want with the help of a search program; the difference is that within Web sites, the search engine is limited to finding matches from that one site. Sites without search engines are asking visitors to spend lots of time exploring the site—something few people are willing to do— when most sites offer a quick-and-easy way to find what they're looking for.

3   Intelligent Agents (Bots)

Intelligent agents, or **software robots** (**bots** for short) are software programs that gather and/or filter information on a specific topic, and then provide a list of results for the user. Intelligent agents were originally invented by computer scientists interested in the development of artificial intelligence (a family of related technologies that attempt to imbue computers with human-like intelligence). However, with the advent of e-commerce on the Web, interest quickly turned to exploiting intelligent agent technology for commercial purposes. Today, there are a number of different types of bots used in e-commerce on the Web, and more are being developed every day.

For instance, as previously noted, many search engines employ *web crawlers* or *spiders* that crawl from server to server, compiling lists of URLs that form the database for the search engine. These web crawlers and spiders are actually bots.

The *shopping bot* is another common type of bot. Shopping bots search online retail sites all over the Web and then report back on the availability and pricing of a range of products. For instance, you can use MySimon.com's shopping bot to search for a Sony digital camera. The bot provides a list of online retailers that carry a particular camera model, as well as report about whether it is in inventory and what the price and shipping charges are.

Another type of bot, called an *update bot*, allows you to monitor for updated materials on the Web, and will e-mail you when a selected site has new or changed information.

News bots will create custom newspapers or clip articles for you in newspapers around the world.

4   Instant Messaging

E-mail messages have a time lag of several seconds to minutes between when messages are sent and received, but **instant messaging (IM)** displays words typed on a computer almost instantaneously. Recipients can then respond immediately to the sender the same way, making the communication more like a live conversation than is possible through e-mail.

America Online (AOL) was the first to introduce a widely accepted Instant Messaging system several years ago, which is credited with the company's sudden surge in users. AOL's system is proprietary. One of the key components of an IM service is a *buddy list*, as AOL called it. The buddy list is a private list of people with whom you might want to communicate. If a person is on your buddy list, AOL will alert you when that individual signs on, enabling an IM to be sent.

The downside is that IM systems are proprietary—no standard has been set yet —so that competing sites have created their own IM services. Yahoo has IM, as does MSN, but neither works in conjunction with the others.

Interestingly, despite the wild popularity of such services, no one seems to know yet how to make money from it. AOL, Yahoo, and MSN have all offered IM free to their users and have no immediate plans to start charging a fee. True, it is a marketing draw that brings in new users, but that doesn't necessarily translate into profits.

Nevertheless, some companies have added IM to their Web sites as a means of offering instant access to customer service. For example, Sotheby's, an auction house, encourages visitors to chat live with a Sotheby's representative online. The hope is that by encouraging consumers' need for immediate gratification—whether in the form of a question answered or product ordered—IM will boost revenues and customer satisfaction.

5　Chat

Like IM, **chat** enables users to communicate via computer in real time, that is, simultaneously. However, unlike IM, which can only work between two people, chat can occur between several users.

For many Web sites, developing a community of like-minded users has been critical for their growth and success. Just look at eBay.com, which would probably have been unsuccessful without its corps of auction fans, or About.com, which exists to serve communities of consumers with similar interests. Once those community members come together on a site, chat can be a service that enables them to further bond and network, endearing them further to the Web site.

Chat is also used frequently in distance learning, for class discussions and online discussions sponsored by a company. When a celebrity appears on an entertainment Web site, for example, they use chat software in order to see and respond to questions from audience members out in cyberspace.

6　Music, Video, and Other Standard Files

Although the low bandwidth of Internet I era connections has made audio and video files more difficult to share, with Internet II, these files will become more commonplace. Today it is possible to send and receive files containing music or other audio information, video clips, animation, photographs, and other images, although the download times can be very long, especially for those using a 56 Kbps modem.

Video clips, Flash animations, and photo images are now routinely displayed either as part of Web sites, or sent as attached files. Companies that want to demonstrate use of their product have found video clips to be extremely effective. And audio reports and discussions have also become commonplace, either as marketing materials or customer reports. Photos, of course, have become an important element of most Web sites, helping to make site designs more interesting and eye catching, not to mention helping to sell products, just as catalogs do.

7　Streaming Media

Streaming media enables music, video, and other large files to be sent to users in chunks so that when received and played, the file comes through uninterrupted. Streamed files must be viewed "live": They cannot be stored on client hard drives. RealAudio and RealVideo are the most widely used streaming tools. Streaming audio and video segments used in Web ads or CNN news stories are perhaps the most frequently used streaming services.

Macromedia's Shockwave is commonly used to stream audio and video for instructional purposes. Macromedia's Flash vector graphics program is the fastest growing streaming audio and video tool. Flash has the advantage of being built into most client browsers; no plug-in is required to play Flash files.

8　Cookies

Cookies are a tool used by Web sites to store information about a user. When a visitor enters a Web site, the site sends a small text file (the cookie) to the user's computer so that information from the site can be loaded more quickly on future visits. The cookie can contain any information desired by the site designers, including customer number, pages visited, products examined, and other detailed information on the behavior of the consumer at the site. Cookies are useful to consumers because the site will recognize returning patrons and not ask them to register again.

Cookies can also help personalize a site by allowing the site to recognize returning customers and make special offers to them based on their past behavior at the site. Cookies can also permit customization and market segmentation—the ability to change the product or the price based on prior consumer information. As we will discuss throughout the book, cookies also can pose a threat to consumer privacy, and at times they are bothersome. Many people clear their cookies at the end of every day. Some disable them entirely.

9   Internet II and E-Commerce: Emerging Features and Services

The Internet II infrastructure will permit the rapid deployment of new services and greatly expand e-commerce opportunities. New technologies, increased bandwidth, and greater reliance on the Internet for communications will create new e-commerce product and service opportunities and potentially replace existing modes of communication. Telephone communication is one area destined for change.

Internet Telephony. Internet telephony is not entirely new. **IP telephony** is a general term for the technologies that use the **Voice Over Internet Protocol (VOIP)** and the Internet's packet-switched network to transmit voice, fax, and other forms of audio communication over the Internet. The major advantage, of course, is the cost:It's free. VOIP avoids the long distance charges imposed by phone companies.

The problem with VOIP has been that breaking calls into packets in order to transmit them via the Internet often results in poor voice quality. However, with new high bandwidth connections, quality problems will diminish; use of VOIP is expected to rise dramatically. New communication services will also be introduced that combine voice and computer functioning, such as call forwarding on Internet lines that can send callers to voice mail or e-mail, or the ability to click on a buddy list member and initiate voice chat, rather than text-based Instant Messaging. Because of these new capabilities, analysts are expecting major increases in the amount and type of VOIP usage in the very near future.

A recent report from market research firm Infonetics Research shows that the global VoIP services market grew 33 percent in 2008 to $30.8 billion.

In the past, voice and fax were the exclusive provenance of the regulated telephone networks. With the convergence of the Internet and telephony, however, this dominance is already starting to change, with local and long distance telephone providers and cable companies becoming ISPs, and ISPs getting into the phone market. Part of the attraction to this market may be that, unlike traditional phone services, IP telephony is currently free of governmental oversight, with the FCC (Federal Communications Commission) stating that it has no immediate intention of stepping in.

Digital Libraries. As bandwidth capabilities of the Internet increase, distribution of software applications by Application Service Providers (ASPs) over the Internet is also expected to increase. Digital libraries of software applications will emerge as companies and individuals elect to rent software rather than buy it. Accessing a Web server will enable a user to download the desired software, paying a subscription fee instead of a purchase price. This service will be especially useful for expensive software packages, such as graphic design or software development tools, that few individuals could afford. Multimedia digital libraries, with automated video and audio indexing, navigation, and search and retrieval, will also be available.

Distributed Storage. ASPs can assist both in processing data and in storing it, dispersing it to multiple servers rather than having it reside on one. Although compiling information from multiple sources used to be a challenge for computers, it has become commonplace today. Sophisticated software, such as XML, can now extract pieces of data from various sources, analyze it, and report the results in a predetermined fashion.

Distance Learning. Perhaps one of the biggest educational initiatives in recent years, the distance learning opportunity has pushed schools, colleges, and universities worldwide to make courses and whole degree programs available online. The sticking point has been the lack of interactivity available through the Internet. Some schools have tried to get around this by providing videos of actual lectures and encouraging regular chat sessions as class supplements, but two-way communication between student and teacher had a significant time lag. Now, through videoconferencing, students can watch in real time as professors give lectures. Student interactions and questions can also incorporate a visual image of the student in action, rather than a text-only message.

Development of the application software required to merge video, audio, and voice at once is a prime opportunity for an ASP, rather than for the schools themselves. Distributing the software from the company's server will also reduce the data load on school computing systems and place the burden for reliability on the ASP.

Digital Video. Ted Hanss, Internet II Director for Applications Development, considers digital video to be the "killer app" for Internet II. Future digital video networks will be able to deliver better-than-broadcast quality video over the Internet to computers and other devices. High quality interactive video and audio will make sales presentations and demonstrations more effective and lifelike and enable companies to develop new forms of customer support. New video, audio, and presentation approaches could also dramatically change the nature of the media and news business.

Video Teleconferencing. Although video teleconferencing has been available for years, few companies and individuals have made use of it simply because both the cost of equipment and rental fees have been high. Internet II will significantly reduce that cost, making it affordable for most workers to use video conferencing to share information that involves either an image or audio component. Meetings of geographically dispersed workers or colleagues will be easy to arrange, using VOIP technology, and the quality of image and audio transmission will be much higher.

Tele-immersion. One of the newest services to come onto the market will be teleimmersion, a merger of virtual reality and video conferencing, where participants can see each other and collaborate on visual projects. For instance, at the University of Illinois at Chicago, researchers are working on CALVIN, a testbed for using virtual reality in architectural design. Researchers believe high-speed connectivity, collaborative design systems that allow customers and vendors to interactively design and develop new products, coupled with virtual reality modeling and simulation such as this could dramatically reduce the time required for new product development.

M-commerce Applications. Combining voice, data, images, audio, and video on one wireless device will become possible during Internet II. As one commentator noted, "when high-bandwidth wireless and the fiber-optic based Internet2 converge, that's when we go from e-business to e-life".

New Words & Phrases

spawn v. 产生	attachment n. 附件，附加装置，配属
Snail Mail 由邮递员分发传递的传统信件，指其速度慢	Spam 兜售信息，垃圾邮件
unsolicited adj. 未被恳求的，主动提供的	defy vt. 不服从，藐视，使……难于
bane n. 毒药，祸害	Search engine 搜索引擎
meta n. 元的	unleash v. 释放
overlap v. 与……交迭	buddy n. <美口>密友，伙伴
chat v. 聊天；n.聊天	Video clip 视频剪辑

chunk　n. 程序块；组块；字节片　　　　　CNN 美国有线新闻网络

patron　n. 赞助人（顾客）　　　　　　　fax　n. vt.传真

sophisticated　adj. 复杂的，久经世故的　　killer app　招人喜爱的应用程序

connectivity　n. 连通性　　　　　　　　virtual reality　n. 虚拟现实

Flash　由 macromedia 公司推出的交互式矢量图和 Web 动画的标准

Cookie　当你访问某个站点时，随某个 HTML 网页发送到你的浏览器中的一小段信息

Abbreviations

MSN (Microsoft Network) 微软提供的网络在线服务

VOIP (Voice Over Internet Protocol) 基于网际协议的声音技术

英语专业词汇的构成

英语的词汇构成有很多种，真正英语的基本词汇是不多的，大部分词汇属于构成型词汇。这里，仅介绍在专业英语中遇到的专业词汇及其构成。目前，各行各业都有一些自己领域的专业词汇，有的是随着本专业发展应运而生的，有的是借用公共英语中的词汇，有的是借用外来语言词汇，有的则是人为构造成的词汇。

一、派生词（derivation）

这类词汇非常多，它是根据已有的词加上某种前后缀，或以词根生成、或以构成成分形成新的词。科技英语词汇中有很大一部分来源于拉丁语、希腊语等外来语，有的是直接借用，有的是在它们之上不断创造出新的词汇。这些词汇的构词成分（前缀、后缀、词根等）较固定，构成新词以后便于读者揣度词义，易于记忆。

1. 前缀

采用前缀构成的单词在计算机专业英语中占了很大比例，通过下面的实例可以了解这些常用的前缀构成的单词。

multi-多	hyper-超级	super 超级
multiprogram 多道程序	hypercube 超立方	superhighway 超级公路
multimedia 多媒体	hypercard 超级卡片	superpipline 超流水线
multiprocessor 多处理器	hypermedia 超媒体	superscalar 超标量
multiplex 多路复用	hypertext 超文本	superset 超集
multiprotocol 多协议	hyperswitch 超级交换机	superclass 超类
inter-相互、在……间	micro-微型	tele-远程的
interface 接口、界面	microprocessor 微处理器	telephone 电话
interlace 隔行扫描	microkernel 微内核	teletext 图文电视
interlock 联锁	microcode 微代码	telemarketing 电话购物
internet 互联网络（因特网）	microkid 微机迷	telecommuting 家庭办公
interconnection 互联	microchannel 微通道	teleconference 远程会议

单词前缀还有很多，其构成可以同义而不同源（如拉丁、希腊），可以互换，例如：

multi, poly　相当于 many　　　如: multimedia 多媒体, polytechnic 各种工艺的

uni, mono　相当于 single　　　如: unicode 统一的字符编码标准, monochrome 单色

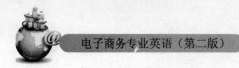

bi, di 相当于 twice   如: binomial 二项式，dibit 双位

equi,iso 相当于 equal   如: equality 等同性, isochromatic 等色的,

simili, homo 相当于 same   如: similarity 类似, homogeneous 同类的

semi,hemi 相当于 half   如: semiconductor 半导体, hemicycle 半圆形

hyper, super 相当于 over   如: hypertext 超文本, supercomputer 超级计算机

2. 后缀

后缀是在单词后部加上构词结构，形成新的单词。如：

-scope 探测仪器	-meter 计量仪器	-graph 记录仪器
microscope 显微镜	barometer 气压表	tomograph X 线体层照相
telescope 望远镜	telemeter 测距仪	telegraph 电报
spectroscope 分光镜	spectrometer 分光仪	spectrograph 分光摄像仪
-able 可能的	-ware 件(部件)	-ity 性质
enable 允许、使能	hardware 硬件	reliability 可靠性
disable 禁止、不能	software 软件	availability 可用性
programmable 可编程的	firmware 固件	accountability 可核查性
portable 便携的	groupware 组件	integrity 完整性
scalable 可缩放的	freeware 赠件	confidentiality 保密性

二、复合词（compounding）

复合词是科技英语中另一大类词汇，其组成面广，通常分为复合名词、复合形容词、复合动词等。**复合词通常以小横杠"-"连接单词构成，或者采用短语构成。有的复合词进一步发展，去掉了小横杠，并经过缩略成为另一类词类，即混成词。复合词的实例有：**

-based 基于，以……为基础	-centric 以……为中心的
rate-based 基于速率的	client-centric 以客户为中心的
credit-based 基于信誉的	user-centric 以用户为中心的
file-based 基于文件的	host-centered 以主机为中心的
Windows-based 基于 Windows 的	
-oriented 面向……的	-free 自由的，无关的
object-oriented 面向对象的	lead-free 无线的
market-oriented 市场导向	jumper-free 无跳线的
process-oriented 面向进程的	paper-free 无纸的
thread-oriented 面向线程的	charge-free 免费的
info-信息，与信息有关的	envent-事件的
info-channel 信息通道	envent-driven 事件驱动的
info-tree 信息、树	envent-oriented 面向事件的
info-world 信息世界	event-based 基于事件的
info-sec 信息安全	
其他	
point-to-point 点到点	point-and-click 点击

plug-and-play 即插即用   drag-and-drop 拖放

easy-to-use 易用的   line-by-line 逐行

off-the-shelf 流行的   store-and-forward 存储转发

peer-to-peer 对等的   operator-controllable 操作员可控制的

leading-edge 领先的   over-hyped 过度宣扬的

end-user 最终用户   front-user 前端用户

sign-on 登录   sign-of 取消

pull-down 下拉   pull-up 上拉

pop-up 弹出

此外，以名词 + 动词-ing 构成的复合形容词形成了一种典型的替换关系，即可以根据需要在结构中代入同一词类而构成新词，它们多为动宾关系。如：

man-carrying aircraft 载人飞船   earth-moving machine 推土机

time-consuming operation 耗时操作   ocean-going freighter 远洋货舱

然而，必须注意，复合词并非随意可以构造，否则会形成一种非正常的英语句子结构。虽然上述例子给出了多个连接单词组成的复合词，但不提倡这种冗长的复合方式。对于多个单词的非连线形式，要注意其顺序和主要针对对象。此外还应当注意，有时加连字符的复合词与不加连字符的词汇词意是不同的，必须通过文章的上下文推断。如：

force-feed 强迫接受（vt.），而 force feed 则为 "加压润滑"。

随着词汇的专用化，复合词中间的连接符被省略掉，形成了一个单词，例如：

videotape 录像带   fanin 扇入   fanout 扇出

online 在线   onboard 在板   login 登录

logout 撤消   pushup 拉高   popup 弹出

三、混成词（blending）

混成词不论在公共英语还是科技英语中也大量出现，也有人将它们称为缩合词（与缩略词区别）、融会词，它们多是名词，也有地方将其作为动词用，对这类词汇可以通过其构词规律和词素进行理解。这类词汇将两个单词的前部拼接、前后拼接或者将一个单词前部与另一词拼接构成新的词汇，实例有：

brunch (breakfast + lunch) 早中饭   smog (smoke +fog) 烟雾

codec (coder+decoder) 编码译码器   compuser (computer+user) 计算机用户

transeiver (transmitter+receiver) 收发机   syscall (system+call) 系统调用

mechatronics (mechanical+electronic) 机械电子学

calputer (calculator+computer) 计算器式电脑

四、缩略词（shortening）

缩略词是将较长的英语单词取其首部或者主干构成与原词同义的短单词，或者将组成词汇短语的各个单词的首字母拼接为一个大写字母的字符串。随着科技发展，缩略词在文章索引、前言、摘要、文摘、电报、说明书、商标等科技文章中频繁采用。对计算机专业来说，在程序语句、程序注释、软件文档、文件描述中也采用了大量的缩略词作为标识符、名称。缩略词的出现方便了印刷、书写、速记、以及口语交流等，但也同时增加了阅读和理解的困难。

缩略词开始出现时，通常采用破折号、引号或者括号将它们的原形单词和组合词一并列出，久而久之，人们对缩略词逐渐接受和认可，作为注释性的后者也就消失了。在通常情况下，缩略词多取自各个组合字（虚词除外）的首部第一、二字母。缩略词也可能有形同而义异的情况。如果遇到这种情况，翻译时应当根据上下文确定词意，并在括号内给出其原形组合词汇。缩略词可以分为如下几种。

1. 压缩和省略

将某些太长、难拼、难记、使用频繁的单词压缩成一个短小的单词，或取其头部、或取其关键音节。如：

flu=influenza 流感　　　　　　lab=laboratory 实验室　　　　　math=mathematics 数学

iff=if only if 当且仅当　　　　rhino=rhinoceros 犀牛　　　　ad=advertisement 广告

2. 缩写（acronym）

将某些词组和单词集合中每个实意单词的第一或者首部几个字母重新组合，组成为一个新的词汇，作为专用词汇使用。在应用中它形成三种类型，即：

1) 通常以小写字母出现，并作为常规单词

radar (radio detecting and ranging) 雷达 sonar (sound navigation and ranging) 声纳

flops (floating-point Operation Per Second) 每秒浮点运算次数

spool (simultaneous peripheral operation on line) 假脱机

2) 以大写字母出现，具有主体发音音节

BASIC (Beginner's All-purpose Symbolic Instruction Code) 初学者通用符号指令代码

FORTRAN (Formula Translation) 公式翻译（语言）

COBOL (Common Business Oriented Language) 面向商务的通用语言

3) 以大写字母出现，没有读音音节，仅为字母头缩写

RISC (Reduced Instruction Set Computer) 精简指令集计算机

CISC (Complex Instruction Set Computer) 复杂指令集计算机

ADE (Application Development Environment) 应用开发环境

PCB (Process Control Block) 进程控制块

CGA (Color Graphics Adapter) 彩色图形适配器

DBMS (Data Base Management System) 数据库管理系统

FDD (Floppy Disk Device) 软盘驱动器

MBPS (Mega Byte Per Second) 每秒兆字节

五、借用词

借用词一般来自厂商名、商标名、产品代号名、发明者名、地名等，它通过将普通公共英语词汇演变成专业词意而实现。有的则是将原来已经有的词汇赋予新的含义。例如：

woofer 低音喇叭　　　　　tweeter 高音喇叭　　　　　flag 标志、状态

cache 高速缓存　　　　　semaphore 信号量　　　　　firewall 防火墙

mailbomb 邮件炸弹　　　　scratch pad 高速缓存　　　fitfall 专用程序入口

在现代科技英语中借用了大量的公共英语词汇、日常生活中的常用词汇，而且，以西方特有的幽默和结构讲述科技内容。这时，读者必须在努力扩大自己专业词汇的同时，也要掌握和丰富自己的生活词汇，并在阅读和翻译时正确采用适当的含义。

Exercises

I. Answer the following questions

1. Discuss the origins of the Internet.

2. Relate the key technology concepts behind the Internet.

3. Please describe the role of Internet protocols and utility programs.

4. What are the main structural elements of Internet today?

5. What are the limitations of today's Internet?

6. Please describe the potential capabilities of Internet II.

7. How does World Wide Web work?

8. Please Describe how Internet and Web features and services support e-commerce.

II. Fill in the blanks in each of the following

1. The basic building blocks of the Internet are _____.

2. _____ is a method of slicing digital messages into parcels called "packets", sending the packets along different communication paths as they become available, and then reassembling the packets once they arrive at their destination.

3. IP addresses are 32-bit numbers that appear as a series of _____ separate numbers marked off by periods.

4. IP addresses can be represented by a natural language convention called _____.

5. An _____ is a TCP/IP network located within a single organization for purposes of communications and information processing.

6. _____ are formed when firms permit outsiders to access their internal TCP/IP networks.

7. The primary purpose of Web _____ is to display Web pages.

8. Cookies are a tool used by Web sites to store information about a _____.

Chapter 3　E-Business Models

学习指导

电子企业可以提供个性化服务、高品质顾客服务及其改进的供应链管理。本章详细分析了各种电子商业模型及其实现技术，通过本章学习，读者应该：
- 理解不同的电子商业模型。
- 探索传统企业向电子商业转变的可行性及其方法。
- 掌握专用术语和电子商务的基本原理。

3.1　Introduction

There are many benefits of bringing your business to the Web. An e-business can offer personalized service, high-quality customer service, and improved supply chain management. In this chapter we explore the different types of businesses operating on the Web, as well as the technologies needed to build and run an e-commerce Web site.

Amazon.com, eBay, Yahoo! and others have helped to define industry categories and business models on the Web. Entrepreneurs starting e-businesses need to be aware of these models and how to implement them effectively. In this chapter, we review the storefront model, the auction model, dynamic pricing models, the portal model and other Web business models. An e-business is defined as a company that has an online presence. E-businesses that have the ability to sell, trade, barter and transact over the Web can be considered e-commerce businesses. The combination of a company's policy, operations, technology and ideology define its business model. In this chapter, we define a number of models and the technologies that make them possible. Businesses within a particular model can leverage these fundamental technologies to differentiate themselves from the competition.

New Words & Phrases

storefront　n. 店头，店面
barter　n. & v. 物品交换，实物交易
leverage　n. 杠杆机构，杠杆作用；v. 利用杠杆作用调节

auction　n. 拍卖；vt. 拍卖
ideology　n. 思想体系，意识形态

3.2　Storefront Model

Shopping online is an increasingly popular activity. A report by eMarketer predicted 72.5% of all web users would shop online in 2009, with the proportion increasing to 75.7% by 2013. The move toward e-commerce presents many benefits, as well as a host of new considerations. The storefront model is what many people think of when they hear the word e-business. The storefront combines transaction processing, security, online payment and information storage to enable merchants to sell their products on the Web. This is a basic form of e-commerce where the buyer and the seller interact directly.

To conduct storefront e-commerce, merchants need to organize an online catalog of products, take orders through their Web sites, accept payments in a secure environment, send merchandise to customers and manage customer data (such as customer profiles). They must also market their sites to potential customers—a topic further explored in "Internet Marketing".

Although the term e-commerce is fairly new, large corporations have been conducting e-commerce for decades by networking their systems with those of business partners and clients. For example, the banking industry uses Electronic Funds Transfer (EFT) to transfer money between accounts. Many companies also use Electronic Data Interchange (EDI), in which business forms, such as purchase orders and invoices, are standardized so that companies can share information with customers, vendors and business partners electronically.

Until recently, e-commerce was feasible only for large companies. However, the Internet and the World Wide Web make it possible for small businesses to compete with large companies. E-commerce also allows companies to conduct business 24-by-7[1], all day, everyday, worldwide.

Some of the most successful e-businesses are using the storefront model. Many of the leading storefront model companies are B2C (business-to-consumer) companies. For example, More.com (www.more.com) is a health and beauty e-commerce site that uses a shopping cart to allow customers to shop, buy and arrange shipment. Products include skin care, eye care, pharmaceuticals and many other products associated with health and wellness.

Ticketmaster.com (www.ticketmaster.com) uses the Internet to sell tickets improve its customer service. Customers have access to seating plans, show listings and price discounts. Ticketmaster uses shopping-cart technology, an advanced database system and a strong supporting infrastructure to make this possible.

Although both companies use a shopping cart and supporting technologies to offer their products and services to customers, each has chosen a different approach to e-commerce.

3.2.1 Shopping-cart Technology

One of the most commonly used e-commerce enablers is the shopping cart. This order-processing technology allows customers to accumulate items they wish to buy as they continue to shop. Supporting the shopping cart is a product catalog, which is hosted on the merchant server in the form of a database. The merchant server is the data storage and management system employed by the merchant. A database is a part of the merchant server designed to store and report on large amounts of information. For example, a database for an online clothing retailer would typically include such product specifications as item description, size, availability, shipping information, stock levels and on-order information. Databases also store customer information, such as names, addresses, credit-card information and past purchases. The Amazon.com feature explains these technologies and how they are implemented.

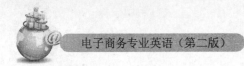

Although the shopping cart is only one method of conducting transactions online, it is an effective way of buying and selling products on the Internet. Many companies combine a number of purchasing methods to give their customers a wide array of options.

While shopping-cart technology offers consumers the convenience of quick and easy transactions, it creates problems regarding consumer privacy and online security. For more examples of e-businesses who have found success using this technology visit www.etoys.com, www.webvan.com, and www.cdnow.com.

3.2.2 Online Shopping Malls

Online shopping malls present consumers with a wide selection of products and services. They are often considered to be more convenient than searching and shopping at independent online storefronts for several reasons. Consumers can search and shop for a variety of products, and rather than making several separate purchases, they can use the mall's shopping-cart technology to purchase items from many stores in a single transaction. Often these sites act as shopping portals, directing traffic to the leading shopping retailers for a specific product.

Leading online malls include Mall.com (www.mall.com), which features many of the same vendors you will find in your local brick-and-mortar[3] mall—offline retailers such as JCrew, Harrods, and the Sharper Image. Shopnow.com, www.shopnow.com and www.DealShop.com are other online malls offering a wide variety of shopping options

New Words & Phrases

merchandise   n. 商品，货物

invoice   n. 发票，发货单，v.开发票，记清单

shipment   n. 发货，装运，装运的货物

pharmaceuticals   n. 医药品

discount   n. 折扣

on-order   已订购

confirmation   n. 证实，确认，批准

Billing Address 账单地址

privacy   n. 秘密，隐私

mall   n. 购物中心，商场

DVD   数字化视频光盘

Abbreviations

EFT   (Electronic Funds Transfer) 电子资金转账

EDI (Electronic Data Interchange)电子数据交换

Notes

1. 24-by-7:   指一天 24 小时、一周 7 天的工作（营业）方式。

2. 1-Click SM system: 网上书店亚马逊公司的"1－click"（一点开）专利技术可以存储网上购物者的票据结算和送货信息，该系统被称为"绿色通道"结算服务系统，顾客下次光顾时可以简化结算过程，以方便回头客。

3. brick-and-mortar: 原意为砖和砂浆，指实体商铺或传统商家。

3.3   Auction Model

An **auction** is a process of buying and selling goods or services by offering them up for bid, taking bids, and then selling the item to the highest bidder. The Web offers many different kinds of auction sites, in addition to sites designed to search existing auction sites in order to pinpoint the lowest prices on an available item.

Usually, auction sites act as forums through which Internet users can log-on and assume the role of either bidder or seller. As a seller, you are able to post an item you wish to sell, the minimum price you require to sell your item and a deadline to close the auction. Some sites allow you to add features, such as a photograph or a description of the item's condition. As a bidder, you may search the site for availability of the item you are seeking, view the current bidding activity and place a bid (bids are usually in designated increments). Some sites allow you to submit a maximum bidding price and will continue bidding for you. Auction technology will be explained in depth in the eBay feature.

The reverse auction model allows the buyer to set a price as sellers compete to match or even beat it. One example of a reverse auction site is Liquidprice.com which processes your auction within two days. A faster option is available when the buyer sets a reserve price. A reserve price is the lowest price that the seller will accept in any type of auction. Sellers can set the reserve price higher than the minimum bid. If no bid meets the reserve price, the auction is unsuccessful. If a seller sets a reserve price at Liquidprice.com, the seller will receive a series of bids within six hours of their initial post. However, if a successful bid is made, the buyer and seller must commit.

Although auction sites usually require a commission on sales, these sites are only a forum for online buying and selling. They do not involve themselves in payment or delivery. After the auction has been completed, both the seller and the bidder are notified, and the method of payment and the cost of delivery is then worked out between the two parties.

There are several other online auction sites. A few of the largest auctions sites are Yahoo! Auctions (auctions.yahoo.com), Amazon Auctions (www.amazon.com), FairMarket, Inc. (www.fairmarket.com) and Sotheby's (www.sothebys.com). If you prefer to see the auction as it happens, visit www.ibidlive.com. There is a demo available on this site.

Auctions are also being employed by business-to-business Web sites. In these auctions the buyer and the seller are companies. Auctions are a good way for a company to sell excess inventory and gain access to new, price-sensitive customers. Three examples of B2B auction sites are DoveBid, Inc. (www.dovebid.com), WorldCall Exchange (www.worldcallexchange. com) and U-Bid-It.com (www.u-bid-it.com).

New Words & Phrases

dwarf　adj. 矮小的；vt. 使矮小；使相形见拙

log on　登录

dispenser　n. 自动售货机

pinpoint　v. 查明

Reverse Auction，反向拍卖，反向标购

bold-face　n. [印刷]粗体铅字，黑体字

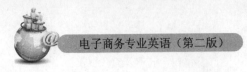
bid　vt. 出价，投标 n. 出价，投标　　　　　downtime　n. 停工期

consistently　adv. 一贯地，始终如一地　　　　addiction　n.　沉溺，上瘾

3.4　Portal Model

Portal sites give visitors the chance to find almost everything they are looking for in one place. They often offer news, sports and weather, as well as the ability to search the Web. When most people hear the word portal they think of search engines. Search engines are horizontal portals, or portals that aggregate information on a broad range of topics. Other portals are more specific, offering a great deal of information pertaining to a single area of interest—these are called vertical portals.

Online shopping is a popular addition to the major portals. Sites such as Hotbot.com, About.com, altavista.com and Yahoo.com provide users with a shopping page that links them to thousands of sites carrying a variety of products.

Portals linking consumers to online merchants, online shopping malls and auction sites provide several advantages. See the feature on Yahoo! for a better example of a shopping portal. Portals help users collect information on the item for which they are looking and allow users to browse independently owned storefronts, unlike some online shopping malls. Yahoo! permits users to browse a variety of sites while maintaining the convenience of paying through their Yahoo! account.

About.com offers its users an individualized experience through GuideSite, a service that acts as a personal shopper for the user. About.com's "guides", each specializing in a particular product type, continually update the Web site and are accessible via e-mail for consumer comments and questions.

Consumers must be savvy when using portals to do their online shopping. Each portal structures its online shopping experience a little differently. Some portals charge merchants for a link, others do not. For example, GoTo.com bills merchants per consumer "clickthrough". The more a business is willing to pay for each consumer "click", the higher that business will appear in GoTo.com's ranks. Because charging merchants may limit the options available to customers, this may not be the best method. Other sites, About.com and altavista.com for example, do not charge merchants to appear in some locations on their sites (About.com's GuideSite and Altavista.com's Shopping and Services Categories) but reserve the best areas of the site for paying customers.

Vertical Portals and Community Sites

Vertical portals offer a large amount of information in one subject area and are often described as community sites (see AOL feature). Community sites for an enormous number of special interest groups can be found online. Community sites create customer loyalty by allowing visitors to contribute to the sites, chat with friends and find information specifically targeted to them. Vertical portals tend to attract repeat visitors.

Many portal sites provide information pertaining to professional fields such as medicine and law. As a medical community site, Healtheon WebMD (www.webmd.com) offers a repository of documentation relating to the medical field. WebMD can also help you find doctors and medical professionals. Physicians can become members of WebMD, joining the specialized practice portal allows them to keep up-to-date with medical announcements, read the latest medical journals and communicate with other members of the medical community. Medscape (www.medscape.com) and Dr. Koop (www.drkoop.com) also offer medical-portal sites.

There are many legal portals on the Web. The services provided by LEXIS (www.lexis.com) and its partner site NEXIS (www.nexis.com) are fee-based and usually purchased on a licence basis by law firms. LEXIS provides access to case and other legal data, as well as relevant news articles. Lexis speeds up the research process for people within the legal profession.

Other types of online communities center themselves around a particular demographic. Bolt.com is an online teen community that offers chat forums, message boards, polls and shopping. Bolt promotes longer visits by giving visitors free access to content targeted to teens and a chance to communicate with others in the same age group. IVillage.com is a portal site for women. News and information on women's health, hobbies and general interest are available for free. Message boards are available for women who need questions answered or who would like to speak out on a given issue. iEmily.com (www.iemily.com) is a similar site designed for teenage women.

Internet.com is a portal site for the Internet and e-commerce. The latest news is offered along with links and a search option. Internet.com is loaded with content. All of the news articles are available free.

Epinions (www.epinions.com) gives visitors a chance to speak out on their hobbies, politics, favorite media, etc. Members are paid a few cents for each opinion they post. Epinions is a good place to find out real opinions on products and services you are considering. Some members have written hundreds of reviews on everything from film to automobiles.

New Words & Phrases

pertain to   v. 属于，关于，附属，适合，相称
clickthrough   n. 点击，点进，同 click-through
descending   n. 递减
merger   n. 合并，联合组织

savvy   v. 知道，了解；n.机智，理解，悟性
sign in   v. 签到，记录到达时间，签收
dorm   n. <俗> 宿舍，同 dormitory

3.5   Dynamic Pricing Models

The Web has changed the way business is done and the way products are priced. Companies such as Priceline (www.priceline.com) and Imandi (www.imandi.com) have enabled customers to name their prices for travel, homes, automobiles and consumer goods.

In the past, bargain hunters had to search out deals by visiting numerous local retailers and wholesalers. Today, a few mouse clicks is all you need to find the lowest price available.

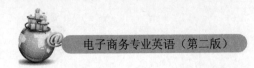

Buying in bulk has always driven prices down, and there are now Web sites that allow you to lower the price by joining with other buyers to purchase products in large quantities. Another pricing strategy used by many e-businesses is to offer products and services for free. By forming strategic partnerships and selling advertising many companies are able to offer their products at a greatly reduced rate and often for free. Bartering and offering rebates are other ways companies are keeping prices down on the Internet.

3.5.1 Name-Your-Price Model

The name-your-price business model empowers customers by allowing them to choose their price for products and services (See the Priceline.com feature). Many of the businesses that offer this service have formed partnerships with leaders of industries such as travel, lending, retail etc. These industry leaders receive the customer's desired price from the intermediary and decide whether or not to sell the product or service. If the customer's price is not reasonable then that customer will be asked to choose another price.

3.5.2 Comparison Pricing Model

The comparison pricing model allows customers to poll a variety of merchants and find a desired product or service at the lowest price (See the Bottomdollar.com feature). These sites often get their revenue from partnerships with particular merchants. Thus, you need to be careful when using these services, because you may not necessarily be getting the best price available on the entire Web. Other similar sites search the most popular stores on the Internet, trying to appeal to the largest audience.

3.5.3 Demand-Sensitive Pricing Model

The Web has enabled customers to demand better, faster service at cheaper prices. It has also empowered buyers to shop in large groups to achieve a group rate.

The concept behind the demand-sensitive-pricing business model is that the more people who buy a product in a single purchase, the lower the cost per person becomes. Selling products individually can be expensive because the vendor must price a product so that it covers selling and overhead cost while still generating a profit. When customers buy in bulk, this cost is shared and the profit margin is increased. Mercata (www.mercata.com) sells products using this business model for the home, electronics, computers and peripherals among many other things. Customers become loyal to Mercata for helping them save money. MobShop (www.mobshop.com) offers comparable services. Because pricing and products do vary between these and other similar sites, so you may want to visit several such sites before making a purchase.

3.5.4 Bartering Model

Another popular method of conducting e-business is bartering, or offering one item in exchange for another. Ubarter.com (www.ubarter.com) is a site that allows individuals and companies wishing to sell a product to post their listings. The seller makes an initial offer with the intention of bartering to reach a final agreement with the buyer. A broad range of products and services is available for barter.

If a business is looking to get rid of an overstocked product, iSolve (www.isolve.com) can help sell it. Products can be sold directly or on a barter basis. Potential customers send their pricing preferences to the merchant who evaluates the offer. Deals are often part barter and part cash. Examples of items typically bartered are overstocked inventory items, factory surplus and unneeded assets.

3.5.5　Rebates

Rebates can help attract customers to your site. Many companies offer "everyday low prices" and specials to keep customers coming back. eBates is a shopping site where customers receive a rebate on every purchase. eBates has formed partnerships with wholesalers and retailers who will offer discounts—the company passes these discounts to customers in the form of rebates. By adding value to a customers visit, eBates builds customer satisfaction and loyalty. eBates retains a portion of the savings.

3.5.6　Offering Free Products and Services

Many entrepreneurs are forming their business models around advertising-driven revenue streams. Television networks, radio stations, magazines and print media use advertising to fund their operations and make a profit. The following sites offer their products for free on the Web. Many of these sites also form partnerships with companies to exchange products and services for advertising space and vise versa.

The Hollywood Stock Exchange (www.hsx.com) is a free gaming site where visitors become traders of entertainment stocks and star bonds. Traders are able to track the value of their movie and music stocks and bonds as they fluctuate. The strongest portfolios are rewarded with prizes. The company is able to offer its services free by selling advertising to sponsors.

iWon.com (www.iWon.com) is a portal site that rewards users with raffle points as they browse the site's content. iWon has the appearance of a traditional search engine, offering links to news, sports, weather, and other topics. However, users registering and surfing the site become eligible for daily, weekly, monthly and annual prizes. Every advertisement and link has a point value and, as your points accrue, so do your chances of winning. iWon.com is able to support its free contests through advertising revenue and partnerships.

Freelotto.com (www.freelotto.com) also offers free contests supported by advertising revenue. After registering with Freelotto.com, you can enter a free lottery. FreeLotto awards tens of millions in cash and prizes through its online lottery system. However, you must visit sponsoring Web sites in exchange for your visit. Freelotto.com generates its income from these sponsors.

Freemerchant.com offers free hosting, a free store builder, a free shopping cart, free traffic logs, free auction tools and all necessary elements for running an e-commerce storefront. Freemerchant makes money from its strategic partnerships and referrals. Freemerchant partners are companies who

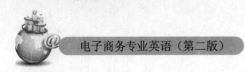
can help small businesses establish a presence on the Web. These partners offer their services free of charge in exchange for advertising.

At Startsampling.com (www.startsampling.com) you can earn prizes for trying and reviewing products. This site allows you to request free samples from companies across the country.

Other Web sites that offer free resources are free-programs.com, freestuffcenter.com and emazing.com.

New Words & Phrases

mouse	n. 鼠标	rebate	n. 回扣，折扣；vt.减少，打折扣
empower	v. 授权与，使能够	catapult	vt. 突然把……捧出名
spotlight	n. 聚光灯	mortgage	n. 抵押；v.抵押
scour	vt.（搜索或追捕时）急速走遍	markup	n. 涨价，涨价幅度
profit margin	n. 利润率	overstock	vt. 进货过多，n.过多的进货，库存过剩
vice versa	adv. 反之亦然	star bond	n. 明星债券
eligible	adj.（常与 for 连用）适合的，被选的	lottery	n. 彩票
referral	n. 提名，推举，被推举的人	raffle	n. 抽彩售货；vt. 抽彩售货；vi. 抽彩

3.6　B2B Exchange

B2B e-commerce is defined as buying, selling, partnering, bartering or trading conducted between two or more businesses. The B2B marketplace is one of the fastest growing segments of e-commerce. Industry leaders have begun using B2B marketplaces and exchanges to improve their business methods on the Web. B2B exchanges allow businesses to buy, sell, auction, barter and distribute products and services. This cuts costs while improving efficiency.

Procurement (acquiring goods or services) and effective supply chain management can be difficult and costly aspects of running businesses. ICG Commerce Systems (www. icgcommerce.com) is a site that enables businesses, customers, suppliers, purchasers and any combination of these to interact and conduct transactions over the Internet. The system supports B2B, B2C and all variations of these models.

TradeAccess (www.tradeaccess.com) helps businesses form relationships and facilitate negotiations. The site aggregates all of the documentation and materials appropriate for a specific contract and negotiates the terms over the Web.

ItoI stands for Industry to Industry. This site, located at www.itoi.com, is designed for inter-industry trading and offers services in the chemical, retail, construction and energy industries. Visitors have the option of buying through traditional methods, auctioning or conducting exchanges. In an exchange, customers make requests and merchants attempt to fill their request at the best price. The business provides a marketplace for raw materials, chemicals, equipments and services.

Another kind of B2B exchange is available online at eWork.com, which allows businesses to exchange employees to complete short-term projects. eWork can search its databases and find qualified professionals to help you complete all of your projects. eWork is just one of many online companies that can help a business exchange human resources.

Other B2B exchanges include www.cynomix.com and www.biz2biz.com.

New Words & Phrases

procurement　n. 购置，采购

exchange　n. 交易市场

marketplace　n. 集会场所，市场，商场

aggregate　vt. 聚集

negotiate　vt. 谈判，处理，转让

3.7　B2B Service Providers

B2B service providers make B2B transactions on the Internet easier. These e-businesses help other businesses improve policies, procedures, customer services and general operations.

Ariba (www.ariba.com) is a B2B service provider. Solutions include supply chain management, procurement, logistics, customer service features and many others.

Freemarkets.com is a B2B marketplace connecting buyers and sellers. Companies with surplus inventory can use Freemarkets to sell extra assets. Freemarkets specializes in hard-to-sell raw materials, property and equipment.

Because of the intense competition among Web sites for customers, the Web makes it more important than ever to keep your customers happy. Customer service and troubleshooting are important. Liveperson.com has found a way to improve customer service on the Internet, by offering a product that connects visitors to your help center through a live text-based chat. By clicking an icon on the site the visitor can speak directly with a company representative. Try the system at www.liveperson.com.

Business travelers who wish to do work often have to pay for time on a computer within a hotel's business center. PCRoomLink (www.pcroomlink.com) provides computers and secure Internet access to business travelers by putting computers in their hotel rooms. Membership is free and required when using the service.

B2B services are also available from www.ceverything.com and www.magnifi.com.

New Words & Phrases

logistics　n. 物流

surplus　n. 剩余；adj.剩余的，过剩的

troubleshooting　n. 发现并修理故障，解决纷争

icon　n. 图标，肖像，偶像

membership　n. 成员资格

3.8　Online Trading and Lending Models

Another fast-growing area of e-commerce is online securities trading. According to U.S. Bancorp Piper Jaffray, Company and Industry Sources (www.piperjaffray.com/re/re_ne2.asp?id =188), "online trading volumes accounted for 37 percent of all retail trades for the first half of 1999, up from 30 percent in the second half of 1998."

Stock trades used to be handled only through brokers who were paid commissions for their services. However, due to the popularity of online trading, many brokerage houses have established a presence on the Web. Trading sites allow you to research securities, buy, sell and manage all of your investments from your desktop. Online trading often costs less than conventional brokerage.

Charles Schwab (www.schwab.com) is becoming one of the leading online trading providers. DLJ Direct (www.dljdirect.com) and Fidelity Investments (www.fidelity.com) offer similar services.

For more information about e-commerce and online trading, check out the latest news reports or review back issues of Business Week at www.businessweek.com and of The Industry Standard at www.thestandard.com. The Motley Fool (www.fool.com) is another good resource for online trading information.

New Words & Phrases

brokerage	n. 经纪业务	securities	n. 有价证券
investment	n. 投资，可获利的东西	Stock Quote	股票报价
broker	n. 掮客，经纪人	portfolio	n. 有价证券，资产组合，证券资产

3.9　Getting a Loan Online

Online lending is a growing segment of e-commerce. You might find a loan with a lower rate online than through traditional lending channels. The following companies make loans to customers over the Web.

E-LOAN (www.eloan.com) offers credit-card services, home equity loans and the tools and calculators to help you make educated borrowing decisions.

Rated the number-one mortgage e-commerce site by Gomez.com, Mortgagebot (www.mortgagebot.com) offers a five-vendor rate search. This allows customers to find a bank in their neighborhood that is willing to offer them the lowest possible interest rate.

E-businesses can seek loans at eCredit (www.ecredit.com). This company has formed partnerships with leading lenders to speed the financing process. Once a business has received funding, eCredit will also help the business manage their new assets. eCredit customers include Hewlett-Packard, Intel and many other Fortune 1000 companies[1]. LoansDirect (www.loansdirect.com) offers a comparable service. It is important to investigate a variety of options when getting a loan. A difference of a few interest points can significantly increase bills.

New Words & Phrases

brokerage n. 经纪业务	securities n. 有价证券
lending n. 出借，出租，贷款，出租物	loan n.（借出的）贷款，借出；v.借，借给
vendor n. 卖主	assets n. 资产

Notes

1. eCredit customers include Hewlett-Packard, Intel and many other Fortune 1000 companies. ECredit 的顾客包括惠普、英特尔和其他许多世界《财富》1000 强公司。

3.10   Recruiting on the Web

Recruiting and job searching can be done effectively on the Web (See the monster.com feature) Whether you are an employer or a job seeker, the Internet can improve your ability to recruit or find a job. Job seekers can learn how to write a resume and cover letter, post it online and search through job listings to find the jobs that best suit their needs. Employers can post jobs that can be searched by an enormous pool of applicants. In this section we will examine some of the recruiting options available on the Web.

Dice.com (www.dice.com) is a recruiting Web site that focuses on the computer industry. Fees are based on the number of jobs a company wishes to post and the frequency with which the postings are updated. Job seekers can post their resumes and search the job database for free.

Guru.com (www.guru.com) is a recruiting site for contract employees. Independent contractors, private consultants and trainers can use guru.com to find short-term and long-term work. Tips, articles and advices are available for contractors who wish to learn more about their industry and the best way to contract their work. Other sections of the site teach you how to run your business, buy the best equipment and manage legal issues. Guru.com includes an online store where you can buy products associated with small business management. Companies wishing to hire contractors need to register.

SixFigureJobs (www.sixfigurejobs.com) is a recruitment site designed for experienced executives. Executive positions are often hard to fill due to the high demands and experience required for the jobs. This site is designed to help fill these executive positions. Resume posting and job searching is free to job seekers.

Refer.com (www.refer.com.) rewards visitors for successful job referrals. Highly sought-after positions can earn thousands of dollars. If you refer a friend or family member and they are hired, you receive a commission.

These are just a few of the many recruiting-related sites on the Web. Some sites are targeted at specific groups of people such as computer programmers or electrical engineers, while others offer their services to anyone. It is worthwhile to search and post on many of the sites at one time.

monster.com

Super Bowl ads[1] and effective marketing have made monster.com one of the most recognizable online brands. monster.com allows people looking for jobs to post their resumes, search job listings, read advice and information about the job-search process and take proactive steps to improve their career. These services are free to job seekers. Employers can post job listings, search resume databases and become featured employers.

Posting your resume at monster.com is simple and free. monster.com has a resume builder that allows you to post a resume to its site in 15-30 minutes; you can store up to 5 resumes and cover letters on the monster.com server. Some companies offer their applications directly on the monster.com site. monster.com has job postings in every state and all major categories. Furthermore, you can decide who gets to see your personal identification information. As one of the leading recruiting sites on the Web, monster.com is a good place to start your job search or to find out more about the search process.

New Words & Phrases

recruit vt，vi 招募，招聘
pool n. 存储池，组合，联合
consultant n. 顾问，商议者，咨询者
commission n. 代理（权），佣金

cover letter n. 自述信，工作申请信
contractor n. 订约人，承包人
referral n. 提名，推举，被推举的人
Super Bowl 超级杯（美式橄榄球赛）

Notes

1. Super Bowl ads 美式足球超级杯(Super Bowl)赛场上的广告，其广告价位最高，多泛指天价的广告。

3.11 Online News Services

As we move into the information age, there is no question that the Web will play a major role in the publishing and news industries. Well-known news organizations such as CNN (see feature), The Wall Street Journal and Newsweek have all found the Web to be a dynamic environment on which to feature their content.

The Wall Street Journal (www.wsj.com), one of the most widely read newspapers in the world, is offered in an online edition which includes full text and 24-hour updates. You can start by trying the online version on a free-trial basis, and, if you choose to subscribe, you will receive full access to the Barrons (www.barrons.com.) database—an online database of commentaries and articles by leading investment analysts.

ESPN.com provides the latest sporting news and allows users to get in-depth information on their favorite players, teams, etc. ESPN.com offers live text, audio and video of games and highlights. Visitors can also enroll in fantasy sporting games, such as football, baseball and golf.

Quality writers with reliable sources can begin publishing their content on the Web. Traditional barriers of entry such as printing and distribution costs do not exist on the Web. This allows independent Web news organizations to compete with traditional news leaders. Matt

Drudge has become a celebrity due to the success of his online news site, the Drudge Report (www.drudgereport.com).

CNN Interactive

CNN Interactive (www.cnn.com) is one of the most visited and most interactive sites on the Web. CNN has a network of sites designed to give current, highly targeted news and information to their visitors. Each of these sites offers streaming audio and video taken from broadcasts on the television network.

CNNallpolitics is a site offering more in-depth articles about politicians and their campaigns, public policy and global politics. CNNSI is the all-sports section of the CNN network. You can follow teams in every league or just catch up on the latest scores and highlights. CNNFN allows you to track financial news and securities data from your Web browser. MyCNN allows you to personalize the news and information that appears on your browser. You can choose text, audio and video in any category. You can then customize the way CNN appears when you visit the site.

CNN has also built sites offering information in foreign languages. They include news and information specific to each country and region. The network of sites that make up CNN Interactive uses the highest quality multimedia and content to add value to customers' experiences.

New Words & Phrases

CNN　美国有线新闻网络

highlights　n. 拔萃，集锦（精采会议文献选辑）

celebrity　n. 名声，名人

multimedia　n. 多媒体，多媒体的采用

enroll　v. [亦作 enrol] 登记，招收，参加，成为成员

fantasy　n. 幻想；狂想；想象，荒诞的想法

commentary　n. 注释，解说词

Wall Street Journal　华尔街日报

3.12　Online Travel Services

Web surfers can search for and arrange all of their travel and accommodations online, and can often save money doing so. The Web gives people access to much of the same information previously accessible only by travel agents(See the Travelocity.com feature). You will find the lowest prices, best times and the best accommodations available to you.

Microsoft offers travel services through www.expedia.com. Microsoft Expedia allows you to book all of your travel arrangements, including transportation and lodging. Membership is free, and members are given access to a database of information offering them the best available options.

Cheaptickets (www.cheaptickets.com) is a similar site that helps customers find discount fares for airline tickets, hotel rooms, cruise vacations and rental cars. Users are given access to a database of up-to-the-minute flight schedule data.

Many travel sites are targeting business travelers specifically. BizTravel.com will reimburse customers in the event of a late or cancelled flight, lost luggage, or poor in-flight service. The rate of reimbursement is based on the severity of the problem. All flights that are cancelled or arrive more than two hours later than scheduled are reimbursed in full. Lost luggage is also paid for in full. This

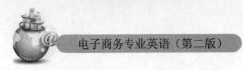

system is designed for business travelers.

Another site designed for business travelers, GetThere.com (www.getthere.com), helps corporate clients cut travel costs by connecting them directly to airlines, hotels and rental cars through its site. GetThere also outsources its technology, allowing portal sites to offer similar services.

New Words & Phrases

cruise	vi. 巡游，巡航；n.巡游，巡航	reimburse	v. 偿还，报销
reimbursement	n. 付还，退还	outsource	v. 外部采办，外购
itinerary	n. 路线	up-to-date	adj. 直到现在的，最近的
criteria	n. 标准		

3.13 Online Entertainment

The Web is based on the communication of high-quality information developed with high-quality multimedia. The entertainment industry has recognized this and has leveraged its power to sell movie tickets, albums and any other entertainment-related content they can fit on a Web page. Some of the Web's greatest controversies surround the online entertainment industry. Internet copyright cases are becoming the norm as individuals begin to use the Internet to trade their media such as music and videos.

iCast.com (www.icast.com) is a multimedia-rich entertainment site. Audio and Video downloads of popular music and films are available for free. Each news article is accompanied by a supporting multimedia file. For instance, news regarding a particular actress may include the trailer of her latest feature film. Visitors to the site will benefit from a high-speed connection. The iCast media player is a free product that allows visitors to play audio and video from the site.

The Internet Movie Database (www.imdb.com) combines a huge database, a well-designed and easily maneuverable site and interesting content to create a highly entertaining site. IMDB helps you to locate and learn more about your favorite films, actors, executives, production companies and news relating to filmed entertainment. A search for any given film will give information pertaining to that film's cast and crew and their personal history. IMDB is part of the Amazon.com network of Web sites.

New Words & Phrases

trailer	n. 预告片，片尾，带尾	multimedia-rich	富媒体
pertaining	adj. 与……有关系的，为……固有的(to)	cast	n. 演员表，演员阵容
crew	n. 摄制组	scour	vt.（搜索或追捕时）急速走遍

3.14 Online Automotive Sites

Various sites allow users to research and purchase new and used cars. Whether or not you actually make your final arrangements for the purchase of a new vehicle online, many of the preliminary steps can be completed. Online auto sites provide users with the ability to explore options more efficiently than traveling among dealerships. Online automobile appraisers also offer users leverage in negotiating a price on a new car by giving them access to instant value estimates.

Autobytel (www.autobytel.com) is a one-stop shop where users buy, sell, maintain and learn more about automobiles. You can search classified ads for used cars or find the best price on a new car. Additionally, if you are looking to service your car, you can contact your local service station and request an estimate. You can also find out where to get the best value on car insurance.

Autoparts.com is an online auction site for people buying and selling auto parts. Once you register, you can begin searching through the database of auto parts. You can search for parts by year, make and model.

Auto.com is an online version of the Detroit Free Press. The site offers news and information regarding the automotive industry. The site is a good place to learn about the automobile industry as well as the car you drive.

New Words & Phrases

dealership　n. 商品经销特殊权，商品特许经销商	appraiser　n. 评价者，鉴定者，估价官
one-stop shop　n. 一站式服务商店	Detroit Free Press 底特律自由报

3.15　Energy Online

A number of companies have set up energy exchanges where buyers and sellers come to communicate, buy, sell, and distribute energy. These companies sell crude oil, electricity and the products and systems for distributing them.

HoustonStreet (www.houstonstreet.com.) is an online market for traders looking to buy energy commodities. Traders can buy and sell crude oil, refined products and electricity from the HoustonStreet Web site.

Altranet (www.altranet.com.) also sells energy commodities. Utility companies can buy natural gas, electricity and heating oil directly from the site. Altranet also facilitates the distribution of products with the help of its subsidiaries.

Retail Energy (www.retailenergy.com) is a directory for the energy industry. This site was designed by the Power Marketing Association and offers a comprehensive listing of energy providers. Current energy prices for both electricity and natural gas are available.

New Words & Phrases

subsidiary　n. 辅助的，子公司

3.16　Selling Brainpower

Companies can buy patents and other intellectual property online. It is often difficult for small

businesses to invest time and money in research and development. Other companies have trouble finding the talent to create such property.

Companies who do not have the human resources to complete complex projects can find help at HelloBrain.com. When merchants post the projects they need completed and the compensation they are willing to pay, proposed answers will be sent from companies and contractors that can help. HelloBrain acts as the middleman offering free postings to merchants.

The Question Exchange (www.questionexchange.com) allows businesses and individuals to access programming-specific troubleshooting as well as customer service. Companies pay a subscription fee to gain access to the system — in exchange, users are able to ask programming-related development questions and access a database of 10,000 archived questions.

Yet2 (www.yet2.com) is an e-business designed to help companies raise capital by selling intellectual property such as patents and trademarks. Yet2 is backed by industry-leading companies who wish to sell intellectual property assets. You must register to get a full view of the properties, but Yet2 does offer a sample listing.

New Words & Phrases

brainpower   n. 科学工作者，智囊

compensation   n. 补偿，赔偿

archive   vt. 存档；n.档案文件

intellectual property   知识产权

patent   n. 专利权，执照，专利品

3.17   Online Art Dealers

The Web offers a new outlet for your favorite supplies and artwork which you can often find at a discount on the Web. Shopping-cart technology and express shipping allow you to have your art and supplies within a few days of your order.

Art.com allows you to choose between fine art, photography, posters and prints, animations and many other media. You can search the art.com database by artist, medium, decor, size, subject, and genre. Artists also list their favorites, for you to peruse.

Guild.com is another art dealer offering pieces in a wide variety of media. The products are well documented, easy to find and range from a few hundred dollars to thousands of dollars. There are more than 7,000 products available to your shopping cart.

Atom Films (www.atomfilms.com) is one of the leading film sites on the Web and has frequently turned down offers to bring their content to the big screen. Members of Atom Films have access to award-winning short films and animations delivered via streaming video.

Art.net (www.art.net) offers links to many art resources on the Web, including artists' home pages, suppliers and supporting services.

New Words & Phrases

dealer   n. 经销商，经销人，经纪人

medium   n. 媒体，方法，媒介

decor　n. 舞台装饰，装饰之格调　　　　　genre　n. 类型，流派

peruse　vt. 细读，研讨

3.18　E-Learning

The e-learning industry is growing rapidly as the number of individuals with access to computers and hand-held-devices increases. Universities and corporate-training companies offer high-quality distance education directly over the Web. There are companies on the Web that aggregate e-learning products and services from content creators and publishers worldwide, and offer them on a subscription basis to individuals and corporations. As technology increases and audio and video quality on the Web improve, so will the quality and availability of e-learning programs.

Click2Learn (www.click2learn.com) has created a database of products and services to help individuals and companies find the education they need. Click2Learn also has a skills assessment feature that helps customers evaluate their e-learning needs. Companies wishing to develop their own training can use the Click2Learn Toolbook product in order to develop and sell courses on the Click2Learn site. Once a customer has developed courseware for the Web, the course can be included within the Click2learn Web site.

Saba (www.saba.com) also aggregates e-learning materials and courses. Companies can create Saba learning e-stores—customized storefronts—to sell their e-learning products. Saba helps their customers turn traditional instructor-led courses into Web-based training courses. Additionally, customers can use Saba as an e-learning portal where they can find training products for themselves and their employees.

Blackboard.com (www.blackboard.com) allows teachers and educational organizations to post their courses on the Web. Once a company has bought a license for the Blackboard.com CourseInfoTM course-development product, they can begin posting and offering their training materials and courses over the Web. For an additional fee, Blackboard.com offers trainers e-commerce capabilities, special marketing opportunities, more server space, and access to customer support.

WebCT (www.webct.com) helps educators and students leverage the power of the Web to improve their educational experience. WebCT sells a course development tool that enables educators to quickly build supplementary course materials or full courses to be offered through the WebCT learning hub. The company has offered courses to more than one million students.

Deitel & Associates, Inc. (www.deitel.com) teaches instructor-led training courses for many of the world's largest organizations. Deitel publications are used in each of its training courses, and in thousands of colleges and universities worldwide.

The Version 1 Deitel Web-based training courses are similar to the Deitel interactive multimedia Cyber Classroom products. The courses include the full content of the text-books as well as complete audio walkthroughs, "live-code" examples and hundreds of solved problems. The products also include course management, scheduling and assessment features. The Version 2

Web-based training courses emulate the instructor-led training experience with more extensive lecture and lab features.

Colleges and universities have also begun integrating e-learning into their curricula. Jones International University (www.getmymba.com), the University of Illinois (www.online.uillinois. edu) and the University of Phoenix (www.universityofphoenix.com) are among the first schools to offer complete degree programs online. Students are able to apply online and take courses at home using the Internet.

Many publishers are beginning to add electronic publishing departments to meet the demand for electronic books. Electronic books, or e-books are publications that can be downloaded onto your computer or to a hand-held device and read at your convenience. Xlibris (www.xlibris.com) specializes in publishing books in electronic form. Other electronic publishing companies include iPublish.com (www.ipublish.com) and netLibrary.com (www.netlibrary.com).

New Words & Phrases

hand-held devices　手持设备	assessment　n. 估价，被估定的金额
license　n. 许可（证），执照；vt.许可，特许	hub　n. 网络集线器，网络中心
supplementary　n. 增补者，增补物；adj.附助的	walkthrough　n. 开拍前的排练，初步排演
curricula　n. 课程	

3.19　Click-and-Mortar Businesses

Brick-and-mortar companies who wish to bring their businesses to the Web must determine the level of cooperation and integration the two separate entities will share. A company that can offer its services both online and offline can add value to the customers' experience. One of the major issues in e-commerce today is how to integrate the Internet into offline businesses. The following companies have all worked out successful answers to this question.

Barnes & Noble (www.bn.com) has established itself as a leader in the booksellers market both online and offline. Customers have access to the same inventory online as they do in the actual stores. In the event that a customer is dissatisfied with a purchase made online, they can return it to their local brick-and-mortar B&N store.

1-800-Flowers (www.1800flowers.com) has established a presence on the Web. Their customers can now view pictures of floral arrangements before making a purchase.

CircuitCity (www.circuitcity.com), a store specializing in consumer electronics, appliances, audio and video, has effectively integrated its online and offline entities. CircuitCity has tied its offline stores to its online store, allowing customers to order online and pick up at their local stores, though shipping is still available.

The Web has created such great opportunities for some companies that they have abandoned their bricks all-together. Egghead.com (www.egghead.com) started out as a company that sold computers and peripherals through small brick-and-mortar stores. Many of their competitors were catalog businesses that often underpriced them. The Web gave Egghead the opportunity to abandon unnecessary property overhead and access a global market.

peripheral   adj. 外围的，n.外围设备   entity   n. 实体

egghead   n. 有知识者，受过高等教育的人，理论家   overhead   n. 企业一般管理费用

Notes

1. Click-and-Mortar 鼠标+水泥，即传统商务(Brick-and-Mortar)与电子商务的结合，可译为虚实结合的混合商务。

数学公式的读法（Pronunciation of mathematical expressions）

下面给出了大部分数学公式的读法。除非需要特别准确地说明，通常最短形式是首选读法。

1 逻辑（Logic）

$\exists$	there exists
$\forall$	for all
$p \Rightarrow q$	p implies q / if p, then q
$p \Leftrightarrow q$	p if and only if q /p is equivalent to q / p and q are equivalent

2 集合（Sets）

$x \in A$	x belongs to A / x is an element (or a member) of A
$x \notin A$	x does not belong to A / x is not an element (or a member) of A
$A \subset B$	A is contained in B / A is a subset of B
$A \supset B$	A contains B / B is a subset of A
$A \cap B$	A cap B / A meet B/ A intersection B
$A \cup B$	A cup B/ A join B / A union B
B/A	A minus B/the difference between A and B
$A \times B$	A cross B / the Cartesian product of A and B （A 与 B 的笛卡尔积）

3 实数（Real numbers）

$x+1$	x plus one
$x-1$	x minus one
$x \pm 1$	x plus or minus one
xy	xy / x multiplied by y
$(x-y)(x+y)$	x minus y, x plus y
$\dfrac{x}{y}$	x over y

=	the equals sign
x=5	x equals 5 / x is equal to 5
x≠5	x (is) not equal to 5
x≡y	x is equivalent to (or identical with) y
x>y	x is greater than y
x≥y	x is greater than or equal to y
x< y	x is less than y
x≤y	x is less than or equal to y
0<x<1	zero is less than x is less than 1
0≤x≤1	zero is less than or equal to x is less than or equal to 1
|x|	mod x / modulus x
x^2	x squared / x (raised) to the power 2
x^3	x cubed
x^4	x to the fourth / x to the power four
x^n	x to the nth / x to the power n
x^{-n}	x to the (power) minus n
$\sqrt{x}$	(square) root x / the square root of x
$\sqrt[3]{x}$	cube root (of) x
$\sqrt[4]{x}$	fourth root (of) x
$\sqrt[n]{x}$	nth root (of) x
$(x+y)^2$	x plus y all squared
$\left(\dfrac{x}{y}\right)^2$	x over y all squared
n!	n factorial
$\hat{x}$	x hat
$\bar{x}$	x bar
$\tilde{x}$	x tilde
x_i	xi / x subscript i / x suffix i / x sub i
$\sum\limits_{i=1}^{n} a_i$	the sum from i equals one to n ai / the sum as i runs from 1 to n of the ai

4　线性代数（Linear algebra）

‖A‖	the norm (or modulus) of x
$\overline{OA}$	OA / vector OA OA
$\overline{OA}$	OA / the length of the segment OA
A^T	A transpose / the transpose of A
A^{-1}	A inverse / the inverse of A

5   函数（Functions）

f(x)	fx / f of x / the function f of x
f : S→T	a function f from S to T
x ↦ y	x maps to y / x is sent (or mapped) to y
f'(x)	f prime x / f dash x / the (rst) derivative of f with respect to x
f''(x)	f double–prime x / f double–dash x / the second derivative of f with respect to x
f'''(x)	f triple–prime x / f triple–dash x / the third derivative of f with respect to x
f(4)	four x / the fourth derivative of f with respect to x
$\dfrac{\partial f}{\partial x_1}$	the partial (derivative) of f with respect to x1
$\dfrac{\partial^2 f}{\partial x_1^2}$	the second partial (derivative) of f with respect to x1
$\displaystyle\int_0^\infty$	the integral from zero to infinity
$\displaystyle\lim_{x\to 0}$	the limit as x approaches zero
$\displaystyle\lim_{x\to +0}$	the limit as x approaches zero from above
$\displaystyle\lim_{x\to -0}$	the limit as x approaches zero from below
$\log_e y$	log y to the base e / log to the base e of y / natural log (of) y
ln y	log y to the base e / log to the base e of y / natural log (of) y

需要注意的是，每个数学家对数学公式常常有各自的读法，在许多情况下，并不存在一个普遍接受的所谓"正确"读法。

一些在书写上有明确区别的公式在口头表达时经常难以区分，如 fx 的发音可以理解为以下任何一种：fx, f(x), f_x, FX, $\overline{FX}$, $\overrightarrow{FX}$。**这种差别通常通过上下文来区分**。只有在可能发生混淆、或要强调其观点时，数学家才使用较长的读法：f 乘以 x，关于 x 的函数 f，f 下标 x，直线 FX，弧 FX 的长度，矢量 FX。

同样，对于下列几对公式，除了有时在音调或停顿长度上有一些差别外，数学家在演讲时不大可能表现出明显的区别：

x+(y+z) and (x+y)+z, $\sqrt{ax+b}$ and $\sqrt{ax}+b$, a^n-1 and a^{n-1}

Exercises

I. State whether the following are true or false. If the answer is false, explain why

1. A shopping cart allows customers to continue to browse after selecting each item they wish to purchase.

2. In a reverse auction the seller sets a price and customers make individual bids to buy the item.

3. A reserve price is the highest bid a customer is willing to make.

4. In the demand-sensitive pricing model, the price decreases as more people buy.

5. The name-your-price model is an auction-based model.

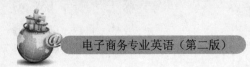

6. Brick-and-mortar companies are businesses that build the infrastructure of an e-commerce Web site.

7. Web-based training is not yet possible, but will be when streaming audio and video technology improve.

8. Priceline.com employs the name-your-price model.

9. B2B exchanges are e-businesses that facilitate the sale, purchase and exchange of goods and services between one or more companies.

10. High-availability computing refers to the minimization of downtime for a company.

II. Fill in the blanks in each of the following

1. A business that has a presence off but, not on the Web is described as a _____ company.

2. The _____ model is designed to bring prices down by increasing the number of customers who buy a particular product at once.

3. Customers can shop for products and store them for later purchase using a _____.

4. Reserve prices are set by a buyer in an _____.

5. The two types of portals are called _____ and _____.

6. iVillage, WebMD and Bolt.com can be described as horizontal portals or _____ sites.

7. Auctions that allow the buyer to set a price and have the merchants compete for the best deal are called _____.

8. _____ are designed to help businesses buy, sell and barter their products and services to other businesses over the Internet.

9. E*trade and Charles Schwab are companies that offer _____.

10. The e-businesses that allows customers to find the lowest price on a particular item are called _____ pricing sites.

III. Categorize each of the following items as it best relates to the storefront model, the auction model or dynamic pricing models

a) reserve price   b) liquidprice   c) shopping cart

d) catalog   e) mercata   f) bottomdollar

IV. Define each of the following terms

a) Web-based training   b) name-your-price model   c) shopping cart

d) reverse auction   e) redundancy   f) high-availability computing

g) merchant server

Chapter 4 Business-to-Business Electronic Commerce

本章介绍了 B2B 电子商务潜在提高生产力的四种类型，分析了在线 B2B 媒介的特点，介绍了 B2B 电子商务在美国的发展、现状及未来。通过本章学习，读者应该：

学习指导

- 掌握 B2B 电子商务的定义与范畴。
- 了解 B2B 电子商务潜在提高生产力的四种类型。
- 理解 B2B 在线 B2B 媒介的特点。
- 了解 B2B 电子商务美国的发展、现状及未来。
- 体会专业论文的组成及其写作的基本方法。

4.1 Introduction

Business-to-business commerce includes a broad range of intercompany transactions, including wholesale trade as well as company purchases of services, resources, technology, manufactured parts and components, and capital equipments. It also includes some types of financial transactions between companies, such as insurance, commercial credit, bonds, securities and other financial assets. The popular phrase B2B e-commerce refers to the substitution of computer data processing and Internet communications for labor services in the production of economic transactions. Many companies engaged in B2B e-commerce are intermediaries between other companies that buy and sell goods and services.

The potential size of B2B e-commerce in the economy is vast, though somewhat difficult to pin down. It is estimated that the annual growth rate of global B2B e-commerce will be maintained at about 45%, and the value of B2B transactions will reach $26 trillion by 2010.

Expectations about productivity gains from B2B e-commerce can be usefully divided into four areas: possible efficiencies from automation of transactions, potential economic advantages of new market intermediaries, consolidation of demand and supply through organized exchanges, and changes in the extent of vertical integration of companies.

New Words & Phrases

pin down v. 使受约束，阻止，压制

intermediary n. 仲裁者，调解者，中间物

consolidation n. 巩固，合并

securities n. 有价证券

bond n. 公债，债券，合同

intercompany n. 公司间的

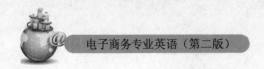
4.2 Cost Efficiencies from Automation of Transactions

Traditionally, interbusiness transactions begin with a buyer looking for inputs or a supplier seeking buyers for its goods and services. Buyers and suppliers search for each other through advertising, trade shows, brokers, and dealers. Suppliers send out sales agents. Buyers then negotiate with potential sellers concerning product specifications and prices, and perhaps conclude a spot transaction or form a long-term contract. After the agreement has been reached, the transaction still involves ordering, billing, arrangements for transportation, confirmation of payments, and acceptance of delivery.

E-commerce innovations aim to reduce the cost of procurement before, during and after the transaction. At every stage, e-commerce avoids the need to translate computer files into paper documents, a process that generally involves errors, delay and costly clerical personnel. E-commerce automates this process by mediating transactions through Web sites and electronic data interchange (EDI).

Before the transaction, Internet technology may lower the cost of searching for suppliers or buyers and making price and product comparisons. Search costs can be significantly relative to the value of the product, particularly for small purchases. Alf Sherk, the founder of e-Chemicals, claims: "When you're dealing with one or two drum quantities, the cost of comparison shopping can be more than the value of the product". Sales personnel acting as sales representatives have traditionally carried out such mundane tasks as tracking product availability and pricing and supplying such information to customers. By automating these information services, e-commerce relieves sales personnel of these tasks, allowing them to concentrate on account management and marketing strategy.

During the transaction, e-commerce can reduce the cost of communicating with counterparts in other companies regarding transaction details. Transactions over computer networks avoid many of the associated costs of inter personal economic exchange, including the costs of travel, times pent on communication, physical space for meetings, and processing paper documents.

After the transaction, electronic commerce allows companies to lower costs of communication, to monitor contractual performance, or to confirm delivery. In addition, companies can apply information generated by the transaction to update their inventory, production and accounting records by automatically linking their transactions to software used for managing all aspects of the firm including sales, purchasing and operations.

The potential cost savings in this area are substantial. Processing a purchase order manually, including paperwork, data entry, phone calls, faxes, and approval requests, can be quite expensive, so online transactions might easily reduce costs by a factor of five or ten or more. There is anecdotal evidence that such cost reductions are possible. British Telecom estimates that by moving external procurement functions to electronic commerce, it has reduced its costs from $113 to $8 per transaction. MasterCard estimates that the cost of processing purchase orders has fallen from $125 to

$40, with the time involved cut from 4 days to 1.25 days. Lehman Brothers finds that a financial transaction is $1.27 for a teller, $0.27 for an ATM and $0.01 for an online transaction. Online brokerage fees have fallen to below $5 in comparison with traditional discount brokerage fees exceeding $50, suggesting a decrease in costs in back-office operations and brokerage transactions with financial exchanges. Even if such estimated savings are greater than average or vary across industries, their aggregate impact is likely to be enormous. By lowering the costs of transactions, e-commerce will change not only operating costs but also the characteristics and scope of feasible transactions.

New Words & Phrases

interbusiness n. 企业间的	confirmation n. 证明，证实，认证，确认
contract n. 合同，契约，婚约	mediate vt. 调停，斡旋
personnel n. 人员，职员	drum n. 盛装大量化学品的桶槽
quantity n. [pl.]大量；大宗；大批	contractual adj. 契约的
anecdotal adj. 轶事	teller n. 柜台职员，出纳员
back office 后台管理	

Abbreviations

ATM (Automated Teller Machine) (银行)自动柜员[出纳]机

4.3   Economic Efficiency Gains from Intermediation in B2B E-Commerce

Intermediation and market-making are central activities in a market-oriented economy, bringing buyers and sellers together. Intermediaries can reduce transaction costs relative to direct exchange, by reducing the costs of search, certifying product quality, mitigating communication costs, and providing guarantees for buyer or seller commitments. Companies acting as market-makers enhance transaction efficiency by creating institutions of exchange, adjusting and communicating prices, clearing markets, allocating goods, and providing liquidity and immediacy.

Business-to-business e-commerce appears likely to transform the traditional patterns of intermediation in ways large and small. Intermediaries reduce search costs by consolidating markets, providing market information and offering an assortment of goods and services, so that buyers obtain the cost efficiency of one-stop shopping, rather than spending time contacting multiple suppliers. Many business-to-business intermediaries seek to offer a broader range of services including communication of price information and price adjustment. Centralized markets often reduce time costs by replacing bilateral negotiation with formal bidding mechanisms and information about transaction prices. B2B e-commerce companies cover a wide spectrum of industries.

Companies have been formed to trade items from advertising to almonds, from lighting fixtures to laboratory equipment, from cattle embryos to circuit boards. Online markets have been established (or at least announced) for aircraft parts, agriculture, apparel, automotive parts, chemicals, computers and electronics, energy, financial instruments, food and beverages, health care, intellectual property, freelance services, laboratory supplies, industrial machinery, advertising, metals, office supplies, plastics, paper, printing services, telecommunications, shipping, and travel services. One market receiving particular attention has been products for maintenance, repair, and operations (MRO) because materials like belts, pumps, and light fixtures are required by almost all firms in all industries, and therefore are seen as a large potential market.

Many business-to-business companies hope to create additional intermediation services. Many B2B companies propose to design innovative procurement transactions between a company and its many suppliers. Other firms are setting up markets that can provide novel types of transactions that aggregate supply and demand. For example, the oil companies BP Amoco, Royal Dutch/Shell Group and Totalfina Elf Group, along with financial services companies Deutsche Bank, Goldman Sachs, Morgan Stanley Dean Witter and Societé Generale, have announced a new global electronic marketplace for over-the-counter energy, metal, and other commodities called the Intercontinental Exchange to replace transactions that were largely conducted bilaterally by telephone. The Inter continental Exchange market will have various novel features including the provision of information to traders regarding the creditworthiness and other characteristics of their counter parties, along with information regarding market aggregates.

A number of online companies described ambitious plans for offering some of the value-added services frequently offered by established dealers: trade credit, supply-chain-management services, appraisal, transportation, storage and other wholesale activities. For example, ChemConnect, an online exchange for chemicals and plastics, arranged for Optimum Logistics to provide transportation services. VerticalNet provides consulting services to complement its intermediation activities on the dozens of specialized websites it operates in different markets. VerticalNet's websites also feature services often referred to as "community and content", including industry news, reviews, and other editorial features.

Popular discussions often suggest that efficiencies in B2B e-commerce are obtained by disintermediation: that is, by "cutting out middlemen" and supplanting presumably costly intermediaries with direct transactions. However, less expensive intermediation and lower transactions costs do not necessarily mean fewer intermediaries. If B2B e-commerce encourages outsourcing to replace some transactions previously internal to the firm, or if firms can use intermediaries to outsource some of the their current external purchasing and sales efforts, or if firms can employ specialized intermediaries to avoid inefficient one-on-one direct meetings between companies and their suppliers, the end result would be a greater number of intermediaries.

E-commerce intermediaries can be classified into four main categories: brokers, auctioneers, dealers, and exchanges. These categories depend on the intermediary's pricing mechanism and whether or not the intermediary takes ownership of the goods and services.

Brokers match buyers and sellers for a fee. Some brokers offer referral services that resemble yellow-page directories, but with more comprehensive information and search facilities. Buyers generally do not pay for access, using the directories to contract sellers who in turn pay listing fees. Examples include Buzzsaw (construction) and Bakery Online (bakery supplies). Sellers also can place product listings that resemble classified ads. At the web sites of some B2B brokers known as "catalog aggregators", buyers can view sets of catalogs that contain information about products and prices from different sellers. Examples are iProcure (office supplies) and Chemdex (laboratory chemicals). Catalog aggregators take orders for products on the sellers' behalf, typically leaving order fulfillment up to sellers.

Auctioneers take a more active role in transactions by setting up a mechanism to determine prices. Internet technology significantly reduces the cost of running an auction relative to using posted prices, and auctions are useful in situations where there is enough uncertainty about market-clearing prices. Some auctioneers hold auctions of surplus inventory for sellers; examples include MetalSite (steel) and One Media Place (advertising space). Other auctioneers hold reverse auctions for buyers, in which sellers compete against each other for a procurement contract. FreeMarkets Online, founded in 1995, is perhaps the largest "reverse auctioneer", their 1999 financial statements report over $2.7 billion in transactions and $20.9 million in corporate revenues. FreeMarkets has conducted procurement auctions for dozens of clients, including Quaker Oats, Deere & Co., and the Pennsylvania Department of Transportation, with bidding from over 4,000 vendors from more than 50 countries in over 70 categories.

Dealers take ownership of goods provided by suppliers and resell them to buyers. Dealers post ask prices for buyers and bid prices for sellers. They earn returns from the bid ask spread, adjusting prices to changes in market conditions. In the early stage of development of B2B e-commerce, few of the new online companies attempted to become dealers. Instead of building the physical infrastructure required for inventory and shipping, most chose to focus on building the electronic infrastructure of markets (broker, auction, or exchange).

Online dealer intermediaries tend to be subsidiaries of "old economy" distributors with existing physical infrastructure. Established distributors have certain advantages, including industry expertise and customer and supplier contacts. W.W. Grainger takes advantage of its long-standing distribution network. Grainger, a distributor of supplies for maintenance, repair, and operations founded in 1927, has made its catalog of hundreds of thousands of items available for online ordering. Interestingly, Grainger negotiates customer-specific contracts, so that each customer views a customized set of prices after logging in to Grainger.com. EnronOnline is an online extension of Enron' s business of buying and selling contracts for natural gas and other commodities with over-the-counter brokers, other wholesale merchants and its own sales and marketing unit. Enron migrated its trading from dealing over the phone to online buying and selling at posted prices. According to Enron's quarterly report for the third quarter of 2000, EnronOnline conducted 350,000 transactions worth $183 billion since their launch in November 1999.

Exchanges are double-sided markets, similar to existing markets for financial instruments and some commodities (such as those traded on the Chicago Mercantile Exchange). B2B firms promise to extend such markets to a variety of new products, including manufactured goods, primary inputs, and services. Exchanges provide a host of services, including rules for trading, price transparency, and centralized clearing. Trading rules can be structured so that buyers and sellers expect to receive the best available price for their transactions. Typically, buyers and sellers can observe the prices of transactions as they occur. Centralized clearing reduces transaction costs because buyers and sellers need only settle with the exchange based on their net position at the end of the day, rather than settling each transaction individually. B2B exchanges typically deal in unregulated forward contracts and thus differ from financial futures exchanges, which are governed by the Commodity Futures Trading Commission and other government agencies.

Examples of B2B companies organized as exchanges are AlmondEx (almonds), Altra Energy (oil and gas), Arbinet (telecommunications bandwidth), CheMatch (chemicals), e-Steel (steel), and PaperExchange (paper and pulp). Cantor Fitzgerald, the parent company of eSpeed, provides an important example of a company establishing an online service that will cannibalize its existing business. Cantor Fitzgerald operates about 50% of the global wholesale market for fixed-income securities such as treasuries, corporate bonds, and municipal bonds.

Centralized clearing is a straightforward service in stock exchanges or with limited numbers of well-defined commodities, but it presents more of a challenge in B2B markets with a proliferation of different specialized products. With many different product specifications possible—say, thousands of types of plastic moldings—exchanges may often look more like small-party negotiations with only two or three participants, rather than like financial double-auction markets with thousands of participants trading shares of the same stock in a given day.

In some of the online B2B markets we have observed, the exchange has been organized like a bulletin board: a buyer may post a bid for a desired commodity, say 4 tons of grade-3 low-density polyethylene to be delivered to St. Louis on October 1, with some bid price in dollars. In response, a seller can post a counteroffer—and rather than merely posting an ask price somewhat higher than the bid on this commodity, the seller may also decide to change the product specifications. For example, the seller might post the information that while it has no grade-3 product available for October 1, it might instead provide a grade-2 product on October 10, at a specified ask price. The original buyer —or a new buyer—could then respond with a new bid on the newly defined commodity.

Perhaps as the market grows and the number of participants increases, there will be enough transaction volume to support a separate double auction for each separate commodity, just as in markets for precious metals or for shares of stock. Another possibility is that intelligently designed computer software will make it less cumbersome to conduct these types of negotiations with lots of permutations of product attributes. Creating an exchange for such products will likely entail specialized auction procedures that adjust prices for multidimensional product attributes. The exchanges also will improve economic efficiency of input markets by creating standardized products, allowing competitive bidding by multiple buyers and sellers, as in commodity futures markets.

Some firms fall into more than one of these categories. For example, PlasticsNet runs auctions for some transactions, but also operates as a broker by allowing its users to place classified ads for products. Similarly, MetalSite runs single-sided auctions for some clients, but operates a double-sided exchange as well.

New Words & Phrases

mitigate v. 减轻	market maker 庄家，市场制造者，做市商
market making 市场开拓，造市	assortment n. 分类
almond n. 杏仁	lighting fixture 照明器材
embryos n. 胚胎	apparel n. 衣服，装饰
freelance n. 自由劳动者	over-the-counter 买卖双方直接交易的
creditworthiness n. 信用，信贷价值	appraisal n. 评价，估价，鉴定
disintermediation n. 不干预，脱媒	supplant vt. 排挤掉，代替
one-on-one adj. 一对一的	auctioneer n. 拍卖商
referral n. 职业分派[介绍]，介绍，指点	subsidiary n. 辅助的，子公司
proliferation n. 增殖	counteroffer n. 还价，还盘，反建议
polyethylene n. 聚乙烯	bilateral adj. 有两面的，双边的
Market-clearing 市场结算	host of 许多，一大群

Abbreviations

MRO (Maintenance Repair and Operating) 维护、修理及运行

4.4   Market Structure and Ownership of B2B Intermediaries

At the formative stage of B2B e-commerce, segments of the intermediary marketplace appeared to be highly competitive. There were hundreds of entrants with projections of thousands more. Rapid initial entry suggests that entry costs were low relative to expected returns. Entry costs also appeared to be low because companies could rent communications and computer facilities without incurring irreversible capital costs. Moreover, market entrants could outsource operation of their website to specialized service providers, the so-called e-commerce platforms. For example, Ariba and CommerceOne developed software platforms for running e-commerce marketplaces (either via fixed-price catalogs or via bidding to determine prices), and they provided the software to a number of companies. A wide variety of software applications became available. Thus, for many B2B companies entry costs were primarily focused on the design of e-commerce services and on marketing and sales expenditures to attract buyers and sellers.

Returns to scale and the importance of liquidity suggest that eventually only one or two markets will operate in each product or service category. Economies of scale result from the fact that creating an Internet-based market involves large fixed costs, while the marginal costs of providing transaction information to market participants appear to be near zero. Moreover, as the number of participants at a site increases, buyers and sellers both find it easier to realize transactions in a market, so that a greater number of sellers attracts more buyers and conversely a greater number of buyer s attracts more sellers. Accordingly, buyers and sellers have an incentive to trade on the highest-volume exchange. These scale and liquidity effects would be reduced if industries managed to settle on open standards for the exchange of information about products because then a smaller exchange could easily gather information and trading partners from a larger exchange, but it is unclear whether such interoperability between markets will materialize.

The history of commodity futures markets demonstrates that new markets often can fail. Carlton observes that between 1921 and 1983, 180 different futures contract markets existed, with an average lifetime of less than 12 years. Those contract markets founded after 1921 had an average lifetime of about nine years, with only three specific commodity contracts continuously listed in the Wall Street Journal for the entire period studied. An individual futures exchange can encompass many futures contract markets, so the failure of an individual market need not alter the lifespan of futures exchanges. Carlton points out that futures exchanges compete with each other for volume, and that the industry has tended to converge to highly concentrated market structures.

The rate at which concentration takes place in B2B e-commerce will depend on the speed at which buying and selling migrates to the Internet, what sorts of intercompany transaction mechanisms prove popular, and what methods evolve for standardizing transactions of goods that come in many closely related varieties. Some concentration appears to be occurring globally in equities exchanges. For example, the Paris, Brussels and Amsterdam exchanges have merged to form the Euronext exchange. This concentration of equities exchanges occur red partly in response to the efficiency of electronic communications networks such as Instinet, Island and Archipelago, which had captured 30 percent of NASDAQ trades in the United States.

Consolidations in financial markets suggest that the proliferation of B2B exchanges is likely to be a short-run phenomenon, with eventual concentration of volume in specific markets through mergers and by the exit of smaller exchanges. Industry reports and our own observations of dozens of e-commerce sites indicate that less than 15 percent of B2B exchanges were actively operating markets. Many were "vaporware", premature announcements designed to stake out market territory for companies before their service was actually available. Some observers predicted substantial shakeouts within several years as the markets become established.

There are several different forms of ownership of B2B e-commerce companies: independent firms that operate a web site, traditional dealers who also operate online markets, and industry-operated exchanges. It is not clear whether one type of ownership structure will be more successful than others.

Many early B2B e-commerce companies were independent startups financed by venture capital. Some, like VerticalNet, became publicly traded companies. By mid- 2000, there were at least 600 online trading exchanges funded by venture-capital firms). ChemConnect also included customers BASF and Dow as equity partners, while PaperExchange included customers International Paper and Staples Many established distributors are shifting part of their business online or taking equity shares of online markets, as noted previously. At least to date, there are no prominent examples of an existing distributor being displaced by a purely online business. DoveBid, a decades-old industrial machinery auctioneer that recently entered into online auctions, has established business arms for value-added transportation, appraisal, and inspection services. The on line chemical marketplace Chempoint is a subsidiary of the traditional distributor Royal Vopak. Other large established dealers entering B2B e-commerce include electronics and computer industry companies such as Arrow Electronics, Avnet, Ingram Micro, and Tech Data.

Alliances of established manufacturers announced plans to sponsor market places. These industry-sponsored exchanges base their strategy on the idea that the technology of Internet marketplaces is relatively easy to reproduce, and that the most important asset of an intermediary is the business of its key buyers and sellers. For example, Weirton Steel, LTV and Steel Dynamics for med MetalSite, which conducts thousands of transactions monthly. Sears, Carrefour, and several other major retailers started GlobalNetExchange to organize purchases from over 50,000 vendors. Boeing, Lockheed Martin, BAE Systems, and Raytheon formed an exchange for aerospace parts and services with the potential for over $70 billion in business with 37,000 suppliers. Similarly, International Paper (despite its previous equity investment in PaperExchange) joined with Georgia Pacific and Weyerhaeuser to announce the ForestExchange trading exchange for paper and forest products. By mid-2000, it was estimated that 60 buyer- dominated consortia, representing over 278 companies and $3 trillion in annual purchasing, planned to establish their own electronic markets rather than relying on independent exchanges.

The establishment of B2B exchanges has raised several critical antitrust issues. Antitrust policy makers are concerned that B2B web sites will allow competitors to exchange price information thus facilitating collusion to fix prices. Also, antitrust authorities worry that B2B web sites will foreclose participation by competitors, leading to their exclusion from segments of the market. The FTC negotiated with the automakers regarding the independence of the industry-sponsored parts exchange Covisint. These concerns recall antitrust scrutiny of airline computer reservation systems that alleged collusion, exclusion and biased listings. Buyer or seller dominated web sites allegedly could become mechanisms for the exercise of market power.

In industry-sponsored exchanges as they have been announced, ownership tends to be on the side of the market with the greatest concentration of market power; for example, few buyers and many suppliers in automotive parts, many buyers and few suppliers in paper products. In contrast, smaller buyers and sellers may favor independently owned exchanges offering transparency in execution of trades and up-to-date pricing information. Competition between exchanges should create incentives to avoid foreclosure or the exercise of market power. Owners of exchanges have incentives to increase volume and to foster liquidity by attracting more buyers and sellers, which should in turn lead to the development of independent neutral exchanges.

New Words & Phrases

marginal cost   边际成本

materialize   v. 物化

vaporware   n. 朦胧件

equity   n. 权益，公平，股票，股权

interoperability   n. 互用性，协同工作的能力

lifespan   n. 寿命，预期使用期限

stake out   v. 立桩标出，置于警察监视下

antitrust   adj. 反托拉斯的

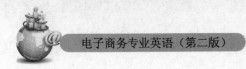

collusion   n. 共谋，勾结

allege   vt. 宣称，断言

incentive   n. 动机；adj.激励的

market power 市场权力，市场势力

foreclose   vt. 排除在外，妨碍，自称，阻止

foreclosure   n. 排斥

venture capital   n. <美>风险资本

Abbreviations

FTC (Fair Trade Commission) 公平贸易委员会

4.5   Effects of E-commerce on the Organization of Firms

Ronald H. Coase's classic article introduced the concept of transaction costs. Coase explained that the costs of using the market were an important determinant of whether firms would carry out an economic activity within their organization or rely on purchases from other firms. When using the market is costly relative to management costs, companies have an incentive to vertically integrate. Yet, outsourcing is compelled by the buyer's need for flexibility and focus, supplier economies of scale and scope, and supplier expertise. To the extent that e-commerce technology lowers the costs of intercompany transactions, it should tip the balance toward greater use of external markets.

The potential effects of B2B e-commerce extend beyond saving money on transactions between existing firms. Cost and allocative efficiencies in e-commerce suggest a more fundamental change in the way that businesses are organized. Vertically integrated firms engage in substantial internal sales and procurement activities. With B2B e-commerce, such vertically integrated companies might reorganize to outsource production of goods and services that were previously produced internally, as well as outsourcing of the management of these transactions. For companies that purchase externally, B2B e-commerce intermediaries would substitute for many of the activities of company purchasing, sales, marketing, and even accounting departments. As market transaction costs fall with the maturation of business-to-business e-commerce, outsourcing and vertical disintegration will occur, resulting in more independent entities along the supply chain.

The automobile industry offers a vivid example of this change. At the beginning of the 20th century, the automobile industry exhibited a strong preference for vertical integration. Ford had a slogan: "From Mine to Finished Car, One Organization". By 1920, General Motors "had extended its scope so that not only all the engines used in its cars, but a large proportion of such units as gears, axles, crank shafts, radiators, electrical equipment, roller bearings, warning signals, spark plugs, bodies, plate glass, and body hardware, were produced either by a General Motors unit or by a subsidiary".

But by the beginning of the 21st century, the automobile industry had begun to reevaluate its organizational structure. GM had spun off its parts manufacturing unit Delphi Automotive Systems Corp., thus creating the world's largest auto parts supplier with over 200,000 employees. Similarly, Ford had spun off its Visteon parts division in summer 2000, converting internal transactions into B2B transactions[2]. GM, Ford, and Daimler Chrysler have announced a plan to start a company called Covisint that will handle auto parts transactions from suppliers. The supply chains of these three companies total almost \$250 billion, so if it succeeds, Covisint has the potential to be one of the largest business on the Internet. The pattern of greater reliance on coordination through markets and less emphasis on vertical integration and organizational governance seems likely to proliferate.

1. From Mine to Finished Car, One Organization. 从矿山到汽车成品，一个企业应有尽有。

2. Ford had spun off its Visteon parts division in summer 2000, converting internal transactions into B2B transactions. 福特汽车公司于 2000 年夏天将零部件部门剥离出来，组成了 Visteon 公司，将内部交易转变为企业间交易。"Spin off" 指 "组成衍生公司" 或 "拆分"。

4.6　Conclusion

Advances in computers and communications clearly hold great promise for reducing transaction costs between businesses. Productivity gains may result from the automation of transactions, the potential economic advantages of intermediation, the organization of centralized exchanges, and the reorganization of firms.

An important research question is the measurement of these economic efficiency gains. Yet, estimation of productivity growth in services such as B2B e-commerce presents some difficulties. Triplett and Bosworth observe that economic changes attributable to e-commerce cross the traditional production boundary used in national accounts. As an example, they compare the purchase of a book from a traditional retailer with the purchase of a book from an online retailer. Comparing the prices in the two settings ignores the costs of travel and time involved in visiting the traditional retailer, while explicitly counting the costs of shipping and handling for the online purchase. In the case of B2B e-commerce, one would like measurement of productivity to reflect total net benefits, including lower search and procurement costs for buyers and sellers. A related question is how much of the current activities of companies in manufacturing, construction, energy, transportation are devoted to production operations and how much are attributable to transactions.

One of the challenges faced by companies in B2B e-commerce is the development of software and communication standards. Extensible Markup Language (XML) is being applied to develop data descriptions and protocols to describe practically all aspects of a transaction, including product features, transportation, prices, and credit terms. If standards are generally adopted, manufacturers, suppliers and distributors will be able to exchange commercial information using generally-recognized formats. Such standardization enables the computers of both parties to a transaction to understand precisely what is being traded, so that each party can automatically update its internal records, such as billing and inventory. Developing such protocols will require extensive cooperation of buyers and sellers within industries. An important question for economic observers is what types of goods and services can be standardized and what types of transaction protocols will emerge.

Business-to-business e-commerce seems likely to engender a significant reorganization of industry, with a certain amount of vertical disintegration and new roles for intermediaries and market makers. The extent to which e-commerce will change the organization of firms has empirical significance for the theory of the firm. Another important issue is what types of market mechanisms will be favored by e-commerce and the relative importance of different types of intermediaries. Will B2B exchanges be owned by industry consortia or will they tend toward independence? The plethora of entrants and business models, and the significant returns to market consolidation, suggest that substantial entry and exit of firms will take place before the benefits of B2B e-commerce are obtained. The economic significance of intercompany transactions suggests that even small enhancements in the efficiency of transactions will eventually produce extremely large overall savings in the economy.

New Words & Phrases

plethora　n. 过剩，过多　　　　　　empirical　adj. 完全根据经验的，经验主义的

engender　v. 造成　　　　　　　　consortia　n. 合作，国际财团

Reading Material——Trust, as a main barrier in adoption to B2C E-Commerce

I. Introduction

By and large, many of the customers who have purchased products through the Internet feel hesitant about the transaction– typically when entering credit card number or receiving unexpected goods. For that reason, trust takes a crucial part in the E-commerce and involves the issues like high uncertainty and lack of legal protection.

Consumers need guarantees that the other party will not mistreat their personal information, while suppliers need guarantees that they will receive payment for the goods delivered. Although security protocols such as the Secure Sockets Layers (SSL) and Security Electronic Transactions (SET) ensure that a credit card number will not be interrupted during transmission, they still cannot guarantee against its misuse by the customers, or against fraud by the suppliers, Consequently causing a number of "dot.coms" to leave from the online markets.

Ever since much consideration has focused upon the importance of trust, the main focus of this paper is to discuss the topic of trust as a fundamental component of B2C E-commerce relationships.

II. Identifying the Elements of Trust Building

In the last ten years there have been conducted a lot of empirical studies on the issue of trust in E-commerce. For example, the role of trust more important than technological restrictions if the purpose is to reduce constraints between merchants and customers in online businesses. Trust is accepted as a main focus among trading partners in e-commerce, which strengthens the prospect of being continuous in a relationship.

The reason more consumers have not yet shopped online is because of a basic lack of faith towards the web. Consumers do not have enough trust in e-business to engage in relationship exchanges that involve money and personal information. There are six combined elements to build a "trust pyramid".

Core elements: State of the art security, Merchant legitimacy, fulfillment

Differentiators: Customer control, tone and ambience, and customer collaboration

They say, to make browsers and everyday customers to site loyalists, the six elements of trust are needed as they create comfort and confidence. When customers trust an e-vendor, they are more likely to share personal information with the vendor. If customers trust that the web is safe, and that personal and transactional information remains private, they will gather to e-commerce in large groups.

Giga Information group (mentioned in) showed that the trust and lack of security is the highest barrier in adoption to the e- commerce.

Later, research done by identified three elements producing the trust in online business operations. The framework including three production elements was mainly based on the work of Zucker where he made a sociological and economic analysis of historical data in the United States from 1840 to 1920.

The three main trust building elements are:
- Character-based trust – focuses on specific to the person or group and defines characteristics such as ethnicity or family background.
- Process-based trust – refers to the type of trust produced from past exchange or expected future exchange. For instance, repeated purchases or gift exchange.
- Institution-based trust – the element is tied to formal societal structures. This type of trust depends either on firm-specific attributes (e.g., certification as an accountant) or on an intermediary mechanism (e.g., use of escrow accounts).

Finally, five main elements representing a sense of trustworthiness to online customers as: web design, encryption, privacy policy, third party endorsement, and feedback were introduced by Sciortino and Mus in 2002.

III. How To Increase Trust in B2C E-Commerce

A. Website Design perhaps is the starting point for businesses to construct the trust for its customers. Since, first thing online consumers face with is website of the company, it affects their sense of trust among the first.

Website must be appropriately designed to the products of company. For example, if a company sells toys, it seems to be good-humoured and colourful look for website would be an appropriate for the children, however the parents who in actual fact buy the products and of course who are the owners of the credit cards. So it would be suitable to design the page without so many colours, rather light background with dark text would be more appropriate.

Another part of web design is construction of the navigation and wide range of browsers. Since main purpose of a customer in visiting the site is to buy the product he/she wants, simple and reliable navigations are usually successful. Web designers have to consider that customers will not like spending their times to learn how to navigate the site to get the desired products; therefore simple and intuitive pages will be successful, as even shopper who visit the site first time can control it without any difficulties.

Finally, company have to regularly check and repair every link in its web site, because by discovering broken links customers can dislike it, thus trust for the page will decrease. An inability to keep the website working does not encourage confidence for businesses that they provide a quality product. The e-commerce site represents business to the whole online population; thus it needs to work correctly, and display promptly and cleanly all of the time.

B. Characteristic-based trust. The focus of this element may be relatively general (e.g., sex, ethnicity, and nationality) or specific (e.g., kinship and clan membership). Here, similarity of kinship and gender indicates similar cultural values, which are the driving force in creating trust. The greater the extent of these cultural similarities, the greater the implied similarity of background expectations, and, hence, the more trust toward the transaction partner.

A number of empirical studies support the effects of similarity on trusting behaviour. Trust was significantly affected by shared values-beliefs about behavior, goal, and polices. For example, www.babycenter.com offers chat rooms, interests groups, and an online doctoring service to parents of children. This creates a family type culture, and builds a relationship between the firm and the Internet users. The resulting trust is believed to boost www.babycenter.com's baby stuff online sales. Besides, Inter customer contact within this community culture will reward an honest manufacturer and enhance the perception that it is a trust-worthy member of the community.

Characteristic-based trust is able to reduce the privacy concerns because customers in a common community such as www.babycenter.com are prone to treat the site as a shared family. They trust the information on the site such as weekly reports of baby growth status and if further information is needed, they can communicate with other parents or even consult online with free pediatricians. Moreover, according to consumer complaining behaviour theory e-retailers are more subject to consumers' voice responses—complaints directed at friends and family relatives—by fast communication tool such as e-mail message in the electronic community. This high risk of voice responses will force the sites to be better self-regulated and, as a result, prevent unauthorized access to or other inappropriate use of personal information.

Online societies offer the participants a forum for exchange of common interests and ideas, the development of a congenial environment, and encouragement for active participation. For example, www.Boschtools.com hosts a meeting regarding power tools, together with prices, brand, and technical advice. Participators in this forum include wholesales, retailers, consumers, and others from all over the world. Above all, this e-forum creates shared values and a mutual trust within the community.

C. Process-based trust – is the category of trust reliant on past transactions, repeated purchases (e.g., reputation), or predictable future exchanges such as gift giving. Unlike characteristic-based trust, process based trust builds on reputation, gift giving, and brand names. A key factor of building this type of trust according to is satisfaction with buying experience and past relations. To such trust through interpersonal interaction, it is important to persuade the trusting party of one that owns trustworthiness, since when one party trusts another, the trusted party often feels bound by the trust placed in them to respond the trust. According to many researchers process based trust can be developed from interpersonal relationships. Communication is another source of building process-based trust.

The process-based trust influences to B2C relationships where e-businesses give free gifts and extra advices about products for its customers. Virtual Vineyards Online for example, provides free advice on wines in an open environment involving both customer and the expert. Consumers notice that the web on the features of different wines advises them personally. They can explore the history of a particular winemaker, learn about the specific taste, receive a complete description of different brands, and post their comments regarding the wine they purchased on the web. It has been mentioned in that 1-800-FLOWERS sends e-mail messages to remind customers of coming birthdays and weddings, in expectancy that flowers will be ordered in the future.

Another good example is Honda, which is using free gifts in building a relationship with its potential customers. In its site Honda gives one dollar to every Internet visitor who clicks through its homepage at www.honda.com. This free gift is proposed to build stronger relationship with the customers and create a comparative advantage over the competitors. As a result Honda may expect some equivalent gift from the customers in the form of voluntarily providing personal data and even purchasing products or services.

Process-based trust is more likely to solve the confidentiality concerns of online customers. Through repeat purchases, interactive communication, and gift exchange with the sites, consumers are willing to provide the sites personal information, expecting a long-term relationship with the sites. This can be further illustrated by an example of purchasing airline tickets via www.priceline.com. Customers are given credit of up to $70 for each ticket when they verify the price and order the tickets online. One at a time, customers provide demographic and general information to the www.priceline.com. This gift-like relational exchange overtime strengthens the trust between the seller and consumers and significantly reduces the consumers' privacy concerns. However, process-based trust is expensive in the relationship exchange because it requires overtime-dynamic interaction and even purchases experience. A comparatively cheap alternative is institution-based trust.

D. Institution-based trust is different from characteristic and process-based trust given that it simplifies beyond both a given transaction and specific sets of exchange partners. According to institution based trust has a formal marketable formation such as institutions and third party sponsors that in fact sell certificates promising truth, capability, and intentions. Such certifications are intentionally proposed and used to build trust in the bearer's ability through external guarantors such as universities and state regulators. This category of trust according to can relate to specific individuals or firms from whom trust can be guaranteed and purchased in the form of certified education and in intermediary mechanisms such as banks, and government regulators.

When comes across from the B2C relationships side this type of trust is probably solving confidentiality fears. Because of the lack of legal protection in the electronic market, customers have no control over the e-vendors, no guarantee of the quality of the online content, and no power to influence the sites' behaviours. However, certification third parties or intermediary protocols such as SSL and SET can balance the power and create the needed trust between the e-vendor and customers.

For example, Amazon.com's SSL software is the industry standard and among the best software available today for secure commerce transactions. It encrypts all of customers' personal information including credit card number, name, and address, so that it cannot be read as the information travels over the Internet. AOL Time Warner even purchased a $100 million stake in the Amazon.com and will use its sophisticated and safe technology in AOL's shopping areas.

More specifically, the most common way to secure the collection of sensitive information words is through a connection secured by a 128-bit SSL server certificate. The order page is then accessed securely via "https://..." rather than typical "http://" and a security icon is normally shown in the browser status bar. The customers have to make sure that the orde page can only be accessed securely when they type in the URL without the "s" the order page needs to automatically redirect to the secure version or not be available at all.

Moreover, TRUSTe and BBBOnLine are good examples of certification third parties, whereas accounts such as MoneySave.com and E-cash.com are examples of intermediary mechanisms in the electronic commerce. According to "E-vendors should purchase institution-based trust to keep in long-term orientated exchange with their customers". It is particularly important when the e-business is not a famous brand, because customers may not trust to stand by its privacy policy. They can find out what endorsements make sense for their site among the logos like: TRUSTe (45%-increase in trust), Visa logo (50%), Master Card (40%), VeriSign (35%), and BBBOnLine (30%), and pursue, because

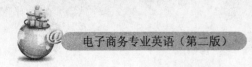

each of them can have a significant impact to the security of the website.

In exhibiting the privacy guaranteed seal trademark on their sites, e-vendors send a clear signal to customers that they have openly agreed to make known their information gathering and distribution practices. Privacy seal programs start websites with unique identifiers to track the uses of private information. As a result buyers may discard the licensee's trust seal mark or even transfer the issue to appropriate law authority such as the FTC and the Consumer Protection Agency, if the sites are broken or disobey the privacy agreement.

VeriSign's (www.verisign.com) trusted identity is through the official approval of the public key in the form of digital certificate. By dealing with e-business with this digital certificate, online consumers are protected and need not be concerned about the invasion of personal privacy. Besides, if the sites neglect personal information, consumers may display third party response type of consumer bad-tempered behaviours—formal complaints directed toward agencies not involved in the exchange process. Because of third party respond actions, e-marketers are better off by sustaining appropriate privacy practices. Accordingly, consumers' confidentiality concerns are significantly reduced in the e-market with guarantee institutions or third parties.

Indeed, as has been illustrated in the reason that institution-based trusts can solve the personal information concerns can also be suggested by the models such as the licensing and the data commissioner model which have been proposed to care for individual confidentiality while building the most of the chances presented by the growth in the communication technology. Basically, privacy control models occupy some governmental institutions performing as peacekeeping troops between the data gatherer and the data provider. These institutions implement regulatory and advisory powers to keep under control in the e-merchant and to help the relatively unskilled e-shopper with the purpose of protecting their privacy interests.

E. Feedback – The role of feedback in the customer-supplier relationship is to guarantee that both parties keep the other informed for events that might disorder the flow of goods or services through the supply chain. When the e-merchant keeps customers fully informed by giving feedbacks to any problems as these arise, it is much more expected that customers will be tolerant and certainly will keep the loyalty towards the merchant.

E-merchant can effectively achieve trust by organizing a flexible respond to unexpected market contingencies, rather than adhering to pre-defined corporate policies. It is necessary for the e- merchant to realize that e-commerce operations often lack the ability to handle unforeseen contingencies because the required feedback has not been programmed into the system. Good example here is that not all websites provide a telephone number, an address or even e-mail address that the customer can use when he or she has made an error placing an on-line order. Obviously the customer with a choice of where to buy will be likely to favour those sites that make contact with the company easy.

By developing feedback company gives potential customers an idea of what to expect if they purchase from them. A great example of this is the eBay auction system, which allows both e-merchants, and buyers to give each other positive, negative, or neutral feedback about the other party upon completion of a transaction. Before requesting on a product to see if they can trust that the seller offers a quality product and prompt service buyers first check this feedback information. Even a small amount of negative feedback may quickly decrease the number of people willing to offer on a seller's auctions. Another example is BizRate.com which lets customers to fill out a survey after completion of e-shopping to rate the company in a number of different areas including ease of ordering, quality of product, speed of delivery, etc. BizRate.com attracts customers to complete the survey by giving a chance to win cash prizes. The outcome as says give opportunity for potential customers to visit BizRate.com to browse high scoring merchants, while e-merchants can use the information gathered to improve their e-commerce sites.

IV. Conclusion

Building trust is one of the key ways to make better e-commerce, at the same time expecting considerable works to be done. After looking through many of these research papers five elements (i.e. website design, characteristic based trust, process based trust, institutional based trust, and feedback) have been identified that can be considered as key elements for enhancing trust.

Website design has been discussed as starting point for businesses to increase trust for its customers.

The focus of characteristic-based trust was that through it e-vendors could use the unique element to build, through a sense of community and similarity, trust with the online customers. The example of babycenter.com has been discussed where they find the trust by offering chat rooms, interests groups, and an online doctoring service to parents of children.

The process-based trust influence to B2C relationships where e-businesses give free gifts and extra advices about products for its customers.

Institution-based trust has a formal marketable formation such as institutions and third party sponsors that in fact sell certificates promising truth, capability, and intentions. In case of pure.coms such as Amazon.com its SSL software is the industry standard and among the best softwares available today for secure commerce transactions. It encrypts all of customers' personal information including credit card number, name, and address, so that it cannot be read as the information travels over the Internet. Lastly, by receiving a good feedback customers have an idea of what to expect if they purchase from them. eBay auction system has been discussed, where it allows both e-merchants, and buyers to give each other positive, negative, or neutral feedback about the other party upon completion of a transaction.

New Words & Phrases

by and large　总的来说，大体而言

legitimacy　n. 合法（性），合理（性）

ambience　n. 环境，气氛

institution　n. 惯例，习俗；制度

intuitive　adj. 有直觉力的；凭直觉获知的

kinship　n. 血族关系

guarantor　n. 保证人

auction　n. vt.　拍卖

neutral　adj. 中立的，不偏不倚的

mistreat　vt. 滥用，虐待

differentiator　n. 区分者

vendor　n.　卖方

good-humoured　adj. 快乐的，愉快的

ethnicity　n. 种族划分

bearer　n. 持票人，运载工具，载体，受力体

feedback　n. 反馈，反馈信息

encrypt　v. 加密，将……译成密码

Abbreviations

SSL (Secure Sockets Layers) 加密套接字协议层

SET (Security Electronic Transactions) 安全电子交易

FTC(Fair Trade Commission)公平贸易委员会

常用英汉互译技巧

英汉两种语言在句法、词汇、修辞等方面均存在着很大的差异，因此在进行英汉互译时必然会遇到很多困难，需要有一定的翻译技巧作指导。常用的翻译技巧有增译法、省译法、转换法、拆句法、合并法、正译法、反译法、倒置法、包孕法、插入法、重组法和综合法等。

一、增译法

指根据英汉两种语言不同的思维方式、语言习惯和表达方式，在翻译时增添一些词、短句或句子，以便更准确地表达出原文所包含的意义。这种方式多半用在汉译英里。

首先，汉语无主句较多，而英语句子一般都要有主语，所以在翻译汉语无主句的时候，除了少数可用英语无主句、被动语态或"There be…"结构来翻译以外，一般都要根据语境补出主语，使句子完整。

第二，英汉两种语言在名词、代词、连词、介词和冠词的使用方法上也存在很大差别。英语中代词使用频率较高，凡说到人的器官和归某人所有的或与某人有关的事物时，必须在前面加上物主代词。因此，在汉译英时需要增补物主代词，而在英译汉时又需要根据情况适当地删减。

其次，英语词与词、词组与词组以及句子与句子的逻辑关系一般用连词来表示，而汉语则往往通过上下文和语序来表示这种关系。因此，在汉译英时常常需要增补连词。英语句子离不开介词和冠词。

另外，在汉译英时还要注意增补一些原文中暗含而没有明言的词语和一些概括性、注释性的词语，以确保译文意思的完整。总之，通过增译，一是保证译文语法结构的完整，二是保证译文意思的明确。如：

例 1. Indeed, the reverse is true

实际<u>情况</u>恰好相反。（增译名词）

例 2. 这是这两代计算机之间的又一个共同点。

This is yet another common point <u>between</u> the computers of the two generations.（增译介词）

例 3.　Individual mathematicians often have their own way of pronouncing mathematical expressions and in many cases there is no generally accepted "correct" pronunciation.

每个数学家对数学公式常常有各自的读法，在许多情况下，并不存在一个普遍接受的<u>所谓</u>"正确"读法。(增加隐含意义的词)

例 4.　只有在可能发生混淆、或要强调其观点时，数学家才使用较长的读法。

It is only when confusion may occur, or where <u>he/she</u> wishes to emphasis the point, that the mathematician will use the longer forms. (增加主语)

例 5. 三个臭皮匠，合成一个诸葛亮。

Three cobblers <u>with their wits</u> combined equal Zhuge Liang <u>the mastermind</u>.（增译注释性词语）

例 6.　Three computers in this section are infected by virus.

这个部门有三<u>台</u>计算机感染了病毒。(增译量词)

二、省译法：

这是与增译法相对应的一种翻译方法，即删去不符合目标语思维习惯、语言习惯和表达方式的词，以避免译文累赘。增译法的例句反之即可。又如：

例 1. You will be staying in this hotel during <u>your</u> visit in Beijing.

你在北京访问期间就住在这家饭店里。(省译物主代词)

例 2. I hope you will enjoy your stay here.

希望您在这儿过得愉快。(省译主语)

例 3. 中国政府历来重视环境保护工作。

The Chinese government has always attached great importance to environmental protection. (省译名词)

例 4.　The development of IC made it possible for electronic devices to become smaller and smaller.

集成电路的发展是电子器件可以做得越来越小。(省译形式主语 it)

三、转换法

转换法指在翻译过程中为了使译文符合目标语的表述方式、方法和习惯而对原句中的词类、句型和语态等进行转换。具体地说，就是在词性方面，把名词转换为代词、形容词、动词；把动词转换成名词、形容词、副词、介词；把形容词转换成副词和短语。在句子成分方面，把主语变成状语、定语、宾语、表语；把谓语变成主语、定语、表语；把定语变成状语、主语；把宾语变成主语。在句型方面，把并列句变成复合句，把复合句变成并列句，把状语从句变成定语从句。在语态方面，可以把主动语态变为被动语态。如：

例 1. Too much exposure to TV programs will do great harm to the eyesight of children.

孩子们看电视过多会大大地损坏视力。(名词转动词)

例 2. 由于我们实行了改革开放政策，我国的综合国力有了明显的增强。

Thanks to the introduction of our reform and opening policy, our comprehensive national strength has greatly improved. (动词转名词)

例 3. In his article the author is critical of man's negligence toward his environment.

作者在文章中，对人类疏忽自身环境作了批评。(形容词转名词)

例 4. 时间不早了，我们回去吧！

We don't have much time left. Let's go back. (句型转换)

例 5. 学生们都应该德、智、体全面发展。

All the students should develop morally, intellectually and physically. (名词转副词)

例 6.　The modern world is experiencing rapid development of information technology.

当今世界的信息技术正在迅速发展。(名词转动词、形容词转副词)

四、拆句法和合并法

这是两种相对应的翻译方法。拆句法是把一个长而复杂的句子拆译成若干个较短、较简单的句子，通常用于英译汉；合并法是把若干个短句合并成一个长句，一般用于汉译英。汉语强调意合，结构较松散，因此简单句较多；英语强调形合，结构较严密，因此长句较多。所以汉译英时要根据需要注意利用连词、分词、介词、不定式、定语从句、独立结构等把汉语短句连成长句；而英译汉时又常常要在原句的关系代词、关系副词、主谓连接处、并列或转折连接处、后续成分与主体的连接处，以及意群结束处将长句切断，译成汉语分句。这样就可以基本保留英语语序，顺译全句，顺应现代汉语长短句相替、单复句相间的句法修辞原则。如：

例 1.　Increased cooperation with China is in the interests of the United States.

同中国加强合作，符合美国的利益。(在主谓连接处拆译)

例 2.　It is common practice the electric wires are made from copper.

电线是铜制成的。(主从句合一)

例 3. 中国是个大国，百分之八十的人口从事农业，但耕地只占土地面积的十分之一，其余为山脉、森林、城镇和其他用地。

China is a large country with four-fifths of the population engaged in agriculture, but only one tenth of the land is farmland, the rest being mountains, forests and places for urban and other uses.（合译法）

例 4. Packet switching is a method of slicing digital messages into parcels called "packets," sending the packets along different communication paths as they become available, and then reassembling the packets once they arrive at their destination.

分组交换是传输数据的一种方法，它先将数据信息分割成许多称为"分组"的数据信息包；当路径可用时，经过不同的通信路径发送；当到达目的地后，再将它们组装起来。（将长定语从句拆成几个并列的分句）

例 5. The URL htttp://www.azimuth-interactive.com/flash_test refers to the IP address 208.148.84.1 with the domain name "azimuth-interactive.com" and the protocol being used to access the address, Hypertext Transfer Protocol (HTTP).

网址 htttp://www.azimuth-interactive.com/flash_test 就是指 IP 地址 208.148.84.1，其域名为 "azimuth-interactive.com"，而访问地址时使用的协议为超文本传输协议 HTTP。（拆分法）

五、正译法和反译法

这两种方法通常用于汉译英，偶尔也用于英译汉。所谓正译，是指把句子按照与汉语相同的语序或表达方式译成英语。所谓反译则是指把句子按照与汉语相反的语序或表达方式译成英语。正译与反译常常具有同义的效果，但反译往往更符合英语的思维方式和表达习惯。因此比较地道。如：

例 1. 你可以从因特网上获得这一信息。

You can obtain this information on the Internet. （正译）

This information is accessible/available on the Internet. （反译）

例 2. 他突然想到了一个新主意。

Suddenly he had a new idea. （正译）

He suddenly thought out a new idea. （正译）

A new idea suddenly occurred to/struck him. （反译）

例 3. 他仍然没有弄懂我的意思。

He still could not understand me. （正译）

Still he failed to understand me. （反译）

六、倒置法

在汉语中，定语修饰语和状语修饰语往往位于被修饰语之前；在英语中，许多修饰语常常位于被修饰语之后，因此翻译时往往要把原文的语序颠倒过来。倒置法通常用于英译汉，即对英语长句按照汉语的习惯表达法进行前后调换，按意群或进行全部倒置，原则是使汉语译句安排符合现代汉语论理叙事的一般逻辑顺序。有时倒置法也用于汉译英。如：

例 1. At this moment, through the wonder of telecommunications, more people are seeing and hearing what we say than on any other occasions in the whole history of the world.

此时此刻，通过现代通信手段的奇迹，看到和听到我们讲话的人比整个世界历史上任何其他这样的场合都要多。（部分倒置）

例2. 改革开放以来，中国发生了巨大的变化。

Great changes have taken place in China since the introduction of the reform and opening policy.（全部倒置）

七、包孕法

这种方法多用于英译汉。所谓包孕是指在把英语长句译成汉语时，把英语后置成分按照汉语的正常语序放在中心词之前，使修饰成分在汉语句中形成前置包孕。但修饰成分不宜过长，否则会形成拖沓或造成汉语句子成分在连接上的纠葛。如：

例1. **IP multicasting** is a set of technologies that enables efficient delivery of data to many locations on a network.

IP 多信道广播是使数据向网络中许多位置高效传送的一组技术。

例2. What brings us together is that we have common interests which transcend those differences.

使我们走到一起的，是我们有超越这些分歧的共同利益。

八、插入法

指把难以处理的句子成分用破折号、括号或前后逗号插入译句中。这种方法主要用于笔译中。偶尔也用于口译中，即用同位语、插入语或定语从句来处理一些解释性成分。如：

如果说宣布收回香港就会像夫人说的"带来灾难性的影响"，那我们将勇敢地面对这个灾难，做出决策。

If the announcement of the recovery of Hong Kong would bring about, as Madam put it, "disastrous effects," we will face that disaster squarely and make a new policy decision.

九、重组法

指在进行英译汉时，为了使译文流畅和更符合汉语叙事论理的习惯，在捋清英语长句的结构、弄懂英语原意的基础上，彻底摆脱原文语序和句子形式，对句子进行重新组合。如：

Decision must be made very rapidly; physical endurance is tested as much as perception, because an enormous amount of time must be spent making certain that the key figures act on the basis of the same information and purpose.

必须把大量时间花在确保关键人物均根据同一情报和目的行事，而这一切对身体的耐力和思维能力都是一大考验。因此，一旦考虑成熟，决策者就应迅速做出决策。

十、综合法

是指单用某种翻译技巧无法译出时，着眼篇章，以逻辑分析为基础，同时使用转换法、倒置法、增译法、省译法、拆句法等多种翻译技巧的方法。如：

例1. Behind this formal definition are three extremely important concepts that are the basis for understanding the Internet: packet switching, the TCP/IP communications protocol, and client/server computing.

在这个正式的定义背后，隐含着三个极其重要的概念：分组交换、TCP/IP（传输控制协议/网际协议）通信协议和客户机/服务器计算技术，它们乃是理解因特网的基础。

例2. Routers are special purpose computers that interconnect the thousands of different computer networks that make up the Internet and route packets along to their ultimate destination as they travel.

路由器是一种特殊用途的计算机，它将组成因特网的成千上万个不同计算机网络互相联接起来，并在信

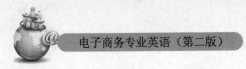

息包旅行时将它们向终极目的地发送。

Exercises

I. Answer the following questions

1. What is B2B E-commerce?

2. How many types of potential productivity gains are expected from B2B E-commerce?

3. Describe the characteristics of B2B online intermediaries.

4. How many categories can e-commerce intermediaries be classified?

II. Translate the following sentences into Chinese

1. Adding more dollars to the bottom line, increasing your company's revenue opportunities, and capturing and maintaining an edge over your competitors—these are what e-business and business-to-business (B2B) e-commerce are all about.

2. The B2B marketplace is a new way to implement an old business practice called *supply chain management*.

3. If you're a bigger company and you want to influence an industry, you become what is called a *market maker*.

III. State whether the following are True or False?

1. B2B e-commerce includes some types of financial transactions between companies.

2. E-commerce innovations can reduce the cost of procurement before, during and after the transactio

3. Less expensive intermediation and lower transactions costs necessarily mean fewer intermediaries.

4. B2B exchanges are double-sided markets.

5. The exercise of market power is occurred in competition between B2B exchanges.

IV. Write an Abstract of "Trust, as a main barrier in adoption to B2C E-Commerce" in about 100 words.

V. Select three consumer-to-consumer (C2C) auction sites, including eBay. Create a chart that compares and contrasts the attributes of each auction site. Under what conditions or circumstances would a seller use an auction site other than eBay?

Chapter 5　Electronic Payment Systems

学习指导

　　电子商务网站的一个重要功能就是处理网上结算业务。本章将简单介绍当前常用的电子支付系统。通过本章的学习，读者应该了解以下内容：
- 支付方式涉及的五个方面。
- 有哪些因素决定一种支付方式是否能得到广泛的接受。
- 什么是虚拟信用卡和电子钱包。
- 什么是智能卡，以及它的分类。
- 什么是电子支票和电子登账。

5.1　Electronic Payments: a Critical Element in EC Support Services

In the off-line world, consumers use cash, checks, and credit cards to make purchases. At a fast-food restaurant, people usually pay with cash. If someone purchases an appliance at a discount store, they are likely to use a credit card. When people pay their bills, most use checks. How do people pay online? Unfortunately, paying online with the same instruments that people use off-line, namely cash, credit card, debit card, or paper check may be too slow, inefficient, or expensive for online payments. When a buyer places an order, the seller wants to make sure they will pay. When a bidder wins an electronic auction, the money must be ready. Therefore, special payment methods were developed for online payments. These are referred to as e-payments (electronic payments). E-payments are payments made electronically rather than by paper (cash, checks, vouchers, etc.). For example, a person can pay their bills electronically or transfer money electronically among their accounts or to their child's college fund.

Electronic payment methods expedite payments online and reduce payment processing costs. However, such methods must be safe and trusted by users. The basic e-payment methods are similar to off-line methods. However, some innovative methods exist only in cyberspace. The major methods that are in use include the following:
- Electronic payment cards (credit, debit, charge)
- Virtual credit cards
- E-wallets (or e-purses)
- Smart cards
- Electronic cash (several variations)
- Wireless payments
- Stored-value card payments
- Loyalty cards

Other methods are used primarily for B2B payments:

- Electronic checks
- Purchasing cards
- Electronic letters of credit
- Electronic funds transfer (EFT)
- Electronic benefits transfer (EBT)

What these diverse e-payment methods share in common is the ability to transfer a payment from one person or party to another person or party over a network without face-to-face interaction.

Whatever the e-payment method, five parties may be involved:

A) Customer/payer/buyer. The party making the e-payment in exchange for goods or services

B) Merchant/payee/seller. The party receiving the e-payment in exchange for goods and services

C) Issuer. The banks or nonbanking institutions that issue the e-payment instrument used to make the purchase

D) Regulator. Usually a government agency whose regulations control the e-payment process

E) Automated Clearing House (ACH). An electronic network that transfers money between bank accounts

Characteristics of Successful E-payment Methods

A crucial element in the success of an e-payment method is the "chicken-and-egg" problem: How do you get sellers to adopt a method when there are few buyers using it? And, how do you get buyers to adopt a method when there are few sellers using it? A number of factors come into play in determining whether a particular method of e-payment achieves widespread acceptance. Some of the crucial factors include the following.

Independence. Some forms of e-payment require specialized software or hardware to make the payment. Almost all forms of e-payment require the seller or merchant to install specialized software to receive and authorize a payment. Those e-payment methods that require the payer to install specialized components are less likely to succeed.

Interoperability and portability. All forms of EC run on specialized systems that are interlinked with other enterprise systems and applications. An e-payment method must mesh with these existing systems and applications and be supported by standard computing platforms.

Security. How safe is the transfer? What are the consequences of the transfer being compromised? Again, if the risk for the payer is higher than the risk for the payee, then the method is not likely to be accepted.

Anonymity. Unlike credit cards and checks, if a buyer uses cash, there is no way to trace the cash back to the buyer. Some buyers want their identities and purchase patterns to remain anonymous. To succeed, special payment methods have to maintain anonymity.

Divisibility. Most sellers accept credit cards only for purchases within a minimum and maximum range. If the cost of the item is too small—say, only a few dollars—a credit card will not do. In addition, a credit card will not work if an item or set of items costs too much—say, an airline company purchasing a new airplane. Any method that can address the lower or higher end of the price continuum or that can span one of the extremes and the middle has a chance of being widely accepted.

Easy of use. For B2C e-payments, credit cards are the standard due to their ease of use. For B2B payments, the question is whether the online e-payment methods can supplant the existing off-line methods of procurement.

Transaction fees. When a credit card is used for payment, the merchant pays a transaction fee of up to about 3 percent of the item's purchase price (above a minimum fixed fee). These fees make it prohibitive to support smaller purchases with credit cards, which leaves room for alternative forms of payment.

Critical mass. A critical mass of vendors must be willing to accept the payment method. Conversely, a critical mass of places to acquire the payment method (i.e., buy payment cards) is also necessary.

New Words & Phrases

bidder   n. 出价人，投标人

voucher   n. 凭证，代金券

innovative   adj. 新发明的；革新的；

portability   n. 可携带，轻便

anonymous   adj. 无名的，匿名的

span   n. 跨度，跨径 vt. 跨越，穿越

procurement   n. 获得

auction   n. 拍卖，拍卖方式 vt. 拍卖

expedite   vt. 加快进展，迅速完成

interoperability   n. 互用性，协同工作的能力

anonymity   n. 匿名，作者不明（或不详）

continuum   n. 连续统一体

supplant   vt. 把……排挤掉，取代

prohibitive   adj. 禁止的

Notes

1. Any method that can address the lower or higher end of the price continuum or that can span one of the extremes and the middle has a chance of being widely accepted. 本句的主干为 "any method …has a chance of being widely accepted"。句中的两个 "that" 引导的都是定语从句，用来修饰 "method"。本句译为："任何一种支付方式都应该有一个消费最低或最高的限用额度，或是能够超出一个极值点和中间点，这样的支付方式才能被广泛接受。"

5.2   Electronic Cards and Smart Cards

Electronic cards are plastic cards that contain digitized information. This information can be used for payment purposes. Electronic cards also can be used for other purposes, such as identification or to access a secure location. Some electronic cards are considered "smart" cards because they can manipulate information.

5.2.1   Payment Cards

If you are an American, you are likely to have at least one electronic payment card, an

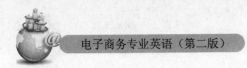

electronic card that contains information used for payment purposes.

There are three types of payment cards:

- Credit cards. A credit card provides the holder with credit to make purchases up to a limit fixed by the card issuer. Credit cards rarely have an annual fee. Instead, holders are charged high interest—the annual percentage rate—on their unpaid balances. Visa, MasterCard, and EuroPay are the predominant credit cards.

- Charge cards. The balance on a charge card is supposed to be paid in full upon receipt of the monthly statement. Such cards usually have annual fees.

- Debit cards. With a debit card, the money for a purchased item comes directly out of the holder's checking account (called a demand-deposit account). The actual transfer of funds from the holder's account to the merchant's takes place within 1 to 2 days. MasterCard, Visa, and EuroPay are the predominant debit cards.

5.2.2　Virtual Credit Cards

One innovation in online credit cards is a virtual credit card. This is an e-payment system in which a credit card issuer issues a special number that can be used in place of regular credit card numbers to make online purchases. This allows users to use a credit card online without having to disclose the actual credit card number.

5.2.3　E-Wallets

Most of the time when a person makes a purchase on the Web they are required to fill out a form with their name, shipping address, billing address, and credit card information. Doing this a few times is fine, but having to do it every time one shops on the Web can be an annoyance. Some merchants solve the problem by having customers fill out a form once and then saving the information on their servers for later use. For instance, this is what Amazon.com has done with its "One-Click" shopping feature. Of course, even if every merchant provided "one-click" shopping, customers would still have to set up an account with every merchant. This would also increase the possibility that the information might fall into the hands of a merchant who wanted to use this information for some other purpose. Also, the merchant wants to be sure of the identity of the buyer.

One way to avoid the problem is to use an electronic wallet (e-wallet). An e-wallet is a software component that a user downloads to their desktop PC and in which the user stores credit card numbers and other personal information. When a user shops at a merchant who accepts the e-wallet, the user clicks the e-wallet, which automatically fills in all the necessary information.

5.2.4　Smart Cards

One of the technologies that is used to support e-payments is smart cards. A smart card looks like any plastic payment card, but it is distinguished by the presence of an embedded microchip. The embedded chip can either be a microprocessor and a memory chip combined or just a memory chip with nonprogrammable logic. The microprocessor card can add, delete, and otherwise manipulate information on the card, whereas a memorychip card is usually a "read only" card like a credit card. Although the microprocessor is capable of running programs like a computer does, it is not a stand-alone computer. The programs and data must be downloaded from some other device (such as an ATM machine).

Smart cards are used for transaction processing, authentication, and authorization, and they can be categorized by the way in which data (and applications) are downloaded and read from the card. Under this scheme there are two major types of smart cards. The first type is a contact card, a card that is inserted in a smart card reader. These cards have a small gold plate about one-half inch in diameter on the front; when the card is inserted in the reader, the plate makes electronic contact and data are passed to and from the chip.

The second type of smart card is the contactless (proximity) card. In addition to the chip, a contactless card has an embedded antenna. In this case, data (and applications) are passed to and from the card through the card's antenna to another antenna attached to a cardreader unit or other device. Contactless cards are used for those applications in which the data must be processed very quickly (e.g., mass-transit applications such as paying in buses and trains) or when contact is difficult (e.g., security-entering mechanisms to buildings). Proximity cards usually work at short range, just a few inches. However, one type of proximity card can be used at a distance of over100 feet.

New Words & Phrases

digitized   n. 将资料数字化

charge cards 签账卡

deposit   vt. 储蓄，存款

disclose   vt. 说出，表明

annoyance   n. 烦恼，可厌之事

microchip   n. 微晶片（微型集成电路片）

nonprogrammable   adj.不可编程序的

stand-alone   n. 单机，卓越

contactless   adj. 不接触的，遥控的

antenna   n. 天线，触角，触须

attach to   （使）贴（系，粘）在……上，（使）相关；（使）依附

predominant   adj. 占主导地位的，显著的

debit cards 借记卡

virtual   adj. 虚拟的

e-wallet   n. 电子钱包

embedded   adj. 植入的，深入的，内含的

chip   n. 集成电路片

microprocessor n. 〈计〉微（信息）处理机

diameter   n. 直径

proximity   n. 接近，附近

Notes

1. An e-wallet is a software component that a user downloads to their desktop PC and in which the user stores credit card numbers and other personal information.句中"that"和"in which"分别引导两个定语从句，都用来修饰"a software component"。本句译为："电子钱包是用户下载到自己电脑上的软件，在这个软件中，用户存入信用卡的号码和其他个人信息。"

2. In this case, data (and applications) are passed to and from the card through the card's antenna to another antenna attached to a cardreader unit or other device. 句中"attached to a cardreader unit or other device"是过去分词做定语用来修饰"another antenna"。本句译为："在这种情况下，数据通过卡和读卡器或

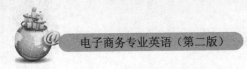

其他设备上的天线进行数据传输。"

5.3　E-Cash and Innovative Payment Methods

E-cash—the digital equivalent of paper currency and coins—makes a lot of sense. It is secure and anonymous, and it can be used to support payments that cannot be economically supported with payment cards. From a practical standpoint, however, the inconvenience of opening an account and downloading software and the difficulty of obtaining a critical mass of users seems to have outweighed the benefits of e-cash.

5.3.1　E-Cash and Alternatives to Credit Cards

Consider the following online shopping scenarios:

- A customer goes to an online music store and purchases a single CD that costs $8.95.
- A person goes online to a leading newspaper or news journal and purchases (downloads) a copy of an archived news article for $1.50.
- A person goes to an online gaming company, selects a game, and plays it for 30 minutes. The person owes the company $3 for the playing time.
- A person goes to a Web site selling digital images and clip art. The person purchases a couple of images at a cost of $0.80.

These are all examples of micropayments, which are small payments, usually under $10. Credit cards do not work well for such small payments. Vendors who accept credit cards typically must pay a minimum transaction fee that ranges from 25 cents to 35 cents. These fees are relatively insignificant for credit card purchases above $10, but are cost-prohibitive for smaller transactions. Also, when the purchase amount is small, consumers are unwilling to type in credit card numbers or wait for a standard credit card authorization. Micropayments are one area where e-cash and other payment card schemes come into play. Here are examples of a few innovative methods.

Wireless Payments

An ideal way to pay for certain types of micropayments is to use wireless devices. Vodafone, for example, has an "m-pay bill" system that enables wireless subscribers to use their mobile phones to make payments of $10 or less. Users respond to a telephone number posted on a Web site by sending a text message (SMS) from their cell phones. A message is then sent back, confirming the payment arrangement and including a PIN number that acts as a password to the specific customer's account. The customer then proceeds with the transaction, and the charge shows up on their monthly Vodafone bill. Other telecommunication companies offer similar services.

Qpass

One micropayment system that avoids some of the e-cash problems and has enjoyed some success is Qpass. Qpass is used primarily to purchase content from participating news services and periodicals such as the New York Times, Wall Street Journal, and Forbs.

A user sets up a Qpass account, creating a user name and password and specifying a credit card against which purchases will be charged. Then, when a purchase is made at a participating site, the user simply enters their Qpass user name and password and confirms the purchase. Instead of immediately billing the user's credit card account, the charges are aggregated into a single monthly statement, which is billed to the user's credit card.

5.3.2 Stored-value Cards

Stored-value smart cards have found greater usage than e-cash schemes as an alternative to credit cards. When used to store cash downloaded from a bank or credit card account, smart cards can be used to purchase items with values ranging from a few cents to hundreds of dollars. Various types of vendors worldwide accept stored-value cards: telephone companies, fast-food restaurants, convenience stores, vending machines, gas stations, transportation facilities, sundries stores, cinemas, parking garages, grocery stores, department stores, taxis, parking meters, cafeterias, and video stores. For example, people can now buy such a card at Kinko's and use it for services such as photocopying and Internet time. A leading vendor of stored-value cards is Visa.

New Words & Phrases

standpoint   n. 立场；观点
scenario   n. 情节，剧本，方案
ideal   adj. 理想的，完满的
bill   n. 账单 vt. 送交某人账单
vend   vt. 出售，贩卖
photocopying   n. 影印服务

outweigh   vt. 在重要性或价值方面超过
archive   v. 存档 n. 档案文件
subscriber   n. 消费者；用户
aggregate   v.（使）聚集   n. 〈正〉数，总计
sundries   n. 杂项，杂物

5.4   E-Checking

An e-check is the electronic version or representation of a paper check. E-checks contain the same information as a paper check, can be used wherever paper checks are used, and are based on the same legal framework. E-checks work essentially the same way a paper check works, but in pure electronic form, with fewer manual steps. Simply put, they are faster and cheaper, and they can be more secure.

E-checks fit within current business practices, eliminating the need for expensive process reengineering and taking advantage of the competency of the banking industry. Using state-of-the-art security techniques, e-checks can be used by all bank customers who have checking accounts, including small and midsize businesses that otherwise have little access to electronic payment systems.

New Words & Phrases

framework. n. 构架；结构
state-of-the-art   n. 艺术级的，最新水平

competency   n. 资格，能力，作证能力

1. Using state-of-the-art security techniques, e-checks can be used by all bank customers who have checking accounts, including small and midsize businesses that otherwise have little access to electronic payment systems. 句中 "who have checking accounts" 是定语从句，用来修饰 "customers"。本句译为："使用最新的安全技术，拥有支票账户的所有银行客户，包括建立不起电子支付系统的小型和中型企业都可以使用电子支票。"

5.5   E-Billing

E-billing is also called electronic bill presentment and payment (EBPP). E-billing enables the presentment, payment, and posting of bills via the Internet. Presentment involves taking the information that is typically printed on a bill and hosting it on a bill-presentment Web server. Once the bill is available on the Web server, a customer can access the bill with a browser, review it, and pay it electronically. Payments are generally transferred from the customer's checking account via the ACH. In e-billing, the customers can be either individuals or companies.

Advantages of E-billing

From the perspective of the billing firm, e-billing has several advantages. The most obvious benefit is the reduction in expenses related to billing and processing payments. The estimate is that paper bills cost between $0.75 and $2.70 per bill. E-billing costs between $0.25 and $0.30 per bill. E-billing also enables better customer service. Not only can customer service representatives see the same presentment that the customer is seeing, but the presentment can also provide access to frequently asked questions and help boxes.

Another advantage relates to advertising. A paper bill can include advertising and marketing inserts. Usually, every customer gets the same ads or materials. With e-billing, electronic inserts can be customized to the individual customer. If a customer responds to the insert, then it is much easier to trace which ads or materials are successful.

There are also advantages from the customer's perspective. E-billing reduces the customer's expenses by eliminating the cost of checks, postage, and envelopes. E-billing simplifies and centralizes payment processing and provides better record keeping. Customers can review and pay bills at virtually any time. In this way, the customer has direct control over the timing of the payment.

perspective n. 观点，想法；前途；希望	representative n. 代表 adj. 有代表性的，典型的
insert vt. 插入，嵌入 n. 添入物	centralize vt. 把……集中于中央

1. The estimate is that paper bills cost between $0.75 and $2.70 per bill. 句中 "that" 引导的是宾语从句。本

句译为："据估计，纸质账单的成本大约在 0.75 到 2.7 美元之间。"

2. Not only can customer service representatives see the same presentment that the customer is seeing, but the presentment can also provide access to frequently asked questions and help boxes. 句中，由于"not only"位于句首，所以使用了倒装句"Not only can customer service representatives…"。本句译为："不仅客户代表看到的账单和客户看到的账单相同，而且电子账单还提供常见问答和帮助框。"

Reading Material——Stored-Value Cards: Tapping The Teen and Preteen Markets

"We're living on a plastic planet, where even vending machines, parking meters and Starbucks branches are now accepting credit and debit cards for everyday transactions. Small wonder that high schoolers—who were expected to spend $195 billion in 2006, according to a study by the Harrison Group—hanker for their own charge cards" (Campbell 2006). According to a 2006 study by the Jump$tart Coalition for Financial Literacy, almost 50 percent of high school seniors in the United States have a credit card. Close to half of the students have a card in their own names, whereas the other half uses their parents' cards. In order to serve the market of children under the age of 18, MasterCard and Visa have introduced a number of preloaded, open-loop stored-value cards. These prepaid cards look like a regular plastic credit card, but the cardholder has no line of credit. Instead, they are more like debit cards where the cardholder can only spend up to the amount loaded on the card. The cards are accepted anywhere a MasterCard credit card or Visa credit card are accepted—at stores, online, and at ATM machines.

For the under-18 market, MasterCard offers the affinity-based MYPlash card, which features images of rock stars and athletes on the cards, as well as the Allow Card (short for allowance card), which is a prepaid debit card. Not to be outdone, Visa offers a variety of cards that cater to the under-18 market. One of these is the RushCard, developed in conjunction with hip-hop mogul Russell Simmons. Besides working anywhere a Visa card is accepted, the card also works with mobile phones and provides discounts on clothing from Simmons' Phat Farm and Baby Phat. Another is the Visa UPside card, which teaches responsible spending. Toward this end, Visa has developed a number of financial literacy programs for teachers and schools (see spendresponsibly.com).

Probably the best known of the Visa offerings aimed at the under-18 market is the Visa Buxx card (pronounced "bucks"). The Visa Buxx program was started in the fall of 1999 by WildCard Systems. WildCard created the system in order to tap into the teen market. In the United States, there are more than 30 million teens between 13 and 18 years of age, and they spend more than $160 billion annually. Most of their spending involves cash provided by their parents.

WildCard was looking for a way to provide a turnkey payment system that would meet the needs of both parents and teens by offering a card that would provide:

- A parent-controlled reloadable payment card that would be accepted anywhere that Visa was accepted, including online and ATM cash machines.
- Stored-value functionality so that teens can only spend up to the amount established by their parents and loaded onto the card.
- A Web site where parents and teens could enroll for the card; add value through checking accounts, savings accounts, credit cards, or debit cards; set up recurring allowance schedules; shop online; and

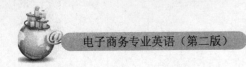

check balances and transaction history.

● Parental-control features so parents could maintain control over the account through the Web site.

● An educational component on the Web site so that teens could learn about financial responsibility and budgeting.

WildCard licensed the Visa Buxx product to Visa. Five Visa card issuers, including Bank of America, Capital One, National City, U.S. Bank, and Wachovia Bank, launched the system in 2000. Today, the card is offered by a wide range of banks throughout the United States. For issuing banks, the card helps build stronger relationships with existing customers (parents) and establishes relationships with new customers (the teens). In 2005, eFunds acquired WildCard.

Although these prepaid cards have a number of benefits, there is also a big downside. Excluding the actual use of the card, card issuers charge users fees for virtually every action. Most card issuers collect fees for enrolling in the program, reloading or replacing the card, and for making inquiries about the balance remaining on the card. Some issuers charge the cardholder if the card is not used for a few weeks or months.

New Words & Phrases

hanker vi. 渴望	coalition n. 结合体，同盟
preloaded n., v. 预载；预加负荷	open-loop 开环，开回路
outdo vt. 胜过 cater to v. 供应伙食，迎合	conjunction n. 连词，结合；联合
mogul n. 大人物；大亨；小雪丘	tap into 利用；开发；打入市场，开拓生意
turnkey adj. 可立即投入使用的	downside adj. 下降趋势的，向下的走向[趋势]

被动语态的翻译技巧

英语中被动语态的使用范围极为广泛，尤其是在科技英语中，被动语态几乎随处可见，凡是在不必、不愿说出或不知道主动者的情况下均可使用被动语态，因此，掌握被动语态的翻译方法是极为重要的。在汉语中，也有被动语态，通常通过"把"或"被"等词体现出来，但它的使用范围远远小于英语中被动语态的使用范围，因此英语中的被动语态在很多情况下都翻译成主动结构。

对于英语原文的被动结构，我们一般采取下列的方法：

一、翻译成汉语的主动句

英语原文的被动结构翻译成汉语的主动结构又可以进一步分为几种不同的情况。

1. **英语原文中的主语在译文中仍做主语。**

在采用此方法时，我们往往在译文中使用"加以"，"经过"，"用……来"等词来体现原文中的被动含义。例如：

例1.   Other questions will be discussed briefly.

其他问题将简单地加以讨论。

例2.   In other words mineral substances which are found on earth must be extracted   by digging, boring holes, artificial explosions, or similar operations   which make them available to us.

换言之，矿物就是存在于地球上，但须经过挖掘、钻孔、人工爆破或类似作业才能获得的物质。

例 3.　Nuclear power's danger to health, safety, and even life itself can be summed up in one word: radiation.

核能对健康、安全, 甚至对生命本身构成的危险可以用一个词——辐射来概括。

2. 将英语原文中的主语翻译为宾语, 同时增补泛指性的词语（人们, 大家等）做主语。

例 1.　It could be argued that the radio performs this service as well, but on television everything is much more living, much more real.

可能有人会指出, 无线电广播同样也能做到这一点, 但还是电视屏幕上的节目要生动、真实的多。

例 2.　Television, it is often said, keeps one informed about current events, allows one to follow the latest developments in science and politics, and offers an endless series of programs which are both instructive and entertaining.

人们常说, 电视使人了解时事, 熟悉政治领域的最新发展变化, 并能源源不断地为观众提供各种既有教育意义又有趣的节目。

例 3.　It is generally accepted that the experiences of the child in his first years largely determine his character and later personality.

人们普遍认为, 孩子们的早年经历在很大程度上决定了他们的性格及其未来的人品。

另外, 下列的结构也可以通过这一手段翻译:

It is asserted that … 有人主张 ……

It is believed that … 有人认为……

It is generally considered that … 大家（一般人）认为

It is well known that … 大家知道（众所周知）……

It will be said … 有人会说……

It was told that … 有人曾经说……

3. 将英语原文中的 by, in, for 等做状语的介词短语翻译成译文的主语, 而英语原文中的主语一般被翻译成宾语。

例 1.　A right kind of fuel is needed for an atomic reactor.

原子反应堆需要一种合适的燃料。

例 2.　By the end of the war, 800 people had been saved by the organization, but at a cost of 200 Belgian and French lives.

大战结束时, 这个组织拯救了八百人, 但那是以二百多比利时人和法国人的生命为代价的。

例 3.　And it is imagined by many that the operations of the common mind can be by no means compared with these processes, and that they have to be acquired by a sort of special training.

许多人认为, 普通人的思维活动根本无法与科学家的思维过程相比, 而且认为这些思维过程必须经过某种专门的训练才能掌握。

4. 翻译成汉语的无主句。

例 1.　Great efforts should be made to inform young people especially the dreadful consequences of taking up the habit.

应该尽最大努力告诫年轻人吸烟的危害, 特别是吸烟上瘾后的可怕后果。

例 2.　By this procedure, different honeys have been found to vary widely in the sensitivity of their inhibit to heat.

通过这种方法分析发现不同种类的蜂蜜的抗菌活动对热的敏感程度也极为不同。

例 3. Many strange new means of transport have been developed in our century, the strangest of them being perhaps the hovercraft.

在我们这个世纪内研制了许多新奇的交通工具，其中最奇特的也许就是气垫船了。

例 4. New source of energy must be found, and this will take time.

必须找到新的能源，这需要时间.

另外，下列结构也可以通过这一手段翻译：

It is hoped that …… 希望……

It is reported that …… 据报道……

It is said that …… 据说……

It is supposed that …… 据推测……

It may be said without fear of exaggeration that …… 可以毫不夸张地说……

It must be admitted that …… 必须承认……

It must be pointed out that …… 必须指出……

It will be seen from this that …… 由此可见……

5. 翻译成带表语的主动句。

例 1.The decision to attack was not taken lightly.

进攻的决定不是轻易做出的。

例 2. On the whole such an conclusion can be drawn with a certain degree of confidence, but only if the child can be assumed to have had the same attitude towards the test as the other with whom he is being compared, and only if he was not punished by lack of relevant information which they possessed.

总的来说，得出这种结论是有一定程度把握的，但必须具备两个条件：能够假定这个孩子对测试的态度和与他比较的另一个孩子的态度相同；他也没有因为缺乏别的孩子已掌握的有关知识而被扣分。

二、译成汉语的被动语态

英语中的许多被动句可以翻译成汉语的被动句。常用"被"，"给"，"遭"，"挨"，"为……所"，"使"，"由……"，"受到"等表示。例如：

例 1. Early fires on the earth were certainly caused by nature, not by Man.

地球上早期的火肯定是由大自然而不是人类引燃的。

例 2. These signals are produced by colliding stars or nuclear reactions in outer space.

这些讯号是由外层空间的星球碰撞或者核反应所造成的。

例 3. Natural light or "white" light is actually made up of many colors.

自然光或者"白光"实际上是由许多种颜色组成的。

例 4. They may have been a source of part of the atmosphere of the terrestrial planets, and they are believed to have been the planetesimal-like building blocks for some of the outer planets and their satellites.

它们可能一直是地球行星的一部分大气的来源。它们还被认为是构成外部行星以及其卫星的一种类似微星的基础材料。

例 5. Over the years, tools and technology themselves as a source of fundamental innovation have largely been ignored by historians and philosophers of science.

工具和技术本身作为根本性创新的源泉多年来在很大程度上被科学史学家和科学思想家们忽视了。

例 6.   Whether the Government should increase the financing of pure science at the expense of technology or vice versa (反之) often depends on the issue of which is seen as the driving force.

政府是以减少技术的经费投入来增加纯理论科学的经费投入，还是相反，这往往取决于把哪一方看作是驱动的力量。

Exercises

I. Answer the following questions

1. List five parties may be involved in the e-payment method.

2. List characteristics of successful e-payment methods

3. What are virtual credit cards?

4. Describe the difference between the contact card and contactless card.

5. List advantages of e-billing.

II. Fill in the blanks in each of the following

1. There are three types of payment cards: _____, _____ and _____.

2. A (an) _____ is a software component that a user downloads to their desktop PC and in which the user stores credit card numbers and other personal information.

3. A _____ looks like any plastic payment card, but it is distinguished by the presence of an embedded microchip. The embedded chip can either be a _____ and a _____ chip combined or just a memory chip with _____ logic.

4. _____ smart cards have found greater usage than e-cash schemes as an alternative to credit cards.

5. A (An) _____ is the electronic version or representation of a paper check. E-checks contain the same information as a paper check.

6. E-billing is also called _____.

III. Questions and Discussion

1. What is the market for MasterCard's MYPlash card and Visa's RushCard?

2. What key characteristics underlie WildCard's Visa Buxx system?

3. What is the major downside of prepaid, preloaded cards for the under-18 market?

Chapter 6　E-Commerce Security

今天，电子商务正在成为大多数公司的基本活动，但这些活动必须采用适当的安全策略来加以保障。通过本章的学习，读者应该了解以下内容：

- 电子商务安全的基本要素。
- 网络安全攻击的基本类型。
- 组织在管理安全问题上的常见错误。
- 电子商务通信安全的一些主要技术手段。
- 电子商务网络安全组件的主要技术手段。

学习指导

6.1　Security is Everyone's Business

As the technology underlying e-commerce has become more complex, the opportunities for intrusion and attack have increased. Not only are the underlying components more vulnerable, they are also harder to administer. Teenage hackers, industrial spies, corporate insiders, agents of foreign governments, and criminal elements have all taken advantage of the situation. The variety of potential perpetrators makes it hard to deter potential attacks and detect them once they have occurred.

The worldwide security software market will total $14.5 billion in 2009, an eight per cent increase from 2008, according to Gartner. Although spending on security has increased significantly, the average company still spends very little of its IT budget on security and very little per employee.

New Words & Phrases

underlie　vt. 位于或存在于（某物）之下，构成…的基础（或起因）；引起

intrusion　n. 闯入；打扰　　　　　　　　　attack　n. v. 攻击，袭击

vulnerable　adj. 易受伤的，脆弱的　　　　　hacker　n. 电脑黑客

spy　n. 间谍　　　　　　　　　　　　　　corporate　adj. 社团的，法人的

insider　n. 知情人　　　　　　　　　　　　take advantage of　v. 利用

perpetrator　n. 犯罪者，作恶者　　　　　　deter　vt. 阻止；制止

detect　vt. 发现；发觉，查明　　　　　　　spending　n. 开销，花费

Notes

1. Not only are the underlying components more vulnerable, they are also harder to administer. 本句中的前半句为倒装句，正常的顺序为 "the underlying components are not only more vulnerable"。本句译为 "技术部分不仅脆弱，而且还难于管理。"

6.2   Basic Security Issues

The following list summarizes some of the major security issues that can occur in EC:

- Authentication. When a person views a Web page from a Web site, how can they be sure that the site is not fraudulent? If a person files a tax return electronically, how do they know that is has been sent to the taxing authority? If a person receives an e-mail, how can they be sure that the sender is who they claim to be? The process by which one entity verifies that another entity is who they claim to be is called authentication. Authentication requires evidence in the form of credentials, which can take a variety of forms, including something known (e.g., a password), something unique (e.g., a signature).

- Authorization. Once authenticated, does a person or program have the right to access particular data, programs, or system resources (e.g., files, registries, directories, etc.)? Authorization ensures that a person or program has the right to access certain resources. It is usually determined by comparing information about the person or program with access control information associated with the resource being accessed.

- Auditing. If a person or program accesses a Web site, various pieces of information are noted in a log file. If a person or program queries a database, the action is also noted in a log file. The process of collecting information about accessing particular resources, using particular privileges, or performing other security actions (either successfully or unsuccessfully) is known as auditing. Audits provide the means to reconstruct the specific actions that were taken and often enable IT personnel to identify the person or program that performed the actions.

- Confidentiality (privacy). The idea behind confidentiality is that information that is private or sensitive should not be disclosed to unauthorized individuals, entities, or computer software processes. It is intertwined with the notion of digital privacy, which is now a regulatory issue in many countries. Some examples of things that should be confidential are trade secrets, business plans, health records, credit card numbers, and even the fact that a person visited a particular Web site. Confidentiality requires that we know what data or applications we want to protect and who should have access to them. Confidentiality is usually ensured by encryption.

- Integrity. Data can be altered or destroyed while it is in transit or after it is stored. The ability to protect data from being altered or destroyed in an unauthorized or accidental manner is called integrity. Financial transactions are one example of data whose integrity needs to be secured. Again, encryption is one way of ensuring integrity of data while it is in transit.

- Availability. If a person is trying to execute a stock trade through an online service, then the service needs to be available in near-real time. An online site is available if a person or program can gain access to the pages, data, or services provided by the site when they are needed. Technologies such as load-balancing hardware and software are aimed at ensuring availability.

- Nonrepudiation. If a person orders an item through a mail-order catalog and pays by check, then it is difficult to dispute the veracity of the order. If the same item is ordered through the company's "1-800" number and the person pays by credit card, then there is always room for dispute. Similarly, if a person uses the company's Web site and pays by credit card, the person can always claim that they did not place the order. Nonrepudiation is the ability to limit parties from refuting that a legitimate transaction took place. One of the keys to nonrepudiation is a "signature" that makes it difficult for a person to dispute that they were involved in an exchange.

New Words & Phrases

authentication n. 证明，认证	fraudulent adj. 欺骗的，不诚实的
file v. 提交，把……归档 n. 文件	tax return 纳税申报单
authority n. 权力，当局	entity n. 实体
verify vt. 证实，核实	credentials n. 资格证书；国书
Authorization n. 授权，认可	registry n. 档案室；登记簿存放处
associated with 与……交往，联系	privilege n. 特权 vt. 给与……特权
reconstruct vt. 重建，重现，重整	confidentiality n. 机密性
privacy n. 私事，隐私	sensitive adj. 敏感的，灵敏的
disclose vt. 揭露，揭开	unauthorized adj. 未被授权的
intertwined v. 缠结在一起	notion n. 概念，观念
encryption n. 加密	availability n. 可用性，有效性
nonrepudiation n. 不可抵赖性，非否认性	mail-order adj. 邮购的
dispute v. & n. 辩论；争论	veracity n. 诚实；真实
refute vt. 驳斥，驳倒	legitimate adj. 合情合理的；合法的

Notes

1. The process by which one entity verifies that another entity is who they claim to be is called authentication. 本句的主干是"The process … is called authentication. "。 which 引导定语从句用来修饰 process。本句译为"一个实体证实另一实体身份与其所声明身份是否一致的过程称为认证。"

2. It is usually determined by comparing information about the person or program with access control information associated with the resource being accessed. 本句译为"通常是通过对比个人或程序的信息与要访问资源的访问控制信息来决定是否具有这种权限。"

3. One of the keys to nonrepudiation is a "signature" that makes it difficult for a person to dispute that they were involved in an exchange. 本句中第一个 that 引导的是定语从句，用来修饰 signature；第二个 that 引导宾语从句。本句译为"不可否认性的关键之一就是签名，这使个人很难否认他们确实进行了交易。"

6.3　Types of Threats and Attacks

Security experts distinguish between two types of attacks—nontechnical and technical. Nontechnical attacks are those in which a perpetrator uses chicanery or other forms of persuasion to trick people into revealing sensitive information or performing actions that can be used to compromise the security of a network. These attacks are also called social engineering attacks.

6.3.1　Nontechnical Attacks: Social Engineering

In social engineering, individual users are tricked by social pressures into providing information or carrying out actions that they feel are innocuous but that inadvertently support hackers in their attempts to attack and compromise the networks to which those individuals have access. Social engineering preys on an individual's desire to help, an individual's fear of getting into trouble, or the general trust among individuals.

Because the key to successful social engineering rests with the victims, the key to combating social engineering attacks also rests with the victims. Certain positions within an organization are clearly more vulnerable than others. These are the individuals who have access to private and confidential information and interact with the public on a frequent basis. Some of the positions with this sort of access and contact are secretaries and executive assistants, database and network administrators, computer operators, call-center operators, and help-desk attendants.

6.3.2　Technical Attacks

In contrast to nontechnical attacks, software and system knowledge are used to perpetrate technical attacks. In conducting a technical attack, an expert hacker often uses a methodical approach. Several software tools are readily and freely available over the Internet that enable a hacker to expose a system's vulnerabilities. Although many of these tools require expertise, novice hackers can easily use many of the existing tools.

We will confine our discussion to two types of attacks that are well known and that have affected the lives of millions—distributed denial of service(DDoS) attacks and malicious code attacks (viruses, worms, and Trojan horses).

1. Distributed Denial of Service Attacks

In a denial-of-service (DoS) attack, an attacker uses specialized software to send a flood of data packets to the target computer, with the aim of overloading it's resources. Many attackers rely on software that has been created by other hackers and made available over the Internet rather than developing it themselves.

With a distributed denial of service(DDoS) attack, the attacker gains illegal administrative access to as many computers on the Internet as possible. Once an attacker has access to a large number of computers, they load the specialized DDoS software onto these computers. The software lays in wait, listening for a command to begin the attack. When the command is given, the distributed network of computers begins sending out requests to the target computer. The requests can be legitimate queries for information or can be very specialized computer commands designed to overwhelm specific computer resources. There are different types of DDoS attacks. In the simplest case, it is the magnitude of the requests that brings the target computer to a halt.

The machines on which the DDoS software is loaded are known as zombies. Zombies are often located at university and government sites. Increasingly, with the rise of cable modems and DSL modems, home computers that are connected to the Internet and left on all the time have become good zombie candidates.

Due to the widespread availability of free intrusion tools and scripts and the overall interconnectivity on the Internet, virtually anyone with minimal computer experience (often a teenager with time on his hands) can mount a DoS attack.

2. Malicious Code: Viruses, Worms, and Trojan Horses

Sometimes referred to as malware (for malicious software), malicious code is classified by the way in which it is propagated. Some malicious code is rather benign, but it all has the potential to do damage.

Malicious code takes a variety of forms—both pure and hybrid. The names of such code are taken from the real-word pathogens they resemble.

（1）Viruses

This is the best known of the malicious code categories. Although there are many definitions of a computer virus, the Request for Comment (RFC) 1135 definition is widely used: " A virus is a piece of code that inserts itself into a host, including the operating systems, to propagate. It cannot run independently. It requires that its host program be run to activate it."

A virus has two components. First, it has a propagation mechanism by which it spreads. Second, it has a payload that refers to what the virus does once it is executed. Sometimes the execution is triggered by a particular event. The Michelangelo virus, for instance, was triggered by Michelangelo's birth date. Some viruses simply infect and spread. Others do substantial damage (e.g., deleting files or corrupting the hard drive).

（2）Worms

The major difference between a worm and a virus is that a worm propagates between systems (usually through a network), whereas a virus propagates locally. RFC1135 defines a worm in this way: " A worm is a program that can run independently, will consume the resources of its host from within in order to maintain itself, and can propagate a complete working version of itself onto another machine."

（3）Macro viruses and macro worms

A macro virus or macro worm is usually executed when the application object (e.g., spreadsheet, word processing document, e-mail message) containing the macro is opened or a particular procedure is executed (e.g., a file is saved). Melissa and ILOVEYOU were both examples of macro worms that were propagated through Microsoft Outlook e-mail and whose payloads were delivered as a Visual Basic for Application (VBA) programs attached to e-mail messages. When the unsuspecting recipient opened the e-mail, the VBA program looked up the entries in the recipient's Outlook address book and sent copies of itself to the contacts in the address book. If you think this is a difficult task, note that the ILOVEYOU macro was about 40 lines of code.

（4）Trojan horses

A Trojan horse is a program that appears to have a useful function but contains a hidden function that presents a security risk.

There are many types of Trojan horse programs. The programs of interest are those that make it possible for someone else to access and control a person's computer over the Internet. This type of Trojan horse has two parts: server and client. The server is the program that runs on the computer under attack. The client program is the program used by the person perpetrating the attack. For example, the Girlfriend Trojan is a server program that arrives in the form of a file that looks like an interesting game or program. When the unsuspecting user runs the program, the Trojan program is installed. The installed program is executed every time the attacked computer is turned on. The server simply waits for the associated client program to send a command. This particular Trojan horse enables the perpetrator to capture user IDs and passwords, to display messages on the affected computer, to delete and upload files, and so on.

New Words & Phrases

distinguish　v. 辨别，区别

chicanery　n. 哄骗；欺骗

reveal　vt. 显示；露出

innocuous　adj. 无害的，不会招致反对的

attempt　vt. n. 试图；尝试

rest with 在于，取决于

combat　n. 战斗，斗争 vt. 与……战斗

in contrast to 相比之下

expertise　n. 专门知识或技能

confine　vt. 限制；局限于；n. 界限，范围

malicious　adj. 恶意的，恶毒的

packet　n. 小包

legitimate　adj. 合情合理的；合法的

magnitude　n. 巨大；重要性

zombie n. 傀儡，行尸走肉

candidate　n. 申请求职者，候选人

on sb.'s hands 由某人负责

benign　adj. 善良的，温和的

hybrid　n. 杂种，混合的

resemble　vt. 像……，类似于

trigger　n. （枪）扳机 vt. 引发

nontechnical　n. 非技术性的

trick into 诱骗……使之采取……

compromise　n. 妥协 vi. 折中解决 vt. 危害

inadvertently　adv. 不注意地

desire　vt. n. 希望，渴望

victim　n. 牺牲者，受害者，受灾者

frequent　adj. 常见的 vt. 光顾，常与……交往

methodical　adj. 有条理的，井然的

novice　n. 新手，初学者

distributed　adj. 分布式的

a flood of　一大批

overloading　vt. 使超载，使过载

overwhelm　vt. 覆盖，淹没

halt　n. 停住，停止，暂停 v. （使）停下来

modem　n. 　调制解调器

script　n. 剧本，脚本，讲稿

propagate　v. 繁衍，增殖 vt. 传播；宣传，普及

potential　adj. 潜在的，有可能的 n. 潜力，可能性

pathogen　n. 病菌，病原体

payload　n. 有效载荷

substantial adj. 重大的，实质的

119

worm　n. 虫；蠕虫

macro　n. 宏；　adj. 巨大的

unsuspecting　adj. 不怀疑的，可信任的

Trojan horse n. 〈希神〉特洛伊木马

DDoS (distributed denial of service) 分布式拒绝服务

DoS (denial-of –service) 拒绝服务

Malware (malicious software) 恶意软件

RFC (Request for Comment) 请求注解

1. Many attackers rely on software that has been created by other hackers and made available over the Internet rather than developing it themselves. 本句的主干是"Many attackers rely on software···rather than developing it themselves."，"that"引导的是定语从句。本句译为"许多攻击者依赖于其他黑客开发的软件而不是自己开发软件，并通过因特网使它们发挥作用。"

2. A worm is a program that can run independently, will consume the resources of its host from within in order to maintain itself, and can propagate a complete working version of itself onto another machine. 本句译为"蠕虫是可以独立运行的程序，为了维护自身，它会消耗主机资源，并能复制一个自身的完整工作版本到另一台计算机上。"

3. The client program is the program used by the person perpetrating the attack. 句中"perpetrating the attack"是定语来修饰 person，"used by···"是过去分词做定语修饰"program"。本句译为"客户端程序由实施攻击的人来使用。"

6.4 Managing EC Security

Although awareness of security issues has increased in recent years, organizations continue to make some fairly common mistakes in managing their security risks (McConnell 2002):

- Undervalued information. Few organizations have a clear understanding of the value of specific information assets.

- Narrowly defined security boundaries. Most organizations focus on securing their internal networks and fail to understand the security practices of their supply chain partners.

- Reactive security management. Many organizations are reactive rather than proactive focusing on security after an incident or problem occurs.

- Dated security management processes. Organizations rarely update or change their security practice to meet changing needs. Similarly, they rarely update the knowledge and skills of their staff about best practices in information security.

- Lack of communication about security responsibilities. Security often is viewed as an IT problem, not an organizational one.

Given these common mistakes, it is clear that a holistic approach is required to secure an EC site. Sites must constantly evaluate and address emerging vulnerabilities and threats. End users must recognize that IT security is as important as physical security and must adopt responsible behavior. Senior management must articulate the need for IT security, play a key role in formulating organizational security policies, and actively support those policies. Those organizations with sound security practices rely on comprehensive risk management to determine their security needs (King 2001; Power 2000).

Security Risk Management

Security risk management is a systematic process for determining the likelihood of various security attacks and for identifying the actions needed to prevent or otherwise mitigate those attacks. It consists of four phases:

- Assessment. In this phase, organizations evaluate their security risks by determining their assets, the vulnerabilities of their system, and the potential threats to these vulnerabilities. One way to evaluate the vulnerabilities and threats facing a specific organization is to rely on the knowledge of the organization's IT personnel or to use outside consultants to make the determination. Another way is to utilize a honeynet to study the types of attacks to which a site is being actively subjected. A honeynet is a network of honeypots, which are production systems (firewalls, routers, Web servers, database servers, and the like) that can be watched and studied as network intrusions occur.

- Planning. The goal of this phase is to arrive at a set of policies defining which threats are tolerable and which are not. A threat is deemed tolerable if the cost of the safeguard is too high or the risk too low. The policies also specify the general measures to be taken against those threats that are intolerable or high priority.

- Implementation. During implementation, particular technologies are chosen to counter high-priority threats. The selection of particular technologies is based on the general guidelines established in the planning phase. As a first step in the implementation phase, generic types of technology should be selected for each of the high priority threats. Given the generic types, particular software from particular vendors can then be selected.

- Monitoring. This is an ongoing process that is used to determine which measures are successful, which measures are unsuccessful and need modification, whether there are any new types of threats, whether there have been advances or changes in technology, and whether there are any new business assets that need to be secured.

New Words & Phrases

undervalued   adj. 售价过低的

dated   adj. 有日期的，陈旧的

holistic   adj. 整体的，全盘的

honeynet 蜜网

tolerable   adj. 可忍受的

counter n. 柜台，计数器 v.对抗，反驳

proactive   adj. 前摄的

lack of 缺乏

articulate   adj. 表达能力强的 v.清楚地表达

honeypot 蜜罐

deem   vt. 认为，相信

ongoing adj. 继续进行的；不断前进（发展）中的

1. Many organizations are reactive rather than proactive focusing on security after an incident or problem occurs. 本句译为"许多组织是在事故或问题发生后才重视安全问题，而不是在事前就进行安全管理。"

2. Security risk management is a systematic process for determining the likelihood of various security attacks and for identifying the actions needed to prevent or otherwise mitigate those attacks. 本句译为"对于确定各种安全攻击的可能性和识别需要防范或减弱攻击来说，安全风险管理是一个系统过程。"

6.5 Securing EC Communications

As the CERT/FBI survey indicates, most organizations rely on multiple technologies to secure their networks. The technologies can be divided into two major groups: those designed to secure communications across the network and those designed to protect the servers and clients on the network. This section considers the first of these technologies.

6.5.1 Authentication

Stronger security is achieved by combining something one knows with something one has, a technique known as two-factor authentication. Tokens qualify as something one has. Tokens come in various shapes, forms, and sizes. Passive tokens are storage devices containing a secret code. The most common passive tokens are plastic cards with magnetic strips containing a hidden code. With passive tokens, the user swipes the token through a reader attached to a personal computer or workstation and then enters their password in order to gain access to the network.

Active tokens are usually small stand-alone electronic devices that generate one-time passwords. In this case, the user enters a PIN into the token, the token generates a password that is only good for a single log-on, and the user then logs on to the system using the one-time password. ActiveCard and Cryptocard are companies that provide active token authentication devices.

Biometric System

Two-factor authentication can also be based on something one is. Fingerprint scanners, iris scanners, facial recognition systems, and voice recognition are all examples of biometric systems that identify a person by something they have.

Biometrics come in two "flavors"—physiological and behavioral. Physiological biometrics are based on measurements derived directly from different parts of the body (e.g., scans of fingerprints, the iris, hand geometry, and facial characteristics). In contrast, behavioral biometrics are derived from various actions and indirectly from various body parts (e.g., voice scans or keystroke monitoring).

In practice, physiological biometrics are used more often than behavioral biometrics. Among the physiological biometrics, the scans of fingerprints, iris scans, hand geometry, and facial characteristics are the most popular.

Fingerprint scanning. Fingerprints can be distinguished by a variety of "discontinuities that interrupt the smooth flow of ridges" (Keroeker 2002) on the bottom tips of the fingers. Ridge endings, dots (small ridges), and ponds (spaces between ridges) are examples of such discontinuities. In fingerprint scanning, a special algorithm is used to convert the scanned discontinuities to a set of numbers stored as a template. The chance that any two people have the same template is one in a billion.

Iris scanning. The iris is the colored part of the eye surrounding the pupil. The iris has a large number of unique spots that can be captured by a camera that is placed 3 to 10 inches from the eye. Within a second, a special algorithm can convert the iris scan to a set of numbers. The numbers can be used to construct an iris-scan template that can be used in iris scanning, in which a camera scans a person's iris, compares the scan to a template, and verifies the person's identity. The chance that any two people have identical iris templates is considerably smaller that the chance that they have the same fingerprint templates.

Voice scanning. Differences in the physiology of speech production from one individual to the next produce different acoustical patterns that can be converted into a template used in voice scanning. In most voice-scanning systems, the user talks into a microphone or telephone. The word that is spoken is usually the user's system ID or password. The next time a user wants to gain access to a system, the user simply repeats the spoken word. It takes about 4 to 6 seconds to verify a voice scan.

Keystroke monitoring. This biometric is still under development. Keystroke monitoring is based on the assumption that the way in which users type words at a keyboard varies from one user to the next. The pressure, speed, and rhythm with which a word is entered are converted through a special algorithm to a set of numbers to form a keystroke template. Again, the word that is employed in most of these systems is the user's system ID or password. When a user wants to gain access to a system, the user simply types in their system ID or password. The system checks the pressure, speed, and rhythm with which the word is typed against the templates in the database. The main problem with these systems is that there is still too much variability in the way an individual types from one session to the next.

6.5.2 Public key infrastructure

The "state of the art" in authentication rests on the public key infrastructure (PKI). PKI has become the cornerstone for secure e-payments. It refers to the technical components, infrastructure, and practices needed to enable the use of public key encryption, digital signatures, and digital certificates with a network application. PKI is also the foundation of a number of network applications, including SCM, VPNs, secure e-mail, and intranet applications.

(1) Private and Public Key Encryption

At the heart of PKI is encryption. Encryption is the process of transforming or scrambling (encrypting) data in such a way that it is difficult, expensive, or time-consuming for an unauthorized person to unscramble (decrypt) it. All encryption has four basic parts: the plaintext, ciphertext, encryption algorithm, and the key.

The two major classes of encryption systems are symmetric systems, with one secret key, and asymmetric systems, with two keys.

（2）Symmetric (Private) Key System

In a symmetric (private) key system the same key is used to encrypt and decrypt the plaintext. The sender and receiver of the text must share the same key without revealing it to anyone else—thus making it a so-called private system.

For years, the Data Encryption Standard (DES) was the standard symmetric encryption algorithm supported by U.S. government agencies. On October 2, 2000, the National Institute of Standards and Technology (NIST) announced that DES was being replaced by Rijndael, the new Advanced Encryption Standard used to secure U.S. government communications.

（3）Public (Asymmetric) Key Encryption

Imagine trying to use one-key encryption to buy something offered on a particular Web server. If the seller's key were distributed to thousands of buyers, then the key would not remain secret for long. This is where public key (asymmetric) encryption comes into play. Public key encryption uses a pair of matched keys—a public key that is publicly available to anyone and a private key that is known only to its owner. If a message is encrypted with a public key, then the associated private key is required to decrypt the message. If, for example, a person wanted to send a purchase order to a company and have the contents remain private, they would encrypt the message with the company's public key. When the company received the order, they would decrypt it with the associated private key.

The most common public key encryption algorithm is RSA. RSA uses keys ranging in length from 512 bits to 1,024 bits. The main problem with public key encryption is speed. Symmetrical algorithms are significantly faster than asymmetric key algorithms. Therefore, public key encryption cannot be used effectively to encrypt and decrypt large amounts of data. In practice, a combination of symmetric and asymmetric encryption is used to encrypt messages.

（4）Digital Signatures

In the online world, how can one be sure that a message is actually coming from the person who they think sent it? Similarly, how one be sure that a person cannot deny that they sent a particular message?

One part of the answer is a digital signature—the electronic equivalent of a personal signature that cannot be forged. Digital signatures are based on public keys. They can be used to authenticate the identity of the sender of a message or document. They also can be used to ensure that the original content of an electronic message or document is unchanged. Digital signatures have additional benefits in the online world. They are portable, cannot be easily repudiated or imitated, and can be time-stamped.

（5）Digital Certificates and Certificate Authorities

If one has to know someone's public key to send them a message, where does the public key come from and how can one be sure of the person's actual identity? Digital certificates verify that the holder of a public and/ or private key is who they claim to be. Third parties called certificate authorities

(CAs) issue digital certificates. A certificate contains things such as the holder's name, validity period, public key information, and a signed hash of the certificate data (i.e., hashed contents of the certificate signed with the CA's private key). Certificates are used to authenticate Web sites (site certificates), individuals (personal certificates), and software companies (software publisher certificates).

There are a large number of third-party CAs. VeriSign (versign.com) is the best known of the CAs. VeriSign issues three classes of certificates: Class 1 verifies that an e-mail actually comes from the user's address. Class 2 checks the user's identity against a commercial credit database. Class 3 requires notarized documents. Companies such as Microsoft offer systems that enable companies to issue their own private, in-house certificates.

（6）Secure Socket Layer

If the average user had to figure out how to use encryption, digital certificates, digital signature, and the like, there would be few secure transactions on the Web. Fortunately, many of these issues are handled in a transparent fashion by Web browser and Web servers. Given that different companies, financial institutions, and governments, in many countries, are involved in e-commerce, it is necessary to have generally accepted protocols for securing e-commerce. One of the major protocols in use today is Secure Socket Layer (SSL), also known as Transport Layer Security (TLS).

The Secure Socket Layer (SSL) was invented by Netscape to utilize standard certificates for authentication and data encryption to ensure privacy or confidentiality. SSL became a de facto standard adopted by the browsers and servers provided by Microsoft and Netscape. In 1996, SSL was renamed Transport Layer Security (TLS), but many people still use the SSL name. It is the major standard used for online credit card payments.

SSL makes it possible to encrypt credit card numbers and other transmissions between a Web server and a Web browser. In the case of credit card transactions, there is more to making a purchase on the Web than simply passing an encrypted credit card number to a merchant. The number must be checked for validity, the consumer's bank must authorize the card, and the purchase must be processed. SSL is not designed to handle any of the steps beyond the transmission of the card number.

New Words & Phrases

token　n. 象征，代币

magnetic strip　磁条

biometric 生物识别技术

iris n. 虹膜

discontinuity　n. 断绝，不连续，中断

tip　n. 尖端，末端

template　n. 模板

identical　adj. 同一的

assumption　n. 假定，臆断

state of the art　n. 技术发展水平

e-payment 电子支付

passive adj. 被动的；消极的

swipe　n. v. 重击，挥击

fingerprint n. 指纹

physiological　adj. 生理的，生理学的

ridge　n. 脊，山脊

pond　n. 池塘，槽

pupil　n. 学生，瞳孔

acoustical　adj. 听觉的，声学的

variability　n. 可变性

cornerstone　n. 奠基石

encryption　n. 加密

scramble　vt. 混杂；把……搅乱	decrypt　v. 解密
plaintext　n. 明码文本	ciphertext　n. 密码，暗记文
symmetric　adj. 相称性的，均衡的	asymmetric　adj. 不均匀的，不对称的
forge　v. 伪造，仿造	repudiate vt.拒绝接受，否认，否定
notarize　vt. 证明，确认	confidentiality n. 机密性
de facto　adj. 〈拉〉实际上存在的	in the case of 至于……，就……来说

Abbreviations

PKI (public key infrastructure) 公钥基础设施　　　DES (Data Encryption Standard) 数据加密标准

CA (certificate authority) 认证中心　　　SSL (Secure Socket Layer) 安全套接层

TLS (Transport Layer Security) 传输层安全

Notes

1. In fingerprint scanning, a special algorithm is used to convert the scanned discontinuities to a set of numbers stored as a template.句中"stored as a template"是过去分词做定语来修饰"numbers"。本句译为"在指纹扫描中，使用特殊的算法来将扫描的不连贯物转换成一组数据以用作模板。"

2. The numbers can be used to construct an iris-scan template that can be used in iris scanning, in which a camera scans a person's iris, compares the scan to a template, and verifies the person's identity.句中"that"引导定语从句用以修饰"iris-scan template"；"in which"是非限定性定语从句用来修饰前面的"iris scanning"。本句译文"这些数据被用来创建虹膜扫描模板，在虹膜扫描中，照相机将扫描的结果和模板数据进行比较以确认人们的身份。"

3. It refers to the technical components, infrastructure, and practices needed to enable the use of public key encryption, digital signatures, and digital certificates with a network application. 本句译为"PKI 指的是技术组件、基础设施和应用，这些应用可以使网络应用所必须的公钥加密、数字签名和数字证书的使用成为可能。"

4. Encryption is the process of transforming or scrambling (encrypting) data in such a way that it is difficult, expensive, or time-consuming for an unauthorized person to unscramble (decrypt) it.本句译为"加密是采用一种方法来改变或杂凑（加密）数据的过程，这种方法对于非授权用户来说，解密数据将是非常困难、昂贵或耗时的。"

6.6　Securing EC Networks

Several technologies exists that ensure that an organization's network boundaries are secure from cyber attack or intrusion and that if the organization's boundaries are compromised that the intrusion is detected.

6.6.1　Firewalls

The term firewall came into use in the 1700s to describe the gaps cut into forests so that fires could be prevented from spreading to other parts of the forest. In the world of networked computing, a firewall is a network node consisting of both hardware and software that isolates a private network form a public network.

Some firewalls filter data and requests moving from the public Internet to a private network based on the network addresses of the computer sending or receiving the request. These firewalls are called packet-filtering routers. On the Internet, the data and requests sent from one computer to another are broken into segments called packets. Each packet contains the Internet address of the computer sending the data, as well as the Internet address of the computer receiving the data. Packet filters are rules that can accept or reject incoming packets based on source and destination addresses and the other identifying information.

6.6.2   Personal Firewalls

Personal firewalls are designed to protect desktop systems by monitoring all the traffic that passes through the computer's network interface card. They operate in one of two ways. With the first method, the owner can create filtering rules (much like packet filtering) that are used by the firewall to permit or delete packets. With the other method, the firewall can learn, by asking the user questions, how particular traffic ought to be handled. A number of personal firewall products are on the market, including Symantec's Norton Personal Firewall.

6.6.3   VPNs

A VPN (virtual private network) uses the public Internet to carry information but remains private by using a combination of encryption to scramble the communications, authentication to ensure that the information has not been tampered with and comes from a legitimate source, and access control to verify the identity of anyone using the network. In addition, a VPN can also be used to support site-to-site communications between branch offices and corporate headquarters and the communications between mobile workers and their workplace. In all these cases, communication costs are drastically reduced.

Three technologies can be used to create a VPN. First, many of the firewall packages hardware and software—support VPN functionality. Second, routers (i.e., special network components for controlling communications) cannot only function as firewalls, but they can also function as VPN servers. Finally, software solutions are available that can be used to handle VPN connections.

6.6.4   Intrusion Detection Systems

Even if an organization has a well-formulated security policy and a number of security technologies in place, it is still vulnerable to attack. This is why an organization must continually watch for attempted, as well as actual, security breaches.

In the past, audit logs, produced by a variety of system components and applications, were manually reviewed for excessive failed log-on attempts, failed file and database access attempts, and other application and system violations. Obviously, this manual procedure had its flaws. Today, a special category of software exists that can monitor activity across a network or on a host computer,

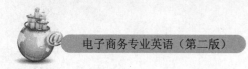

watch for suspicious activity, and take automated action based on what it sees. This category of software is called intrusion detection systems (IDSs).

IDSs are either host-based or network-based. A host-based IDS resides on the server or other host system that is being monitored. Host-based systems are particularly good at detecting whether critical or security-related files have been tampered with or whether a user has attempted to access files that they are not authorized to use.

A network-based IDS uses rules to analyze suspicious activity at the perimeter of a network or at key locations in the network. It usually consists of a monitor—a software package that scans the network—and software agents that reside on various host computers and feed information back to the monitor.

New Words & Phrases

segment n. 部分，片段	packet n. 小包，小盒
tamper vt. 窜改；玩弄	flaw n. 缺点，瑕疵

Abbreviations

VPN (virtual private network) 虚拟专用网   IDS (intrusion detection system) 入侵检测系统

Notes

1. Some firewalls filter data and requests moving from the public Internet to a private network based on the network addresses of the computer sending or receiving the request. 句中"moving …a private network"是现在分词做定语，修饰"data and requests"。本句译为"一些防火墙是基于发送或接收请求的计算机网络地址来过滤那些从公共网络进入私有网络的数据和请求。"

Reading Material——Spyware: A Financial Assault Weapon

Defending against targeted cyber assaults requires multiple security layers. The building up, layering on, and overlapping of security measures is called *defense in depth*. The strength of any system is only as good as its weakest link. A defense-in-depth strategy is crucial, because if one defensive measure fails, other defensive measures are in place to provide protection. Consider the risks posed by spyware and the importance of backup defensive measures.

Spyware is a targeted attack directed at very specific people to gather account numbers and passwords. Spyware attackers can intercept sensitive communications by monitoring keystrokes, e-mail, and Internet activity. Spyware can install itself through pop-up ads from visited Web sites. Once installed, the spyware waits for the computer to visit a targeted bank site and captures the log-in keystrokes. The passwords are captured before the browser software encrypts the information.

Spyware is so prevalent that most computers contain at least some intrusive code. A multiyear study by Webroot and Earthlink, which tested over 4.6 million systems, reported that 55 percent had some form of spyware. They also identified more than 4,000 Web sites that contained some form of spyware for distribution. According to several organizations, spyware is among the fastest-growing online threats. Other reports on spyware provide the following information:

- The National IT Security Alliance predicts that spyware infections may surpass computer viruses.
- A Gartner report notes that theft from personal bank accounts is the fastest-growing financial fraud.
- The FTC reports that the combination of Internet fraud and identity theft cost consumers $437 million in 2003 and spiked to over $8 billion in 2006.
- The FDIC issued guidance on mitigating risks from spyware to inform financial institutions about the risks posed by spyware within an institution's network and on customers' computers.

Some of the risks of spyware are that it:

- sets new channels that circumvent firewalls.
- consumes system resources and productivity and may compromise a company's ability to conduct business by disrupting Internet connections.
- provides the attacker the ability to control corporate computers to send unsolicited spam or malicious software.
- compromises confidentiality by rerouting communications through third-party servers, circumventing encrypted communication methods.
- increases vulnerability to various types of redirected attacks that can damage a company's reputation.

Defensive Procedures

Effective defenses to spyware require a layered approach. For financial institutions, the Federal Financial Institutions Examination Council (FFIEC) (*ffiec.gov*) recommends using several best practices, because no one solution is sufficient. Those best practices include:

- Monitoring inbound and outbound traffic on firewalls and IDS to analyze traffic for actual attacks, new threats, and vulnerabilities
- Updating software patches and antivirus and antispyware software
- Scanning e-mail for spam and blocking it
- Assessing and verifying that controls are effective
- Expanding audits to consider spyware threats
- Implementing acceptable use polices for nonwork-related browsing and software installation
- Requiring users to carefully read licensing agreements and staying away from peer-to-peer file-sharing networks and sites that offer pirated software or adult material
- Scanning systems for infiltration
- Setting browser security settings to "high" to avoid software being surreptitiously installed while the Internet is browsed
- Reviewing installed trusted root certificates on Web servers
- Using multifactor authentication for online banking.

The FFIEC released new guidance on Internet banking that set 2006 as the deadline for achieving two-factor authentication compliance for institutions offering Internet-based financial services.

New Words & Phrases

spyware   n. 间谍软件   assault   n. 攻击，突袭 vt. 袭击，殴打；

intercept　vt. 拦截，截住，截击　　　　circumvent　vt. 设法克服或避免（某事物）；回避

unsolicited　adj. 未被恳求的，主动提供的　　spam　n. 垃圾邮件，香火腿

inbound　adj. 内地的，归航的　n. 入站　　outbound adj. 开往外地的，开往外国的

license　vt. 批准，许可，颁发执照　　　　surreptitiously adv. 秘密地

复杂定语（从句）的翻译技巧之一

科技英语中，句子的某个中心词常常被若干个后置定语或定语从句所修饰。这是因为英语句法结构重"形合"，任何一个名词或名词词组，为了对它进行完整而明确的阐述，可以借助各种修饰结构（介词短语、不定式短语、分词短语、定语或同位语从句等）像滚雪球那样引出一长串修饰成分。而汉语讲"意合"，各个成分用意义串联，往往不需要连接词，一般句子较短。汉语中，对于一个名词，通常不用"叠床架屋"式的多重修饰语，因为过长的前置定语会使句子拖泥带水、冗长臃肿、晦涩难懂。

由于英汉两种语言的修饰方式有很大差别，所以对于科技英语中含有多重定语或长定语从句的中心词（组）没有现成的对应译法，也就难以用规范的汉语，简练地译出原文复杂的修饰关系。

实际上，翻译复杂的多重定语（从句），不但许多初学英语者视为畏途，常常感到"只能意会，难以言传"，就是对于具有一定经验的译者，也是一个难题。例如：

例 1. A stack is a data type whose major attributes are determined by the rules governing the insertion and deletion of its elements.

译文：栈是主要性质由支配其元素的插入与删除的规则来决定的一种数据类型。

译文中，动宾之间所含内容过多，形成"大肚子"句，行文不畅。

改译：栈是这样一种数据类型，其主要性质由支配其元素的插入与删除的规则来决定。

例 2. A fast and accurate symbol manipulating system that is organized to accept, store, and process data and produce output results under the direction of a stored program of instruction is a computer.

原译：一种能够接收、存储、和处理数据，并能在存储指令程序控制下产生输出结果的快速而准确地处理符号的系统叫做计算机。

由于译文主语较长，所以句子显得有点"头重脚轻"，读起来感到不够顺畅。

改译：一种快速而准确地处理符号的系统叫做计算机，它能够接收、存储、和处理数据，并能在存储指令程序控制下产生输出结果。

由上述一些例句可以发现，翻译科技英语中含有复杂定语或长定语从句的中心词(组)时，一般容易犯的"通病"是：把原文机械地译成汉语的偏正词组，以致出现"重负荷"修饰语，影响译文的畅达。下文讲述一些技巧，在不少情况下，可以避免译文中出现"头重脚轻"的现象。

一、先提后述法

此译法适用于结构复杂的并列长定语（从句）。翻译时，首先用"这样（的）"、"这样一些"、"下列（的）"等词语概括所有修饰成分，然后分别叙述各个修饰内容。用这种方法翻译的译文，重点突出、条理清楚。在许多情况下，这是一种翻译并列长定语（从句）行之有效的方法。例如：

例 1. A computer is an electronic device that can receive a set of instructions, or program, and then carry out this program by performing calculations on numerical data or by compiling and correlating other forms of information.

译文：计算机是一种电子装置，它能接受一套指令或程序，并通过数据运算，或收集和联系其他形式的信息来执行该程序。

（比较：计算机是一种能接受一套指令或程序，并通过数据运算，或收集和联系其他形式的信息来执行该程序的电子装置）

例 2. A sound card is a printed circuit board that can translate digital information into sound and back, that plug into a slot on the motherboard (the main circuit board of a computer) and is usually connected to a pair of speakers.

译文：声卡是一块印刷电路板，它能把数字信息译为声音，也能把声音变为数字信息，它插在母板(计算机主电路板)上的槽内，而且通常连接一对喇叭。

（比较：声卡是一块能把数字信息译为声音，也能把声音变为数字信息，插在母板（计算机主电路板）上的槽内，而且通常连接一对喇叭的印刷电路板。）

例 3. The transistor meant more powerful, more reliable, and less expensive computers that would occupy less space and give off less heat than did vacuum-tube-powered computers.

译文：使用晶体管可做成功能更强、更可靠、更价廉的计算机，它与真空管计算机相比，占地面积小，产生的热量少。

（比较：使用晶体管可做成功能更强、更可靠、更价廉的，与真空管计算机相比，占地面积小，产生的热量小的计算机。）

例 4. The World Wide Web is one of the Internet's most popular services, providing access to over one billion Web pages, which are documents created in a programming language called HTML and which can contain text, graphics, audio, video, and other objects, as well as "hyperlinks" that permit a user to jump easily from one page to another.

万维网是因特网最流行的服务之一，提供对超过 10 亿网页的访问，这些网页是由一种叫做 HTML（超文本链接标示语言）的编程语言生成的文件，它们可以包含本文、图形、声频、视频和其它的对象、以及允许用户容易地跳跃到其他网页的"超链接"。

二、先述后提法

此译法是"先提后述法"的倒置。也就是先叙述中心词（组）的修饰内容，最后用"这样的"、"这一切"、"这种"、"这些"等词语予以呼应。对于科技英语文献，这往往也是一种翻译长定语或定语从句的有效方法。例如：

例 1. The fact that the Government may have formulated, furnished, or in any way supplied the said drawings, specifications, or other data is not to be regarded by implication …

译文：政府可能已经系统地阐述、提供或以某种方式供应了上述图纸、规范或其它资料，但这样的事实并非暗示……

（比较：政府可能已经系统地阐述、提供或以某种方式供应了上述图纸、规范或其他资料的这一事实，并非暗示是……）

例 2. The way in which a number of processor units are employed in a single computer system to increase the performance of the system in its application environment above the performance of single processor is an organizational technique.

译文：将许多处理器组成单一的计算机系统，从而提高该系统在其运行环境中的性能，使其超过单个处理器的性能，这种方法称为组织技术。

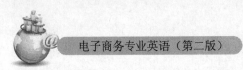

（比较：将许多处理器组成单一的计算机系统，从而提高该系统在其运行环境中的性能，使其超过单个处理器的性能的方法称为组织技术。）

例 3. The developer must be aware of certain basic acoustic principles which must all be taken into account during the design stages of the office and which, at certain points, can conflict other requirements posed by the office layout, decor, environmental control, etc.

译文：某些基本的声学因素，在办公室的设计阶段就必须予以考虑，因为它们在某些方面可能与办公室的布局、室内装饰、环境控制等方面的其他要求相抵触。因此，对于这些声学因素，设计人员务必注意。

（比较：设计人员必须注意在设计阶段应该予以考虑的并且在某些方面可能与办公室的布局、室内装饰、环境控制等方面的其他要求相抵触的某些基本声学因素。）

例 4. Each publication maintains its own editorial policy but, by and large, articles that report research results from a practical viewpoint or describe application of new technology or procedures to existing problem merit publication.

译文：每种出版物都有各自的编辑原则，但一般来说，从实用观点报道研究成果，或描述新技术的应用，或描述存在问题的过程，这样的文章都是值得出版的。

（比较：每种出版物都有各自的编辑原则，但一般来说，文章从实用观点报道研究成果，或描述新技术的应用，或描述存在问题的过程是值得出版的。）

Exercises

I. Answer the following questions

1. Describe the difference between a nontechnical and a technical cyber attack.

2. How are DDoS attacks perpetrated?

3. What are the major forms of malicious code?

4. What are some common mistakes that EC sites make in managing their security?

5. Describe the difference between physiological biometrics and behavioral biometrics.

6. Describe the basic components of encryption.

7. What are the basic differences between symmetric and asymmetric encryption?

8. What is a personal firewall?

II. Questions and Discussion

1. Explain how spyware can be used as an assault tool?

2. Can spyware be stopped or protected against? Explain it.

Chapter 7　Pricing

学习指导

　　互联网对旧经济下的定价策略产生了巨大的影响，并且创造了全新类别的定价工具用于新经济公司：动态定价策略。动态定价彻底改变了 B2B 以及 C2C 交易，并为 B2C 公司创造了全新的机会。通过本章学习，读者应掌握以下内容并能够用英语表达：

- 个性化和交互性对定价的影响。
- 用于产品定价的基本、动态和高级定价策略。
- 互联网对动态定价的影响。
- 拍卖的类型以及它们在互联网上的实现方式。

7.1　The Effects of the 2Is on Pricing

7.1.1　The 2Is: Individualization and Interactivity

Two very important concepts need to be introduced to fully understand the profound implications that the Internet has for business. These two concepts are individualization (or customization) and interactivity.

Customers expect to have a personal experience with the firm, but broadcast approaches send the same messages to all members of the target audience. The Internet enables the firm to engage in customer-specific actions—a broadcast to an audience of one. Equally important, the customer can control the degree of customization by taking action to set the level of customization he or she desires. Hence, the amount of individualization can be controlled either by the firm or by the customer.

Interactivity is defined as the extent to which a two-way communication flow occurs between the firm and customers. The Internet enables a level of customer dialogue that has not previously been experienced in the history of business. Certainly, customers could have conversations with retail store clerks, sales reps, or managers; however, it was not possible at the scale that the Internet affords. Hence, the fundamental shift is one from broadcast media such as television, radio, and newspapers to one that encourages debate, exchange, and conversation.

7.1.2　The Effects of the 2Is on Pricing

The individualization force of the Internet has affected pricing in the following manner:

• By informing companies of their pricing and product desires, consumers make it easier for firms to convey prices of products in which they have an interest.

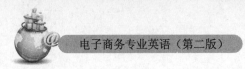

• Customers can register their preferences with firms, making it easier for those firms to offer targeted, individualized pricing promotions.

• Customers can more easily participate in dynamic pricing processes. Sites that practice dynamic pricing can notify customers via e-mail when their bids are no longer the highest.

• The Internet offers many different distribution outlets (i.e., websites) that cater to different segments, which allows firms the flexibility to set prices specifically for the segment(s) being served by the website.

The interactivity force of the Internet has affected pricing by making it:

• Easier to reach wider audiences. New markets are created, or existing markets are made more efficient, by bringing together disparate groups of buyers and sellers in a low-cost manner. Sellers who offer their products over the Internet have the potential to reach buyers from around the world. By increasing the number of potential bidders, firms benefit in both the selling of product (more customers can translate into increased bidding for products) and procuring supplies (more potential bidders can result in lowering price bidding for supply contracts).

• Easier and cheaper to implement dynamic pricing strategies. Auctions, for instance, can be implemented in a less costly and more efficient manner. While auctioning is an effective selling process, it has often been difficult to implement auctions in a manner that encourages many buyers and sellers to participate. The Internet allows auctions to be implemented in a very cost-efficient manner.

• Easier and cheaper to adjust prices in accordance with demand conditions and to remain competitive with other firms. Prices can be changed instantly on websites.

• Cheaper for consumers to investigate prices. With an easy click, consumers can check prices instantly. Customers can also register with sites to receive e-mail notification of changes in product prices.

• Easier to understand and measure consumers' reactions to price promotions. Tracking consumers electronically makes it easier to understand what types of customers are stimulated by price promotions and then develop strategies to best design and implement pricing promotions.

• Easier to receive customer feedback on price, understand customer willingness to pay for a product, and implement price-discrimination strategies. By better understanding how customers navigate a website or by requiring information such as the consumer's zip code, firms can more easily customize prices for individuals.

New Words & Phrases

individualization n. 个性化	interactivity n. 交互性
customization n. 定制	two-way communication 双向沟通
sales reps 销售代表	register v. 注册，登记
promotion n. 促销	preference n. 偏好
participate in 参加，参与	dynamic pricing 动态定价
bid n. 出价；v. 投标	distribution outlet 分销点
segment n. 细分（市场）	disparate adj. 根本不同的

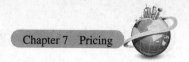

procure v. 采购

in accordance with 根据

auction n. 拍卖

price-discrimination strategy 价格歧视策略

Notes

1. By increasing the number of potential bidders, firms benefit in both the selling of product (more customers can translate into increased bidding for products) and procuring supplies (more potential bidders can result in lowering price bidding for supply contracts). 通过增加潜在竞标者的数量，公司将从产品出售（更多的客户能提高产品出价）和获取供应（更多的潜在竞标者导致供应合同的出价降低）上获得利益。

2. Tracking consumers electronically makes it easier to understand what types of customers are stimulated by price promotions and then develop strategies to best design and implement pricing promotions. 通过电子方式跟踪消费者能够更容易理解价格促销激励哪些类型的顾客，从而制定策略最好地设计和实施定价促销。

7.2　Basic Pricing Strategies

7.2.1　Cost Plus

This basic pricing strategy involves simply adding a fixed markup to the product cost. This markup is added to the firm's total or variable costs. Total cost includes both variable costs—the incremental costs of producing an additional good—and an appropriate allocation of fixed costs. Variable costs often include the raw material and labor necessary to produce an extra good. Fixed costs—factory, management, and general overhead costs—do not vary with the level of output. In general, manufacturers add a 15 percent markup to their total costs; wholesalers add a 20 percent markup; and retailers add a 40 percent markup.

（1）Target Profit Growth Pricing

Target profit growth pricing is a close relative of cost-plus pricing and is most often used in mature industries. The sole focus of managers is to meet or exceed the growth target. If the target growth-rate goal is met, managers are considered successful.

To increase profits, managers have three levers to consider: reduce costs, grow sales, and change (increase or decrease) prices. In mature industries, costs are generally considered fixed. Thus, managers can either increase marketing efforts or experiment with price. Effective marketing will help to grow demand in current markets and create demand in new markets. From a pricing perspective, based on the shape/slope of the demand curve and competitor reaction, a manager can experiment with price in the following ways:

• Decrease price with the hope that the increase in units sold will more than cover the decrease in profit margin per unit.

• Increase price in hopes that the decrease in product sales (due to the increase in price) will be more than covered by the increased profit margin per product.

（2）Target Return Pricing

Also a close relative of cost-plus pricing, target return pricing aims to maximize the return on capital for a company and its shareholders. Consider a firm that has a cost of capital of 15 percent. The firm is funded by a variety of types of investors and investing instruments that on average are charging (or demanding) a 15 percent return on their invested capital. Thus, managers are given the mandate to produce financial returns that exceed 15 percent. This financial return is computed by dividing total profit by total capital. If a company is targeting an 18 percent return on capital, managers must price products with the goal of meeting this target rate of return.

7.2.2　Brand Pricing

Pricing strategists have argued that buyers feel a sense of prestige when they purchase and consume a high-priced product. More realistically, the customer derives that sense of prestige from the implicit value and image that is conveyed by owning the good. This value is typically associated with the perceived value of the brand.

The brand value associated with prestige pricing is the result of the concerted efforts of the firm to create a high-end brand. The firm has often invested significantly in building its brand in hopes that there will be a customer market that values the brand and will pay for it. This brand-building work has influenced consumers to pay a premium for such items as a specially colored credit card, a meal at a trendy restaurant, or a standard cotton T-shirt with a brand name or logo displayed on it.

Under certain circumstances, sellers can use price to signal high quality to consumers. This strategy is most effective when consumers are not well informed about the product and its attributes, such as when they purchase the product infrequently or the product is insignificant in terms of price. Then consumers often use price as an indicator of product quality.

Is price a good indicator of quality? Sometimes—but it may depend on how a consumer measures quality. Hotels rated highly by Zagat, for example, are usually expensive. However, consumers evaluate the quality level of a hotel using many different criteria. Some customers might be most concerned with room quality; others might rate a hotel on the quality of its room service or whether or not it has a swimming pool. Thus, the fact that a hotel is expensive does not guarantee that the hotel represents high quality to each consumer.

7.2.3　Promotion Pricing

Stores and manufacturers often significantly decrease prices for the following reasons:

（1）Trial

Marketers often offer low prices on new products in order to gain trial. The theory is that a low price will induce consumers to purchase a product, then realize its differentiating attributes. The hope is that in the future, consumers will pay the regular (higher) product price. While price lowering is a relatively easy strategy to implement, it does have significant long-term implications. Trial consumers, nurtured on a product's low introductory price, may use that introductory price to form a reference price and therefore may balk at paying the full price at a later date. Alternative trial pricing strategies to consider include free samples and manufacturer coupons.

（2）Benefits of Rapid Acceptance

There are many benefits to being a first mover in a new product category. However, while being a first mover is important, gaining market acceptance is critical. The frenzy pricing associated with the less-than-market clearing price that Sony set for the PlayStation 2 is an example. One possible explanation for the low price is that Sony knew that Microsoft and Nintendo planned to release their own advanced game systems in the near future. Sony's long-term strategy may have been to set the below-market clearing price of $299 as a reference in consumers' minds so that as supply increases, consumers would not hesitate to purchase the product. If Sony had capitalized on the initial high demand by setting a high price, that price may have become coded as the reference price. As supply increased, Sony could have lowered its price, but it would be difficult to communicate the price change to consumers. This could have resulted in fewer consumers adopting the PlayStation 2 before Microsoft and Nintendo introduced their products.

（3）Switching Costs

A firm may set a low cost to make its product part of the consumer's routine. Once that happens, switching products might prove costly to the consumer. Once a customer has signed up for an ISP service and circulated his or her e-mail address to friends, there is a significant cost associated with changing services. There are similar switching costs associated with stock brokerages. Once a consumer has created a portfolio, there is significant paperwork associated with moving that portfolio to a rival brokerage firm.

（4）Loss Leaders

Retailers often discount prices with the hope that once customers come to the store to purchase these low-price loss-leader products, they will also purchase other high-margin products. The types of loss leaders that retail stores offer tend to fall into three product categories:

• Well-known brand goods. While consumers enjoy discounts on well-known brands, upscale-product producers often dislike it when their brands are used as loss leaders because discounting can damage their established brand.

• Staples for price-sensitive customers. Price-sensitive customers are often keenly aware of staple-good prices, and a lower price on staple goods is likely to draw customers to the store. Duncan Simester maintains that a store has two primary types of customers: regulars and price shoppers (customers who will purchase from the cheapest seller) . Given that regular shoppers will patronize a store regardless of promotions, the types of products selected to be loss leaders should be staples, because those are the discounts that attract price shoppers to the store.

• Seasonal/holiday/special-demand items. During a particular holiday or season, demand is often high for specific items—champagne on New Year's Eve, for example. Given their high demand, retailers often discount those items to induce customers to visit their stores.

New Words & Phrases

cost plus 成本加成，成本加利润	markup n. 加价，毛利
variable cost 可变成本	fixed cost 固定成本
manufacturer n. 制造商	wholesaler n. 批发商

retailer   n. 零售商

prestige pricing   声望定价

be concerned with   关心

first mover   先行者

market clearing price   保证市场供求平衡的价格

portfolio   n. 投资组合

staple   n. 主要产品，销路稳定的商品，常用品

mandate   n. 委托，命令，要求

premium   n. 额外的费用

balk at   畏缩，回避

frenzy pricing   疯狂定价

switching cost   转移成本，转换成本

loss-leader   n. 为招徕顾客而亏本销售的商品

patronize   vt. 光顾，惠顾

Notes

1. Total cost includes both variable costs—the incremental costs of producing an additional good—and an appropriate allocation of fixed costs.   总成本包括可变成本（额外生产一件商品的增量成本）和适当的固定成本分摊。

2. Trial consumers, nurtured on a product's low introductory price, may use that introductory price to form a reference price and therefore may balk at paying the full price at a later date.   用产品的低导入价格来培育试用消费者，可能使消费者将导入价格作为参考价格，并因此在以后支付全价时望而却步。

7.3　Dynamic Pricing Strategies

Dynamic pricing is one of the most significant contributions the Internet and the 2Is have made to pricing strategy. Dynamic pricing is a pricing environment in which prices are not set but are fluid. The Internet has enhanced the attractiveness of dynamic pricing in two primary ways:

• Decreased menu costs. Menu costs are the costs associated with changing the price of a good. When a retail store changes its product prices, there is a cost associated with physically changing all of the price tags. Likewise, when a mail-order catalog changes its prices, there are considerable costs associated with reprinting the catalog with the new prices. For goods advertised on the Internet, it is easy and virtually costless to change product prices. Given this environment, it is very attractive for firms to change their prices based on demand and supply conditions.

• Interactivity. The Internet makes it easy for sellers and buyers around the world to interact and negotiate prices. In the old economy, it was costly to create a dynamic pricing market due to the costs associated with bringing together sellers and buyers to negotiate. The fact that buyers and sellers can easily interact from their homes or workplaces via the Internet makes it easy to conduct dynamic pricing structures.

In the new economy, forecasters view auctions as a key pricing strategy. This section discusses the wide variety of auction types and how they are being implemented on the Internet.

7.3.1 English Auctions

English auctions are the most common auction type. Also known as ascending or oral auctions, English auctions are open auctions in which buyers successively raise their bids until only one buyer remains. The term open auction indicates that all of the bidders know the amount of the highest bid at all times. English auctions can occur in person or via the Internet, proprietary data network, or phone. In many instances, the product seller can maintain a reserve price; if the final bid does not equal or exceed the reserve price, the item is not sold. Depending on the auction structure, this reserve price is either known or unknown to bidders.

7.3.2 Reverse-Price English Auctions

Many auction sites—B2B sites, in particular—use reverse-price auctions to help firms save on supply costs. On these sites, firms often submit a request for proposal (RFP) or request for quotation (RFQ) to initiate a supply auction. The auction winner is the firm that provides the lowest bid to supply the requested goods or services. FreeMarkets has become well known in the B2B space as a site that helps firms significantly lower their supply costs by implementing reverse auctions. One analysis of B2B auctions estimated that from November 1995 to January 1998, firms saved between 1 percent and 43 percent (with an average of 17 percent) on their supply costs by using FreeMarkets' reverse auction to procure supplies. Imandi.com is a B2C site that facilitates reverse-price English auctions in which potential suppliers bid to serve customers. Registered imandi.com customers can post what goods they are searching for and select which suppliers they would like to have bid on their requests. The customer-selected retailers then proceed to bid for the customer's business. At the end of the process, the customer can review the bids and decide which retailer to use.

7.3.3 Dutch Auctions

There is a difference between how economists and eBay define a Dutch auction, which gets its name from the process by which flowers have been sold in the Netherlands for the last century. Typically, at Dutch flower auctions, an auctioneer will start by announcing a high price for the product and then begin to slowly decrease the product price until a bidder accepts the price. This auction is the exact opposite of an English auction. Dutch auctions have two key drawbacks:

• The process does not allow the price to be increased when buyers reveal their interest in goods. In English auctions, when a buyer reveals interest in a product by bidding, other parties may reevaluate the worth of the good and increase their bids.

• It is important for Dutch auctions to start at a price that is higher than the market clearing price, or else profit has been left on the table.

On eBay, Dutch auction refers to a special auction format in which a seller sells multiple identical items. The seller specifies the minimum price (the starting bid) and the number of items available. Buyers bid at or above that minimum price for the quantity they are interested in purchasing. At the close of the auction, the highest bidders purchase the items at the price offered by the lowest winning bidder. This derivative of Dutch auctions is called a new-economy Dutch auction.

Suppose a seller has two pens, and the seller is demanding a minimum bid of $20 for each pen. In the simplest case, two buyers will bid $20 for one pen—thus each bidder will end up purchasing one pen for $20. Now consider a more difficult case. Suppose Buyer A bids $20 for one pen, Buyer B bids $20 for one pen, and Buyer C bids $21 for one pen. At the end of the auction, Buyer C will

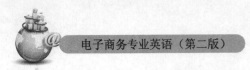

get to purchase the pen for $20, Buyer A will get to purchase the pen for $20 (because Buyer A was the first to bid $20), and Buyer B will not be able to purchase the pen.

7.3.4　First-Price Sealed-Bid Auctions

This is a very straightforward type of auction. Sellers offer a good for buyers to evaluate and consider bidding on. Potential buyers have the option to submit one sealed bid for the product by a specified time. One implication of this auction is that since the bidding is sealed, buyers do not know the amount of competing bids. After the deadline, the product is sold to the highest bidder. The seller also has the right to specify a minimum reserve price. If the bidding does not reach this reserve price, the seller does not have to sell the good. Sellers have the option of making the minimum reserve price either known or unknown to potential bidders.

Priceline has created a new-economy variant of the first-price sealed-bid auction. In Priceline's auction model, bidders might submit a price (guaranteed by a credit card) for a roundtrip airline ticket on specified days. Once they submit their bids, bidders agree that Priceline can place them on any airline flight (the bidder has some control over the number of connecting flights) departing anytime between 6AM and 10PM, and that the tickets are nonrefundable. Once a bid has been submitted, Priceline automatically checks if the bid price is in line with the fares and restrictions that participating airlines have offered to Priceline for its customers. After Priceline checks if an airline is willing to sell a ticket at or below the customer's bid price, the airline then checks to see if it has available seat inventory for the specified travel dates. If the airline does, it charges the bidder's credit card and notifies him or her of the itinerary. Priceline derives revenues from this process in two primary ways:

• Priceline makes money on the spread—the difference between the airline's ticket price and the bid price.

• Priceline charges a nominal ticketing fee.

The Priceline auction is a unique variant of the standard auction. The interactivity offered by the Internet affords Priceline the opportunity to offer these types of auctions efficiently. Priceline was able to capitalize on its first-mover advantage in this space by patenting this unique-to-the-Internet "name your own price" auction process.

7.3.5　Reverse First- Price Sealed-Bid Auctions

In a similar fashion, firms can use reverse first-price sealed-bid auctions to purchase goods. The U.S. government often uses this auction method to procure supplies. A federal agency will post an RFP or RFQ on which potential suppliers can bid. Suppliers can submit only one sealed bid to fulfill the supply request; they do not know the prices that other bidders have submitted. At the end of the auction, the federal agency awards the contract to the lowest bidder.

7.3.6　Exchanges

Electronic exchanges are marketplaces that have arisen to bring buyers and sellers together.

Typically, an electronic exchange acts as the middleman for a sale, and collects a percentage of the total sale price. Exchanges serve as a meeting ground where sellers can post goods that they have for sale for a set time period. During this time period, prospective buyers can submit product bids. In a similar fashion, prospective buyers can post a request for a specific product. During a fixed time period, potential suppliers can post bids to supply the product. A key advantage for buyers using the exchange is the exposure to a large number of sellers. Given the increased number of sellers, economic theory posits that the average buying price should be lower than it would be if fewer sellers bid for the project. Similarly, a seller's products are exposed to more potential buyers through such an exchange. Given that there are more buyers when a seller uses an exchange, sellers will theoretically receive higher prices for their products.

FastParts.com is an example of an electronic exchange designed to give its members access to a global marketplace in which to more efficiently buy and sell electronic components. FastParts .com prequalifies all buyers and sellers to ensure integrity within its trading community, and buyers and sellers negotiate anonymously online to arrive at a mutually agreeable price. Because buyers and sellers are anonymous, FastParts.com acts as an intermediary, providing a one-year warranty on all parts bought and sold and guaranteeing payment before the seller ships the product.

New Words & Phrases

fluid　adj. 流动的，可改变的	menu cost　菜单成本
reserve price　（拍卖时的）保留价格	request for proposal　投标申请书
request for quotation　报价邀请函	reverse auction　反向拍卖，逆向拍卖
derivative　adj. 派生的；n. 派生物	variant　n. 变体；adj. 不同的
revenue　n. 收入，收益	spread　n. 进出差价
exchanges　n. 交易市场	prospective　adj. 未来的，预期的
anonymous　adj. 匿名的	

Notes

1. FastParts.com is an example of an electronic exchange designed to give its members access to a global marketplace in which to more efficiently buy and sell electronic components. FastParts.com 是电子交易所的一个例子，该网站的设计旨在帮助其成员进入高效买卖电子元器件的全球市场。

7.4　Advanced Pricing Strategies

7.4.1　Bundling

If there is one pricing strategy best suited for true Internet products, it is bundling. Indeed, bundling can be thought of both as a product strategy and a pricing strategy. There are two primary types of bundling strategies: pure bundling and mixed bundling. Pure bundling occurs when a firm offers its products only as part of a bundle. Mixed bundling is a popular marketing strategy that involves selling goods both individually and in bundles. The bundle price is generally less than the sum of the individual component prices. Mixed bundling is a particularly easy and profitable pricing strategy to implement for Internet electronic service products.

The Internet has made bundling a more attractive pricing/product strategy for the following reasons:

• Internet content is easier to package. Most products being revolutionized by the Internet involve content delivered in the form of bits. This content can be music, news, research reports, software, and, with the adoption of broadband, movies and television shows.

• There is low friction between consumers and firms on the Internet. For both consumers and firms, it is often far easier to interact online than offline. The interactivity of the Internet makes it easier for customers to create their own bundles and convey their preferences to firms.

• Online content is a fungible product, and the costs associated with adding new customers are low. Given the relative ease of creating new product bundles and the low marginal costs often associated with selling content, firms have an incentive to create many different bundles to serve as many segments as possible.

7.4.2 Frenzy Pricing

Firms often implement pricing schemes that result in significant excess demand due to low prices. This can occur for a variety of reasons:

• Fairness pricing. Firms faced with excess demand may opt to keep prices below the market clearing price in an effort to maintain goodwill. This can create a buying frenzy.

• Demand uncertainty. When a firm brings a new product to market, there may be uncertainty about whether the market will accept the product. If demand is unexpectedly high, retailers and manufacturers are often risk-averse in terms of increasing prices once some products have been sold at a lower price. Consumers often accuse firms of price gouging when they raise prices during periods in which demand exceeds supply. While it may be more profitable to increase prices, the potential for adverse publicity may dissuade firms from doing so.

• Marketing. A key derivative of frenzy pricing is the frenzied nature of the consumers who are trying to obtain a good. This frenzy often leads hopeful consumers to sleep outside of stores, bid on auction sites, or frantically drive from store to store to find the product. During the 2000 holiday shopping season, one of the "must have" gifts was the Sony PlayStation 2. The buying frenzy began in late October 2000, when Sony announced that, due to production problems, it was only going to ship half of the 1 million units that it had promised to release in the United States. This announcement created a frenzy among consumers eager to purchase the machines. Despite the significant demand and low supply, Sony maintained its suggested retail price of $299. After the late October release of half a million units, Sony added an additional 100,000 units per month. Many consumers capitalized on the shortage and took to reselling brand new PlayStation 2s on Internet auction sites such as eBay. AuctionWatch.com reported that when the PlayStation 2 was released, its average selling price on auction sites was $950. By mid-December, after initial demand had been satisfied and supply had increased, the average auction selling price dropped to $445. The result of the tremendous consumer frenzy surrounding the PlayStation 2 was an unprecedented amount of free publicity. With the media playing up the PlayStation 2 as the must-have product of the season, consumers became aware of the product and demand significantly increased.

• Signal of quality. If prices are set so that there is excess demand, many may view this as a signal or verification of high quality. For consumers, there are often high search costs involved in determining product quality.

• Efficient selling method. Disney has created buying frenzies with the release of several of its classic animated movies by announcing that the films would be sold for a limited time. This type of strategy creates hype in the media and encourages consumers to purchase the item immediately. It also allows Disney to concentrate its marketing in a very finite phase and efficiently sell as many or more videos than it would if it made the videos constantly available.

New Words & Phrases

bundling　n. 捆绑
pure bundling　纯捆绑
marketing strategy　营销策略
revolutionize　vt. 使革命化，彻底改革
friction　n. 摩擦，矛盾，冲突
marginal cost　边际成本
due to　由于，应归于
risk-averse　adj. 不愿承担风险的
accuse　v. 指责，控告
adverse　adj. 方向相反的，敌对的，不利的
frantically　adv. 狂暴地，疯狂似地

think of…as…　把……看作……
mixed bundling　混合捆绑
package　vt. 打包
broadband　n. 宽带
fungible　adj. 代替的；n. 代替物
incentive　n. 动机，刺激，鼓励
opt　vi. 选择，抉择
in terms of　在…方面
gouge　v. 欺诈
publicity　n. 名声，宣传，广告，推销
verification　n. 证实，证据，确认，确定

Notes

1. Given the relative ease of creating new product bundles and the low marginal costs often associated with selling content, firms have an incentive to create many different bundles to serve as many segments as possible.　由于创建新产品捆绑相对容易，而且与出售内容相关的边际成本很低，这激励公司创建许多不同的捆绑以服务于尽可能多的细分市场。

Reading Materials——eBay France: The Price (Increase) is Right.

If you don't think that pricing can be a powerful marketing tool, consider the case of eBay France. Launched by the online auction giant in late 2000 and bolstered by the quick purchase of its largest European rival , iBazar, eBay France was hosting a healthy 300 , 000 listings by early 2002.

Then the company announced a radical pricing change: instead of paying only a transaction fee after a successful sale, sellers would also be charged an upfront listings fee. The fee was modest (ranging from about $ 0.13

to just over $ 2), but the impact was massive: Within days, the number of listings on the site dropped by nearly 50 percent. After three weeks, the site was hosting a mere 37, 000 auctions—a precipitous 90 percent plunge. Meanwhile, eBay's main rivals in Europe, Yahoo! France and QXL France, were enjoying a listings boom as sellers fled eBay.

Disaster, right? Not necessarily. It turns out that with no upfront fees to worry about, many sellers had been clogging the site with items that had little chance of selling. With those sellers gone, eBay France was a leaner site, but a more attractive one for serious buyers and sellers. And in fact, slowly but surely the number of listings began to rebound. As Deutsche Banc Alex Brown analyst Jeetil Patel told CNet News, the imposition of listing fees functioned "as a self-policing mechanism to encourage sellers to clean up poor inventory and poorly merchandised product on the site." In other words, eBay's pricing policy led to less. And oftentimes less, as we all know, is actually more.

New Words & Phrases

surge   v. 汹涌，涌现

precipitous   a. 突然的，急转直下的

listings fee   列名费

imposition   n. 征收

复杂定语（从句）的翻译技巧之二

三、解环法

这种方法适用于翻译"连环式"后置定语或定语从句，也就是当原文中的一个中心词（组）被若干个定语（从句）一环扣一环地修饰时，可先将中心词（组）译出，或把中心词（组）与靠近它的一个或两个后置定语（从句）译成汉语偏正词组，然后顺着"修饰环"依次翻译其余成分。

采用这种方法译出的句子层次分明，脉络清楚。由于科技英语中"连环式"修饰语出现较多，所以"解环法"具有较大的实用价值。例如：

例 1. A flight simulator is a perfect example of programs that create a virtual reality, or computer-generated "reality" in which the user dose not merely watch but is able to actually participate.

译文：飞行模拟器是创造虚拟现实的程序的一个完美例子，或者也可以叫它计算机生成的"现实"，在这个"现实"中，用户不仅能看，而且能实际参与。

（比较：飞行模拟器是创造虚拟现实，或者也可以叫它计算机生成的，用户不仅能看，而且能实际参与的"现实"的程序的一个完美例子。）

例 2. In fact, the Internet is a giant example of client/server computing in which over 70 million host server computers store Web pages and other content that can be easily accessed by nearly a million local area networks and hundreds of millions of client machines worldwide.

事实上，因特网是客户机/服务器计算技术的一个巨大实例，其中，超过 7000 万部主机服务器计算机储存网页和其他内容，这些网页和内容能被全世界接近一百万个局域网和数亿台客户机容易地访问。

（比较：事实上，因特网是客户机/服务器计算技术的一个巨大实例，其中，超过 7000 万部主机服务器计算机储存能被全世界接近一百万个局域网和数亿台客户机容易地访问的网页和其他内容。）

例 3. Object-oriented databases store and manipulate more complex data structures, called "object", which are organized into hierarchical classes that may inherit properties from classes higher in the chain; this database structure is the most flexible and adaptable.

译文：面向对象的数据库可以存储并处理更加复杂的数据结构，这种数据结构称为"对象"，"对象"可以按层次组成"类"，低层的"类"可以继承上层"类"的属性；这是一种最灵活，最具适应性的数据结构。

（比较：面向对象的数据库可以存储并处理更加复杂的、称为"对象"的、可以按层次组成"类"的，低层的"类"可以继承上层"类"属性的数据结构；这是一种最灵活，最具适应性的数据结构。）

在英语科技文献中，对于某些连环式修饰语，有时还需同时借助"先提后叙法"，才能使语句顺畅。例如：

例4. It (chapter 2) provides numerous solutions for protecting problems associated with any type of instruments using microprocessors that must be protected when voltage supply fluctuates.

就修饰关系而言，这个句子属于连环式修饰。由于各个修饰环扣得很紧——原文中，protecting problems 并非仅仅与 associated with … instruments 有关，而且与修饰 instruments 的分词短语 using microprocessors 及修饰 microprocessors 的定语从句 that … fluctuates 密切相关。(定语从句本身带有一个较长的状语)。因此，译成汉语时，为了使修饰成分紧扣修饰对象，既不宜直接译成偏正词组——这会造成"大肚子"句，见译文(1)；也不宜用"解环法"法逐个翻译修饰环——这会导致修饰语与中心词关系松弛，见译文(2)。此时可采用"解环法+先提后叙法"，也就是先译出一两个修饰环，再用"这样的"、"这样一些"等词语"扣"住中心词，最后叙述具体修饰内容。这样，不但句子修饰关系明确，而且行文较为流畅，见译文(3)。

（1）第二章提供与使用当供电电压波动时必须加以保护的微处理器的任何类型仪器有关的保护问题的许多解决办法。

（2）第二章提供与任何类型仪器有关的保护问题的许多保护办法，这类仪器使用微处理器，这些微处理器当供电电压波动时必须予以保护。

（3）第二章提供解决某些保护问题的许多办法，这些保护问题与任何使用这样一些微处理器的仪器有关：当供电电压波动时时，必须予以保护。

例5. This is a software of flight simulator running on personal computers, intended primarily for computer-aided instruction which requires providing practice navigation and instruments reading while users immerse in the virtual environment.

这个句子中的修饰关系也是"连环式"。由于某些修饰环（如 of …和 running …, intended … 和 which … ）扣得紧，加上 which 引导的定语从句本身含有一个 while 引导的状语从句，所以此句也适于采用"解环法+先提后叙法"。全句可译为：

这是一个运行于个人计算机的飞行模拟器软件，这种软件主要用于如下计算机辅助教学：当用户投入虚拟环境时，它必须提供导航和仪表读数。

由此可见，翻译"连环式"修饰成分要因句制宜，灵活处理，不能只着眼于表面的修饰关系，还要考虑"修饰环"之间的紧密程度。通常，如果"修饰环"彼此关系较松，适于采用"解环法"；要是"扣"得很紧，则可采用"解环法+先提后叙法"。

四、句子结构调整法

有时，原文句中一个中心词带有若干修饰成分，但它们既不是纯"并列"关系，也不是规则的"连环"关系，而是"并列"中有"连环"（例1），或"连环"中含不规则"修饰环"（例2）；或者句中各有一个分别被"连环式"定语和"并列式"定语所修饰的中心词（例3）；或者中心词的定语从句本身又含有其他修饰成分（例4）。由于这类句子所含的修饰关系比较复杂，很难纳入上述几种译法予以表达，此时就应该根据上下文的逻辑关系，调整句子结构。常用的方法是："化整为零"，将带有多重定语（从句）的长句拆译成若干汉语短句，然后按汉语表达习惯组织译文句子。例如：

例 1. An operating system is a master control program, permanently stored in memory, that interprets user commands requesting various kind of service, such as display, print, or copy a data file, list all files in a directory, or execute a particular program.

译文：操作系统是主控程序，永久地驻留在内存中，它理解用户的各种指令：如显示、打印文件，将目录中所有文件列表，或者执行一个特殊的程序。

（比较：操作系统是永久地驻留在内存中的；理解用户的各种指令：如显示、打印文件，将目录中所有文件列表，或者执行一个特殊的程序主控程序。）

例 2. The users of such a system control the process by means of a program, which is a set of instruction that specify the operation, operands, and the sequence by which processing has to occur.

译文：该系统用户通过程序控制处理过程，所谓程序是一套指定操作、操作数和处理序列的指令集。（比较：该系统用户通过一套指定操作、操作数和处理序列的指令集即程序控制处理过程。）

例 3. Indeed, today's products—most of all, the latest in speech recognition—are a roll-out of technologies that have been percolating for years and that are based on an understanding of speech that has taken several decades to accumulate.

译文：的确，今日的产品，尤其是语音识别方面最新的产品，是过去多年技术渗透的延伸，也是基于几十年来对语音理解的结果。

（比较：的确，今日的产品，尤其是语音识别方面最新的产品，是过去多年的渗透和基于几十年来对语音理解的积累的技术延伸。）

例 4. The computer family, in computer science, is a term commonly used to indicate a group of computers that are built around the same microprocessor or around a series of related microprocessors, and that share significant design feature.

译文：在计算机科学中，计算机系列是常用的一个术语，通常指一组用相同的或者一系列相关的微处理器制造的计算机。

（比较：在计算机科学中，计算机系列是一个常用来指一组用相同的或者一系列相关的微处理器制造的计算机的术语。）

了解科技英语中复杂定语或长定语从句的译法，对提高科技英语翻译水平和译文质量具有重要意义。由于语言现象丰富多彩，修饰关系错综复杂，上述几种译法虽然适用于多数复杂定语或长定语从句，但不能包括一切场合，读者应根据特定的原文句子，灵活处理。

Exercises

I. True or False

1. Demand pricing is a pricing environment in which prices are not set but are fluid.

2. Forecasters view auctions as a key pricing strategy in the new economy.

3. B2B sites particularly use Dutch auction to help firms save on supply costs.

4. Electronic exchanges are marketplaces that have arisen to bring buyers and sellers together.

5. The practice of selling goods both individually and in bundles is called pure bundling.

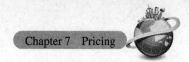

II. Fill the blanks

1. In_____, the financial return is computed by dividing total profit by total capital.

2. The internet has made bundling more attractive because_____, _____, _____.

3. Low prices intended to stimulate "excess" demand is called_____.

III. Answer the following questions

1. Identify the six results of the interactivity force of the Internet on pricing.

2. In what ways has the individualization force of the Internet affected pricing?

3. What is a loss leader?   What types are most likely to be used?

4. Describe the two primary ways that the Internet has enhanced the attractiveness of dynamic pricing.

IV. Questions and Discussion

1. Is pricing a powerful marketing tool? Why?

2. Should eBay France's competitors increase price? Explain why or why not.

3. Identify the difference between the last-minute bidding rules of Amazon and eBay. Discuss how auction rules affect bidding strategies.

Chapter 8　Internet Marketing

本章主要介绍了网络营销的概念、步骤及其特征，通过学习，读者应该掌握以下内容：

- 网络营销的定义。
- 网络营销的七个阶段。
- 客户关系的四个阶段。
- 交互性与个性化在网络营销中的意义。
- 市场空间矩阵的概念。
- 网络营销成功的关键因素。

8.1　Introduction

At its core, the mission of marketing is to attract and retain customers. To accomplish this goal, a traditional bricks-and-mortar marketer uses a variety of marketing variables—including pricing, advertising, and channel choice—to satisfy current and new customers. In this context, the standard marketing-mix toolkit includes such mass-marketing levers as television advertising, direct mail, and public relations, as well as customer-specific marketing techniques such as the use of sales reps[1].

With the emergence of the Internet and its associated technology enabled *screen-to-face* interfaces (e.g., mobile phones, interactive television), a new era of marketing has emerged. Well-respected academics and practitioners have called for new rules and urged debate about fundamental tenets of marketing, including segmentation, mass marketing, and regionalized programs. At the other extreme, pundits and academics alike have argued that both the basic building blocks of marketing strategy and the pathways to competitive advantage have remained the same.

The approach taken in the current volume falls between these polar views. That is, new levers have been added to the marketing mix, segments have been narrowed to finer gradations, consumer expectations about convenience have forever been altered, and competitive responses happen in real time. In short, these are new, exciting changes that have a profound impact on the practice of marketing. At the same time, some of the fundamentals of business strategy—seeking competitive advantage based on superior value, building unique resources, and positioning in the minds of customers—have remained the same.

The intent of this text is to provide a clear indication of what has changed and what has not changed. At the same time, the text would not be complete (and indeed might be actionable from the standpoint of business practice!) if it did not propose a broader framework to understanding the practice of Internet marketing. Frameworks such as the 4Ps of marketing or the five forces of competitive analysis are important because they provide easy-to-remember, simplifying structures for complex problems[2]. They also serve as guides to managerial action. Thus, understanding the five forces enables firms to comprehensively map their competitive environment while simultaneously identifying specific actions for their managers (e.g., reduce buyer power by increasing the number of buyers). This opening chapter provides a simple seven-stage framework for Internet marketing. But first it offers a brief review of the basics of marketing and the scope of Internet marketing.

New Words & Phrases

toolkit　n. 工具包，工具箱

lever　n. 杆，杠杆，控制杆，v.抬起

rep　n.（同 reps）代表，推销员

academic　n. 学者

pundit　n. 博学者，印度学者，梵文学家

gradation　n. 分等级，顺序，阶级

standpoint　n. 立场，观点

marketing-mix　市场营销组合

customer-specific　针对特定客户

practitioner　n. 专业人员

tenet　n. 原则

mass-marketing　大众营销

positioning　n. 配置，布置

sales rep　销售代表

Notes

1. the standard marketing-mix toolkit includes such mass-marketing levers as television advertising, direct mail, and public relations, as well as customer-specific marketing techniques such as the use of sales reps. 标准的营销组合工具包括诸如电视广告、直接邮寄广告和公众关系等大众营销手段，以及针对特定客户的营销技巧如销售代表。本句主语为"toolkit"，由"as well as"联接的两个并列成分"mass-marketing levers"和 "customer-specific marketing techniques"作宾语。

2. Frameworks such as the 4Ps of marketing or the five forces of competitive analysis…: "4Ps of marketing" 即 4P 原则——市场营销战略的因素：价格、宣传、地点、和产品；"five forces of competitive analysis" 即 5 个影响力分析模型，为米歇尔·博德提出的分析一个行业战略吸引力的模型。

8.2　Definition and Scope of Internet Marketing

It is perhaps best to begin with the basic American Marketing Association definition of marketing: *Marketing is the process of planning and executing the conception, pricing, promotion, and distribution of ideas, goods, and services to create exchanges that satisfy individual and organizational goals.*[1]

8.2.1　The Basics: What Is Marketing?

The definition summarized above has four critical features. These are:

Marketing Is a Process. A process is a particular method of doing an activity, generally involving a series of steps or operations. The classical marketing approach involves four broad steps: market analysis, market planning, implementation, and control.　Market analysis involves searching for opportunities in the marketplace, upon which a particular firm—with unique skills—can

capitalize. Market planning requires segmentation, target market choice, positioning, and the design of the marketing mix (also termed the 4Ps, or marketing program). Market implementation includes the systems and processes to go to market with the marketing program. Finally, marketing control refers to the informal and formal mechanisms that marketing mangers can use to keep the marketing program on course. Analysis, planning, implementation, and control collectively provide a process for marketing managers to follow in the design and execution of marketing programs.

It Involves a Mix of Product, Pricing, Promotion, and Distribution. Strong marketing programs do not involve one action, such as the design of a great product. Rather, the most successful marketing programs involve *mixing* the ingredients of marketing to deliver value to customers. This mixing entails blending the right amounts of the 4P ingredients, at the right time, and in the right sequence. Too often, marketing programs fail because they allocate too many (or too few) resources in an uncoordinated way. How often have you witnessed the hot Christmas toy advertised—but not found it on the shelf? In the Internet environment, this translates into significant problems with order fulfillment at the most pressing times of the year.

It Is About Exchange. Marketing is not successful unless two parties exchange something of value. The *buyer* may exchange time, money, or services, while the *seller* must exchange something of value to the buyer. The traditional retail context provides the simplest illustration of this principle. A given consumer exchanges money for a particular good or service. However, exchange also occurs in a wide variety of contexts, many of which are nonmonetary. These include bartering, volunteering services, and political donations.

It Is Intended to Satisfy Individual and Organizational Needs. The aim of marketing is to provide a satisfactory outcome for both the firm and the customer. Firms can have highly satisfied customers if they provide services for free. However, those organizations are not likely to have a long life. The key to modern marketing is simultaneously satisfying the customer, the firm, and its shareholders. In the long run, the firm must have a positive cash flow or show a clear path to profitability for investors to maintain confidence.

8.2.2   What Is Internet Marketing?

If traditional marketing is about creating exchanges that simultaneously satisfy the firm and customers, what is Internet marketing? *Internet marketing is the process of building and maintaining customer relationships through online activities to facilitate the exchange of ideas, products, and services that satisfy the goals of both parties.*[2]

This definition can be divided into five components:

A Process. Like a traditional-marketing program, an Internet-marketing program involves a process. The seven stages of the Internet-marketing program process are setting corporate and business-unit strategy, framing the market opportunity, formulating the marketing strategy, designing the customer experience, designing the marketing program, crafting the customer interface, and evaluating the results of the marketing program. These seven stages must be coordinated and internally consistent. While the process can be described in a simple linear fashion, the marketing strategist often has to loop back and forth during the seven stages.

Building and Maintaining Customer Relationships. The goal of marketing is to build and create lasting customer relationships. Hence, the focal point shifts from *finding* customers to *nurturing* a sufficient number of committed, loyal customers. Successful marketing programs move target customers through three stages of relationship building: awareness, exploration, and commitment. It is important to stress that the goal of Internet marketing is not simply building relationships with online customers. Rather, the goal is to build offline (as relevant) as well as online relationships. The Internet marketing program may well be part of a broader campaign to satisfy customers who use both online and offline services.

Online. By definition, Internet marketing deals with levers that are available in the world of the Internet. However, as noted above, the success of an Internet marketing program may rest with traditional, offline marketing vehicles. Consider, for example, the recruiting and job-seeking service Monster.com. Monster's success can be tied directly to the effectiveness of its television advertising and, in particular, its widely successful Super Bowl ads of the past two years.

Exchange. At the core of both online and offline marketing programs is the concept of exchange. In both the online and offline worlds, exchange is still the heart of marketing. In the new economy, firms must be very sensitive to cross-channel exchanges. That is, an online marketing program must be evaluated according to its overall exchange impact—not just the online exchange impact. Hence, online marketing may produce exchanges in retail stores. Firms must be increasingly sensitive to these cross-channel effects if they are to measure the independent effects of online and offline marketing programs.

Satisfaction of Goals of Both Parties. One of the authors of this book is a loyal user of the website weather.com. Each day he arises and checks the weather in his city as well as the weather in cities he will be traveling to during the week. He is clearly satisfied with and loyal to the site. To the extent that weather.com can monetize this loyalty—most likely, in the form of advertising revenue—both parties will be satisfied. However, if the firm is unable to meet its financial obligations to employees, suppliers, or shareholders, then the exchange is unbalanced. Customers are still happy, but the firm is unable to sustain its revenue model. Both parties must be satisfied for exchange to continue.

New Words & Phrases

capitalize vt. 列为长期投资项目，资本化	promotion n. 促销
entail vt. 使必需，使蒙受，使承担	allocate vt. 分派，分配
uncoordinated adj. 不协调的	nonmonetary adj. 非货币的，非金融的
outcome n. 结果，成果	shareholder n. 股东
profitability n. 收益性，利益率	craft vt. 手工制作，构思
nurture n.养育；vt. 培养，养育	commitment n. 承诺，委托
monetize vt. 定为货币，货币化	sustain vt. 维持，持续，支撑，撑住
in the long run: 从长远看来，归根到底，结局	back and forth: 往返；来回

1. It is perhaps best to…*organizational goals.* 或许以美国市场营销协会（AMA）对市场营销所下的基本定开始为妙："市场营销是对构思、产品及服务进行设计、定价、促销及分销的计划与实施的过程，其目的是产生满足个人和组织目标的交换。"

2. *Internet marketing is the process…both parties.* 网络营销就是通过在线活动促进构思、产品及服务的交换，以实现双方的目标，从而建立并维护客户关系的过程。

8.3   The Seven Stages of Internet Marketing

The seven stages of Internet marketing are these: setting corporate and business-unit strategy, framing the market opportunity, formulating the marketing strategy, designing the customer experience, designing the marketing program, crafting the customer interface, and evaluating the results of the marketing program.

8.3.1   Stage One: Setting Corporate and Business-Unit Strategy

Corporate strategy addresses the interrelationship between the various business units in a firm, including decisions about which units should be kept, sold, or augmented. Business-unit strategy focuses on how a particular unit in the company attacks a market to gain competitive advantage. Consider, for example, Amazon.com. Corporate-strategy issues relate to the choice, mix, and number of business units such as kitchen, music, electronics, books, and tools/hardware. Once these business units are established and incubated in Amazon's corporate headquarters, the senior leadership team of each unit sets the strategic direction and steers the business unit toward its goals.

8.3.2   Stage Two: Framing the Market Opportunity

Stage two entails the analysis of market opportunities and an initial first pass of the business concept—that is, collecting sufficient online and offline data to establish the burden of proof of opportunity assessment. Let's say, for example, that you are running a major dot-com business such as Amazon. The senior management team is continually confronted with go/no-go decisions about whether to add a new business unit or develop a new product line within an existing business unit. What mechanism do they put in place to evaluate these opportunities? In this second part of the Internet-marketing process, a simple six-step methodology helps evaluate the attractiveness of the opportunity (see Figure 8-1).

The six steps include: seeding the opportunity, specifying unmet or underserved customer needs, identifying the target segment, declaring the company's resource-based opportunity for advantage, assessing opportunity attractiveness, and making the final go/no-go decision. The final go/no-go choice is often a corporate or business-unit decision. However, it is very important to stress that marketing plays a critical role in this market-opportunity assessment phase.

In order for the firm to make an informed choice about the opportunity, the management team needs to obtain a sufficient picture of the marketplace and a clear articulation of the customer experience that is at the core of the opportunity. Thus, during the market-opportunity assessment phase, the firm also needs to collect sufficient market research data.

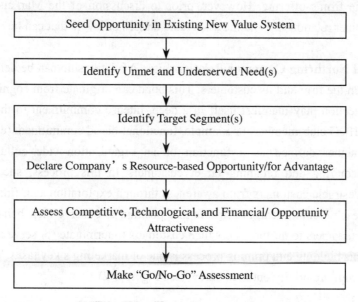

Figure 8-1　Framework for market opportunity

8.3.3　Stage Three: Formulating the Marketing Strategy

Internet marketing strategy is based upon corporate, business-unit, and overall marketing strategies of the firm. The marketing strategy goals, resources, and sequencing of actions must be tightly aligned with the business-unit strategy. Finally, the overall marketing strategy comprises both offline and online marketing activities. Even for pure-play online businesses such as Amazon's tools and hardware group, two of the four cells of activity must be coordinated in a systematic go-to-market strategy.

8.3.4　Stage Four: Designing the Customer Experience

Firms must understand the type of customer experience that needs to be delivered to meet the market opportunity. The experience should correlate with the firm's positioning and marketing strategy. Thus, the design of the customer experience constitutes a bridge between the high-level marketing strategy (step three) and the marketing program tactics (step five).

8.3.5　Stage Five: Designing the Marketing Program

The completion of stages one through four results in clear strategic direction for the firm. The firm has made a go/no-go decision on a particular option. Moreover, it has decided upon the target segment and the specific position that it wishes to own in the minds of the target customer. Stage five entails designing a particular combination of marketing actions (termed levers) to move target customers from awareness to commitment. The framework used to accomplish this task is the Marketspace Matrix. Simply put, the Internet marketer has six classes of levers (e.g., pricing, community) that can be used to create target customer awareness, exploration, and, it is hoped, commitment to the firm's offering. However, prior to discussion of the Marketspace Matrix, the stages of the customer relationship and the associated classes of levers that can be employed must be defined.

Building and Nurturing Customer Relationships. A relationship can be defined as a bond or connection between the firm and its customers. This bond can originate from cognitive or emotional sources. The connection may manifest itself in a deep, intense commitment to the brand (e.g., the Harley-Davidson HOG club-member) or a simple, functional-based commitment (e.g., regular use of weather.com). Whether defined as a function or an organization-wide culture, marketing is responsible for acquiring and retaining target customers. In this process, successful marketers manage to move desirable customers from awareness through exploration and, finally, commitment. Once customers reach commitment, the firm is in a position to observe their behavior patterns and determine which customers to nurture and which customers to terminate (or serve at a lower level of cost). Managing this building and pruning process is one of marketing's key tasks. The four stages of customer relationships are briefly outlined below (see Figure 8-2).

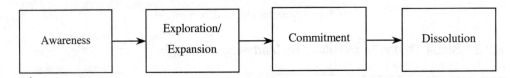

Figure 8-2   The Four Key Stages of Customer Relationships

Awareness. When customers have some basic information, knowledge, or attitudes about a firm or its offerings but have not initiated any communications with the firm, they are in the awareness stage. Consumers become aware of firms through a variety of sources, including word-of-mouth, traditional marketing such as television advertising, and online marketing programs such as banner ads. Awareness is the first step in a potentially deeper relationship with the firm. However, as one can imagine, awareness without action is not in the best interests of the firm.

Exploration. In the exploration stage, the customer (and firm) begin to initiate communications and actions that enable an evaluation of whether or not to pursue a   deeper connection. This stage is also likely to include some trial on the part of the customer. Exploration is analogous to sampling songs, going on a first date, or test driving a car. In the online world, exploration may take the form of frequent site visits, some e-commerce retail exchanges, and possibly even the return of merchandise. It may include phone call follow-ups on delivery times or e-mails about product inventory. The exploration stage may take only a few visits or perhaps years to unfold.

Commitment. In this context, commitment involves feeling a sense of obligation or responsibility for a product or firm. When customers commit to a website, their repeated, enduring attitudes and behaviors reflect loyalty. Commitment is a state of mind (e.g., I strongly prefer

Amazon.com over Barnes & Noble.com) as well as a pattern of behavior (e.g., 9 out of 10 of my book purchases are made through Amazon). One direct measure of commitment to a particular site is the extent to which the individual has invested in customizing the site (e.g., creating a My weather page on weather.com).

Dissolution. Not all customers are equally valuable to the firm. In an industrial marketing context, managers often refer to the 80/20 rule of profitability. That is, 20 percent of customers provide 80 percent of the profit. By implication, therefore, a large number of customers are unprofitable or have high cost to serve. Firms should segment their most valuable and less valuable customers. The most valuable customers may be identified based on profit, revenue, and/or strategic significance (e.g., a large well-regarded customer may not be profitable but opens the door to new accounts). The firm does not want this set of customers to terminate the relationship. Unprofitable, nonstrategic customers are a different matter. Often it is in the best interests of the firm to terminate the relationship or encourage this set of customers to disengage with the firm.

The four stages vary by the intensity of the connection between the firm and the customer. Intensity of connection may be defined as the degree or amount of connection that unfolds between the firm and its target customers. Three dimensions capture intensity:

1. The frequency of the connection. (How often does the customer visit the site?)

2. The scope of the connection. (How many different points of contact does the customer have with the firm?)

3. The depth of contact. (How thoroughly is the customer using the site?)

A customer might visit a website such as Amazon on a regular basis, but only to purchase books. This visitor would have a high level of frequent contact but a low level of scope. Another customer might visit Amazon frequently but not stay on the site for a long duration or engage in deeper connections such as writing reviews, commenting on products, or communicating with other Amazon users. This customer would have high frequency but low depth. In all cases, relationship intensity is correlated with the stage of the relationship.

The Internet Marketing Mix. The traditional 4Ps of marketing are product, price, promotion, and place/distribution. All four of these choices are part of the Internet marketing mix, plus two new elements: community and branding. Community is the level of interaction that unfolds between users. Certainly, the firm can encourage community formation and nurture community development. However, community is about user-to-user connections. Branding is a critical component of building long-term relationships on the Web. Thus, rather than viewing branding as a subcomponent of the product, it is developed here as a moderating variable upon the levers—product, pricing, communication, community, and distribution.

Product. The product is the service or physical good that a firm offers for exchange. A wide range of product forms are being offered on the Internet, including physical goods (e.g., clothing), information-intensive products (e.g., *The Wall Street Journal* online), and services (e.g., online grocers). Frequently, the offerings are a combination of all three forms. In the course of building customer relationships, the firm can use a variety of product levers to build enduring customer relationships. Product packaging is often used to build customer awareness, upgrades and complementary services enable customers to explore a deeper connection, and customized offerings strengthen commitment. The key point is that specific product levers can be used to encourage a stronger connection.

Pricing. Price is the amount the firm charges customers for a particular market transaction. This would include the price of the product, shipping, handling, warranty, and other financial costs incurred by the customer. Price is critical because it influences the perceived customer value (the complete product offering minus cost is often termed customer value). While a casual observer might view the pricing levers quite narrowly (there is only one choice: the price to charge for the good), there is a wide variety of traditional and new-to-the-world levers that emerge on the Internet. Traditional levers include such potential choices as tiered loyalty programs, volume discounts, subscription models, and targeted price promotions. The Internet has created an entirely new category of pricing tools for new-economy firms to use, including dynamic pricing strategies.

Communication. Chapter 10 defines marketing communication as activities that inform one or more groups of target customers about the firm and its products. This text takes a broad view of market communication to include all types of firm level communications, including public relations, the use of sales representatives, and online advertising. Everyone knows how advertising and other forms of communication such as television and direct mail can make target customers aware of the offerings of the firm. However, marketing communication can also encourage exploration, commitment, and dissolution. For example, viral marketing (where one user informs another user about a site through e-mails) often leads to exploration of a firm's offerings by new customers. Also, permission marketing (where customers opt to receive communications from the firm) is intended to encourage commitment to the firm. Both offline and online communication levers can encourage customers to build a stronger bond with the firm and should be integrated in any marketing program.

Community. Community is defined as a set of interwoven relationships built upon shared interests, which satisfy members' needs otherwise unattainable individually. One of the unique aspects of the Internet is the speed with which communities can be formed. Equally important is the impact that these communities can have on the firm. A critical question confronting Internet marketers is how communities should be leveraged to build deep customer relationships. Communities can be leveraged to build awareness (e.g., user-to-user communication to make others aware of a product promotion), encourage exploration (e.g., user groups discussing which automotive options to purchase—or not purchase), and commitment (e.g., bonds between users lead to deepening involvement with the site).

Distribution. The Internet is simultaneously a completely new form of commerce— a revolution in how customers and firms interact—and a distribution channel for the firm's products. With respect to the role as a distribution channel, the Internet has the power to shift customers to a new channel—or to use this channel in combination with other channels (e.g., search the Internet and then purchase at the retail store). Distribution levers include the number of intermediaries (both online and offline), the breadth of channel coverage, and the messaging from the channels. Broad levels of distribution impact both customer awareness and the potential for more customer exploration of the firm and its offerings.

Branding. Branding plays two roles in marketing strategy. First, branding is an outcome or result of the firm's marketing activities. Marketing programs affect how consumers perceive the brand, and hence its value. Second, branding is a part of *every* marketing strategy. That is, each marketing activity is enhanced if the brand is strong, or suppressed if the brand is weak. Thus, a strong advertising program for Travelocity.com is likely to produce better results than a strong advertising program for a site with a weaker brand, such as Travel.com. Branding levers work in concert with other marketing levers to produce positive financial and/or customer results for the firm.

In sum, the Internet marketing mix comprises six classes of levers. Figure 8-3 uses a cloud metaphor to show how branding mixes with each of these elements to produce an interactive effect. This interactive, or multiplier, effect of the brand can be positive or negative. Importantly, this does not mean that the other mix elements do not interact, because they do. However, branding is unique insofar as it is both a lever and an outcome of marketing actions.

Individualization and Interactivity. The previous section provided an overview of the six variables in the Internet marketing mix. However, simply specifying that the firm is able to manage these six classes of variables in an online environment does not do full justice to the uniqueness of the Internet environment. Two very important concepts need to be introduced to fully understand the profound implications that the Internet brings to business. These two concepts are individualization (or customization) and interactivity.

The first concept is individual-level marketing exchange. In addition to high levels of interactivity, customers expect to have a personal experience with the firm. Broadcast approaches send the same messages to all members of the target audience. The Internet enables the firm to engage in customer-specific actions—a broadcast to an audience of one. Equally important, the customer can control the degree of customization by taking action to set the level of customization he or she desires. Hence, the amount of individualization can be controlled either by the firm or by the customer.

Interactivity is defined as the extent to which a two-way communication flow occurs between the firm and customers. The Internet enables a level of customer dialogue that has not previously been experienced in the history of business. Certainly customers could have conversations with retail-store clerks, sales reps, or managers; however, it was not possible at the scale that the Internet affords. Hence, the fundamental shift is one from broadcast media such as television, radio, and newspapers to one that encourages debate, exchange, and conversation.

Figure 8-3 shows how the 2Is (interactivity and individualization) impact the design of all of the levers of the Internet marketing mix. Pricing can be both interactive and individualized--indeed, that is the essence of dynamic pricing. And market communications can be both interactive and individualized—that is the purpose of real-time customer service on the Web. Furthermore, products and services can be designed in real time by the customer, maximizing both interactivity and

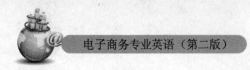

customization. This level of custom dialogue has revolutionized the impact of the Internet on marketing.

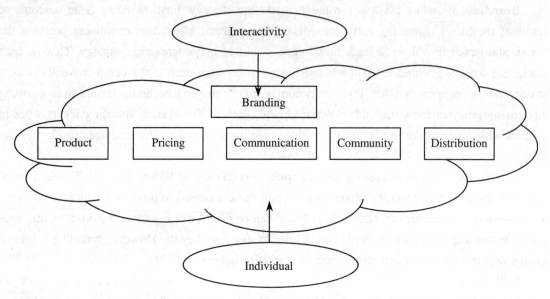

Figure 8-3   Impact of the 2Is on the Internet marketing mix

The Marketspace Matrix. Having touched upon customer relationships, the Internet marketing mix, and the 2Is, attention now turns to the Marketspace Matrix. The Marketspace Matrix is a framework illustrating the levers that the Internet marketer may choose to use at each stage of the customer relationship. These levers are the six classes of variables in the Internet marketing mix including: product, pricing, communication, community, distribution, and branding, and the stages of customer relationships are awareness, exploration, commitment, and dissolution mentioned above. The design of the marketing program—or, to put it differently, the process of filling in the relationship-levers matrix—must be guided by a series of principles.

8.3.6   Stage Six: Crafting the Customer Interface

The Internet has shifted the locus of the exchange from the marketplace (i.e., face-to-face interaction) to the marketspace (i.e., screen-to-face interaction). The key difference is that the nature of the exchange relationship is now mediated by a technology interface. This interface can be a desktop PC, subnotebook, personal digital assistant, mobile phone, wireless applications protocol (WAP) device, or other Internet-enabled appliance. As this shift from people-mediated to technology mediated interfaces unfolds, it is important to consider the types of interface design considerations that confront the senior management team.

8.3.7   Stage Seven: Evaluating the Marketing Program

This last stage involves the evaluation of the overall Internet marketing program. This includes a balanced focus on both customer and financial metrics.

New Words & Phrases

interrelationship   n. 相互关系，干扰

business unit   n. 营业单位

incubate   vt. 把……酝酿成熟；策划

no-go   adj. 不宜继续进行的；非经特许不能进入的

put in   vt. 提交，任命，插入

unmet   adj. 未满足的，未相遇的

articulation   n. 清晰度

comprise   v. 包含，由……组成

manifest   vt. 表明，显现；adj.明白的

word-of-mouth   adj. 口头的，口述的

follow-up   跟踪，随动

enduring   adj. 持久的，不朽的

unprofitable   adj. 无利益的，赚不到钱的

subscription   n. 捐献，订金，订阅，签署

breadth   n. 宽度，（布的）幅宽，（船）幅

insofar   adv. 在……的范围

subnotebook   笔记本（电脑）

address   vt. 专注于，致力于，从事；忙于

steer   v. 驾驶，掌舵

senior   adj. 高级的，年长的，资格较老的

entail   v. t. 承担，伴随

methodology   n. 方法学，方法论

underserved   adj. 服务不周到的，服务水平低下的

align with   v. 与……结盟

bond   n. 结合（物），粘结（剂），联结，债券，合同

pruning   adj. 修剪的

be analogous to   类似于，与……相似

unfold   vt. 打开，显露，阐明；vi.伸展，呈现

dissolution   n. 分解，解散

warranty   n. 正当理由，合理根据，授权，担保

unattainable   adj. 难到达的，做不到的

metaphor   n. 隐喻，暗喻，比喻说话

locus   n. 地点，所在地，[数]轨迹

8.4   Critical Success Factors for Internet Marketing Executives

Marketers have always been in the business of anticipating and managing change, and technology has been their principle tool for managing it[1]. The Internet presents an adaptive challenge for the marketing executive. Today's Internet marketing executive must have all the traditional skills of the offline marketing professional, but must place extra emphasis on some of them to account for the new economy. These critical new skills include customer advocacy and insight, integration, balanced thinking, and a willingness to accept risk and ambiguity.

8.4.1   Customer Advocacy and Insight

An insatiable curiosity for customers and marketplaces is a bare necessity for today's marketing professional. This innate curiosity fuels an individual's desire to transform mounds of customer data into meaningful and actionable insights, which in turn become a platform for advocacy. Because the Internet enables a much greater degree of interaction with customers, designing and promoting these interactions around customers' needs and progressively gaining deeper insights are critical components of creating positive customer experience. A true customer advocate will be looking to provide demonstrable added value to each customer interaction to form the basis for a meaningful relationship. As both customer behaviors and enabling technologies simultaneously evolve, a deep understanding of customer needs should serve as the guidepost driving marketing decisions.

Marketing professionals will need to strategically collect information from many disparate sources, create insightful customer mosaics, and effectively translate them into marketing strategies and tactics.

8.4.2　Integration

The Internet represents both a new channel and a new communication medium. The new-economy marketing professional needs to have an integrated or holistic view of the customer and the enterprise in order to create a uniquely advantaged strategic plan. In today's multichannel environment, a consistent message and experience must be maintained across customer touchpoints in order to create a consistent brand image[2]. Beyond strategy, a marketing manager must fundamentally understand how to integrate these new tools into the overall marketing mix. Managers who are able to hone their marketing plan in a highly integrated fashion are more likely to capitalize on the synergies between marketing elements and thus drive greater effectiveness.

8.4.3　Balanced Thinking

An Internet marketing professional needs to be highly analytical and very creative. Culling specific customer insights from a veritable fire hose of data is critically important for new-economy managers. It requires understanding the dynamic tension between one-to-one marketing and mass marketing and being able to strike a strategic balance between them. It also requires determining the appropriate customer data requirements. Internet marketing professionals must also be technologically savvy. Understanding the strategic and tactical implications of the Internet, leveraging the rapid learning environment and accelerated decision-making process it creates, and then creatively applying the insights gleaned from analysis are critical success factors for all Internet marketing professionals.

8.4.4　Passion and Entrepreneurial Spirit

Although very hard to objectively assess, passion, or fire in the belly, is what will differentiate leaders from followers in the new economy. Trying to change the status quo is never easy, and only people with conviction and passion will be heard over the din of the inevitable naysayers. Successful marketing managers use this passion to fuel their entrepreneurial instincts and vision, creating "bleeding edge" tools as they lead their teams to success.

8.4.5　Willingness to Accept Risk and Ambiguity

In the new economy, Internet marketing professionals need to retool themselves and their companies to enter into a whole new era of customer-centric marketing. The Internet has enabled customers to have much more information and many more choices than ever before, thus shifting the balance of power toward the customer and creating the need for a whole new set of "pull"-based marketing tools. Successful Internet professionals need to rely on a whole new set of marketing tools that work in an extraordinarily dynamic environment. Having the courage to try new things is the key to developing breakthrough Internet marketing. The risk and ambiguity of managing in such uncharted territory is tremendous, and the most successful Internet marketers will be willing to play at the edges.

Today's online marketing professionals must have the basic skill set of the offline marketing professional. But they must also react more quickly and manage more information and channels in order to stay one step ahead of the competition. The skill set has not changed tremendously, but the tools need to be applied with more vigor and sometimes with greater speed. Successful Internet marketers will build their business models and value propositions around a deep understanding of customer needs—not around the product.

New Words & Phrases

customer advocacy and insight 对客户的鼓动与了解	willingness n. 自动自发，积极肯干
ambiguity n. 不明确，不确定	insatiable adj. 不知足的，贪求无厌的
innate adj. 先天的，天生的	guidepost n. 路标，路牌
tactics n. 战术，策略	mosaic n. 镶嵌细工，拼花工艺，马赛克
holistic adj. 整体的，全盘的	multichannel adj. 多通道的，多波段的
touchpoints n. 触摸屏	hone vt. 用磨刀石磨，磨练
synergy n. (=synergism)协同，配合	cull vt. 拣出，挑选，选拔，撮取，采集
veritable adj. 真实的；真正的；确实的	fire hose 灭火水龙带
status quo n. 现状	conviction n. 深信，确信
din n. 喧嚣；v. 絮絮不休地说，喧闹	naysayer n. 反对者，老爱唱反调的人
entrepreneurial adj. 企业家的	

Notes

1. Marketers have always been in the business of anticipating and managing change, and technology has been their principle tool for managing it. 此句是由 "and" 联接的并列句。市场商人总是在预见和处理变革，而技术则总是他们管理的原则工具。

2. a consistent message and experience must be maintained across customer touchpoints in order to create a consistent brand image. 必须贯穿于顾客接触面上保持稳定的信息与经验，以便创立稳定的品牌形象。

英语长句的翻译

在翻译英语长句时，首先不要因为句子太长而产生畏惧心理，因为无论是多么复杂的句子，它都是由一些基本的成分组成的。其次要弄清英语原文的句法结构，找出整个句子的中心内容及其各层意思，然后分析几层意思之间的相互逻辑关系，再按照汉语的特点和表达方式，正确地译出原文的意思，不必拘泥于原文的形式。

一、英语长句的分析

一般来说，造成长句的原因有三方面：（1）修饰语过多；（2）并列成分多；（3）语言结构层次多。在分

析长句时可以采用下面的方法：

（1）找出全句的主语、谓语和宾语，从整体上把握句子的结构。

（2）找出句中所有的谓语结构、非谓语动词、介词短语和从句的引导词。

（3）分析从句和短语的功能，例如，是否为主语从句，宾语从句，表语从句等，若是状语，它是表示时间、原因、结果、还是表示条件等。

（4）分析词、短语和从句之间的相互关系，例如，定语从句所修饰的先行词是哪一个等。

（5）注意插入语等其他成分。

（6）注意分析句子中是否有固定词组或固定搭配。

下面我们结合一些实例来进行分析：

例 1. Behaviorists suggest that the child who is raised in an environment where there are many stimuli which develop his or her capacity for appropriate responses will experience greater intellectual development.

分析：（1）该句的主语为 behaviorists，谓语为 suggest，宾语为一个从句，因此整个句子为 Behaviorist suggest that-clause 结构。（2）该句共有五个谓语结构，它们的谓语动词分别为 suggest, is raised, are, develop, experience 等,这五个谓语结构之间的关系为：Behaviorist suggest that-clause 结构为主句；who is raised in an environment 为定语从句，所修饰的先行词为 child；where there are many stimuli 为定语从句，所修饰的先行词为 environment；which develop his or her capacity for appropriate responses 为定语从句，所修饰的先行词为 stimuli；在 suggest 的宾语从句中，主语为 child，谓语为 experience，宾语为 greater intellectual development。

在作了如上的分析之后，我们就会对该句具有了一个较为透彻的理解，然后根据我们上面所讲述的各种翻译方法，就可以把该句翻译成汉语为：

行为主义者认为，如果儿童的成长环境里有许多刺激因素，这些因素又有利于其适当反应能力的发展，那么，儿童的智力就会发展到较高的水平。

例 2. For a family of four, for example, it is more convenient as well as cheaper to sit comfortably at home, with almost unlimited entertainment available, than to go out in search of amusement elsewhere.

分析：（1）该句的骨干结构为 it is more … to do sth than to do sth else.是一个比较结构，而且是在两个不定式之间进行比较。（2）该句中共有三个谓语结构，它们之间的关系为：it is more convenient as well as cheaper to … 为主体结构，但 it 是形式主语，真正的主语为第二个谓语结构: to sit comfortably at home，并与第三个谓语结构 to go out in search of amusement elsewhere 作比较。（3）句首的 for a family of four 作状语，表示条件。另外，还有两个介词短语作插入语：for example，with almost unlimited entertainment available，其中第二个介词短语作伴随状语，修饰 to sit comfortably at home。

综合上述翻译方法，这个句子我们可以翻译为：

譬如，对于一个四口之家来说，舒舒服服地在家中看电视，就能看到几乎数不清的娱乐节目，这比到外面别的地方去消遣又便宜又方便。

二、长句的翻译

英语习惯于用长的句子表达比较复杂的概念，而汉语则不同, 常常使用若干短句，作层次分明的叙述。因此，在进行英译汉时，要特别注意英语和汉语之间的差异，将英语的长句分解，翻译成汉语的短句。在英语长句的翻译过程中，我们一般采取下列的方法。

1. 顺序法

当英语长句内容的叙述层次与汉语基本一致时，可以按照英语原文的顺序翻译成汉语。

例 1. Even when we turn off the beside lamp and are fast asleep, electricity is working for us, driving our refrigerators, heating our water, or keeping our rooms air-conditioned.

分析：该句子由一个主句，三个作伴随状语的现在分词以及位于句首的时间状语从句组成，共有五层意思：A.既使在我们关掉了床头灯深深地进入梦乡时；B.电仍在为我们工作；C. 帮我们开动电冰箱；D. 加热水；E.或是室内空调机继续运转。上述五层意思的逻辑关系以及表达的顺序与汉语完全一致，因此，我们可以通过顺序法，把该句翻译成：

即使在我们关掉了床头灯深深地进入梦乡时，电仍在为我们工作：帮我们开动电冰箱，把水加热，或使室内空调机继续运转。

例 2. But now it is realized that supplies of some of them are limited, and it is even possible to give a reasonable estimate of their "expectation of life", the time it will take to exhaust all known sources and reserves of these materials.

分析：该句的骨干结构为"It is realized that…"，it 为形式主语，that 引导着主语从句以及并列的 it is even possible to …结构，其中，不定式作主语，the time …是 "expectation of life" 的同位语，进一步解释其含义，而 time 后面的句子是它的定语从句。五个谓语结构，表达了四个层次的意义：A. 可是现在人们意识到；B. 其中有些矿物质的蕴藏量是有限的；C. 人们甚至还可以比较合理的估计出这些矿物质"可望存在多少年"；D. 将这些已知矿源和储量将消耗殆尽的时间。根据同位语从句的翻译方法，把第四层意义的表达作适当的调整，整个句子就翻译为：

可是现在人们意识到，其中有些矿物质的蕴藏量是有限的，人们甚至还可以比较合理的估计出这些矿物质 "可望存在多少年"，也就是说，经过若干年后，这些矿物的全部已知矿源和储量将消耗殆尽。

2. 逆序法

英语有些长句的表达次序与汉语表达习惯不同，甚至完全相反，这时必须从原文后面开始翻译。例如：

例 1. Aluminum remained unknown until the nineteenth century, because nowhere in nature is it found free, owing to its always being combined with other elements, most commonly with oxygen, for which it has a strong affinity.

分析：这个句子由一个主句，两个原因状语和一个定语从句，"铝直到 19 世纪才被人发现"是主句，也是全句的中心内容，全句共有四个谓语结构，共有五层意思：A. 铝直到 19 世纪才被人发现；B. 由于在自然界找不到游离状态的铝；C.由于它总是跟其他元素结合在一起；D. 最普遍的是跟氧结合；E. 铝跟氧有很强的亲和力。按照汉语的表达习惯通常因在前，果在后，这样，我们可以逆着原文的顺序把该句翻译成：

铝总是跟其他元素结合在一起，最普遍的是跟氧结合；因为铝跟氧有很强的亲和力，由于这个原因，在自然界找不到游离状态的铝。所以，铝直到 19 世纪才被人发现。

例 2. It therefore becomes more and more important that, if students are not to waste their opportunities, there will have to be much more detailed information about courses and more advice.

分析：该句由一个主句，一个条件状语从句和一个宾语从句组成，"……变得越来越重要"是主句，也是全句的中心内容，全句共有三个谓语结构，包含三层含义：A. ……变的越来越重要；B. 如果要使学生充分利用他们的机会；C. 得为他们提供大量更为详尽的信息，作更多的指导。为了使译文符合汉语的表达习惯，我们也采用逆序法，翻译成：

因此，如果要使学生充分利用他们（上大学）的机会，就得为他们提供大量关于课程的更详尽信息，作更多的指导。这个问题显得越来越重要了。

例 3. It is probably easier for teachers than for students to appreciate the reasons why learning English seems to become increasingly difficult once the basic structures and patterns of the language have been understood.

一旦了解英语的基本结构和句型，再往下学似乎就越来越难了，这其中的原因，也许教师比学生更容易理解。

例 4. For our purposes we will say e-commerce begins in 1995, following the appearance of the first banner advertisements placed by ATT, Volvo, Sprint and others on Hotwired.com in late October 1994, and the first sales of banner ad space by Netscape and Infoseek in early 1995.

伴随着 ATT、Volvo、Sprint 等公司所做的第一例横幅广告于 1994 年 10 月下旬出现在 Hotwired.com 上，和 1995 年初 Netscape 与 Infoseek 领先出售横幅广告空间，我们会说电子商务是从 1995 年开始的。

3. 分句法

有时英语长句中主语或主句与修饰词的关系并不十分密切，翻译时可以按照汉语多用短句的习惯，把长句的从句或短语化成句子，分开来叙述，为了使语意连贯，有时需要适当增加词语。例如：

例 1. The number of the young people in the United States who can't read is incredible about one in four.

上句在英语中是一个相对简单的句子，但是如果我们按照原文的句子结构死译，就可能被翻译成："没有阅读能力的美国青年人的数目令人难以置信约为 1/4。"这样，就使得译文极为不通顺，不符合汉语的表达习惯，因此，我们应该把它译为：

大约有 1/4 的美国青年人没有阅读能力，这简直令人难以置信。

例 2. Television, it is often said, keeps one informed about current events, allow one to follow the latest developments in science and politics, and offers an endless series of programs which are both instructive and entertaining.

分析：在此长句中，有一个插入语 "it is often said"，三个并列的谓语结构，还有一个定语从句，这三个并列的谓语结构尽管在结构上同属于同一个句子，但都有独立的意义，因此在翻译时可以采用分句法，按照汉语的习惯把整个句子分解成几个独立的分句，结果为：

人们常说，通过电视可以了解时事，掌握科学和政治的最新动态。从电视里还可以看到层出不穷、既有教育意义又有娱乐性的新节目。

例 3. All they have to do is press a button, and they can see plays, films, operas, and shows of every kind, not to mention political discussions and the latest exciting football match.

他们所必须做的只是按一下开关。开关一开，就可以看到电视剧、电影、歌剧，以及其他各种各样的文艺节目。至于政治问题的辩论、最近的激动人心的足球赛更是不在话下。

4. 综合法

上面我们讲述了英语长句的逆序法、顺序法和分句法，事实上，在翻译一个英语长句时，并不只是单纯地使用一种翻译方法，而是要求我们把各种方法综合使用，这在我们上面所举的例子中也有所体现。尤其是在一些情况下，一些英语长句单纯采用上述任何一种方法都不方便，这就需要我们的仔细分析，或按照时间的先后，或按照逻辑顺序，顺逆结合，主次分明地对全句进行综合处理，以便把英语原文翻译成通顺忠实的汉语句子。例如：

例 1. People were afraid to leave their houses, for although the police had been ordered to stand by in case of emergency, they were just as confused and helpless as anybody else.

分析：该句共有三层含义：A：人们不敢出门；B：尽管警察已接到命令，要作好准备以应付紧急情况；C：警察也和其他人一样不知所措和无能为力。在这三层含义中，B 表示让步，C 表示原因，而 A 则表示结果，按照汉语习惯顺序，我们作如下的安排：

尽管警察已接到命令，要作好准备以应付紧急情况，但人们不敢出门，因为警察也和其他人一样不知所措和无能为力。

例 2. Modern scientific and technical books, especially textbooks, requires revision at short intervals if their authors wish to keep pace with new ideas, observations and discoveries.

对于现代书籍，特别是教科书来说，要是作者希望自己书中的内容能与新概念、新观察到的事实和新发现同步发展的话，那么就应该每隔较短的时间，将书中的内容重新修改。

例 3. Napster.com, which was established to aid Internet users in finding and sharing online music files known as *MP3 files*, is perhaps the most wellknown example of peer-to-peer e-commerce, although purists note that Napster is only partially peer-to-peer because it relies on a central database to show which users are sharing music files.

Napster.com 建立的目标是帮助因特网用户发现并分享在线音乐文件，即人所共知的 MP3 文件。尽管纯化论者强调：因为它依赖中央数据库来显示哪一位用户正在分享音乐文件，所以 Napster 仅仅是部分对等。但 Napster 或许是对等电子商务最著名的实例。

Exercises

I. Answer the following questions

1. What is Internet marketing?

2. What are the seven stages of Internet marketing?

3. What are the four stages of the customer relationship?

4. What are the six classes of variables in the Internet marketing mix?

5. What is the Marketspace Matrix?

6. How do interactivity and individuality come into play in the design of the marketing program?

7. What are the critical success factors for the Internet marketing professional?

II. Translate the following into Chinese

The Internet and the World Wide Web provide marketers with new tools and added convenience that can increase the success of their marketing efforts. Components of an *Internet marketing campaign* include marketing research, e-mail marketing, online advertising, promotions, public relations, search engine marketing and so on.

While generating Web-site traffic is important to the success of an e-business, it is not enough. Keeping user profiles, recording visits and analyzing promotional and advertising results are key to measuring the effectiveness of marketing campaigns. By discovering your *target market*—the group of people toward whom it is most profitable to aim your marketing campaign—you can focus your campaign and increase the number of visits, responses and purchases. Internet marketing should be used with traditional marketing to create the most effective corporate marketing strategy. This strategy includes a focus on attracting new customers to your site and bringing them back repeatedly.

Chapter 9 Legal Issues of E-Commerce

电子商务带来了一些新问题，对于这些问题而言，是非对错的界限已不再清晰。因此，从事电子商务的人员需要新的规范来确定在特定环境下，哪些行为是合法的，哪些行为是非法的。本章将分析一些主要的电子商务法律问题，并提出解决方案。

通过本章学习，读者应掌握以下内容并能够用英语表达：
- 在互联网上建立管辖权的困难。
- 电子商务中合同的签订和履行。
- 电子商务隐私权的保护。
- 知识产权在电子商务环境下的主要类型。

9.1   Jurisdiction on the Internet

Defining, establishing, and asserting jurisdiction are much more difficult on the Internet than they are in the physical world, mainly because traditional geographic boundaries do not exist. For example, a Swedish company that engages in electronic commerce may have a Web site that is entirely in English and a URL that ends in ".com," thus not indicating to customers that it is a Swedish firm. The server that hosts this company's Web page could be in Canada, and the people who maintain the Web site might work from their homes in Australia.

If a Mexican citizen buys a product from the Swedish firm and is unhappy with the goods received, that person might want to file a lawsuit against the seller firm. However, the world's physical border-based systems of law and jurisdiction do not help this Mexican citizen determine where to file the lawsuit. The Internet does not provide anything like the obvious international boundary lines in the physical world.

Governments that want to enforce laws regarding business conduct on the Internet must establish jurisdiction over that conduct. A contract is a promise or set of promises between two or more legal entities—people or corporations—that provides for an exchange of value (goods, services, or money) between or among them. A tort is an intentional or negligent action taken by a legal entity that causes harm to another legal entity. People or corporations that wish to enforce their rights based on either contract or tort law must file their claims in courts with jurisdiction to hear their cases. A court has sufficient jurisdiction in a matter if it has both subject-matter jurisdiction and personal jurisdiction.

9.1.1 Subject-Matter Jurisdiction

Subject-matter jurisdiction is a court's authority to decide a particular type of dispute. For example, in the United States, federal courts have subject-matter jurisdiction over issues governed by federal law (such as bankruptcy, copyright, patent, and federal tax matters), and state courts have subject-matter jurisdiction over issues governed by state laws (such as professional licensing and state tax matters). If the parties to a contract are both located in the same state, a state court has subject-matter jurisdiction over disputes that arise from the terms of that contract. The rules for determining whether a court has subject-matter jurisdiction are clear and easy to apply. Few disputes arise over subject-matter jurisdiction.

9.1.2 Personal Jurisdiction

Personal jurisdiction is, in general, determined by the residence of the parties. In the United States, a court has personal jurisdiction over a case if the defendant is a resident of the state in which the court is located. In such cases, the determination of personal jurisdiction is straightforward. However, an out-of-state person or corporation can also voluntarily submit to the jurisdiction of a particular state court by agreeing to do so in writing or by taking certain actions in the state. One of the most common ways that people voluntarily submit to a jurisdiction is by signing a contract that includes a statement, known as a forum selection clause, that the contract will he enforced according to the laws of a particular state. That state then has personal jurisdiction over the parties who signed the contract regarding any enforcement issue that arises from the terms of that contract.

In the United States, individual states have laws that can create personal jurisdiction for their courts. The details of these laws, called long-arm statutes, vary from state to state, but generally create personal jurisdiction over nonresidents who transact business or commit tortious acts in the state. For example, suppose that an Arizona resident drives recklessly while in California and, as a result, causes a collision with another vehicle that is driven by a California resident. Due to the driver's tortious behavior in the state of California, the Arizona resident can expect to be called into a California court. In other words, California courts have personal jurisdiction over the matter.

Businesses should he aware of jurisdictional considerations when conducting electronic commerce over state and international lines. In most states, the extent to which these laws apply to companies doing business over the Internet is unclear. Because these procedural laws were written before electronic commerce existed, their application to Internet transactions continues to evolve as more and more disputes arise from online commercial transactions. The trend in this evolving law is that the more business activities a company conducts in a state, the more likely it is that a court will assert personal jurisdiction over that company through the application of a long-arm statute.

9.1.3 Jurisdiction in International Commerce

Jurisdiction issues that arise in international business are even more complex than the rules governing personal jurisdiction across state lines within the United States. The exercise of jurisdiction across international borders is governed by treaties between the countries engaged in the dispute. In general, U.S. courts determine personal jurisdiction for foreign companies and people in much the same way that these courts interpret the long-arm statutes in domestic matters. Non-U.S.

corporations and individuals can be sued in U.S. courts if they conduct business or commit tortious acts in the United States. Similarly, foreign courts can enforce decisions against U.S. corporations or individuals through the U.S. court system if those courts can establish jurisdiction over the matter.

Courts asked to enforce the laws of other nations sometimes follow a principle called judicial comity, which means that they voluntarily enforce other countries' laws or judgments out of a sense of comity, or friendly civility. However, most courts are reluctant to serve as forums for international disputes. Also, courts are designed to deal with weighing evidence and making findings of right and wrong. International disputes often require diplomacy and the weighing of costs and benefits. Courts are not designed to do cost-benefit evaluations and cannot engage in negotiation and diplomacy. Thus, courts (especially U.S. courts) prefer to have the executive branch of the government negotiate international agreements and resolve international disputes.

Jurisdictional issues are complex and change rapidly. Any business that intends to conduct electronic commerce should consult an attorney who is well versed in these procedural issues. However, there are a number of resources online that can be useful to non-lawyers who want to do preliminary investigation of a legal topic such as jurisdiction. The Harvard Law School's Berkman Center for Internet & Society Web site includes links to many current Internet-related legal issues.

New Words & Phrases

Jurisdiction	n. 司法权，裁判权，管辖权	lawsuit	n. 诉讼
intentional	adj. 有意图的，故意的	negligent	adj. 疏忽的，粗心大意的
legal entity	法人实体	tort	n. 民事侵权行为
dispute	n. 争论，争端	arise from	由……而引起，由……而产生
defendant	n. 被告	submit to	使服从，服从
statute	n. 法令，法规，成文法	transaction	n. 办理，交易
judicial comity	司法礼让	deal with	安排，处理
cost-benefit	adj. 成本效益（分析）的	engage in	使从事于，参加
attorney	n. 律师	preliminary	adj. 预备的，初步的

Abbreviations

URL (Uniform Resource Locator)   统一资源定位器，因特网地址

Notes

1. One of the most common ways that people voluntarily submit to a jurisdiction is by signing a contract that includes a statement, known as a forum selection clause, that the contract will he enforced according to the laws of a particular state.   人们自愿服从管辖权最常用的方式之一是在签署合同中包括一个声明（即所谓的法院选择条款），指明合同将按照某个特定州的法律执行。

2. In general, U.S. courts determine personal jurisdiction for foreign companies and people in much the same way that these courts interpret the long-arm statutes in domestic matters.   总的说来，美国法院按照类似于法院在国内事务中解释长臂法令的方式来决定国外公司或个人的属人管辖权。

9.2 Contracting and Contract Enforcement in Electronic Commerce

Any contract includes three essential elements: an offer, an acceptance, and consideration. The contract is formed when one party accepts the offer of another party. An offer is a commitment with certain terms made to another party, such as a declaration of willingness to buy or sell a product or service. An offer can be revoked as long as no payment, delivery of service, or other consideration has been accepted. An acceptance is the expression of willingness to take an offer, including all of its stated terms. Consideration is the agreed upon exchange of something valuable, such as money, property, or future services. When a party accepts an offer based on the exchange of valuable goods or services, a contract has been created. An implied contract can also be formed by two or more parties that act as if a contract exists, even if no contract has been written and signed.

People enter into contracts on a daily, and often hourly, basis. Every kind of agreement or exchange between parties, no matter how simple, is a type of contract. For example, every time a consumer buys an item at the supermarket, the elements of a valid contract are met:

• The store offers an item at a stated price.

• The consumer accepts this offer by indicating a willingness to buy the product for the stated price.

• The store exchanges its product for another valuable item: the consumer's payment.

Contract is a key element of traditional business practice, and it is equally important on the Internet. Offers and acceptances can occur when parties exchange e-mail messages, engage in electronic data interchange (EDI), or fill out forms on Web pages. These Internet communications can be combined with traditional methods of forming contracts, such as the exchange of paper documents, faxes, and verbal agreements made over the telephone or in person. An excellent resource for many of the laws concerning contracts is the Cornell Law School Web site, which includes the full text of the Uniform Commercial Code (UCC).

When a seller advertises goods for sale on a Web site, that seller is not making an offer, but is inviting offers from potential buyers. If a Web ad were a legal offer to form a contract, the seller could easily become liable for the delivery of more goods than it has available to ship. When a buyer submits an order, which is an offer, the seller can accept that offer and create a contract. If the seller does not have the ordered items in stock, the seller has the option of refusing the buyer's order outright or counteroffering with a decreased amount. The buyer then has the option to accept the seller's counteroffer.

Making a legal acceptance of an offer is quite easy to do in most cases. When enforcing contracts, courts tend to view offers and acceptances as actions that occur within a particular context. If the actions are reasonable under the circumstances, courts tend to interpret those actions as offers and acceptances. For example, courts have held that various actions—including mailing a check, shipping goods, shaking hands, nodding one's head, taking an item off a shelf, or opening a wrapped package—are all, in some circumstances, legally binding acceptances of offers. Although the case

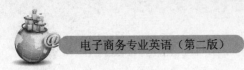

law is limited regarding acceptances made over the Internet, it is reasonable to assume that courts would view clicking a button on a Web page, entering information in a Web form, or downloading a file to be legally binding acceptances.

9.2.1　Written Contracts on the Web

Most courts will hold that a writing exists when the terms of a contract have been reduced to some tangible form. Courts have held that tape recordings of spoken words, computer files on disks, and faxes are writings. Thus, the parties to an electronic commerce contract should find it relatively easy to satisfy the writing requirement. Courts have been similarly generous in determining what constitutes a signature. A signature is any symbol executed or adopted for the purpose of authenticating a writing. Courts have held names on telegrams, telexes, and faxes to be signatures. Even typed names or names printed as part of a letterhead have served as signatures. The United States now has a law that explicitly makes digital signatures legally valid for contract purposes. Similar laws have been enacted in several European and Asian countries.

Firms conducting international electronic commerce do not need to worry about the signed writing requirement in most cases. The main treaty that governs international sales of goods, Article 11 of the United Nations Convention on Contracts for the International Sale of Goods (CISG), requires neither a writing nor a signature to create a legally binding acceptance.

9.2.2　Warranties on the Web

Most firms conducting electronic commerce have little trouble fulfilling the requirements needed to create enforceable, legally binding contracts on the Web. One area that deserves attention, however, is the issue of warranties. Any contract for the sale of goods includes implied warranties. A seller implicitly warrants that the goods it offers for sale are fit for the purposes for which they are normally used. If the seller knows specific information about the buyer's requirements, acceptance of an offer from that buyer may result in an additional implied warranty of fitness, which suggests that the goods are suitable for the specific uses of that buyer. Sellers can also create explicit warranties by providing a specific description of the additional warranty terms. It is also possible for a seller to create explicit warranties, often unintentionally, by making general statements in brochures or other advertising materials about product performance or suitability for particular tasks.

Sellers can avoid some implied warranty liability by making a warranty disclaimer. A warranty disclaimer is a statement declaring that the seller will not honor some or all implied warranties. Any warranty disclaimer must be conspicuously made in writing, which means it must be easily noticed in the body of the written agreement. On a Web page, sellers can meet this requirement by putting the warranty disclaimer in larger type, a bold font, or a contrasting color. To be legally effective, the warranty disclaimer must be stated obviously and must be easy for a buyer to find on the Web site.

9.2.3　Authority to Form Contracts

A contract is formed when an offer is accepted for consideration. Problems can arise when the acceptance is issued by an imposter or someone who does not have the authority to bind the company to a contract. In electronic commerce, the online nature of acceptances can make it relatively easy for identity forgers to pose as others.

Fortunately, the Internet technology that makes forged identities so easy to create also provides the means to avoid being deceived by a forged identity. Companies and individuals can use digital signatures to establish identity in online transactions. If the contract is for any significant amount, the parties should require each other to use digital signatures to avoid identity problems. In general, courts will not hold a person or corporation whose identity has been forged to the terms of the contract; however, if negligence on the part of the person or corporation contributed to the forgery, a court may hold the negligent party to the terms of the contract. For example, if a company was careless about protecting passwords and allowed an imposter to enter the company's system and accept an offer, a court might hold that company responsible for fulfilling the terms of that contract.

Determining whether an individual has the authority to commit a company to an online contract is a greater problem than forged identities in electronic commerce. This issue, called authority to bind, can arise when an employee of a company accepts a contract and the company later asserts that the employee did not have such authority. Digital signatures and certificates from a certification authority is a good electronic solution.

New Words & Phrases

offer   n. 要约
consideration   n. 约因
implied contract   默认契约，默示合同
liable   adj. 有责任的，有义务的
authenticate   vt. 鉴别，鉴定，认证
disclaimer   n. 放弃，拒绝，不承诺
imposter   n. 冒名顶替者
pose   v. 伴装

acceptance   n. 承诺
revoke   v. 撤回，废除，宣告无效
stated   adj. 定期的，规定的，一定的
in stock   有库存，有现货
digital signature   数字签名
conspicuously   adv. 显著地
forger   n. 伪造者

Abbreviations

EDI (electronic data interchange)   电子数据交换   UCC (Uniform Commercial Code)   统一商业法典
CISG(United Nations Convention on Contracts for the International Sale) 联合国国际货物销售合同公约

Notes

1. If the seller knows specific information about the buyer's requirements, acceptance of an offer from that buyer may result in an additional implied warranty of fitness, which suggests that the goods are suitable for the specific uses of that buyer.   如果卖方知道买方要求的具体信息,接受买方要约会产生另一个隐含担保,即所售商品适合买方的特殊用途。

2. When a buyer submits an order, which is an offer, the seller can accept that offer and create a contract. 买方提交的一份订单就是一份要约,卖方可以接受这份要约并达成一份合同。

9.3　Privacy

Privacy means different things to different people. In general, privacy is the right to be left alone and the right to be free of unreasonable personal intrusions.

The right to privacy is recognized today in virtually all U.S. states and by the federal government, either by statute or by common law. The definition of privacy can be interpreted quite broadly. However, the following two rules have been followed fairly closely in past U.S. court decisions: (1) The right of privacy is not absolute. Privacy must be balanced against the needs of society. (2) The public's right to know is superior to the individual's right of privacy. These two rules show why it is difficult, in some cases, to determine and enforce privacy regulations.

9.3.1　Collecting Information about Individuals

In the past, the complexity of collecting, sorting, filing, and accessing information manually from several different government agencies was, in many cases, a built-in protection against misuse of private information. It was simply too expensive, cumbersome, and complex to invade a person's privacy. The Internet, in combination with large-scale databases, has created an entirely new dimension of accessing and using data. The inherent power in systems that can access vast amounts of data can be used for the good of society. For example, by matching records with the aid of a computer, it is possible to eliminate or reduce fraud, crime, government mismanagement, tax evasion, welfare cheats, employment of illegal aliens, and so on. The question is: What price must every individual pay in terms of loss of privacy so that the government can better apprehend these types of criminals?

The Internet offers a number of opportunities to collect private information about individuals. Here are some of the ways that the Internet can be used to find information about an individual:

• By reading an individual's newsgroup postings.

• By looking up an individual's name and identity in an Internet directory.

• By reading an individual's e-mail.

• By conducting surveillance on employees.

• By wiretapping wireline and wireless communication lines and listening to employees.

• By asking an individual to complete a Web site registration.

• By recording an individual's actions as they navigate the Web with a browser, usually using cookies.

Of these, the last two are the most common ways of gathering information on the Internet.

（1）Web Site Registration

All B2C and marketing Web sites ask visitors to fill out registration forms. During the process, customers voluntarily provide their names, addresses, phone numbers, e-mail addresses, sometimes their hobbies and likes or dislikes, and so forth in return for information, for the chance to win a lottery, or for some other item of exchange. There are few restraints on the ways in which the site can use this information. The site might use it to improve customer service or its own business. Or, the site could just as easily sell the information to another company, which could use it in an inappropriate or intrusive manner.

（2）Cookies

Another way that a Web site can gather information about an individual is by using cookies. A cookie is a small piece of data that is passed back and forth between a Web site and an end user's browser as the user navigates the site.

Originally, cookies were designed to help with personalization and CRM. However, cookies also can be used to invade an individual's privacy. Cookies allow Web sites to collect detailed information about a user's preferences, interests, and surfing patterns. The personal profiles created by cookies are often more accurate than self-registration because users have a tendency to falsify information in a registration form.

9.3.2   Protection of Privacy

The ethical principles commonly used when it comes to the collection and use of personal information also apply to information collected in e-commerce. These principles include the following:

• Notice/awareness. Consumers must be given notice of an entity's information practices prior to collection of personal information. Consumers must be able to make informed decisions about the type and extent of their disclosures based on the intentions of the party collecting the information.

• Choice/consent. Consumers must be made aware of their options as to how their personal information may be used, as well as any potential secondary uses of the information. Consent may be granted through opt-out clauses, which require steps to prevent collection of information. In other words, no action equals consent. Or, consumers may grant consent through opt-in clauses, which require steps to allow the collection of information.

• Access/participation. Consumers must be able to access their personal information and challenge the validity of the data.

• Integrity/security Consumers must be assured that their personal data are secure and accurate. It is necessary for those collecting the data to take whatever precautions are required to ensure that data are protected from loss, unauthorized access, destruction, and fraudulent use, and to take reasonable steps to gain information from reputable and reliable sources.

• Enforcement/redress. A method of enforcement and remedy must be available. Otherwise, there is no real deterrent or enforceability for privacy issues.

In the United States, these principles are supported by specific pieces of legislation. For example, the Federal Internet Privacy Protection Act prohibits federal agencies from disclosing personal records or making identifying records about an individual's medical, financial, or employment history. Probably the broadest in scope is the Consumer Empowerment Act, which requires the FTC to enforce online privacy rights in EC, including the collection and use of personal data.

In 1998, the European Union passed a privacy directive (EU Data Protection Directive) reaffirming the principles of personal data protection in the Internet age. Member countries are required to put this directive into effect by introducing new laws or modifying existing laws in their respective countries. The directive aims to regulate the activities of any person or company that controls the collecting, holding, processing, or use of personal data on the Internet.

In many countries, the debate continues about the rights of the individual versus the rights of society. Some feel that the ISPs should be the regulators; others feel that self-regulation is the best alternative. However, some empirical data suggest that self-regulation does not work. For instance, in 1998, the U.S. FTC audited 1,400 commercial Web sites in the United States to measure the effectiveness of self-regulation. They found that privacy protection at these sites was poor. Additionally, few sites provided end users with the following privacy protections: details about the site's information-gathering and dissemination policies; choice over how their personal information is used; control over personal information; and recourse for resolving user complaints.

New Words & Phrases

common law 习惯法，不成文法
cumbersome adj. 讨厌的，麻烦的
in combination with 与……结合
tax evasion 逃税，漏税
newsgroup 新闻组
wiretap v. 搭线窃听，窃听
browser n. 浏览器
disclosure n. 泄露，暴露
opt-in 选择性加入
empirical adj. 实证的

access vt. 访问，存取
invade v. 侵入，侵犯
fraud n. 欺骗，欺诈行为
apprehend v. 逮捕
surveillance n. 监视，监督
registration n. 注册
back and forth 来回地
opt-out 选择性退出
Consumer Empowerment Act 消费者授权法
dissemination n. 传播，散布

Abbreviations

CRM(Customer Relationship Management) 客户关系管理
FTC(Federal Trade Commission)联邦贸易委员会
EU Data Protection Directive 欧盟数据保护指令
ISP(Internet service provider) 互联网服务提供商

Notes

1. The site might use it to improve customer service or its own business. Or, the site could just as easily sell the information to another company, which could use it in an inappropriate or intrusive manner. 网站可能会利用这些信息提高其客户服务水平，或者，网站只是简单将这些信息卖给其他公司，这些公司可能会以不恰当或侵犯性的方式使用这些信息。

2. The ethical principles commonly used when it comes to the collection and use of personal information also apply to information collected in e-commerce. 收集和使用个人信息时通常所遵循的道德原则同样适用于电子商务环境下收集的信息。

9.4   Intellectual Property Rights

According to the World Intellectual Property Organization (WIPO), intellectual property refers to "creations of the mind: inventions, literary and artistic works, and symbols, names, images, and designs used in commerce." Whereas privacy protection is the major concern for individuals, intellectual property protection is the major concern of those who own intellectual property. Intellectual property rights are one of the foundations of modern society. Without these rights, the movie, music, software, publishing, pharmaceutical, and biotech industries would collapse. There are four main types of intellectual property in EC: copyrights, trademarks, domain names, and patents.

9.4.1   Copyrights

A copyright is an exclusive grant from the government that confers on its owner an essentially exclusive right to: (1) reproduce a work, in whole or in part, and (2) distribute, perform, or display it to the public in any form or manner, including the Internet.

Copyrights usually exist in the following works:

• Literary works (e.g., books and computer software)
• Musical works (e.g., compositions)
• Dramatic works (e.g., plays)
• Artistic works (e.g., drawings, paintings)
• Sound recordings, films, broadcasts, cable programs

On the Web, copyrights also can be used to protect images, photos, logos, text, HTML, JavaScript, and other materials.

Various international treaties provide global copyright protection. Of these, the Berne Union for the Protection of Literary and Artistic Property (Berne Convention) is one of the most important. The Berne Convention dates to 1886. It is administered by the WIPO and is supported by over 90 percent of the world's countries.

A copyright owner may seek a court injunction to prevent or stop any infringement and to claim damages. Certain kinds of copyright infringements also incur criminal liabilities. These include: commercial production of infringing works, selling or dealing in infringing works, possessing infringing works for trade or business, and manufacturing and selling technology for defeating copyright protection systems.

It is possible to use software to produce digital content that cannot be copied. Two approaches are used to design effective electronic copyright management systems:

• Preventing copyright violations by using cryptography
• Tracking copyright violations

One other successful method is digital watermarks. Similar to watermarks on fine paper, which indicate the maker of the paper, digital watermarks are unique identifiers that are imbedded in the digital content. Although they do not prevent an individual from making illegal copies, they do make it possible to identify pirated works. If a pirated copy is placed on the Internet, then sophisticated search programs can be used to locate the illegal copies and notify the rightful owner.

9.4.2   Trademarks

A trademark is a symbol used by businesses to identify their goods and services. The symbol can be composed of words, designs, letters, numbers, shapes, a combination of colors, or other such identifiers. Trademarks need to be registered in a country in order to be protected by law. To be eligible for registration, a trademark must be distinctive, original, and not deceptive. Once registered, a trademark lasts forever, as long as a periodic registration fee is paid.

The owner of a registered trademark has exclusive rights to:

• Use the trademark on goods and services for which the trademark is registered.

• Take legal action to prevent anyone else from using the trademark without consent on goods and services (identical or similar) for which the trademark is registered.

On the Internet, fake brand names and products can be sold or auctioned from anywhere. In the United States, the Federal Dilution Act of 1995 protects famous trademarks from dilution. Trademark infringement carries criminal liabilities. In particular, it is a crime for anyone to fraudulently use a registered trademark, including the selling and importing of goods bearing an infringing trademark, and to use or possess equipment for forging registered trademarks.

9.4.3   Domain Names

A variation of a trademark is a domain name. Two controversies surround domain names. One is whether additional top-level domain names (similar to .com, .org, and .gov) should be added. The other is the use of trademarked names that belong to other companies as domain names.

At the heart of the controversies is Network Solutions, Inc.(NSI), a subsidiary of VeriSign, which has been contracted by the U.S. government to assign domain addresses. Until 1998, NSI exclusively assigned domain names for several top levels: .com, .net, .gov, .edu, and org. The United States, as well as the rest of the world, had been subject to NSI for domain names, and critics in Europe and elsewhere were ready to relieve the United States of that responsibility. Europe was weary of the United States assuming the right to direct Internet governance, subjecting the Internet to U.S. law. On June 1, 1998, the monopoly of NSI over domain names ended. NSI created a registration system that it shares with several other competing companies. The new registration system is handled by ICANN, an international nonprofit corporation.

The Council of Registrars (CORE) and the Global Internet Project want to increase the number of top-level names. One of the objectives is to create an adult-only top-level name that will prevent pornographic material from getting into the hands of children.

Both CORE and the Global Internet Project also want to repair the disputes over domain names. Companies are using trade names of other companies as their domain address to help attract traffic to their Web site. For example, DC Comics is suing Brainiac Services, Inc. for using one of its comic book names, Brainiac. Private-sector groups will have to resolve this issue in the future before more lawsuits begin to surface. Major disputes are international in scope, because the same corporate name may be used in different countries by different corporations.

In order to avoid legal battles, the Internet community created a speedy way to resolve domain name disputes using arbitration. Three arbitration organizations have been given the authority to make determinations regarding domain name disputes. They are Disputes.org/eResolution Consortium, the National Arbitration Forum, and the WIPO. If one of these organizations makes a determination regarding a domain name dispute, NSI/ICANN will respect the decision.

In addition to the resolution of disputes by submission to arbitration, a legal action can also be initiated in various jurisdictions. Legal action provides a more potent protection, because in addition to an organization's winning the right to use a certain domain name, courts can also grant monetary damages and enforce specific anticybersquatting legislation.

Cybersquatting refers to the practice of registering domain names in order to sell them later at a higher price. The Consumer Protection Act of 1999 is aimed at cybersquatters who register Internet domain names of famous companies or people and hold them hostage for "ransom" payments from the person or company. In the past, several private individuals were given the right by the governing bodies of the Internet to use Web site (domain) names that involved trademarked names. For example, in 1998, a New Jersey dealer named Russell Boyd applied for and was given the rights to 50 domain names, including juliaroberts.com and alpacino.com. He then proceeded to auction the names on eBay. In that same year, Julia Roberts complained to WIPO. In the summer of 2000, WIPO's Complaint and Arbitration Center, which coordinates international patents, copyrights, and trademarks, upheld the actress's claim. It ruled that Boyd had no rights to the domain name juliaroherts.com even though the actress by that name was not using it at that time. The Anticybersquatting Consumer Protection Act of 1999 lets trademark owners sue for statutory damages.

9.4.4 Patents

A patent is a document that grants the holder exclusive rights on an invention for a fixed number of years (e.g., 17 years in the United States and 20 years in the United Kingdom). Patents serve to protect tangible technological inventions, especially in traditional industrial areas. They are not designed to protect artistic or literary creativity. Patents confer monopoly rights to an idea or an invention, regardless of how it may be expressed. An invention may be in the form of a physical device or a method or process for making a physical device.

Thousands of IT-related patents have been granted over the years. For example, Juno Online Services received an interactive ad patent (5809242). IBM has many patents, including 5870717, a system for ordering from electronic catalogs, and 5926798, a system for using intelligent agents to perform online commerce.

Certain patents granted in the United States deviate from established practices in Europe. For example, Amazon.com has successfully obtained a U.S. patent on its One-Click ordering procedure.

Using this patent, Amazon.com sued Barnes and Noble in 1999 and in 2000, alleging that its rival had copied its patented technology. Barnes and Noble was enjoined by the courts from using the procedure. Similarly, in 1999, Priceline.com filed a suit against Expedia.com alleging that Expedia was using Priceline's patented reverse auction business model. The suit was settled on January 9, 2001, when Expedia.com agreed to pay Priceline.com royalties for use of the model. However, in Europe and many Asian, African, and South American countries, it is almost impossible to obtain patents on business methods or computer processes.

New Words & Phrases

copyright n. 版权，著作权	trademark n. 商标
domain name 域名	patent n. 专利（权）
exclusive adj. 排他的，专有的	logo n. 标识，商标，标识语
treaty n. 条约，协议	Berne Convention 伯尔尼公约
injunction n. 命令，禁令	infringement n. 违反，侵害
criminal adj. 犯罪的，刑事的	cryptography n. 密码学，密码术
digital watermark 数字水印	pirate v. 盗印，盗版
fake adj. 假的	the Federal Dilution Act 联邦商标反淡化法
subsidiary adj. 附属的	monopoly n. 垄断，垄断者
pornographic adj. 色情的，色情作品的	arbitration n. 仲裁，公断
the National Arbitration Forum 国家仲裁论坛	Cybersquatting n. 域名抢注
intelligent agent 智能代理	the Global Internet Project 全球互联网计划联盟
Disputes.org/eResolution Consortium 电子争端解决同盟	

Abbreviations

WIPO (World Intellectual Property Organization) 世界知识产权组织

NSI (Network Solutions, Inc.) 网络解决方案公司

ICANN(the Internet Corporation for Assigned Names and Numbers) 互联网名称与地址分配机构

CORE (The Council of Registrars) 欧洲注册委员会

Notes

1. Similar to watermarks on fine paper, which indicate the maker of the paper, digital watermarks are unique identifiers that are imbedded in the digital content. 与印制在精美纸张上显示纸张制造者的水印一样，数字水印是嵌入到数字内容中的独特标识。

2. Legal action provides a more potent protection, because in addition to an organization's winning the right to use a certain domain name, courts can also grant monetary damages and enforce specific anticybersquatting legislation. 法律诉讼可以提供更有力的保护，因为除了帮助组织赢得使用域名的权利外，法院还可以判决赔偿经济损失并执行特定的反域名抢注法律。

Reading Materials——Information Privacy and Computer Security

A diverse range of legal obligations associated with information privacy and computer security are now in place. In general, information privacy requirements focus on protection of personal information that can be identified with a specific individual ("personally identifiable" information). Information privacy obligations often carry requirements for computer system security, as the protected information is commonly stored and processed on computers. In this way, information privacy and computer security are interrelated.

Several different privacy regulations targeted to protect specific forms of personal information have been enacted at the federal level in the United States. For example, the Health Insurance Portability and Accountability Act ("HIPAA") established privacy requirements regarding personally identifiable health and medical information. The HIPAA requirements are enforced by the federal Department of Health and Human Services, and they apply to all organizations that collect or process personal health care information.

Another example of targeted federal privacy legislation is the Gramm Leach Bliley Act. The Act establishes privacy protection for certain forms of personally identifiable information collected by financial services institutions individual consumers. Gramm Leach also imposes notice requirements associated with the transfer of personal financial information. Regulations developed under the Act are enforced by a variety of federal organizations, including the Department of the Treasury and the Securities and Exchange Commission.

HIPAA and the Gramm Leach Bliley Act regulations also establish security requirements for computer systems that process information protected under those regulations. Computer security is a critical aspect of information privacy, thus privacy requirements are commonly linked to security obligations. Organizations that must comply with HIPAA or Gramm Leach requirements rely on their information technology professionals to ensure compliance with those legal obligations.

Other countries apply information privacy requirements that are more stringent than those enacted at the federal level in the U.S. For example, the European Community and Canada have implemented sweeping information privacy protections, in contrast to the targeted approach applied in the U.S. Information system professionals working for organizations that do business in Europe or other jurisdictions with comprehensive information privacy laws play a key role in compliance with those legal obligations.

Some jurisdictions have now implemented notification requirements when the integrity of personal information has been compromised. California's statute, SB 1386 for example, requires notice to individuals when their personal information has been compromised. Technology professionals working for organizations that fall within the scope of the California statute are actively involved in preventing unauthorized access to personal information which invokes the notification requirement. They also play a key role in identifying when information has been compromised, thus triggering the notice requirement of the law.

Legal issues associated with the integrity of information have a significant impact on computer professionals. A leading example of this connection is provided by the Sarbanes-Oxley Act, federal legislation in the United States. Generally, Sarbanes-Oxley places requirements on senior management of publicly-traded companies to take personal responsibility for disclosure and accuracy of financial information of their companies. The information disclosure and verification requirements of Sarbanes-Oxley have a significant impact on information system professionals. Public companies now require more rigorous financial recordkeeping, auditing, and reporting. These additional legal compliance obligations place an extra set of demands on corporate computer systems. Information technology professionals who develop, maintain, and manage those systems are thus at the center of Sarbanes-Oxley compliance efforts.

Information technology professionals have a significant role to play in compliance with legal requirements associated with information privacy and integrity, and the computer security obligations associated with management of the protected information. Those professionals are called upon to devise information systems that provide the requisite levels of privacy and security. They are also the people who will bear the burden of managing the operations of the systems to ensure compliance, and of developing and implementing remedial measures when compliance problems arise.

New Words & Phrases

legal obligation　法律义务　　　　　　　enact　vt. 制定法律，颁布

comply with　遵守，服从　　　　　　　compromise　v. 危害，危及……的安全

学术论文的英文写作简介

用英语写学术论文的目的主要有两个，一是参加国际学术会议，在会议上宣讲，促进学术交流；二是在国际学术刊物上发表，使国外同行了解自己的研究成果，同样也是出于学术交流的目的。

一、科技论文的结构

不同的学科或领域、不同的刊物对论文的格式有不同的要求，但各个领域的研究论文在文体和语言特点上都有许多共性。一般来说，一篇完整规范的学术论文由以下各部分构成：

<blockquote>

Title（标题）

Abstract（摘要）

Keywords（关键词）

Table of contents（目录）

Nomenclature（术语表）

Introduction（引言）

Body（正文）{
Method（方法）
Results（结果）
Discussion（讨论）
Conclusion（结论）
}

Acknowledgement（致谢）

Notes（注释）

References（参考文献）

Appendix（附录）

</blockquote>

其中，Title，Abstract，Introduction，Method，Result，Discussion，Conclusion 和 Reference 八项内容是必不可少的，其他内容则根据具体需要而定。在这八项内容中，读者最多的是 Title，Abstract 和 Introduction

部分，读者会根据这些内容来决定是否阅读全文。也就是说，一篇研究论文赢得读者的多少，在很大程度上取决于 Title，Abstract 和 Introduction 的写作质量，这三部分内容的写作技巧将在以后章节中分别介绍。下面简单介绍一下科技论文的正文、结论和结尾等内容。

二、正文

学术论文的正文一般包括 Method，Result，Discussion 三个部分。这三部分主要描述研究课题的具体内容、方法，研究过程中所使用的设备、仪器、条件，并如实公布有关数据和研究结果等。Conclusion 是对全文内容或有关研究课题进行的总体性讨论。它具有严密的科学性和客观性，反映一个研究课题的价值，同时提出以后的研究方向。

为了帮助说明论据、事实，正文中经常使用各种图表。最常用的是附图（Figure）和表（Table），此外还有图解或简图（Diagram）、曲线图或流程图（Graph）、视图（View）、剖面图（Profile）、图案（Pattern）等。在文中提到时，通常的表达法为：

如图 4 所示　　As (is) shown in Fig.4,

如表 1 所示　　As (is) shown in Tab.1,

三、结论

在正文最后应有结论（Conclusions）或建议（Suggestions）。

（1）关于结论可用如下表达方式：

① The following conclusions can be drawn from …（由……可得出如下结论）

② It can be concluded that …（可以得出结论……）

③ We may conclude that…或 We come to the conclusion that…（我们得出如下结论……）

④ It is generally accepted (believed, held, acknowledged) that…（一般认为…）（用于表示肯定的结论）

⑤ We think (consider, believe, feel) that…（我们认为……）（用于表示留有商量余地的结论）

（2）关于建议可用如下表达方式。

① It is advantageous to (do)

② It should be realized (emphasized, stressed, noted, pointed out) that …

③ It is suggested (proposed, recommended, desirable) that …

④ It would be better (helpful, advisable) that…

四、结尾部分

1. 致谢

为了对曾给予支持与帮助或关心的人表示感谢，在论文之后，作者通常对有关人员致以简短的谢词，可用如下方式：

I am thankful to sb. for sth

I am grateful to sb. for sth

I am deeply indebted to sb. for sth

I would like to thank sb. for sth

Thanks are due to sb. for sth

The author wishes to express his sincere appreciation to sb. for sth.

The author wishes to acknowledge sb.

The author wishes to express his gratitude for sth.

2. 注释

注释有两种方式，一种为脚注，即将注释放在出现的当页底部；另一种是将全文注释集中在结尾部分。两种注释位置不同，方法一样。注释内容包括：

（1）引文出处。注释方式参见"参考文献"。

（2）对引文的说明,如作者的见解、解释。

（3）文中所提到的人的身份，依次为职称或职务、单位。如：

  Professor, Dean of Dept⋯ University（教授，……大学……系主任）

  Chairman, ⋯ Company, USA（美国……公司董事长）

（4）本论文是否曾发表过。

3. 参考文献

在论文的最后应将写论文所参考过的主要论著列出，目的是表示对别人成果的尊重或表示本论文的科学根据，同时也便于读者查阅。参考文献的列法如下：

（1）如果是书籍，应依次写出作者、书名、出版社名称、出版年代、页数。如：

Dailey, C.L. and Wood, F.C., **Computation curves for compressible Fluid Problems**, *John Wiley & Sons, Inc. New York*, 1949, pp.37-39

（2）如果是论文，应依次写出作者、论文题目、杂志名称、卷次、期次、页数。如：

Marrish Joseph G.,**Turbulence Modeling for Computational Aerodynamics**, *AIAA J.Vol-21,No.7*, 1983, PP.941-955

（3）如果是会议的会刊或论文集，则应指出会议举行的时间、地点。如：

Proceedings of the Sixth International Conference on Fracture Dec.4-10,1984, New Delhi, India

（4）如果作者不止一人，可列出第一作者，其后加上 et al。如：Wagner, R.S. et al, ⋯

（5）在印刷上，论文或著作名称用黑体字，出版社、杂志名称用斜体字。

Exercises

I. True or False

1. The rules for determining whether a court has subject-matter jurisdiction are clear and easy to apply.

2. Most courts don't mind to serve as forums for international disputes.

3. The United States now has a law that explicitly makes digital signatures legally valid for contract purposes.

4. Determining whether an individual has the authority to commit a company to an online contract is not a problem.

5. A cookie is a small piece of data that is passed back and forth between a Web site and an end user's browser as the user navigates the site.

6. In 1998, the U.S. FTC audited 1,400 commercial Web sites in the United States to measure the effectiveness of self-regulation. They found that privacy protection at these sites was good.

7. A copyright owner may seek a court injunction to prevent or stop any infringement and to claim damages.

8. The Internet community created a speedy way to resolve domain name disputes using legal action.

II. Answer the following questions

1. List some of the ways that the Internet can be used to collect information about individuals.

2. List four types of intellectual property.

3. List the legal rights covered by a copyright.

4. List the legal rights of a trademark owner.

III. Questions and Discussion

1. Discuss the relationship between information privacy and computer security.

2. What are some of the things that EC websites can do to ensure that personal information is safeguarded?

3. Check the latest on domain names by visiting sites such as internic.net. Prepare a report.

4. In about 100 words, explain why online business might have difficulty limiting the effects of their actions to a relatively small geographic area.

5. In about 300 words, describe the differences between subject-matter jurisdiction and personal jurisdiction.

Chapter 10   E-Logistics

学习指导

　　对不少人而言，物流不过是将商品拿来送去。这种简单化的认识断送了他们对物流的深刻探讨以及对其中商业机会的发掘能力。事实上，物流是公司整个营销过程中的一个环节，电子商务时期的物流管理不仅需要被革新，而且物流本身也孕育着巨大的商机。

　　本章首先介绍了物流管理委员会关于物流的定义，随后介绍了电子商务中物流的地位、作用、面临的问题及前面的路。读者应掌握相关定义和术语，并了解物流的地位、作用及其面临的问题。

10.1   The CLM Definition of Logistics

The Council of Logistics Management has adopted this definition of logistics:

Logistics is that part of the supply chain process that plans, implements, and controls the efficient, effective flow and storage of goods, services, and related information between the point of origin and the point of consumption in order to meet customers' requirements.

What is Supply Chain Management?

If the difference between logistics and supply chain is confusing, discussions about the phenomenon of "supply chain management" (SCM) can be thoroughly bewildering. The problem, according to the Supply Chain Research Group at The University of Tennessee, is one of trying to define two concepts with one term, i.e., supply chain management. The idea of viewing the coordination of a supply chain from an overall system perspective with each of the tactical activities of distribution flows viewed within a broader strategic context (which has been called SCM as a management philosophy) is more accurately called a Supply Chain Orientation[1]. The actual implementation of this orientation across various companies in the supply chain is more appropriately called Supply Chain Management.

Supply Chain Orientation is defined as "the recognition by an organization of the systemic, strategic implications of the tactical activities involved in managing the various flows in a supply chain." A company possesses a supply chain orientation (SCO) if its management can see the implications of managing both the upstream and downstream flows of products, services, finances, and information across their suppliers and their customers.

However, this does not mean that every firm with an SCO can implement it because such implementation requires an SCO across several companies, directly connected in the supply chain. The firm with an SCO may implement individual, disjointed supply chain tactics (such as Just-In-Time delivery or Electronic Data Interchange with suppliers and customers), but this is not

Supply Chain Management unless those tactics are coordinated (a strategic orientation) across the supply chain (a systemic orientation).

Supply Chain Management is the implementation of a supply chain orientation across suppliers and customers. Companies implementing SCM first must have a supply chain orientation. In other words, a Supply Chain Orientation is a management philosophy and Supply Chain Management is the sum total of all the overt management actions undertaken to realize that philosophy.

Supply Chain Management is defined as "the systemic, strategic coordination of the traditional business functions and tactics across these business functions within a particular company and across businesses within the supply chain for the purposes of improving the long-term performance of the individual companies and the supply chain as a whole[2]."

New Words & Phrases

logistics n.物流，后勤学，后勤
tactical adj.策略上的，战术上的，作战的

bewildering adj.令人困惑的，使人混乱的
disjointed adj.脱节的，杂乱的

Abbreviations

SCM (Supply Chain Management) 供应链管理
JIT delivery (Just-In-Time delivery) 准时制发送
CLM (Council of Logistics Management) 物流管理委员会

SCO (Supply Chain Orientation) 供应链定向
EDI (Electronic Data Interchange) 电子数据交换

Notes

1. The idea of viewing the coordination of a supply chain ⋯ with each of the tactical activities ⋯is more accurately called a Supply Chain Orientation. 这是这个长句的主体，大意为：将供应链与每一次战术行动看作协调的概念更准确地叫做供应链定位。

2. Supply Chain Management is defined as "⋯ coordination of the traditional business functions and tactics ⋯" 这是这个长句的主体，大意为：供应链管理定义为传统企业功能与战术的协调。

10.2   E-Logistics: Delivering the Goods in E-Commerce

10.2.1   Why Logistics Services are Critical to the Success of E-Commerce

Logistics services for e-commerce (e-logistics) have proved to be an area that requires major improvements if e-commerce is to achieve its full potential. The failure of many e-tailers, for example in the United States, to fulfill orders during peak demand periods and the reluctance of some sellers to engage in international e-commerce because of the complex logistics requirements clearly demonstrate the critical role of e-logistics.

The existing e-logistics problems arise largely from the fact that e-commerce and the demand for related logistics services have grown at a much faster rate than that at which suitable logistics services and solutions have been developed.

10.2.2　Solutions Being Used to Improve Logistics for E-Commerce

Traders have responded to the increased demand for logistics services that arises from e-commerce by adopting a variety of methods. These include handling of order fulfillment by companies themselves using in-house logistics services, outsourcing fulfillment to third-party logistics service providers (3PLs), drop-shipping and various combinations of these methods. Concurrently, considerable efforts have been made to develop software applications in order to automate logistics functions such as order management, cargo and equipment tracking, transportation management and planning, customer service management and returns management. It is estimated for that by 2000 worldwide sales of software, hardware and services used in electronic logistics had reached US$ 277 billion, and they are expected to reach US$ 1 trillion by 2005. While these figures appear to be on the high side, they nevertheless provide a useful indication of the importance being given to the issue of logistics in e-commerce.

10.2.3　Difficulties Faced

Technology plays a critical role in providing systems that can enhance the ability of logistics service providers to satisfy customer demands. The main weakness of the efforts to develop applications for improving logistics is the general lack of integration between the various applications used for different logistics functions. Many of the applications are designed to handle different types of logistics functions, and this tends to lead to the existence of incompatible systems being applied to related logistics functions.

Another factor that impedes the effectiveness of e-logistics services is the existence of a multitude of constraints brought about by inefficient trade facilitation. The major problems in this area include:

The existence of a considerable number of disparate documentation requirements, which include government documents, commercial documents and those relating to transportation;

The lack of harmonization of customs procedures and tariff classification systems;

The existence of custom valuation of exports and imports in many countries that is characterized by such problems as double invoicing and undervaluation, thus making assessment of the true value difficult;

The existence of outdated trade procedures such as exchange controls, long retention of goods in customs custody and regulations that require paper documents;

Lack of transparency in many regulations, leading to the inability to predict costs and delivery times;

Customs administrations that are poorly equipped, as regards physical infrastructure and human resources and also lack of cooperation between customs administration of different countries. Many customs administrations are also prone to corruption, which leads to delays, high costs and a distortion in trade information;

Limited use of automation and information technology in trade facilitation functions, leading to delays, high costs and inefficiencies.

10.2.4　The Way Forward

To achieve more efficient e-logistics and e-fulfillment, it is desirable to have a trading environment in which there is sufficient information about goods as regards their description and origins, and destinations. Sellers and buyers should be able to monitor and track goods at every point along the way from the supplier to consumer. All stakeholders should be able to check on the Internet the availability and status of orders. All this can be achieved if trade information is simplified, automated and fully harmonized in all countries and when all restrictive government export/import regulations and practices have been eliminated. It also requires sophisticated supply chain management systems for compiling and enabling global end-to-end monitoring of trade information.

To accomplish these broad objectives and also to take into account the special problems of developing countries, it is recommended that Governments, the international community and the private sector cooperate in promoting the following specific measures:

To take advantage of the great potential provided by the Internet technology in order to capture, transfer and monitor trade information over global networks of supply chains in an open fashion;

To enhance and improve the harmonization of the classification of commodity tariffs and facilitate the identification of individual consignments;

To automate trade processing and particularly customs declaration systems in order to develop customs-to-customs information exchange and thereby provide a basis for the elimination of unnecessary export/import requirements, which can instead be replaced by fully integrated international transactions. In this context, the International Trade Prototype (ITP) project created by the United Kingdom and the United States customs administrations to develop a system that could enable information provided for export declaration to be used to fulfill the data requirements for import entry in the country of destination could provide a model to be developed at the international level. This system, however, could only be implemented if all government customs requirements could be simplified and harmonized and the transmission of trade information based on internationally agreed standards. A preliminary evaluation has shown widespread support for further development of the project, and the international community should lend its support to the project as well;

To harmonize and simplify trade facilitation regulations and procedures, and in particular to encourage greater harmonization of customs procedures through wide adoption and implementation of the revised Kyoto Convention on the Simplification and Harmonization of Customs Procedures;

To encourage greater transparency in trade processing activities and take measures to reduce corruption and other forms of malpractice in customs administration;

To promote greater integration of software applications for logistics functions, including the use of such systems as XML (eXtensible Markup Language);

To promote partnerships between logistics service providers of developing countries and those of developed countries that are applying e-logistics systems;

To provide technical cooperation programs to developing countries in promoting services that support e-logistics, for example in customs, transportation services, cargo terminals and related services and also in the automation of trade information.

New Words & Phrases

logistics	n.后勤学，后勤	e-tailer	n.电子零售商
engage in	v.使从事于，参加	arise from	起于，由……出身
in-house	adj.内部的；adv.内部地	concurrently	adv.同时
incompatible	adj.性质相反的，矛盾的，不调和的	cargo	n.船货，货物
impede	v.阻止	multitude	n.许多
tend to	v.注意，趋向	lead to	导致
harmonization	n.调和化，一致，融洽	bring about	使发生，致使
outdated	adj.过时的，不流行的	undervaluation	n.低估，看轻
custody	n.保管，存仓	prone to	v.倾向于……
end-to-end	端对端，端到端	tariff	n.关税，关税表，税则
revise	vt.修订，校正，修正，修改	Kyoto Convention	京都公约
customs procedures	海关手续	malpractice	n.渎职，舞弊
exchange control	外汇控制，外汇管理，外汇管制	retention	n.留存
private sector	私营成分，私营部门	consignment	n.交运货物，交付，寄售
in this context	关于此点，就此而论	export declaration	出口申报单
customs declaration	海关申报单，申报关税，报关单	import entry	报关，报进口
drop-shipping	直达货运，指不经批发商直达零售商		

Abbreviations

3PLs（third-party logistics service）第三方物流服务　　ITP（International Trade Prototype）国际贸易原型

科技论文标题的写法

论文标题是全文内容的缩影。读者通过标题便能够预测论文的主要内容和作者的意图，从而决定是否阅读全文。因此，为了使文章赢得有关领域里众多的读者，论文的标题必须用最精炼的语言恰如其分地体现全文的主题和核心。

学术文章的标题主要有三种结构：名词性词组（包括动名词），介词词组，名词词组＋介词词组。间或也用一个疑问句作标题（多用在人文社会科学领域），但一般不用陈述句或动词词组作标题。

一、名词性词组

名词性词组由名词及其修饰语构成。名词的修饰语可以是形容词、介词短语，有时也可以是另一个名词。名词修饰名词时，往往可以缩短标题的长度。以下各标题分别由两个名词词组构成。例如：

Latent demand and the browsing shopper（名词词组＋名词词组）

Cost and productivity（名词＋名词）

二、介词词组

介词词组由介词十名词或名词词组构成。如果整个标题就是一个介词词组的话，一般这个介词是"on"，意思是"对……的研究"。例如：

From Knowledge Engineering to Knowledge Management（介词词组+介词词组）

On the correlation between working memory capacity and performance on intelligence tests

三、名词/名词词组+介词词组

这是标题中用得最多的结构。例如：

Simulation of Controlled Financial Statements（名词+介词词组）

The impact of internal marketing activities on external marketing outcomes（名词+介词词组+介词词组）

Diversity in the Future Work Force（名词+介词词组）

Models of Sustaining Human and Natural Development（名词+介词词组）

标题中的介词词组一般用来修饰名词或名词词组，从而限定某研究课题的范围。这种结构与中文的"的"字结构相似，区别是中文标题中修饰语在前，中心词在后。英文正好相反，名词在前，而作为修饰语的介词短语在后。例如：

Progress on Fuel Cell and its Materials（燃料电池及其材料进展）

四、其它形式

对于值得争议的问题，偶尔可用疑问句作为论文的标题，以点明整个论文讨论的焦点。例如：

Is B2B e-commerce ready for prime time?

Can ERP Meet Your eBusiness Needs?

有的标题由两部分组成，用冒号（：）隔开。一般来说，冒号前面一部分是研究的对象、内容或课题，比较笼统，冒号后面具体说明研究重点或研究方法。这种结构可再分为三种模式。

模式 1 研究课题：具体内容。例如：

Microelectronic Assembly and Packaging Technology：Barriers and Needs

The Computer Dictionary Project：an update

模式 2 研究课题：方法/性质。例如：

B2B E-Commerce：A Quick Introduction

The Use of Technology in Higher Education Programs：a National Survey

模式 3 研究课题：问题焦点。例如：

Caring about connections：gender and computing

Exercises

I. Choose the correct answer

1. What does the SCO mean?

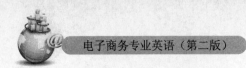

A. Supply Chain Optimization   B. Supply Chain Orientation

C. Supply Chain Organization

2. What does the SCM mean?

A. Supply Chain Management   B. Supply Chain Manager

C. Supply Control Management

3. What is the relation between the SCO and SCM?

A. SCM is the implementation of a SCO   B. SCO is the implementation of a SCM

C. SCM is part of the SCO

4. What does the 3PLs mean?

A. Peer-Peer Protocol Logistics   B. Third-Party Logistics service

C. Production Process Program Languages

5. What does the ITP mean?

A. International Trade Problem   B. International Transactional Prototype

C. International Trade Prototype

6. What does e-logistics really mean?

A. Logistics services for e-commerce   B. Logistics services for electronic engineering

C. Logistics in Electronic Industry

7. How does the existing e-logistics problems arise from?

A. e-commerce and the demand for related logistics services have grown at a much faster rate than that at which suitable logistics services and solutions have been developed

B. e-commerce and the demand for related logistics services have grown at a much slower rate than that at which suitable logistics services and solutions have been developed

II. Translate the following sentences into Chinese

1. Logistics is the time-related positioning of resource, or the strategic management of the total supply chain.

2. The supply chain is a sequence of events intended to satisfy a customer. It can include procurement, manufacture, distribution and waste disposal, together with associated transport, storage and information technology.

3. Transport is an integral part of the supply chain, not only between the sequence of the events but during the process.

III. Write a report on development of E-Logistics in China

Chapter 11　Introduction to M-Business Applications

学习指导

　　本章介绍了移动电子商务的应用，包括价值定位、应用、技术和面临的挑战。通过学习，应掌握以下内容：
- 了解移动电子商务的动力。
- 了解移动电子商务的价值定位。
- 了解移动电子商务的主要应用领域。
- 了解移动电子商务的相关技术。
- 了解移动电子商务公司面临的挑战。

11.1　Introduction

Leung and Antypas (2001) defined mobile business (m-business) as both "content delivery (notification and reporting) and transactions (purchasing and data entry) on mobile devices". Another term often used for m-business is "wireless e-commerce", as such business activities often leverage wireless and Internet technologies. During 2009 USA wireless revenues will continue to enjoy strong growth, following growth of nearly 50% in 2008 according to a Latest Study. The major factors that drive the growth of m-business include:

- Mobile devices such as Internet-enabled handsets, personal digital assistants (PDA), and portable computers are gaining popularity among business and consumer users.
- The wireless infrastructure and support are constantly being upgraded by vendors in order to provide seamless and affordable access. Advances in mobile and wireless technologies are making anywhere, anytime computing a reality.
- Companies want to remove delays and inefficiencies from traditional business processes and explore new business opportunities by allowing employees and consumers to access critical business information from anywhere at anytime.

New Words & Phrases

m-business（mobile business）移动电子商务　　　notification　n.通知，通知单，通知书
delivery　n. 投递，送交，交货　　　　　　　　　transactions　n. 业务
handset　n. 电话听筒，手机，手持机　　　　　　seamless　adj. 准确无误的；无缝的
critical　adj. 决定性的，关键性的

Abbreviations

PDA（personal digital assistants）掌上电脑，个人数字助手

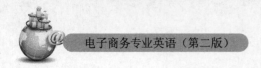
11.2　Value Proposition

Before investing in a mobile project, an organization needs to identify the business drivers behind the project and demonstrate how m-business solutions will help solve existing problems, capitalize new opportunities, or create a competitive edge. Therefore, it is imperative for organizations to understand the value produced by m-business. Evidence has shown that m-business offers organizations the benefits of new channels to reach customers, cost reduction, increased customer satisfaction and revenues, and reduced cycle time by redesigning workflows.

Balasubramanian, Peterson, and Jarvenpaa (2002) conclude that the reason m-business offers values unattainable by conventional business practices is because mobile technologies relax spatial and/or temporal constraints of activities. For example, with mobile technologies, a field worker can check and reply e-mails at any time. Without the right mobile technologies, the activity can only be performed at a location where a computer and a network connection are present. In the same vein, Chen and Nath (2003) believe that the value of m-business is a function of the user's immediacy of information needs and user mobility. As the user's immediacy of information needs and/or mobility increase, the value of m-business solutions that can address the user's needs increases (see Figure 1). At one extreme, we have a traveling stock trader whose ability to access real time market information and transact on the go is crucial. M-business applications that can offer the trader these capabilities will prove to be very valuable. On the other hand, when there is no pressing need for information and the receiver of information is mostly stationary, m-business offers minimal value.

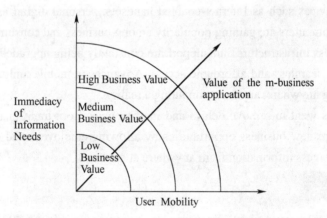

Figure 11-1　Value proposition of m-business

The value can be further enhanced by m-business applications that demonstrate high levels of personalization and context-awareness. Timely information or services based on the user's location and interests are offered by these applications, which can help organizations to better target the right customer and seize business opportunities at the right time. However, the two crucial components of these applications, location identification technologies and database marketing techniques, have provoked a great deal of controversy in the recent years due to consumers' privacy concerns.

Value Proposition   价值定位

competitive edge 竞争优势

spatial   adj. 空间的

field worker 现场调查员；实地调查员

controversy   n. 争论，论战

capitalize   vt. 资本化；转作资本；资本还原

imperative   adj. 必要的，紧急的，极重要的

temporal   adj. 世俗的；现世的，时间的

on the go   活跃，忙个不停

11.3   M-Business Applications

The number of m-business applications is on the rise. Generally, these applications can be categorized into these four categories: business-to-consumer (B2C), business-to-business (B2B), business-to-employee (B2E), and consumer-to-consumer (C2C). M-business creates an effective B2C market by utilizing the intimate nature of mobile devices and communication channels.

Examples of these applications include mobile banking, stock trading, retailing, content delivery, and concierge services. While many of the lessons learned from B2C e-commerce pervade, new business opportunities can be found in m-business. As Paul May (2001) suggested in his book, Mobile Commerce, early experience in B2C m-commerce had taught us the following three lessons:

- Successful mobile commerce services depend on the value perceptions of consumer groups.

- Mobile commerce is most suited for accommodating consumers' impulse buying.

- The relevance of an offer to the user's current position (e.g., location, time and mission) will take precedence over price.

B2B and B2E m-business will likely generate the most revenue as we have seen in the e-commerce arena. Mobile applications for asset and personnel management, collaboration, inventory management, supply chain management, and corporate data access are increasingly seen in organizations today. C2C m-business embodies personal communication applications such as wireless voice communication, short message services, buddy lists, peer-to-peer file sharing, and mobile games.

M-business applications can be found in a wide array of industries ranging from healthcare to transportation. A meaningful categorization of these applications will be helpful to managers in identifying new m-business opportunities. We have developed a technology-independent and application-oriented impact/value framework for m-business applications that will help readers sort through existing m-business applications (See Table 11-1). The model posits that m-business applications are likely to dramatically compress the time required for accessing information and completing business processes, allow individuals and organizations to overcome geographic limitations by making information accessible from anywhere at anytime, help restructure relationships between the provider and the recipient of the information, and proactively seize business opportunities by providing location-specific services. These impacts will result in increased efficiency in operation, improved effectiveness in decision making, and innovative business processes that generate competitive advantage. Each cell in the framework represents a unique business opportunity enabled by m-business. The forthcoming sections briefly discuss each m-business opportunity and representative applications that take advantage of these opportunities.

Table 11-1　A framework for m-business applications

		Value		
		Efficiency	Effectiveness	Innovation
Impact	Time	Reduce Business Process Cycle Time	Reduce Information Float	Enhance Service Quality
	Mobility	Capture Information Electronically Anytime-Anywhere	Access Critical Information Anytime-Anywhere	React to Problems and Opportunities Anytime-Anywhere
	Relationship	Enhance Connectivity and Communication	Increase Collaboration	Increase Information Transparency to Improve Supply Chain
	Location Leverage	Track and Surveillance	Alert and m-Marketing Campaigns	Localize

11.3.1　Reduce Business Process Cycle Time

These applications allow a task's critical information to be delivered to the user wirelessly when requested, resulting in a significant business process cycle-time reduction. For example, at Embassy Suites hotels, maintenance and housekeeping crews are equipped with mobile text messaging devices. Using a silent page, the front desk can inform the crew the location and nature of the repair without physically locating them (McGarvey, 2002b). Also, at the Las Vegas Four Seasons, customer food orders are wirelessly transmitted from the poolside to the kitchen (Terry, 2002). Yet another example where wireless systems have significantly enhanced efficiency involves Johns Hopkins Hospital where pharmacists use a wireless system for accessing critical information on clinical interventions, medication errors, adverse drug reactions, and prescription cost comparisons (Keane, 2002). Cost savings of over $1,000 a day, per pharmacist, have been reported as the system allows each pharmacist to perform an average of six more interventions a day.

11.3.2　Reduce Information Float

Getting the right information to the right persons at the right time has always been one of the top concerns of businesses. Wireless systems reduce information float by delivering needed and relevant information to field decision makers so that time-sensitive business decisions can be made on the spot. For example, at Carlson hotels, managers use Pocket PCs to access all the information they need to manage the properties in real-time. The wireless system compiles information from the hotel's various information systems and delivers it to the manager. This information ranges from how many minutes it takes room service to fill an order to the night's occupancy level. Equipped with such critical information, managers can quickly spot any problems or opportunities at their hotel and react to them (McGarvey, 2002b).

11.3.3 Enhance Service Quality

The wireless technology allows organizations to bring their services to where their customers are, hence a higher level of customer convenience and service quality can be achieved. For example, the Sheraton hotel in New Jersey is experimenting with a new wireless check-in technology in order to reduce the waiting time for guests during check-in and check-out (McGarvey, 2002b). Employees carrying wireless devices will be able to check guests in the lobby, parking area, meeting rooms, and any other hotel facilities. The system also allows a key to be issued at the time of check-in from a portable imprint device. This application offers the hotel guests a real and visible convenience. Industry analysts also predict a 25 percent annual growth rate for the sales of wireless point-of-sale (POS) terminals in the next few years.

11.3.4 Capture Information Electronically Anytime-Anywhere

Paper-based business processes often result in data reentry, repetitive tasks, increase in errors, and waste of human and natural resources. M-business applications allow data capture anywhere in the field and the ability to interact with the company headquarters in resolving problems and answering client questions. For example, consider the operating efficiencies achieved by many utility companies by virtue of employing wireless systems for maintenance inspectors. With a wireless infrastructure, maintenance inspectors can send in the repair request by checking a few boxes on the screens of their hand-held devices. A work request is automatically generated and dispatched to the repair technician. The new and improved process saves time, reduces errors, and leads to a quicker and more proactive maintenance approach (Kuchinskas, 2002). It is reported that due to these advantages, most utility companies expect to recuperate their costs on the mobile systems within 6 to 18 months.

11.3.5 Access Critical Information Anytime-Anywhere

M-business allows users to have access to critical information from anywhere at anytime resulting in greater abilities to seize business opportunities. Target opportunities of this type can be found in situations where a large portion of the workforce is geographically dispersed and highly mobile, and where rapid access to information creates competitive advantages and business opportunities. Producer Lloyds Insurance Company specializes in crop insurance. Since September 2001, it has equipped its field agents with laptops and a host of mobile devices to provide remote access to the company's Policy Administration & Services System (PASS) and Online Policy Update System (OPUS). This remote access has dramatically mobilized the field agents, which is a critical success factor for the insurance industry. This system allows the agents to get instant quotes, create policies in-the-field, prepare various insurance forms, and determine claim status. Such services effectively improve the agents' chance of closing a deal which would otherwise slip away. Some

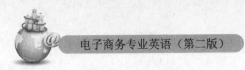

insurance companies project a 17 to 21 percent increase in annual revenue due to the implementation of such systems (Rachel, 2001).

11.3.6 React to Problems and Opportunities Anytime-Anywhere

Besides allowing user access to critical information from anywhere at anytime, some wireless systems let users react to the information. These innovative systems have changed the way businesses operate and the way employees work. Opportunities abound where resolving problems quickly and onsite avoids significant loss and shut down of operations, and where constantly changing conditions require close monitoring and quick reaction. A number of software companies offer wireless network management tools so that network managers can react to problems from any location (Yokomizo, 2002). These wireless network management tools are designed to remotely solve some of the most common problems that bring down corporate networks. The cost savings, convenience, and quick resolution to network problems these tools offer have enticed both large and small companies without an onsite IT crew.

11.3.7 Enhance Connectivity

It is well known that meaningful improvements in customer-firm communication result in enhanced customer loyalty. Wireless access allows customers to receive value-added services when they need them. Consequently, as the customer's dependence on the service increases, so does the cost of switching to another company. Gartner Group estimates that the percentage of North American banks that offer wireless services will increase from the current 5 percent to 29 percent by 2003. A number of banks, such as Citibank and Juniper Bank, send their customers alerts on balance level, bill payments, and check clearances. As customers get more and more comfortable with wireless security, many banks plan to offer wireless bill payments so that customers can act on the alerts (Fox, 2002). Brokerage firms like Fidelity Investments offer their customers stock quote alerts.

Opportunities for revenue-enhancement can also be found in situations where consumer awareness can be translated into sales. Marketers are seeking opportunities to convert cellular phones into an efficient advertising channel. In Europe, businesses are experimenting with sending short message to consumers' wireless devices to promote their products and services. Survey shows that most consumers in Europe and U.S. are willing to receive relevant advertisements via wireless communication (McDonough, 2002). In addition, businesses are using permission-based marketing to target the most receptive group of consumers without alienating them, while some companies, such as BTcellnet, are exploring consumers' reactions to non-opt-in advertisements. Marketers for companies like 20th Century Fox and Pepsi are using mobile games to entice consumers. Mobile games that can be easily played on the small screens of mobile devices increase interaction levels between business and consumer (Rendon, 2002a).

11.3.8 Increase Collaboration

Wireless systems are restructuring and improving relationships within organizations and between business partners. Information can be synchronized centrally and shared with every employee and business partner. Such systems result in more effective business processes. As Paul May indicated in his book, Mobile commerce, wireless collaboration tools will be especially useful in "outdoor" sectors such as architecture, construction, and engineering (ACE) projects (2001). Historically, the construction industry has struggled with the lack of coordination among many subcontractors collaborating on a project. When the right information and building materials are not in the right hands at the right time, it affects the builder's bottom line by wasting time and materials. A family of new mobile project management tools enables contractors to track project workflow and share information with subcontractors. With vital project information readily available via mobile devices, contractors and subcontractors can collaborate in an effective fashion. As a result, human errors are prevented and cost savings are significant (McGarvey, 2002a).

11.3.9 Increase Information Transparency to Improved Supply Chain

High levels of information transparency in the supply chain can be achieved with wireless systems. In some cases, supply chain parties gain timely information about orders and shipments. In other cases, the supply chain is totally revolutionized by new wireless technologies. The new wireless supply chain software allows business customers to access information regarding order status and inventory level, and also to execute transactions using a wide array of handheld devises (Nelson, 2000). This will soon become common practice in supply chain management enabling suppliers to build closer relationships with their customers. The Massachusetts Institute of Technology Auto ID Field Center is developing a globally standardized and low-cost radio frequency identification (RFID) technology. The new RFID has the potential to replace the Universal Product Code (UPC) on products as it can wirelessly provide all retail supply chain parties with real-time information about the location of a product. The RFID will improve the accuracy and speed of inventory management, and most importantly, it will significantly increase the information transparency between the retailer and the manufacturer. The right amount of the product can be supplied to the right place at the right time, thus reducing a retailer's loss in revenues resulting from out-of-stock products (Rendon, 2002b).

11.3.10 Track and Surveillance

By leveraging the location information, organizations that manage mobile assets are achieving unprecedented efficiency. These opportunities are abound in situations where the management of mobile assets is crucial to the success of the business. For example, in the trucking industry truck drivers depend on the global positioning systems (GPS) to determine the best route. These GPS based systems also provide the driver with information pertaining to the nearest restaurant, gas station, or a rest area. Furthermore, fleet managers at the headquarters can dispatch the mobile workforce more efficiently and react to any changes in the shipment since they know exactly where the shipment/truck is at any given moment. Consequently, customers can get a highly accurate status report of their shipments and can be informed of any schedule changes due to unexpected heavy

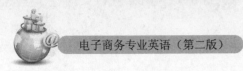

traffic or severe weather conditions. Overall, such wireless systems lead to efficient operations, better utilization of mobile workforce, and higher customer satisfaction (Stevens, 2001). Similar applications can be developed to track any mobile personnel and assets, control inventory, and manage supply chain.

11.3.11   Alert and M-Marketing Campaigns

For the U.S. Army, it is important to get real-time weather alerts to the field as weather conditions significantly impact the performance of weapon systems and personnel. Newly developed hand-held devices enable soldiers in the field to access real-time weather alerts and evaluate the effects of the weather on the mission. The vendor is also considering the possibility of combining this technology with the GPS systems so that the information can be automatically retrieved for the location of the mission (Sauter & Torres, 2002). The same can be done for businesses where location information is crucial. The nationwide implementation of the E911 Act will provide businesses and carriers with a new dimension of customer data-real-time location data. This capability will allow marketers to push relevant alerts and advertisements to the consumer when he or she is at a certain location. Businesses are seeking opportunities to leverage the location data to provide their customers with more targeted advertisements and enhanced services. Alert systems and m-marketing campaigns based on the customer's location are promising applications. Imagine getting an alert on your mobile phone that you have a prescription to pick up when you drive within a one-mile radius of the pharmacy. One day, a consumer may get a reminder on a mobile device that his or her car is due for an oil change and that there is an auto service shop 500 feet away that is running an oil change special. Experience gained by retailers suggests that location-based m-marketing campaigns are most effective for promoting last minute offers and attracting impulse buys.

11.3.12   Localize

Opportunities for localizing information on the fly can be found in situations where consumers in different geographic regions have significantly different needs; and where business opportunities may arise as location changes. Businesses have realized that consumers in different geographic areas respond to different product advertisements. Vert, a technology company, has found a way to integrate electronic billboards on top of taxicabs with the GPS system to create a more powerful promotional tool. Based on the location of the taxicab detected by the GPS system, the central server will wirelessly transmit electronic advertisements to be displayed on the top of the taxicab. The type of advertisements displayed depends on the information the company has about the area. This tool allows marketers to better target their customers (Schibsted, 2001).

New Words & Phrases

content delivery	内容分发	concierge	n. 委托代办
value perceptions	价值观念	posit	vt. 假定，设想，假设
pharmacist	n. 药剂师	proactive	adj. 前摄的，主动的

recuperate　vt. & vi. 恢复（健康、体力等）；复原　　in the field　在田野里，在实地

transparency　n. 透明（度），幻灯片　　non-opt-in　非选入

surveillance　n. 盯梢，监视

Abbreviations

POS (point-of-sale) 销售点

OPUS (Online Policy Update System) 在线正常更新系统

PASS (Policy Administration & Services System) 正常管理与服务系统

RFID (radio frequency identification) 无线电频率识别

GPS (global positioning systems) 全球定位系统

11.4　M-Business Technologies

Wireless technology refers to the hardware and software that allows transmission of information between devices without using physical connections. The successful delivery of m-business applications relies on the reliability and availability of wireless network technologies. Today's wireless network solutions include Wireless Personal Area Networks (WPANs), Wireless Local Area Networks (WLANs), and Wireless Wide Area Networks (WWANs). Each of these wireless network solutions serves its unique purpose and embodies an array of attendant technologies. With a wide range of mobile devices and multiple technical platforms coexisting, it is important to put all these in perspective. Table 11-2 summaries the attendant technologies for different types of wireless networks.

Table 11-2　Wireless networks and their attendant technologies

Wireless Networks	Attendant Technologies
WPANs	Line-of-sight infrared, radio frequency (RF), and Bluetooth
WLANs	Spread spectrum technology (802.11b), Orthogonal Frequency Division Multiplexing (802.11a and 802.11g), Infrared, and narrowband technology
WWANs	Analog cellular networks, digital cellular systems and Personal Communications System (PCS), Cellular Digital Packet Data (CDPD), Code Division Multiple Access (CDMA), Time Division Multiple Access (TDMA), Global System for Mobile Communications (GSM), General Packet Radio Service (GPRS), Enhanced Data Rates for GSM Evolution (EDGE), CDMA2000, W-CDMA, and satellites

Within personal areas (e.g., an office and an automobile), traditional wireless communication technology such as infrared can be found in devices ranging from remote controls to PDAs. One of this area's most promising new technologies is Bluetooth. Bluetooth is a global standard for wireless connectivity that was quickly adopted by many device manufacturers. It uses short range radio technology to connect small devices, such as laptops, PDAs, mice, and other peripheral devices, to each other and other networks. The technology has the potential to replace the cables that connect digital devices and offers users a higher level of freedom within their personal areas. The Bluetooth technology was especially designed for making ad hoc interactions between different devices in a heterogeneous computing environment easy. Its relatively high data transfer speed and extremely low power consumption have made it the ideal technology for many business situations.

Analogous to a traditional wired local area network (LAN), many organizations have adopted the Wi-Fi (e.g., IEEE802.11b) technology to provide wireless access to users within a local geographical area (e.g., a building, campus, airport, coffee shop, and hotel). According to a recent study, the market penetration of WLAN in the U.S. has reached 10 percent, and users have credited WLAN with attainment of convenience, flexibility, mobility, time saving, and productivity gains (Cisco Systems, 2001).

WLAN technologies allow both peer-to-peer communications between devices and point-to-multipoint communications through access points that cover a radius of 50-100 meters. The most widely adopted Wi-Fi standard today, IEEE802.11b, transmits data at the 2.4 GHz spectrum at a speed of 11 Mbps using direct sequence spread spectrum (DSSS). Recently, IEEE802.11a and IEEE802.11g have become commercially available. In contrast to IEEE802.11b, both IEEE802.11a and IEEE802.11g use orthogonal frequency division multiplexing (OFDM) and transmit data at the speed of 54 Mbps.

Today's WLAN technology still has its weaknesses. A recent investigation by Businessweek (Green, Rosenbush, Crockett, & Holmes, 2003) found that the challenges faced by Wi-Fi technology included unclear standards, spotty security, limited range, hidden costs, and lack of inter-operability. In addition to technical difficulties, it is still too early for organizations to determine the real return on investment (ROI) of WLAN and many organizations are seeing little usage of WLAN after its implementation.

Wireless wide area networks (WWAN) allow users to communicate and access resources within a wide geographical area such as a city, a region, an entire country, or even around the world. This achieved through the use of cellular networks and satellites. Throughout the history of wireless communications, several generations of cellular network technologies were developed, and different regions have adopted different, and sometimes incompatible, technology standards. While WWAN offers users unprecedented freedom and many m-business opportunities, in many regions, the absence of new generation cellular networks (2.5G or 3G) with high data transmission rates has impeded the growth of m-business. Furthermore, the incompatible regionally adopted technology standards have limited the globalization of m-business applications. Nevertheless, today, many innovative m-business applications are capable of providing value such as wireless banking, wireless stock trading, remote monitoring, and location-based wireless services.

WWAN technologies can be categorized by generation. Early generations of cellular networks were designed primarily for voice communication using circuit switching. Introduced in 1978, the first-generation (1G) cellular wireless networks were analog networks called Advanced Mobile Phone Systems (AMPS). Compared to newer generations of cellular technologies, AMPS networks were inefficient in the use of limited wireless spectrum and supported limited encryption and advanced services (Agrawal, Chari, & Sankar, 2003). These limitations prompted the development of the second-generation (2G) cellular wireless networks. The basic 2G technologies include Time Division Multiple Access (TDMA), Code Division Multiple Access (CDMA), and Global System for Mobile Communications (GSM). These technologies are widely used around the world today. GSM was adopted by most Asian and European countries, while CDMA, the building block for the 2.5G and third generation (3G) networks, was adopted in the U.S. Although a huge improvement over the 1G technologies, 2G cellular networks are voice-centric and circuit-switching. The data transmission rate of 2G networks was limited to 14.4kbps.

As the need for wireless data communication increased, newer generations of cellular technologies were designed to make data communication more efficient. 2.5G technologies, such as General Packet Radio Service (GPRS), CDMA 2000 1x, and Enhanced Data Rates for GSM Evolution (EDGE), offer data transmission rates of up to 384kbps. The 3G wireless networks offer broadband, packet-based transmission of multimedia data at a rate of up to 2Mbps for stationary users. The two most popular 3G cellular technologies are Wideband CDMA (W-CDMA) and CDMA 2000 3x.

Besides terrestrial cellular networks, satellites also provide support for WWAN. They are especially useful in remote locations where cellular services are sparse. Satellites are also crucial components of the global positioning system (GPS). Widely used in commercial devices today, GPS uses satellites to track the latitude, longitude, and altitude of a person or object using a technique called triangulation. While it is highly accurate, it is expensive to operate and does not work well indoor.

New Words & Phrases

attendant n. 随从，伴随物   infrared adj. 红外线的

spectrum n. 光谱，波谱，范围，系列

Bluetooth n. 蓝牙，一种无线通信的标准，蓝牙的目标是要提供一种通用的无线接口标准，用微波取代传统网络中错综复杂的电缆，在蓝牙设备间实现方便快捷、灵活安全、低成本低功耗的数据和话音通信

Abbreviations

WPAN (Wireless Personal Area Networks) 无线个人局域网

WLAN(Wireless Local Area Network) 无线局域网络

WWAN(Wireless Wide Area Network)无线广域网

WiFi (Wireless Fidelity) 基于 IEEE 802.11b 标准的无线局域网

DSSS(Direct Sequence Spread Spectrum) 直接序列展频

OFDM (orthogonal frequency division multiplexing) 正交频分复用

ROI(return on investment)投资回报

AMPS (Advanced Mobile Phone Systems) 高级移动电话服务

TDMA(Time Division Multiple Access) 时域多重访问系统

CDMA (Code Division Multiple Access) 码分多址

GSM(Global System for Mobile Communications) 全球移动通信系统

General Packet Radio Service (GPRS) 通用分组无线业务

11.5 M-Business vs. E-Business Applications

M-business applications are different from e-business applications in many aspects; therefore, developing m-business applications requires a different set of tools, techniques, and strategies. Most e-business applications cannot be readily transferred to the mobile platforms. When a company attempts to replicate their e-business success by simply moving its Web applications to a wireless environment, the environment often fails to provide the support the applications need to be successful or usable. To successfully move a Web application to a wireless environment, the scope of the application must be redefined, the user interface must be redesigned, and its network and processing requirements must be reassessed. To do this, developers need to start by understanding the differences between e-business and m-business applications.

Singhal, Alvinen, Bridgman, Bevis, Suryanarayana, Chan, Mauney, and Hild (2001) pointed out that m-business applications differed from e-business applications in three areas: device, network, and user. Table 11-3 summarizes some of these differences outlined by Singhal et al. (2001). The differences require developers to think creatively about how to deliver the benefits of m-business applications to users while addressing the constraints of client devices and wireless networks. At the same time, developers must also recognize the unique opportunities m-business applications present. For example, the personal nature of client devices (e.g., handsets and PDAs) allows applications to be more personalized and targeted; location identification technologies have created many new and exciting opportunities to provide context-based products and services; wireless networks make it possible to deliver timely information to users anytime anywhere.

Table 11-3 Differences between e-business applications and m-business applications

	E-Business Applications	M-Business Applications
Device	Monitor resolutions range from 640×480 to 1600×1200	Client devices have capable CPU and considerable memory
	Monitor displays hundreds to millions of colors	Vast majority of handset displays are gray-scale or support limited number of colors
	Keyboard and mouse are the primary input devices	Input methods (keypad and stylus) are laborious to use
	Client devices have capable CPU and considerable memory	Client devices have little processing power and memory
Network	Network speeds range from 28.8KB per second to more than 1MB per second	Data speeds range from less than 100 bits per second to 28.8KB per second
	Networks are stable	More latency, less connection stability and less predictable availability are expected from networks

cont.

	E-Business Applications	M-Business Applications
User	The user is likely to be computer literate	The user may not necessarily have any desktop computing experience
	The user may spend extended periods of time "surfing the net"	The user expects to complete the task within a few minutes
		The user tends to be engaged in other activities at the same time

The key to successful m-business applications is to have a good understanding of the values of m-business application and realistic expectations. Phatak (2001) suggested that the four steps to implement the right wireless applications for a company are:

1. Select an application where the return from providing mobile access will be high.

2. Throughout the development process, focus on the unique characteristics of mobile devices.

3. Select a development and integration partner with experience in both mobile and enterprise systems.

4. Keep in mind that handheld devices will become an even more compelling platform in the near future as the 3G technologies provide higher bandwidths and significant performance improvements.

New Words & Phrases

vs.   versus 对（比），比较   compelling   adj. 使人非注意不可的，必须接受的

11.6   Challenges in M-Business

As Patrick Brans pointed out in his book, Mobilize Your Enterprise, companies that do not consider mobilizing will be at a serious disadvantage in today's fast-paced business environment. Nevertheless, many obstacles that hinder the adoption of m-business still exist. These obstacles mainly include high costs of wireless mobile Internet access, concerns over privacy and security, device limitations, and the lack of global standards for wireless communication. Consumers and businesses have not embraced m-business as enthusiastically as previously predicted. As a result, the actual adoption of m-business has been much slower, especially in the U.S. and Europe. Based on the current adoption data, one source suggests that m-commerce will only account for 1.2 percent of total carrier revenues in 2006 (Luna, 2002). Many have also attributed much of the slow adoption to the slowdown in the U.S. and global economy in the recent years.

Still in its infancy, m-business needs to address many of the challenges that lie ahead. To better illustrate these challenges, Tarasewich, Nickerson, and Warkentin (2002) identified three dimensions of m-business issues: technical, application, and global issues. Managers as well as developers must take these issues into consideration while designing m-business solutions.

In order for m-business to continue to grow, technical issues such as device limitations, usability, standardization, and integration of different wireless technologies must be addressed. The m-business field is governed by a chaotic array of platforms, devices, and standards. Each device class differs tremendously from other classes in terms of screen resolution and button functions. Developing business applications for such a diverse group of client devices proves to be extremely difficult. Furthermore, the small screens of mobile devices and their limited input capabilities have created many design challenges. The miniaturization of mobile devices has resulted in many devices with screens that are too small to display any meaningful data. The limited data entry capabilities of mobile devices have also made m-business applications clumsy and hard to use. In addition, most devices are only useful in bandwidth-limited applications due to the low bandwidth and unreliability of wireless data services today.

Among the application-related issues, the most daunting challenges are identifying killer applications, maintaining data integrity, ensuring data security, and attending to legal and privacy issues. While most of the Internet security threats and privacy issues pervade m-business applications, m-business applications introduce new risks due to its mobility and communication medium, and managers and developers must be sensitive to these attributes when designing m-business solutions.

Global issues raise the question of what impact social, legal, and cultural characteristics of different nations will have on the globalization of m-business. Issues such as the lack of global standards, the disparity in wireless technology adoption, and global access-pricing variations must be addressed.

New Words & Phrases

enthusiastically adv. 热心地，狂热地   data integrity 数据完整性

disparity n. 不同，不等；不一致；悬殊

英文摘要的写作技巧

英文摘要（Abstract）的写作应用很广。不仅参加国际学术会议、向国际学术刊物投稿要写摘要，国内级别较高的学术期刊也要求附上英文摘要。学位论文更是如此。论文摘要是全文的精华，是对一项科学研究工作的总结，对研究目的、方法和研究结果的概括。

一、摘要的种类与特点

摘要主要有以下四种。

第一种是随同论文一起在学术刊物上发表的摘要。这种摘要置于主体部分之前，目的是让读者首先了解一下论文的内容，以便决定是否阅读全文。一般来说，这种摘要在全文完成之后写。字数限制在100～150字之间。内容包括研究目的、研究方法、研究结果和主要结论。

第二种是学术会议论文摘要。会议论文摘要往往在会议召开之前几个月撰写，目的是交给会议论文评审委员会评阅，从而决定是否能够录用。所以比第一种略为详细，长度在200～300字之间。会议论文摘要的开头有必要简单介绍一下研究课题的意义、目的、宗旨等。如果在写摘要时，研究工作尚未完成，全部研究结果还未得到，那么应在方法、目的、宗旨、假设等方面多花笔墨。

第三种为学位论文摘要。学士、硕士和博士论文摘要一般都要求用中、英文两种语言写。学位论文摘要

一般在 400 字左右，根据需要可以分为几个段落。内容一般包括研究背景、意义、主旨和目的；基本理论依据，基本假设；研究方法；研究结果；主要创新点；简短讨论。不同级别的学位论文摘要，要突出不同程度的创新之处，指出有何新的观点、见解或解决问题的新方法。

第四种是脱离原文而独立发表的摘要。这种摘要更应该具有独立性、自含性、完整性。读者无需阅读全文，便可以了解全文的主要内容。

二、摘要的内容与结构

摘要内容一般包括：

➢ 目的(objectives，purposes)：包括研究背景、范围、内容、要解决的问题及解决这一问题的重要性和意义。

➢ 方法(methods and materials)：包括材料、手段和过程。

➢ 结果与简短讨论(results and discussions)：包括数据与分析。

➢ 结论(conclusions)：主要结论，研究的价值和意义等。

概括地说，摘要必须回答"研究什么"、"怎么研究"、"得到了什么结果"、"结果说明了什么"等问题。

无论哪种摘要，语言特点和文体风格也都相同。首先必须符合格式规范。第二，语言必须规范通顺，准确得体，用词要确切、恰如其分，而且要避免非通用的符号、缩略语、生偏词。另外，摘要的语气要客观，不要做出言过其实的结论。

三、学术期刊论文摘要

清华大学学报（自然科学版）就如何写好科技论文英文摘要、提高 EI 收录率，概括了论文摘要的写作规则，值得一读：

1. 摘要的目的

摘要是论文的梗概，提供论文的实质性内容的知识。摘要的目的在于：给读者关于文献内容的足够的信息，使读者决定是否要获得论文。

2. 摘要的要素

1）目的——研究、研制、调查等的前提、目的和任务，所涉及的主题范围。

2）方法——所用的原理、理论、条件、对象、材料、工艺、结构、手段、装备、程序等。

3）结果——实验的、研究的结果、数据，被确定的关系，观察结果，得到的效果、性能等。

4）结论——结果的分析、研究、比较、评价、应用，提出的问题等。

3. 摘要的篇幅

摘要的篇幅取决于论文的类型。但无论哪一种论文，都不能超过 150 单词。可采用以下方法使摘要达到最小篇幅：

1）摘要中第一句的开头部分，不要与论文标题重复。

2）把背景信息删去，或减到最少。

3）只限于新的信息。过去的研究应删去或减到最小。

4）不应包含作者将来的计划。

5）不应包含不属于摘要的说法，如："本文所描述的工作，属于……首创"，"本文所描述的工作，目前尚未见报道"，"本文所描述的工作，是对于先前最新研究的一个改进"等。

6）相同的信息不要重复表达。如 at a temperature of 250 ℃ to 300 ℃，应改为 at 250~300℃；at a high pressure of 1.2 Mpa，应改为 at 1.2 Mpa。

7）以量的国际单位符号表示物理量单位（例如，以"kg"代替"kilogram"）。

8）以标准简化方法表示英文通用词（以"NY"代替"New York"）。

9）删去不必要的短语，如："A method is described"，"In this work"，"It is reported that"，"This paper is concerned with"，"Extensive investigations show that"等。

4. 摘要的英文写作风格

要写好英文摘要，就要完全地遵从通行的公认的英文摘要写作规范。其要点如下：

1）句子完整、清晰、简洁。

2）用简单句。为避免单调，改变句子的长度和句子的结构。

3）用过去时态描述作者的工作，因它是过去所做的。但是，用现在时态描述所做的结论。

4）避免使用动词的名词形式。如：

正："Thickness of plastic sheet was measured"

误："measurement of thickness of plastic sheet was made"

5）正确地使用冠词，既应避免多加冠词，也应避免蹩脚地省略冠词。如：

正："Pressure is a function of the temperature"

误："The pressure is a function of the temperature"

正："The refinery operates …"

误："Refinery operates…"

6）使用长的、连串的形容词、名词、或形容词加名词来修饰名词。为打破这种状态，可使用介词短语，或用连字符连接名词词组中的名词，形成修饰单元。例如：

应写为"The chlorine-containing propylene-based polymer of high melt index"

而不写为"The chlorine containing high melt index-propylene based polymer"

7）使用短的、简单的、具体的、熟悉的词。不使用华丽的词藻。

8）使用主动语态而不使用被动语态，"A exceeds B"读起来要好于"B is exceeded by A"。使用主动语态还有助于避免过多地使用类似于"is"，"was"，"are"和"were"这样的弱动词。

9）构成句子时，动词应靠近主语。避免形如以下的句子：

"The decolorization in solutions of the pigment in dioxane, which were exposed to 10 hr of UV irradiation, was no longer irreversible."

改进的句子，应当是：

"When the pigment was dissolved in dioxane, decolorization was irreversible, after 10 hr of UV irradiation."

10）避免使用那些既不说明问题，又没有任何含意的短语。例如： "specially designed or formulated"，"The author discusses"，"The author studied" 应删去。

11）不使用俚语、非英语的句子，慎用行话和口语，不使用电报体。

5. 学术期刊论文摘要实例

Optimization of Electromagnetic Devices
Using Intelligent Simulated Annealing Algorithm

Abstract—Intelligent simulated annealing algorithm for the optimal design of electromagnetic devices is presented in this paper.[目的] The algorithm is implemented by assembling fuzzy inference into improved simulated annealing algorithm, which makes SA algorithm has the ability to reject infeasible solutions prior to objective function computation.[方法，结论] The algorithm is applied to the optimal design of a brushless dc motor and about 60 percents CPU time of SA can be saved.[结果] —— IEEE Transactions on Magnetics, September 1998

四、学位论文摘要

学位论文摘要也叫内容提要（summary）。一般单独占一页，装订在学位论文目录之前。这种摘要也是介绍研究背景、内容、目的、方法、结果等。但是，学位论文摘要与科技论文摘要的不同之处是，它必须指出研究结果的独到之处或创新点。关于研究的内容也可以稍加详细介绍，摘要的长度一般在 400 字左右。如有必要，可以分为几个段落。学位论文摘要可以分以下四步写。

开头部分可以先介绍一下研究的背景、宗旨、意义，提出问题，说明解决某一问题的必要性或重要性等。

第二步介绍本研究的目的、范围。

第三步介绍论文的主要内容。

最后对研究的主要内容，特别是新创造、新突破、新见解或新方法加以概括总结。当然，不同级别的学位论文(学士、硕士、博士)，对创新性的衡量标准是不同的。

下面给出了一篇硕士学位论文摘要（略有改动），供读者参考。

E-Commerce and E-Payment System

The thesis makes analysis and research upon the payment system of e-commerce, especially upon e-cash, one of the means of electronic payment. With reference to other cash system, it proposes its own off-line divisible and anonymous e-cash system. The above-mentioned system put sophisticated calculation section of the ordinary e-cash system into e-license phase and use advanced OSS blind signature system in the phase of cash, thus it is less complicated, much safer and easily applied compared with other system. The thesis is composed of three parts: firstly, a brief introduction and analysis over e-commerce; secondly, narration upon the security problems of e-commerce and e-payment, citing knowledge on cryptology; thirdly, also the important section, bringing forward a new system after thoroughly studying and analyzing e-cash.

Keywords: e-commerce, e-cash, data encryption technology, blind signature, cut&choose protocol

电子商务和电子支付体制

本文对电子商务（e-commerce）中的支付系统进行了分析和研究，特别是对作为电子支付手段之一的电子现金（e-cash）做了深入的分析和研究，并结合其它现金体制提出了一种新的离线、可分、匿名和电子现金体制。该体制把一般现金体制中计算复杂度较高的部分放到电子凭证阶段，而在获得电子现金阶段使用了改进的 OSS 盲签名体制，这样使得整个体制的复杂度降低，安全性提高，实现起来方便、简单。文章的内容包含三个部分：第一部分是对电子商务的介绍和分析，第二部分结合密码学知识论述了电子商务和电子支付中的安全问题，最后一部分，也就是该文的重点，对电子现金进行了重点研究和分析，并提出了一种新的体制。

关键词：切割-选择协议　盲签名　数据加密技术　电子现金　电子商务

Exercises

I. Answer the following questions

1. Define what is m-business.

2. Describe the benefits of m-business applications to businesses and consumers.

3. Identify the major differences between e-business and m-business applications.

4. How can a developer address the constraints and unique features of mobile client devices during the development process?

5. What are the disadvantages of wireless LANs compared to wired LANs?

II. Read literatures in professional periodicals and try to write abstract

III. Questions and discussion

1. Identify a problem at work that can be solved using m-business applications.

2. Discuss the impact of Wi-Fi technology on businesses and consumers.

3. Outline the obstacles for m-business adoption. Discuss which obstacle will prove to be the most difficult to overcome.

Chapter 12   Launching a Successful Online Business and EC Projects

在在线市场获得成功并非易事。虚拟空间的风险和不确定性加上缺乏经验导致了在线企业很高的失败率。创业者建立一个盈利的在线企业都需要注意哪些问题？如何实现向电子商务企业转型？如何建设网站以及开设网上店面？这些都是值得我们关注的问题。

学习指导

通过本章学习，读者应掌握以下内容并能够用英语表达：
- 创办在线企业所需的基本要求。
- 启动以及投资于一家新的电子商务企业或大型电子商务项目的流程。
- 网站建设的步骤。
- 如何开设网上店面。

12.1   Starting a New Online Business

Success in the online marketplace is never an assured outcome. As in the brick-and-mortar marketplace, the failure rate for online companies is high. Why do so few online companies succeed while many others fail? What does the entrepreneur need to know to launch a profitable online business?

Online businesses may be pure-play companies or click-and-mortar companies that add online projects, such as e-procurement or selling online, as additional marketing channels.

12.1.1   Creating a New Company or Adding an Online Project

Most new businesses—brick-and-mortar, pure play, or click-and-mortar—begin in a similar manner. The following three steps describe the process:

Step 1: Identify a consumer or business need in the marketplace. Many businesses simply begin with a good idea. A magazine article, a personal observation, an unsolved problem, a small irritation, or a friend's suggestion may trigger an idea, and the prospective business owner sees a gap between what people want and what is available.

Step 2: Investigate the opportunity. Just because a person perceives that an opportunity exists does not mean that it is real. Perhaps the potential number of individuals interested in purchasing the product or service is too small. Perhaps the cost of manufacturing, marketing, and distributing the product or providing the service is too large. The revenue model may be wrong, others may have tried already and failed, satisfactory substitute products may be available, and so on. For example, online grocery shopping would seem like a wonderful opportunity—relieving busy professionals of the time-consuming and tiresome task of regular visits to a grocery store. Many have tried to provide large- and small-scale online grocery ventures, but most have failed or continue to lose money because they misjudged the logistical problems associated with grocery warehousing and delivery. This is why it is so important to develop a business plan. One of the purposes of a business plan is to determine the feasibility and viability of a business opportunity in the marketplace.

Step 3: Determine the business owner's ability to meet the need. Assuming that a realistic business opportunity exists, does the prospective business owner have the ability to convert the opportunity into success? Some personal qualities are important: Is the business in an industry the prospective business owner knows well? Is it something the entrepreneur loves doing? Are family and friends supportive? Business skills in staff recruitment, management, negotiation, marketing, and financial management are required, as well as entrepreneurial attitudes such as innovation, risk taking, and being proactive. Many good ideas and realistic initiatives have failed in the execution stage because the owners or principals of the business lacked sufficient business skills to make it a reality.

The process for developing EC projects in existing companies is similar, except that step 3 changes to: "Determine the organization's ability to meet the need."

Beyond these general platitudes about what it takes to start any prosperous business, the owner of an online business must consider some requirements that reflect the online nature of the business. The first of these is the need to understand Internet culture. Activities such as spam, extensive use of graphics, forced visitor registration, and intrusive pop-up browser windows are counter to the accepted norms of behavior on the Internet. Businesses that ignore the cultural and behavioral norms of the Internet do so at their peril. A second requirement that the owner of an online business must consider is the nature of appropriate products and services. Although virtually anything is available for sale on the Internet, the degree of sales success is somewhat dependent on the type of item or service being offered. For example, digitized products (e.g., information, music, software) sell well and are delivered easily. Similarly, services (e.g., stock brokering, travel ticket sales) and commodities (e.g., books, CDs) also have been quite successful. In contrast, experiential products, such as expensive clothes, do not sell well. One of the greatest opportunities the Internet offers is in niche marketing. Rare and quirky sales ideas, such as gadgets for left-handed individuals (anythingleft-handed.co.uk), toys for cats and dogs (cattoys.com), would rarely succeed in a physical storefront, but the Internet offers the owners of these sites an opportunity to pursue their business idea and be successful.

12.1.2　Online Business Planning

Online business planning is similar to any start-up planning. It includes two components: the business plan and the business case.

（1）The Business Plan

Every new online business needs at least an informal business plan. A business plan is a written document that identifies a company's goals and outlines how the company intends to achieve those goals and at what cost. A business plan includes both strategic elements (e.g., mission statement, business model, value proposition, and competitive positioning statement) and operational elements (e.g., operations plan, financial statements) of how a new business intends to do business. Medium and large businesses, as well as those seeking external funding, must have a formal business plan.

The primary reason an entrepreneur writes a business plan is to use it to acquire funding from a bank, an angel investor, a venture capitalist, or the financial markets. Similarly, in an existing business a business case needs to be written for any new large EC project, so management can decide whether to fund it. A business plan also is important for a new venture as a tool to recruit senior management and to convince business partners to make a commitment to the business. A business plan helps ensure a thriving business by encouraging an entrepreneur to set goals, anticipate problems, set measures for success, and keep the business on track after starting it. A business plan forces the entrepreneur to be realistic about the business's prospects. Sometimes the most successful outcome of a business plan is a decision not to proceed.

（2）The Business Case

An existing brick-and-mortar business looking to move online (either to add EC projects or to transform itself into an e-business) also needs a business case—a document that is used to justify the investment of internal, organizational resources in a specific application or project. A business case for a large, resource-intensive EC project resembles a business plan. For a small or medium-size project, the business case can be much simpler.

12.1.3   Funding a New Online Business

Launching an online business can be expensive. The brave entrepreneur usually is willing to invest personal funds from savings, personal lines of credit, or from a second house mortgage; however, these sources of "bootstrap funding" are unlikely to be enough.

The new venture involves significant risk, so some traditional sources of debt financing, such as a bank loan, are difficult or impossible to get. What are other sources of funding for a start-up?

（1）First Round of Initial Funding: Angel Investors and Incubators

When the entrepreneur's personal funds are insufficient, the entrepreneur will go to friends, family members, or to angel investors. An angel investor is a wealthy individual who contributes personal funds and possibly expertise at the earliest stage of business development. Angel investors can be found through organizations such as the Angel Capital Association (angelcapitalassociation.org).

Another important source of support is an incubator. An incubator is a company, university, or nonprofit organization that supports promising businesses in their initial stages of development. Although some incubators offer start-up funding, the primary purpose of most incubators is to offer a variety of support services—office space, accounting services, group purchasing schemes, reception services, coaching, and information technology consulting—at little or no cost. In return, the incubator receives a modest fee, equity in the company, or both.

（2）Second Round of Financing: Venture Capital

One major source of funding during the dot-com boom was venture capital. Venture capital (VC) is money invested in a business by an individual, a group of individuals (venture capitalists), or a funding company in exchange for equity in the business.

Venture capitalists tend to invest in companies that have identified what seems to be an outstanding business opportunity, have taken some action to make the opportunity happen, and need an infusion of funds and management expertise to expand and launch the business.

It is important to match your VC with your business. Venture capitalists usually invest large sums of money and expect in return some management control and a profit on their investment within 3 to 5 years when the successful start-up goes public (an IPO) or a larger company merges with it or acquires it. The start-up receives the funds and experienced management guidance it needs during its launch and expansion stages.

The downside for the start-up to acquire VC is minimal; it loses some control over the business in return for funds it is unlikely to acquire from any other source. The more difficult problem is finding VC. Due to the many dot-com failures in 2000 and onward, many VC sources have disappeared, and competition for venture capital is fierce.

（3）Additional Funding: A Large Partner

As part of a VC investment or after the depletion of VC money, one or more large companies may step into the process. For example, Yahoo!, IBM, Microsoft, Motorola, Google, and Oracle have invested in hundreds of EC startups.

Such investments are frequently done in complementary or competing areas. For example, News Corp. acquired MySpace.com; and Google has invested in dozens of companies related to advertisement, including YouTube in 2006.

（4）The IPO

Once the company is well known and successful, it will go to a stock exchange to raise money via an initial public offer (IPO). In such offerings, investors will pay a much larger amount of money per share than that paid by the initial and secondary funding source, sometimes 5 or 10 times more per share.

New Words & Phrases

launch v. 开办，创办	entrepreneur n. 企业家，创业者
pure-play company 纯在线公司	brick-and-mortar company 传统实体公司
e-procurement n. 电子采购	distribute v. 分销
revenue model 收入模式	viability n. 生存力，活力
spam n. 垃圾邮件	pop-up adj. 弹出的
experiential product 经验性产品	niche marketing 利基营销
business plan 商业计划	business case 商业论证
competitive position 竞争能力	Angel Investor 天使投资者
venture capitalist 风险资本家	venture n. 冒险事业，创立新企业
lines of credit n. 信用贷款的最高限额	Angel Capital Association 天使投资协会
promising adj. 有希望的，有前途的	merge v. 合并，并入
stock exchange n. 证券交易所	make a commitment to 对……作出承诺
click-and-mortar company "鼠标加水泥"公司，指网上与传统业务兼有的公司	

Abbreviations

VC（venture capital）风险资本   IPO(Initial Public Offerings) 首次公开募股

Notes

1. Online businesses may be pure-play companies or click-and-mortar companies that add online projects, such as e-procurement or selling online, as additional marketing channels. 在线企业可以是纯网络公司或是增加了在线项目(如电子采购或在线销售)作为其额外的营销渠道的网上与传统业务兼有的公司。

2. The downside for the start-up to acquire VC is minimal; it loses some control over the business in return for funds it is unlikely to acquire from any other source. 创业企业获得风险资本的弊端是较小的，创业企业损失对公司的控制来获得不太可能从其它渠道获得的资金。

12.2　Adding E-Commerce Initiatives or Transforming to an E-Business

Creating an e-business start-up certainly is exciting, but it also is very risky. As with any other business, the failure rate is very high. However, in cyberspace the risks and uncertainties, plus lack of experience, result in an even higher rate of failure. Nevertheless, thousands of new online businesses have been created since 1995, mostly small ones. A much more common option is adding one or several EC initiatives to an existing business.

12.2.1　Adding Initiatives to an Existing Business

Almost all medium-to-large organizations have added or plan to add EC initiatives to the existing business. The most common additions are:

（1）A storefront.

Adding an online sales channel is common in both B2C and B2B. The required investment is fairly low because storefront hosting is available from many vendors. Customers like the option of buying online, and gradually more of them will use the storefront. You can build a storefront fairly quickly, and the damage in case of failure may not be too large. Because the required investment is not large, it may not be necessary to expend the time and money in developing a formal business case. This is a practical strategy for an SME. For a large-scale storefront, a company will need to follow the steps suggested in Section 12.1, especially the preparation of a business case, in order to secure internal funding and the blessing of top management.

（2）A portal.

There are several types of corporate portals. Almost all companies today have one or several portals that they use for external and/or internal collaboration and communication. Adding a portal (or several portals) may be a necessity, and it may not be preceded by a formal business case. Issues of content and design, as well as security, are of utmost importance. Because many vendors offer portal-building services, vendor selection may be an important issue.

（3）E-procurement.

E-procurement frequently requires a business plan and extensive integration (both internally and externally), so an EC architecture must be in place.

（4）Auctions and reverse auctions.

Large corporations need to consider building their own auction or reverse auction sites. Although forward auctions can be added to a storefront at a reasonable cost, a reverse auction usually requires more integration with business partners and, consequently, a larger investment and a business case.

12.2.2　Transformation to an E-Business

As the brick-and-mortar organization implements more EC projects, it becomes a click-and-mortar organization and eventually an e-business. Being an e-business does not imply that the organization is a pure online company, it just means that it conducts as many processes as possible online. A rapid or large-scale change from brick-and-mortar to e-business involves organizational transformation.

（1）What is Organizational Transformation?

Organizational transformation is a comprehensive concept that implies a major organizational change. According to McKay and Marshall (2004), a transformation is not only a major change, but also a sharp break from the past. The key points in understanding organizational transformation are as follows:

• The organization's ways of thinking and vision will fundamentally change.

• There will be revolutionary changes to the process and context involved in creating a new organizational vision and rethinking business models and business strategy.

• The change must involve a substantial break from previous ways of acting. It will likely involve discovering and developing new opportunities and new ways of doing things.

• The change must permeate through and impact on the behavior of a majority of organizational members.

• The change will involve creating new systems, procedures, and structures that not only enable and dictate how new processes function, but that will also impact on the deeply embedded business models and understandings that drive the organization.

An e-business transformation is not solely about technology. Technologies must be integrated with possible changes in business strategy, processes, organizational culture, and infrastructure.

（2）How an Organization Can Be Transformed into an E-Business

Transforming an organization, especially a large company, into an e-business can be a very complex endeavor. For an organization to transform itself into an e-business, it must transform several major processes, such as procurement, sales, CRM, and manufacturing, as well as deal with change management.

（3）Software Tools for Facilitating Transformation into E-Business

Several vendors offer methodologies and tools to facilitate transformation into e-business. A methodology developed by Northrup Grumman includes a framework for e-strategy, solution development and deployment, a guide for organizational change, a framework for project management, and a systematic approach to quality management.

（4）Change Management

Transforming an existing business into an e-business or adding a major e-commerce initiative means a manager must change business processes and the manner in which people work, communicate, and are promoted and managed. According to Ash and Burn (2006), this requires systematic attention to learning processes, organizational culture, technology infrastructure, people's thinking, and systems.

New Words & Phrases

storefront	n. 店头，店面	large-scale	adj. 大规模的
secure	v. 得到	blessing	n. 批准；同意
forward auction	正向拍卖	reverse auction	逆向拍卖，反向拍卖
comprehensive	adj. 全面的，广泛的	major	adj. 较大的，较多的
sharp	adj. 强烈的，急剧的	substantial	adj. 实质的
permeate	v. 渗透，渗过	integrate with…	与……结合
infrastructure	n. 基本设施	endeavor	n. 努力，尽力
methodology	n. 方法学，一套方法	deployment	n. 展开，部署

Abbreviations

SME（Small and medium enterprise） 中小企业

Notes

1. For an organization to transform itself into an e-business, it must transform several major processes, such as procurement, sales, CRM, and manufacturing, as well as deal with change management. 一个想要转变为电子商务企业的组织必须转变主要的流程，比如采购、销售、客户关系管理以及制造流程，而且还要做好变革管理。

12.3   Building a Web Site

Every online business needs a Web site. A Web site is the primary way any firm doing business on the Internet advertises its products or services and attracts customers. Many Web sites also sell products and services, and businesses with digital products usually deliver their products via the Web site as well. The Web site may be a storefront, a portal, an auction site, and so on.

Assuming that a business has completed the preparatory work of business formation, writing a business plan, deciding what type of site they want to build, and acquiring initial funding, the process of building a Web site is as follows:

Step 1: Select a Web host. One of the first decisions that an online business will face is where to locate the Web site on the Internet. The Web site may be included in a virtual shopping mall, such as activeplaza.com, or hosted in a collection of independent storefronts, as at Yahoo! (smallbusiness.yahoo.com), amazon.com, or ebay.com (even if you do not do auctions). However, many medium-size and large businesses will build a stand-alone Web site either with an independent hosting service or through self-hosting arrangements.

Step 2: Register a domain name. Nearly concurrent with the selection of a Web host will be the domain name decision. Selecting a domain name is an important marketing and branding consideration for any business. The domain name will be the business's online address, and it provides an opportunity to create an identity for the business.

Step 3: Create and manage content. The Web site also needs content—the text, images, sound, and video that deliver the information that site visitors need and expect. Content can come from a variety of sources, but getting the right content in place, making it easy for viewers to find, delivering it effectively, and managing content so it remains accurate and up-to-date are crucial to the success of the online business.

Step 4: Design the Web site. This is the critically important and creative part of the process that determines what the site will look like (e.g., color schemes, graphics, typography) and how visitors will use it (e.g., information architecture, navigation design). Mall or storefront businesses may have limited options, but the design choices for the stand-alone Web site are nearly unlimited. Successful Web site design is about meeting customer expectations. Design starts with identifying customer needs, expectations, and problems. Then a site is designed to meet those needs and expectations or to solve the customers' problems. Table 12-1 presents a list of important Web site design criteria, with relevant questions.

Table 12-1　Web Site Design Criteria

Navigation	Is it easy for visitors to find their way around the site? Does the site comply with the three-click rule?
Consistency	Are design elements, especially look and feel, consistent across all pages? Will the Web site and contents appear the same on all visitors' screens?
Response time	How long does it take for the page to appear? Does the site comply with the 12-second rule (download)? With the 4-second rule (upload)?
Appearance	Is the site aesthetically pleasing? Are the colors pleasant? Does the site's look and feel express the company's desired image? Is the site easy to read, easy to navigate, and easy to understand?
Quality assurance	Do the site's calculators, navigation links, visitor registration processes, search tools, etc., work properly?
Availability	Are all dead links fixed promptly or removed? Is the site available for full service 24 hours a day, 7 days a week?
Interactivity	Does the site encourage the visitor to play an active role in learning about the business's products or services? Are all appropriate contact details available on the Web site so that visitors can submit feedback and ask questions?
Content	How much multimedia? How timely and relevant is the content? Is it easy to read? Informative?

cont.

Usability	How easy is it to use the site? How easy is it to learn the site?
Security	Is customer information protected? Does the customer feel safe in actions such as submitting credit card information?
Scalability	Does the site design provide a seamless path for enhancements or upgrades in the future?

Step 5: Construct the Web site and test. Businesses must also decide whether to design and construct the Web site internally, contract it out to a Web design firm, or some combination of both. When the business owners are satisfied with the Web site, it is transferred to the Web site host. At this point, the Web site is open for business, but it requires final testing to ensure that all the links work and that the processes function as expected (e.g., acceptance of credit cards).

Step 6: Market and promote the Web site. At this stage, the business promotes the location, or URL, of the Web site widely on products, business cards, letters, and promotional materials. A business can use any of the advertising strategies—banner exchanges, e-mail, chat rooms, viral marketing, or other methods. Another key strategy for attracting customers is increased visibility via search engine optimization. Search engine optimization (SEO) is the application of strategies intended to position a Web site at the top of Web search engines' results such as Google, AllTheWeb, and Teoma. Search engines are the primary way many Web users find relevant Web sites; an online business cannot ignore SEO strategies. The strategies to optimize a Web site's ranking in search engines should be part of content creation, Web site design, and site construction. Optimizing search engine rankings through keyword placement and link building is much easier, less time consuming, and less expensive if it is integrated into the Web site development process.

New Words & Phrases

storefront　n. 店头，店面
a collection of　一些，一批
in place　在适当的位置
color schemes　配色方案
navigation　n. 航海，导航
aesthetically　adv. 审美地，美学观点上地
seamless　adj. 无缝的
link　n. 链接
viral marketing　病毒营销
three-click rule　三次点击原则，是指网站用户在寻找任何信息时都不应该超过三次鼠标点击

preparatory　adj. 预备的
concurrent　adj. 并发的，一致的
template　n. 模板
typography　排版，版面，排版式样
consistency　n. 一致性
scalability　n. 可扩展性
contract out　立约把……包出
banner　n. 旗帜广告
ranking　n. 排名

Abbreviations

SEO（search engine optimization）　搜索引擎优化

1. Content can come from a variety of sources, but getting the right content in place, making it easy for viewers to find, delivering it effectively, and managing content so it remains accurate and up-to-date are crucial to the success of the online business. 内容可以从各种不同的来源获得，但让合适的内容放在合适的位置，让访问者方便查找内容，高效地传递内容以及管理内容使之准确及时则是在线企业成功的关键。

12.4　Opening a Web Storefront

The most common EC project on the Internet is the storefront. Millions of storefronts exist on the Internet, mostly those of small businesses. However, large corporations, as well as many individuals, including students and even children, have storefronts as well. Storefronts appear in all different shapes, and their construction and operating expenses vary greatly.

Storefronts can be acquired in several ways:

（1）Build them from scratch.

Pioneering storefronts, such as hothothot.com, wine.com, and amazon.com, built their stores from scratch. Specifically, they designed them and then hired programmers to program all the necessary software. The major advantage of this approach is that the site owner can customize the site to his or her liking. The disadvantages are that the process is slow, expensive, and error prone and requires constant maintenance. Consequently, only large corporations build their storefronts from scratch today.

（2）Build them from components.

This option is faster and less expensive than the first one. The site owner purchases off-the-shelf components (or sometimes obtains them for free), such as a shopping cart, an e-catalog, and a payment gate, and then assembles them. The site owner can replace the components if they become obsolete; therefore, the site owner can save on maintenance. The downside is that the resulting site might not fit the online business owner's needs very well. This approach allows for adapting the application design to the specific needs of the business and for differentiating the storefront from those of the competitors. This approach, however, is usually more costly than building from templates and may take longer. In addition, it usually requires some in-house technical expertise for installation of the required hardware and software as well as for continued operation and maintenance.

（3）Build with templates.

Several vendors provide storebuilding templates. Some provide them free, free for 30 days, or for a nominal monthly fee that includes hosting the site on their servers. Using this approach is especially attractive to small businesses because the cost is relatively low (usually $10 to $99 per month), the business can construct the store in one or a few days, and it does not require extensive programming skills. The site owner basically fills out forms and attaches pictures. Another major benefit of this approach is that hosting is usually provided, as well as support services, such as payment collection, shipments, and security. Furthermore, the vendor will take care of all software maintenance. Finally, and perhaps most important, if the site owner uses a vendor such as Yahoo!, eBay, or Amazon.com, the site will be included in these vendors' e-marketplace, which provides a great deal of exposure. The downside of this approach is that it limits the site owner to the available templates and tools. However, some vendors provide a professional version that allows customization. The following are just a few of the many vendors that provide templates:

- Yahoo! Small Business and Yahoo! Merchant
- eBay (Prostores)
- Hostway (hostway.com)
- GoEmerchant.com
- StoreFront (storefront.net)
- 1and1.com
- Shopping.com
- ShoppingCartsPlus.com
- MonsterCommerce (monstercommerce.com)
- Amazon.com

New Words & Phrases

from scratch 从零开始	error prone 易于出错的
maintenance n. 维护，保持	off-the-shelf adj. 成品的
obsolete adj. 陈旧的，过时的	save on 节省
allow for 虑及，体谅	in-house adj. 内部的
nominal adj. 微不足道的，不重要的	programming n. 节目的计划，编制程序
collection n. 托收，收款	

Notes

1. This approach allows for adapting the application design to the specific needs of the business and for differentiating the storefront from those of the competitors. 这种方法考虑到了调整应用设计来满足企业具体的需要以及与竞争对手的店面差异化。

Reading Materials——Akamai Technologies

An Internet company decided to name itself after a Hawaiian word that means "intelligent, clever, or cool"—Akamai. And indeed, the company has created a clever product. Let's explain.

As user interest in high-speed Internet connections has grown, demand for bandwidth-heavy applications and media also has begun to surge. Paul Kagen Associates estimated that revenues from streaming media services will total $1.5 billion by 2002 and $21 billion by 2008 (as reported at Three Squared Inc. 2000). Finally, Accustream iMedia Research reported that the streaming video market grew to over $25 billion in 2006 (reported by Internet Marketing Newswatch 2007).

However, user connection speeds are only part of the streaming media picture. How will the networks handle the

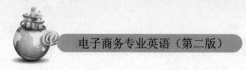

influx of bandwidth-chewing material? With a growing number of users and an abundance of rich media, the Internet is becoming extremely congested. Network traffic control is needed. Akamai and its competitors (Digital Island, Ibeam, and Mirror Image) are stepping in to manage Internet traffic.

Akamai products act as Internet traffic cops by using complicated mathematical algorithms to speed Web pages from the closest Akamai-owned server to a customer's location, thereby passing through fewer router hops. This process also helps to eliminate Internet gridlock. Today, caching and content distribution are the only practical ways to reduce network delay.

How does it work? To provide the service, Akamai maintains a global network of over 20,000 servers in 71 countries (in 2007) and leases space on them to giant portals, such as Yahoo! and CNN. These sites use the servers to store graphic-rich information closer to Internet users' computers in order to circumvent Web traffic jams and enable faster page loads; therefore, reducing delivery time to the users by 20 percent to 30 percent. If a company's Web server is in Germany and a user in the United States visits the Web site, the multimedia content of the site has to be transmitted halfway around the globe.

Akamai's FreeFlow technology speeds the delivery of images, multimedia, and other Web content by placing that content on servers worldwide. Using the FreeFlow Launcher, Web site designers "Akamaize" their sites by marking content for delivery using the Akamai network. FreeFlow takes this content and stores it on Akamai Web servers around the world. When a user visits a Web site that has been "Akamaized," the images and multimedia content are downloaded from an Akamai server near the user for faster content delivery. Akamai allows customer data to move to and from big Web sites through its global network for a fee.

Unfortunately, the service is not 100 percent reliable. The speed for the end user depends on how many people are using the user's LAN at any given point in time and also on the speed of the server downloading any given Web site. A number of competing technologies are trying to provide the same solutions, and only a limited number of large companies that use lots of rich media are willing to pay for the service.

In 2001, Akamai started to diversify, offering a comprehensive suite of content delivery, streaming audio and video, traffic management, and other services, such as dynamic page view, bundled in a package called EdgeAdvantage. Akamai and its competitors were losing money in early 2001, but their revenues were increasing rapidly. By January 2008, the company had 25,000 servers in 69 countries, storing data for its worldwide clientele (Junnarkar 2003; Akamai 2008).

One advantage of using Akamai or a similar service is the added security. For example, on June 15, 2004, a hacker attacked some of Akamai's major clients, including Microsoft, Google, and Apple using a DoS attack (see Chapter 10). Within minutes, Akamai deleted the attacks and solved the problem (Fogarty 2005). According to Pallis and Vakali, Akamai controls 80 percent of the content delivery networks.

New Words & Phrases

surge   v. 汹涌，涌现   influx   n. 流入，注入，涌进
congest   vt. 使充满，使拥塞，充满   gridlock   n. 拥塞，停滞
circumvent   vt. 防止，避免

英文论文引言的写作技巧

学术论文中的引言（Introduction）是对全文内容和结构的总体勾画。引言尽管不像摘要那样有一定的篇幅限制和相对固定的格式，但在内容和结构模式上也有需要遵循的规律。

一、引言的内容与结构布局

引言的主要任务是向读者勾勒出全文的基本内容和轮廓。它可以包括以下五项内容中的全部或其中几项：

➢ 介绍某研究领域的背景、意义、发展状况、目前的水平等；

➢ 对相关领域的文献进行回顾和综述，包括前人的研究成果，已经解决的问题，并适当加以评价或比较；

➢ 指出前人尚未解决的问题，留下的技术空白，也可以提出新问题、解决这些新问题的新方法、新思路，从而引出自己研究课题的动机与意义；

➢ 说明自己研究课题的目的；

➢ 概括论文的主要内容，或勾勒其大体轮廓。

如何合理安排以上这些内容，将它们有条有理地给读者描绘清楚，并非容易之事。经验告诉我们，引言其实是全文最难写的一部分。这是因为作者对有关学科领域的熟悉程度，作者的知识是渊博、还是贫乏，研究的意义何在、价值如何等问题，都在引言的字里行间得以充分体现。

我们可以将引言的内容分为三到四个层次来安排：

第一层由研究背景、意义、发展状况等内容组成，其中还包括某一研究领域的文献综述；

1）Introducing the general research area including its background, importance, and present level of development

2）Reviewing previous research in this area

第二层提出目前尚未解决的问题或急需解决的问题，从而引出自己的研究动机与意义；

Indicating the problem that has not been solved by previous research, raising a relevant question

第三层说明自己研究的具体目的与内容；

Specifying the purpose of your research

最后是引言的结尾，可以介绍一下论文的组成部分。

1）Announcing your major findings

2）Outlining the contents of your paper

值得注意的是，引言中各个层次所占的篇幅可以有很大差别。这一点与摘要大不一样，摘要中的目的、方法、结果、结论四项内容各自所占的篇幅大体比例一样。而在引言中，第一个层次往往占去大部分篇幅。对研究背景和目前的研究状况进行较为详细的介绍。研究目的可能会比较简短。

引言与摘要还有一点不同的是，摘要中必须把主要研究结果列出，而在引言中（如果摘要与正文一同登出）结果则可以省略不写，这是因为正文中专门有一节写结果（results），不必在引言中重复。

下面这段引言的例子摘自一篇关于混合电动汽车的研究论文，大部分篇幅介绍研究背景。

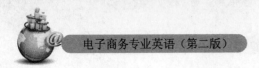

A Hybrid Internal Combustion Engine/Battery Electric Passenger Car for Petroleum Displacement

I. Forster and J. R. Bumby

INTRODUCTION

The finite nature of the world's oil resources and the general concern about automobile emissions（排放） have prompted the adoption of energy conservation policies and emphasized the need to transfer energy demand from oil to other sources of energy, such as natural gas, coal and nuclear. A transfer of energy from oil to electricity can be achieved to a limited extent in the road transport sector by the increased use of electric vehicle. However, such vehicles are limited in range due to the amount of energy that can he realistically stored on-board（在车上） the vehicle without affecting payload（有效载荷）. As a consequence of this, electric vehicles must he used in situations where daily usage is well defined, for example, in urban delivery duty. Indeed, it has been in such vehicles as the urban milk delivery vehicles that electric traction drives have been traditionally applied with a great deal of success. Currently the demand is for urban electric vehicles to he developed with greater traffic compatibility in terms of speed and range.

Although urban delivery vehicle applications will help to reduce the dependence of the road transport sector on petroleum-based fuels, the major part of this market requires vehicles that are not limited in range and have a performance compatible with internal combustion（内燃机）, i.e. engine vehicles. The use of advanced traction battery technology to overcome the range limitation of electric vehicles is one possible solution. However, this would still result in a vehicle limited in range and may in itself create additional problems. For example, due to the much greater on-board stored energy, the charging time required will be greater than at present. The range limitations of the pure electric vehicle can be overcome by using a hybrid i.e. engine/electric drive which incorporates both an i.e. engine and an electric traction system. Although such a vehicle can be designed to meet a number of objectives, it has been argued that a vehicle which seeks to remove the range limitation of the electric vehicle while substituting a substantial amount of petroleum fuel by electrical energy is the vehicle most worth pursuing. With the emphasis of the vehicle design on the electric drive train, the intention may be to operate in an all-electric mode under urban conditions and to use the i.e. engine for long-distance motorway driving. The hybrid mode could then he used for extending urban range and/or improving vehicle accelerative performance on accelerator kick-down. The concept of a hybrid electric vehicle capable of substituting petroleum fuel is' not new, Bosch and Volkswagen(大众汽车)having built vehicles in the 1970s. More recently, the advent of the Electric and Hybrid Vehicle Research, Development and Demonstration Program in the United States of America initiated the design and construction of a Near Term Hybrid Vehicle (NTHV) with the principal aim of substituting petroleum fuel by ' wall plug' electricity. As part of the NTHV program, a large number of conceptual studies were conducted but on vehicles aimed at the American passenger car market. In this paper optimization studies were conducted, but now on a vehicle suitable for the European medium-sized passenger car market. Such optimization studies are important as, with two sources of traction power available, the way in which they are controlled, and their relative sizing, is fundamental to the way the vehicle performs. Before examining in detail the optimum control strategy for the drive train, Section 2 defines the hybrid arrangement under study. A description of the optimization process using an appropriate cost function is then presented in Section 3 followed by a method of translating the resulting control structure into a sub-optimum algorithm capable of being implemented in real time. Using the optimum control structure the effect of component ratings on the vehicle's performance is evaluated in Section 4, while Section 5 discusses the practical implementation of an overall vehicle control algorithm. Finally, in Section 6, an indication of the vehicle's potential for substituting petroleum fuel by electricity is given.

分析：第一层（第 1～5 段）：介绍混合电动汽车的研究背景、意义、目前的发展水平，需要解决的问题等。第 1 段：指出混合电动汽车的研究背景。世界石油资源的有限性及人们对汽车排放问题的广泛关注使得能源转换问题尤为重要。第 2 段：使用电动汽车能够从某种程度上实现能源转换。但问题是电动汽车的续驶里程比内燃机车短。所以目前要解决的问题是提高电动汽车的速度和连续行驶里程。第 3 段：市场要求电动汽车的续驶里程及工作性能与内燃机汽车媲美，但是，即使先进电池可以提高电动汽车的续驶里程，但还会有一些问题不能解决。第 4 段：续驶里程可以通过使用混合电动汽车来提高。混合电动汽车上既装有内燃机，又装有电动驱动系统，在必要时使用其中一种系统。第 5 段：回顾并评述前人关于混合电动汽车的研究成果。第二层（第 6 段第 1 句话）：指出前人研究的范围具有局限性。关于混合电动汽车的研究只针对美国市场。针对欧洲市场的研究还是空白。第三层（In this paper）本文的研究目的及意义：对欧洲中型客车市场进行优化研究。第四层为第 7 段：本文的组成部分及各部分的主要内容。

比较简短的论文，引言也可以相对比较简短。为了缩短篇幅，可以用一两句话简单介绍一下某研究领域的重要性、意义或需要解决的问题等。接着对文献进行回顾。然后介绍自己的研究动机、目的和主要内容。至于研究方法、研究结果及论文的组成部分则可以完全省略。

二、如何写引言的开头

引言开头（即第一层）最主要目的是告诉读者论文所涉及的研究领域及其意义是什么，研究要解决什么问题，目前状况或水平如何。也就是说，开头要回答如下问题：

What is the subject of the research?

What is the importance of this subject?

How is the research going at present?

In what way is it important, interesting, and worth studying?

What problem does the research solve?

引言的开头常用句型有：

句型 1：研究主题+谓语动词 be…

例: Fuel cell（燃料电池）is a technology for the clean and efficient conversion from chemical energy in fossil fuels to electricity.

句型 2：研究主题+ has become …

例：Semiconductor based industry （基于半导体的工业）has be come the largest industry for the USA and it has influenced every other industry and every aspect of human life.

句型 3：研究主题+ 被动语态

例：b. Air pollution has been extensively studied in recent years.

句型 4：Recently, there has been growing interest in / concern about + 研究主题

例：In the 1990s there has been growing interest in the development of electric vehicles in response to the public demand for cleaner air.

句型 5：Recently there have / has been extensive / increasing /numerous publications / literature / reporting on + 研究领域

例：There has been increasing reporting about forest decline in North America.

句型 6：Researchers have become increasingly interested in +研究领域

或:Researchers have recently focused their attention on +研究领域

Researchers are recently paying more attention to + 研究领域

例：Researchers have become more interested in environmental indicators.

三、如何写文献综述

文献综述是学术论文的重要组成部分，是作者对他人在某研究领域所做的工作和研究成果的总结与评述，包括他人有代表性的观点或理论、发明发现、解决问题的方法等。在援引他人的研究成果时，必须标注出处，即这一研究成果由何人在何时何地公开发表。

1. 文献出处的标注

引用文献时，不同的学科或领域可能采用各自约定俗成的体系或格式。在写论文时，应该了解自己学科采用的固定格式。目前最常见的体系有两种，一种是作者+出版年体系，另一种是顺序编码体系。下面对这两种体系分别加以介绍。

第一种体系的主要框架模式如下：

模式 1：作者(年代)十谓语动词主动语态+研究内容／成果

例：Hanson et al. (1976) noted that oak mortality and decline were associated with drought and insects throughout a multi-state region of the mid-west.

模式 2：研究内容／成果+谓语动词被动语态+（作者年代）

例：Success at this Science Day was found to be linked to parental support (Czemiak 1996).

模式 3：It has been 十谓语动词被动语态+by 作者（年代）+that 从句

或：It has been+谓语动词被动语态+that 从句（作者年代）

研究内容／成果+谓语动词被动语态+by 作者（年代）

例：It was found by Czemiak (1996) that success at this Science Day was linked to parental support.

如果引用的文献有两个以上的作者，只标明第一作者，后面用拉丁文 et al 表示，意思是"等人"、"其他人"。

如果在综述中涉及几个项目或文献时，则将这些文献并列标注，必要时用逗号隔开。标注参考文献另一种常见体系是按文献出现的先后顺序编号，置于方括号中，标在指引部分的右上角。被引用的作者、文献名、出版时间、地点等列入论文后面的参考文献中。其顺序要与正文中标注的顺序一致。

2. 文献综述中的动词运用技巧

（1）两类动词

从例中我们可以发现，文献综述中常用 state， note，observe，discuss，establish，find，present 等动词。这些动词有两种特性，一种是描述性动词，客观地向读者介绍他人的工作；另一种是评价性动词，在一定程度上代表了作者对他人的工作的理解、解释或态度。文献综述中常用的描述性动词有：describe，discuss，explain，examine，present，state 等。常见的评价性动词有：affirm，allege，argue，assume，claim，imply，maintain，presume，reveal，suggest 等。

（2）动词时态

文献综述中最常见的时态是一般现在时、一般过去时和现在完成时三种时态。使用不同的动词时态会给句子的意义带来变化，基本原则如下：

原则 1：当作者引用某人过去某个时间所做过的某一项具体的研究时，用一般过去时。如：It was found that

success at this Science Day was linked to parental support (Czemiak 1996)···

原则 2：在概括或总结某一研究领域里所做过的一些研究时，用现在完成时。

原则 3：在谈及目前的知识水平、技术水平或存在的问题时，用一般现在时态。

四、如何写研究动机与目的

在介绍了他人在某领域的工作和成果之后，下一步便介绍作者自己的研究动机、目的与内容。介绍研究动机可以从两个角度入手，一是指出前人尚未解决的问题或知识的空白，二是说明解决这一问题，或填补知识空白的重要意义。

主要句型有：

句型 1：用表示否定意义的词例 little，few，no 或 none of+名词作主语，表示"在特定的范围中还没有······"的意思，由此来暗示知识的空白部分。如：

However, there exists little research on science fair projects.

句型 2：用表示对照的句型。如：

a. The research has tended to focus on···, rather than on···

b. These studies have emphasized···, as opposed to···

c. Although considerable research has been devoted to···, rather less attention has been paid to···

d. Although there is much hope that three-dimensional coupled models will lead to better understanding of the factors that control hurricane intensity and to increased reliability of hurricane intensity forecasts, the present generation of models may not have enough horizontal resolution to capture the full intensity of extreme storms.

句型 3：提出问题或假设。如：

a. However, it remains unclear whether···

b. It would thus be of interest to learn how···

c. If these results could be confirmed, they would provide strong evidence for ···

d. These findings suggest that this treatment might not be so effective when applied to···

e. It would seem, therefore, that further investigations are needed in order to···

指出或暗示了知识领域里的空白，或提出了问题或假设之后，下一步理所当然应该告诉读者本研究的目的和内容，要解决哪些问题，以填补上述空白，或者证明所提出的假设。如何写摘要中的目的部分。这里只略举几例：

a. The aim of the present paper is to give ···

b. This paper reports on the results obtained···

c. In this paper we give preliminary results for···

d. The main purpose of the experiment reported here was to···

e. This study was designed to evaluate···

f. The present work extends the use of the last model by···

g. We now report the interaction between···

h. The primary focus of this paper is on···

i. The aim of this investigation was to test···

j. It is the purpose of the present paper to provide···

从暗示知识的空白到本研究的目的与内容一般需要用一些过度词，以提示一下读者。如上面这些例句中，用了 this paper，here，the present work，now，this investigation，the present paper 等词或词组。为了引起读者的注意，这些词或词组一般放在句首。

如果一项研究、一篇论文不止一个目的，应该按目的的主次排列顺序，并用连接词或词组。常见的连接词还有 additionally, in addition to this, besides this, also, not only…but also…, further, furthermore, moreover 等

五、如何写引言的结尾

研究目的完全可以作为引言的结尾。也可以简单介绍一下文章的结构及每一部分的主要内容，从而起到画龙点睛的作用，使读者了解文章的轮廓和脉络。

至于研究结果，在引言中完全可以不写。研究结果是结论部分最主要的组成部分。下面的例子是引言的结尾，介绍文章的结构。

…Before examining in detail the optimum control strategy for the drive train, Section 2 defines the hybrid arrangement under study. A description of the optimization process using an appropriate cost function is then presented in Section 3 followed by a method of translating the resulting control structure into a sub-optimum algorithm capable of being implemented in real time. Using the optimum control structure the effect of component ratings on the vehicle's performance is evaluated in Section 4, while Section 5 discusses the practical implementation of an overall vehicle control algorithm. Finally, in Section 6, an indication of the vehicle's potential for substituting petroleum fuel by electricity is given.

在介绍全文的结构时，要避免使用同一个句型结构，如，Sections l describes…Section2 analyses…Section3 discusses…Section 4 summarizes…这样，每句话用同样的词开头，句型结构显得单调、枯燥乏味。

Exercises

I. True or False

1. One of the purposes of a business plan is to determine the feasibility and viability of a business opportunity in the marketplace.

2．Although virtually anything is available for sale on the Internet, the degree of sales success is somewhat dependent on the type of item or service being offered.

3．A business plan is a document that is used to justify the investment of internal, organizational resources in a specific application or project.

4. Creating an e-business start-up is exciting, and the failure rate is very low.

5. Sometimes the most successful outcome of a business plan is a decision not to proceed.

II. Fill the blanks

1. E-procurement frequently requires_____ and extensive integration (both internally and externally), so _____ must be in place.

2. Nearly concurrent with the selection of a Web host will be the _____ decision.

3. _____ is the application of strategies intended to position a Web site at the top of Web search engines' results.

4. Although forward auctions can be added to a storefront at a reasonable cost, _____ usually requires more integration with business partners and, consequently, a larger investment and a business case.

III. Answer the following questions

1. What is a business case?
2. Which EC initiatives are brick-and-mortar organizations most likely to add?
3. List the major characteristics (key points) of organizational transformation.
4. List eight criteria used to judge Web site design.

IV. Questions and discussion

1. What services does Akamai provide?
2. What is the company's revenue model?
3. What are the service's limitations?

V. Form two teams, a client team and a Web design team. After suitable preparation, both teams meet for their first Web site planning meeting. Afterward, both teams critique their own and the other team's performance in the meeting.

Chapter 13　Building E-Commerce Applications and Infrastructure

创办一个成功的电子商务网站是每个企业所希望的，如何才能实现这个愿望呢？本章将向读者阐述创建电子商务网站的步骤和如何管理电子商务等内容。通过本章的学习，读者应该了解以下内容:

- 五步法开发电子商务项目。
- 如何选择开发方法。
- 销售商和软件的选择。
- 电子商务网站的使用情况分析和网站的管理。

学习指导

13.1　A Five-Step Approach to Developing an E-Commerce Landscape

A well-developed Web site not only adds to the value of the product or service being offered; it also enhances the worth of the company. Therefore, it is important that a firm choose the correct development strategy in order to obtain the greatest return on its investment. The diversity of e-business models and applications, which vary in size from small stores to global exchanges, requires a variety of development methodologies and approaches.

For example, small storefronts with a few key components can be developed with HTML, Java, or another programming language. They also can be implemented with commercial packages, leased from an application service provider (ASP), or purchased from a site builder. Larger or special EC applications can be developed in-house or outsourced. Building medium to large applications requires extensive integration with existing information systems, such as corporate databases, intranets, enterprise resource planning (ERP), and other application programs. Therefore, although the process of building EC systems can vary, in many cases, it tends to follow a fairly standard format.

The traditional system development life cycle (SDLC) systematically leads developers through six analysis and design stages: problem identification, analysis, logical design, physical design, implementation, and maintenance. The SDLC is the basis for development of the majority of traditional business systems. However, innovative new software and hardware are enabling a move to a more streamlined approach to e-commerce development. Figure 13-1 shows the five major steps needed to develop a typical e-commerce application.

STEP 1: IDENTIFYING, JUSTIFYING, AND PLANNING EC SYSTEMS

EC applications, like all other information systems, are usually built to enable one or more business processes. Consequently, their planning must be aligned with that of the organization's overall business plan and the specific processes involved. Always remember that existing processes may need to be restructured to take full advantage of the benefits of the supporting IT. Furthermore, each application must be carefully analyzed, using different methods, such as the methodology, to ensure that it will have the needed functionality to meet the requirements of the business processes and the users and that its benefits will justify its cost. Both of these activities may be complex, but they are necessary, especially for systems that require high investment to acquire, operate, and maintain. This first step is typically performed in-house (with consultants if needed). All other steps can be completed either in-house or outsourced.

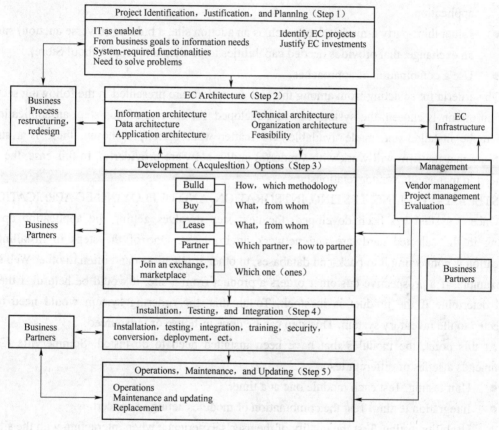

Figure 13-1　The EC Applications Development Process

STEP 2: CREATING AN EC ARCHITECTURE

An EC architecture is a plan for organizing the underlying infrastructure and applications of a site. The plan specifies the following:

- Information and data required to fulfill the business goals and vision.
- Application modules that will deliver and manage the information and data.
- Specific hardware and software on which the application modules will run.
- Necessary security, scalability, and reliability required by the applications.
- Human resources and procedures for implementing the architecture.

STEP 3: SELECTING A DEVELOPMENT OPTION

EC applications can be developed through several alternative approaches. The major options are:

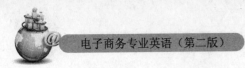

- Build the system in-house.
- Have a vendor build a customized system.
- Buy an existing application and install it, with or without modifications, by yourself or through a vendor.
- Lease standard software from an application service provider (ASP), lease as a service (SaaS), or lease via utility computing.
- Enter into a partnership or alliance that will enable the company to use someone else's application.
- Join a third-party e-marketplace, such as an auction site, a bidding (reverse auction) site, or an exchange, that provides needed capabilities to participants (e.g., Yahoo! Store).
- Use a combination of approaches.

The criteria for selecting from among the various options are presented in the following section. Once an option is chosen, the system can be developed. At the end of this step, an application is ready to be installed and made available. No matter what option is chosen, there is a strong possibility that the firm will work with vendor(s) and/or software provider(s). In this case, the firm will need to manage its vendor relationships.

STEP 4: INSTALLING, TESTING, INTEGRATION, AND DEPLOYING EC APPLICATIONS

Once a system has been developed, the next step involves getting the application up and running in the selected hardware and network environment. One of the steps in installing an application is connecting it to back-end databases, to other applications, and often to other Web sites. For example, if a prospective customer orders a product from a site, it would be helpful if the site could determine if the product is in stock. To do this, the ordering system would need to be connected to the inventory system. This step can be done in-house or outsourced.

At this point, the modules that have been installed need to be tested. Sommerville (2004) recommends a series of different tests:

- Unit testing. Test each module one at a time.
- Integration testing. Test the combination of modules acting in concert.
- Usability testing. Test the quality of the user's experience when interacting with the site.
- Acceptance testing. Determine whether the site meets the firm's original business objectives and vision.

Once all the Web site applications pass all of the tests, they can be made available to the end users. At this stage, issues such as conversion strategies, training, and resistance to change may need to be addressed.

STEP 5: OPERATIONS, MAINTENANCE, AND UPDATING

It usually takes as much time, effort, and money to operate and maintain a site as it does to build and install it in the first place. To enjoy continual usage, a site needs to be updated continually. For example, at a B2C site new products need to be added to the catalog, prices need to be changed, and new promotions need to be run. These changes and updates need to undergo the same testing procedures used during the installation process. Additionally, usage patterns and performance need to be studied to determine which parts of the underlying applications should be modified or eliminated from the site.

MANAGING THE DEVELOPMENT PROCESS

The development process can be fairly complex and must be managed properly. For medium-to-large applications, a project team is usually created to manage the process and the vendors. Collaboration with business partners also is critical. For example, a firm can install a superb e-procurement system, but if its vendors will not use it properly the system will collapse. Projects can be managed with project management software. Best practice management also includes periodic evaluations of system performance. Standard project management techniques and tools are useful for this task. Finally, do not rule out the possibility that implementing an EC project may require restructuring one or more business processes.

New Words & Phrases

diversity   n. 多样化；多样性

in-house   adj. 内部的   adv. 内部地

integration   n. 结合；整合；一体化

systematically   adv. 系统地，有系统地

align with 与……结盟

consultant   n. 顾问

scalability   n. 可量测性，可扩展性

criteria   n. 标准

back-end   n. 后端

inventory   n. 详细目录，存货清单

e-procurement 电子采购

methodology   n. 一套方法，方法学，方法论

outsource   vt. 外购，外包（工程）

intranet   n. 内联网

consequently   adv. 所以，因此

restructure   vt. 重建，改建，重组

module   n. 单元，单位

utility   n. 公用事业，功用，效用

deploy   vt. 使展开；施展；部署

prospective   adj. 预期的；未来的；可能的

acting in concert 一致行动，合谋

rule out 排除……的可能性；用直线划掉

Abbreviations

ASP (application service provider) 应用服务提供商

ERP (enterprise resource planning) 企业资源计划

SDLC (systems development life cycle) 系统开发生命周期

SaaS (software as a service) 软件服务化，软件即服务

Notes

1. It usually takes as much time, effort, and money to operate and maintain a site as it does to build and install it in the first place. 本句译为："通常要花费和起初创建、安装一样多的时间、努力和金钱去运转和维护网站。"

13.2 Criteria for Selecting a Development Approach

Regardless of the complexity of the site, three basic options for developing an EC Web site are available: (1) develop the site in-house, either from scratch or with off-the-shelf components; (2) buy a packaged application designed for a particular type of EC site; or (3) lease the application from a third party.

If a company decides to buy or lease an EC application, the following representative selection criteria need to be considered:

- Flexibility. Commercial packages need to be modified or adapted to the specific requirements of an application. Therefore, it is important to evaluate the extent to which a package can be adapted and the willingness of the vendor to perform or support the adaptation.

- Information requirements. The selected package should satisfy the information requirements of the EC application under development. Information collection, storage, and retrieval capabilities and the database structure should be examined carefully.

- User friendliness. User friendliness is especially important for B2C, G2C, and some B2B sites. In these cases, if an application is difficult for the average visitor or customer to use, then it will have an immediate impact on its use.

- Hardware and software resources. The computer type (e.g., desktop, laptop, mainframe) and the operating system (e.g.,Windows, LINUX, Mac) required by the package must be compatible with the existing platform. The CPU and storage requirements must also be compatible with existing specifications or easily accommodated.

- Installation. The installation effort required to implement the package is another important consideration. Some packages are complex, and their installation requires extensive consultation. The installation process may also take a considerable amount of time and expertise.

- Maintenance services. Because EC application requirements are changing constantly, ongoing maintenance is required. It is important to consider how often the package needs to be updated and whether the vendor provides assistance for its maintenance.

- Vendor quality and track record. It is less risky to acquire an EC package from a vendor who has a good reputation and track record than from one with a less-than-stellar or unknown reputation.

- Estimating costs. The costs of EC projects are usually difficult to assess and often underestimated. In addition to the obvious costs associated with EC development, it also is important to factor in the costs of installation, integration, customization, training, and maintenance.

- Personnel. Staffing requirements should be planned for in advance to ensure that the organization has the appropriate human resources for systems development (in the case of in-house development), implementation, operation, and maintenance. Currently, it is difficult to recruit and retain IT personnel with appropriate knowledge and experience in EC application development. Special expertise acquired from external consultants can be expensive.

- Technological evolution. Planning ahead for technological evolution facilitates the upgrade of EC applications and enables the organization to adopt innovations more quickly than the competition. Given the rapid pace of IT evolution, it is sometimes preferable to develop EC applications incrementally to take advantage of the latest developments in the technology.

- Scaling. System scalability refers to how big a system can grow in various dimensions to provide more service. Scalability can be measured in several ways, including the total number of users, the number of simultaneous users, and the transaction volume. These dimensions are not independent because scaling up the size of the system in one dimension can affect the other dimensions.

- Sizing. The required size and performance of an application are difficult to predict because the growth of the user population of certain EC applications is hard to anticipate. Overloading the application decreases performance. For regular IT applications, deterioration in performance may affect productivity and user satisfaction; for EC applications, it could result in a major loss of business.

- Performance. System performance is a critical factor for business success, particularly when the system is used for EC. In addition to convenience, good performance also brings customers and competitive advantages. Performance is measured by two main metrics: latency and throughput. Latency measures the time required to complete an operation such as downloading a Web page. Throughput measures the number of operations completed in a given period of time. Throughput and latency are interrelated. An increase in either measure directly affects the other.

- Reliability. Reliability is an essential requirement for a successful system. System failures and downtime are costly. When an EC application fails, business is interrupted; at best, the company loses sales; at worst, it loses customers. System reliability can be enhanced through the use of backup systems.

- Security. Security is critical to the adoption and diffusion of EC. Data and information flow in EC, as well as stored data, may include private and/or proprietary information. Thus, a selected package must meet strict security requirements. Systems, communication, and data security must be addressed early in the design of EC applications, not after their implementation. In addition to technological solutions such as firewalls and encryption, physical and procedural security measures must also be enforced.

New Words & Phrases

from scratch 从头做起，从零开始

compatible　adj. 可以并存的，相容的，协调的

reputation　n. 名气，名声，名誉

evolution　n. 演变；进化；发展

predict　v. 预言；预测；预示

off-the-shelf 现货供应

ongoing　adj. 前进的；进行的

less-than-stellar 并非大成功

simultaneous　adj. 同时发生的；同时存在的

anticipate　vt. 预感，期望，先于……行动

deterioration	n. 变坏，堕落；衰退	metrics	n. 韵律学，作诗法，度量
latency	n. 潜伏，反应时间	throughput	n. 生产量，生产能力，吞吐量
downtime	n. 停工期	backup	n. 替代物；支援人员，后备
diffusion	n. 传播，普及	proprietary adj. 私有的

Notes

1. Therefore, it is important to evaluate the extent to which a package can be adapted and the willingness of the vendor to perform or support the adaptation. 本句译为："评价软件包能够适应以及销售商执行或支持这种改变的意愿的程度是很重要的。"

13.3　Vendor and Software Selection

Few organizations, especially SMEs, have the time, financial resources, or technical expertise required to develop today's complex e-business systems. This means that most EC applications are built with hardware, software, hosting services, and development expertise provided by outside vendors. Thus, a major aspect of developing an EC application revolves around the selection and management of these vendors and their software offerings. Martin et al. identified six steps in selecting a software vendor and a package, as illustrated in Figure 13-2.

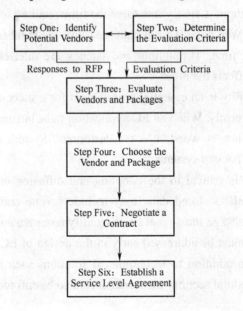

Figure 13-2　The Process of Selecting a Software Vendor and an EC Package

STEP 1: IDENTIFY POTENTIAL VENDORS

Potential vendors can be identified from software catalogs, lists provided by hardware vendors, technical and trade journals, consultants experienced in the application area, peers in other companies, and Web searches. These sources often yield so many vendors and packages that one must use some preliminary evaluation criteria to eliminate all but a few of the most promising ones from further consideration. For example, one can eliminate vendors that are too small or that have no track record or that have a questionable reputation. Also, packages may be eliminated if they do not have the required features or will not work with available hardware or the operating system, communication network, or database management software.

STEP 2: DETERMINE THE EVALUATION CRITERIA

The most difficult and crucial task in evaluating a vendor and a packaged system is to determine a weighted set of detailed criteria for choosing the best vendor and package. Some areas in which detailed criteria should be developed are vendor characteristics, functional requirements of the system, technical requirements the software must satisfy, the amount and quality of documentation provided, and vendor support of the package.

These criteria should be documented in a request for proposal (RFP), which is sent to potential vendors to invite them to submit a proposal describing their software package and how it would meet the company's needs. The RFP provides the vendors with information about the objectives and requirements of the system, the environment in which the system will be used, the general criteria that will be used to evaluate the proposals, and the conditions for submitting proposals. It may also request a list of current users of the package who may be contacted.

STEP 3: EVALUATE VENDORS AND PACKAGES

Vendor responses to an RFP generate massive volumes of information that must be evaluated to determine the gaps between the company's needs and the capabilities of the vendors and their application packages. Often, the vendors and packages are given an overall score by assigning an importance weight to each of the criteria, ranking the vendors on each of the weighted criteria and then multiplying the ranks by the associated weights. A short list of potential suppliers can be chosen from those vendors and packages with the highest overall scores.

STEP 4: CHOOSE THE VENDOR AND PACKAGE

Once a short list has been prepared, negotiations can begin with vendors to determine how their packages might be modified to remove any discrepancies with the company's desired EC application. Thus, one of the most important factors in the decision is the additional development effort that may be required to tailor the system to the company's needs or at least to integrate it into the company's environment. Additionally, the opinions of the users who will work with the system and the IT personnel who will have to support the system must be considered.

STEP 5: NEGOTIATE A CONTRACT

The contract with the software vendor is very important. Not only does it specify the price of the software, but also it determines the type and amount of support to be provided by the vendor. The contract will be the only recourse if the system or the vendor does not perform as specified. Furthermore, if the vendor is modifying the software to tailor it to the company's needs, the contract must include detailed specifications of the modifications. Also, the contract should describe in detail the acceptance tests the software package must pass.

Contracts are legal documents, and they can be quite tricky. Experienced contract negotiators and legal assistance may be needed.

STEP 6: ESTABLISH A SERVICE LEVEL AGREEMENT

Service level agreements (SLAs) are formal agreements regarding the division of work between a company and its vendors. Such divisions are based on a set of agreed-upon milestones, quality checks, "what-if " situations, how checks will be made, and what is to be done in case of disputes. If the vendor is to meet its objectives of installing EC applications, it must develop and deliver support services to meet these objectives. An effective approach to managing SLAs must achieve both facilitation and coordination. SLAs do this by (1) defining the partners' responsibilities, (2) providing a framework for designing support services, and (3) allowing the company to retain as much control as possible over their own systems.

New Words & Phrases

revolve   v.（使）旋转，细想   preliminary   adj. 初步的，开端的 n. 准备工作，初步行动
promising   adj. 有希望的，有前途的   weighted   adj. 有利的；加重的；加权的；受力的
discrepancy   n. 差异，不符合（之处）；   tailor   n. 裁缝 v. 裁制，调整使适应
dispute   n. 辩论，争端，争执 v. 辩论；争论

Abbreviations

SME（Small Medium Enterprise）中小企业   RFP（request for proposal）投标申请书
SLA（Service level agreement） 服务水平协议，服务等级协议，服务品质协议

Notes

1. Vendor responses to an RFP generate massive volumes of information that must be evaluated to determine the gaps between the company's needs and the capabilities of the vendors and their application packages. 句中"that"引导定语从句，用来修饰"information"。本句译为："销售商会给出大量的信息以对投标申请书做出回应，这些信息要被评估以确定公司的需求和销售商及他们的应用软件包的能力之间的差距。"

13.4   Usage Analysis and Site Management

To improve EC Web sites, it is advisable to monitor what customers are doing there (usage analysis). Both B2C and B2B Web sites require a thorough understanding of the usage and patterns—the who, what, where, when, and how. This can be done by analyzing Web log files.

13.4.1   Log Files

Every time a user accesses a Web server, the server logs the transaction in a special access log file. Access logs are text files in which each line of the file details an individual access. Regardless of the type of Web server, access logs use a common log file format. This makes them easy to analyze and compare. Because log files can become quite voluminous, it is hard to analyze the accesses by hand. For this reason, most Web server EC software vendors provide free software for analyzing access log files.

Access logs provide a variety of statistics that can be used for analyzing and improving marketing and advertising strategies. Among the more valuable statistics are:

- Pageviews by time slot. Pageview statistics allow frequent review of the number of site accesses. Grouping pageviews by "time bucket" (time slot) also enables a company to ascertain the time slots, such as morning, afternoon, or evening, during which customers visit the site.
- Pageviews by customers' log-in status. This information helps determine whether requiring customers to log in is worthwhile. For instance, if the number of pageviews of customers who log in is substantially greater than those who do not, the company may find the login requirement effective and worthwhile.
- Pageviews by referrers. Some customers are drawn or referred to the site by clicking on banners or links on other Web sites. Knowing the source of such referrers is useful for assessing the effectiveness of the location of banners; customers' interests can also be determined from the nature of the Web site with those banners.
- Pageviews by visitor's hardware platform, operating system, browser, and/or browser version. These types of pageviews enable a company to obtain information on the hardware platform (e.g., Mac or PC) and browser type (e.g., Internet Explorer or Mozilla Firefox) used by the viewer.
- Pageviews by visitor's host. This type of pageview provides information on the customers' host sites. Knowing where customers are coming from can enable the company to target potential customers via popular hosts such as Yahoo!

13.4.2 E-Commerce Management Tools

Managing the performance of a Web site is a time-consuming and tedious administrative task. Several vendors offer suites of products or individual packages that can assist with the management process. One of the more prominent vendors of IT and Web management tools is BMC Software, Inc. (bmc.com). Some of the products offered by BMC include:

- Patrol for E-Business Management. This package includes Patrol for Internet Services, which measures Web response time; Patrol for Firewalls, which provides firewall administration; and Patrol for Microsoft or Netscape application servers.
- MainView for E-Business Management. This package includes MainView for WebSphere, which aids in the management of mainframe-based EC applications; MainView for Network Management, to monitor mainframe network connections; and MainView for Systems Management, to provide systems administration.

Other EC management tools include site version control tools, combined utilities/tools, server management and optimization tools, and authoring/publishing/deployment tools that include significant site management or testing capabilities.

New Words & Phrases

advisable adj. 明智的；可取的

log n. 原木，日志 v. 砍伐，把……记入航海日志

voluminous adj. 宽松的，容量大的，篇幅长的

time slot n. 时间空档

ascertain vt. 弄清，确定，查明

worthwhile adj. 值得的，值钱的，有价值的

patrol n. 巡逻[查、视]；巡逻队；v. 巡逻[查，视]

thorough adj. 彻底的，考虑周到的

regardless of 不管，不顾

pageview 页面浏览量，浏览页数

time bucket 时间段

log-in 登录系统，开始工作

tedious adj. 乏味的，单调的

mainframe n. （大型电脑的）主机，中央处理机

Notes

1. Both B2C and B2B Web sites require a thorough understanding of the usage and patterns—the who, what, where, when, and how. 本句译为："B2C 和 B2B 网站都要求对网站的使用和方式——什么人、做了什么么、在什么地方、什么时间、如何做的——有彻底的了解。"

Reading Materials——Molding a New Vision for E-Commerce at D-M-E

D-M-E Company may not be a household name, but for mold-makers, mold designers, and molders who make parts for the plastics industry, D-M-E is one of the world's leading manufacturers and suppliers of mold-base assemblies and components, mold-making equipment and supplies, and other specialized systems. Offering the industry's broadest and deepest line of mold-tooling technologies, D-M-E's mission is to help its customers produce better parts, reduce their costs, and accelerate time-to-market, as well as enable mold-makers to devote more time to refining their molds. D-M-E has five machining facilities in North America and Europe and direct and joint venture operations worldwide.

Web Site Grows in Stature

D-M-E's current Web site plays an increasingly important role as a greater number of customers go online to purchase products. Approximately 5 percent of D-M-E's sales come from the Web, a number that is growing at the rate of 20 percent a year. To accommodate this growth and encourage more customers to use the Web site, D-M-E realized it needed a more robust online environment. It decided to upgrade to IBM WebSphere Commerce Professional Edition while leveraging the iSeries environment—providing the scalability and stability required to support the business-to-business environment. The solution includes IBM's DB2 Universal Database, WebSphere Application Server, and HTTP server.

Out-of-the-Box Functionality

Although D-M-E's IT staff is small and has limited experience in Web development, it found IBM's WebSphere Commerce an easy-to-use, complete solution for the Web. In configuring a new store for its Web site, D-M-E only had to modify the sample store template to customize it for its needs. D-M-E also was able to migrate its product catalog, because WebSphere Commerce imports the necessary HTML and JavaServer Pages files, catalog information, payment and tax details, and shipper information to build a complete store archive template that is ready for customization. Todd Oliver, a system programmer for D-M-E, pointed out that "WebSphere Commerce is a great product for companies like ours because it didn't require that we have a lot of experience with Java technologies and JavaServer Pages."

Easy Administration, Better Customer Service

D-M-E has leveraged WebSphere Commerce catalog management tooling to simplify the management of its product catalog, the main feature of its Web site. Internally, D-M-E's business users can now make changes to catalog products and pricing without requesting help from the IT department, making both groups more productive. The workload on the customer service department has also decreased, because more customers are checking product pricing and order status online.

On the customer side, users have the assurance that the D-M-E Web site will be available 24/7. This encourages more customers to use the site, in turn creating greater efficiencies internally as customers and D-M-E affiliates rely more upon the Internet to place orders. D-M-E still has customers who place orders by phone and fax, but now the stability and robustness of the site provides customers with another reliable sales channel.

Improvements Drive Incremental Sales

Customers can now easily order multiple products at a time online. "With the old system, customers had to know the SKU number for a product, type it in, click 'go,' and repeat the same process for each product they wanted," explains Oliver. "With WebSphere Commerce, we added a quick order page that allows customers to add up to 10 products at a time."

Order processing speed has also increased sevenfold, and the search capabilities of WebSphere Commerce allow customers to define and limit their searches for better results. Also popular with customers is the automated e-mail notification containing forgotten password information, a capability of WebSphere Commerce.

Since the introduction of the Web site, incremental sales have increased 23 percent due to faster order processing and the capability for customers to order more than one product at a time. One measure of success of the new D-M-E Web site is the absence of customer complaint calls fielded by the IT department. Instead of three to four calls per week from customers with questions and/or concerns about the Web site, D-M-E now rarely receives calls.

Application Development Environment Gets Kudos

When D-M-E migrated its Web site to WebSphere Commerce, it faced two hurdles: a small IT staff and limited experience in Web development. Working with IBM Business Partner Dynamik Technologies, Jay Stobbe, D-M-E's manager of IT systems and administration, and Oliver designed, constructed, tested, and deployed the new site using IBM Rational Application Developer for WebSphere (formerly known as WebSphere Studio Application Developer). Although the group faced some development challenges, its work was simplified by the Rational development environment.

As an integrated development tool, Rational Application Developer for WebSphere accelerates Java 2 Enterprise Edition (J2EE) technology-based application development with a comprehensive set of visual productivity tools, templates, and wizards. D-M-E found the search capabilities, self-help, debugging tools, and built-in test environment to be the most useful. Stobbe estimated that IBM WebSphere Commerce cut D-M-E's Web development time by at least half.

The Future Looks Bright

In the near future, D-M-E plans to take advantage of the marketing tools available in the IBM WebSphere Commerce Professional Edition to increase revenues and grow its customer base. "We have not even begun to explore all the possibilities WebSphere Commerce provides," says Stobbe. The D-M-E marketing department is excited about leveraging capabilities, such as support for running promotions and executing special offers by automatically presenting targeted cross-selling, up-selling, and advertisements to new and existing customers, as well as the analytics and business intelligence tools. Thanks to WebSphere Commerce, D-M-E has the opportunity to explore areas it had not even dreamed of and has the flexibility to easily add new applications.

New Words & Phrases

household name n. 家喻户晓的事或人

time-to-market 上市时间

stature n. 才干，高境界，高水平；身高

out-of-the-Box 拆盒即可使用的，开箱即用，盒外

Workload n. 工作量，劳动负荷（量）

kudos n. 荣誉，光荣，赞誉

mission n. 使命，任务，代表团，使节团

refine vt. 精炼；使文雅高尚；使变得完善

leverage n. 力量，影响 vt. 促使……改变

migrate vi. 迁移；移往

sevenfold adj. 七倍的，七重的 adv. 七倍地

Abbreviations

SKU（Stock Keeping Unit） 库存单位，单品，存货单元

求职英语简介

一、个人简历

个人简历（resume / curriculum vitae）是升学、求职过程中的重要文件。英文个人简历的格式比较固定，一般应包括个人信息、联系地址、求职愿望、学历、工作经历、证明人等部分，也可以根据具体情况，适当增加有关条目。内容的安排要求清晰易读、层次分明，学历和工作经历一般可从最近开始，逐渐向后追述。从语言方面来看，个人简历多以名词词组为主，也可以使用动词词组，但是要求结构整齐对称。

以下是某位学生的个人简历，他申请的工作职位是某计算机公司的售后服务技术员。一般来说，他还需另外撰写一份求职信，介绍一下本人的基本情况、特长及对该公司业务的熟悉程度，同时重申个人的工作愿望，并提出面试请求。请大家阅读以下简历，注意其格式及语言特点，然后分析一下自己的情况，撰写一份个人简历。

Resume

Personal details	Name: Li Jian
	Age: 20
	Date of Birth: May 21,1981
	Marital Status: single
	Address: 36 Yanshan Street, Jinan, Shandong 250014, P. R. China
	Tel: 0531-8937777
	E-mail: lijian@hotmail.com

Position applied for   After-sale Service Technician

Education：

September 1995 to present   Shandong Institute of Electronic Technology,

Major in Applied Computing with special interest in

networking & website implementation.

Courses taken: C Programming, Software Engineering,

Visual Foxpro, Microsfot Office, Data Structures in C,

English for Computing, Computer Networks,

Internet Application, etc.

September 1992 to July 1995 Jinan No.14 Middle School, Jinan, Shandong.

Monitor of class, outstanding in math & physics.

Work experience：

Summer 1998   Company: ABC Computer Corp.

Post: Sales Promotion

Responsibility: organizing product exhibition tours & market survey.

Summer 1997   Company: Hope Co., Ltd

Post: System Integration

Responsibility: assembling PCs according to customer requirements; fixing hardware

problems; on-the-spot installation & testing.

Summer, 1996   Company: Eastsoft Co., Ltd

Post: Reception

Responsibility: understanding customer needs; explaining Eastsoft products & services;

highlighting Eastsoft after-sale service.

Honors   Top Prize in Homepage Design Contest, 1998.

Other information   Fluent in English with a TOEFL score of 590.

References

Mr. Liu Xinhua	Ms. Wang Ying
Sales Manager	Manager of Customer Relations
ABC Computer Corp.	Eastsoft Co., Ltd
38 Heping Street	135 Wenhua Avenue
Jinan, Shandong, 250014	Jinan, Shandong 250014
P. R. China	P. R. China

二、求职申请信

求职信实质上是一种推销自己的商业函件，它通常与简历等一块儿寄出。其主要目的是说服雇主或招聘单位雇用你，或至少为你赢得面试的机会，是求职成功与否很关键的第一步。

求职可分为毕业后求职、跳槽求职和业余兼职三大类。无论是哪一种求职申请信，都应该认真撰写，做到简明扼要，重点突出，千万不要在信中罗列过多的琐碎事实，或对自己百般吹嘘炫耀，因为你在随信寄出的简历中已说明了最重要的资料。

一般来讲，求职信主要应包括以下几项内容：

（1）点明你所要申请的工作职位；

（2）说明你从何得知这份工作的信息（如从同事朋友处或从报纸的招聘广告等）；

（3）引起招聘者对简历中相关内容的注意；

（4）说明你是此项工作的最佳人选。

前两项通常在信函的第一段中开门见山加以说明。后两项是申请信的主要内容，放在第二段。本段表达成功与否起着很重要的作用，对求职者的能力和个性也是一种检验。在写作时，应指出你的简历中与工作特别相关的内容，以引起招聘者的注意和兴趣。在求职信的收尾段中，应说明联络方式并表达希望得到面试的机会。

求职申请信写好之后，应选用优质白纸打印出来。布局排版要美观大方，给人以整洁清新之感。求职申请信的格式与普通书信的格式基本一致。在寄发求职申请信时，应按招聘要求随函附上个人简历或和自传等有关材料。一个考虑周到的求职者还会随函附上一个已写好自己的通讯地址并贴好邮票的信封或明信片，供招聘单位复函之用。

总之，注意求职申请信从内容至形式的每一个细节，将为你赢得面试机会，最终找到称心如意的工作。下面是一篇毕业求职范例，供读者参考。

谋求证券经纪人之职 (Application for a Position of Stock Broker)

Gentlemen:

Your advertisement for stockbrokers in "China Daily" of May 2 has interested me very much. I feel I can fit one of the vacancies you have.

I am twenty-two years of age and female. I will graduate in July. My specialty at college is none other than securities business. I have gained some practical experience in brokerage in recent years acting as a part-time broker for Beijing Commodities Futures Exchange. At college, I have participated in a lot of activities both at the collegiate level and the departmental level. I have attended a large number of symposia and conferences on the business of stockbroking. I am young and energetic and maintain good interpersonal relations. I mention these because I know my line off work is a demanding one and I am willing to show that I can face up to any challenge placed before me.

Should this application meet with your favorable consideration, I will do my utmost to satisfy the confidence you may repose in me. I am looking forward to hearing from you as soon as possible.

Faithfully yours, Jing Jimei

Enclose:　　（1）My resume

　　　　　　（2）My academic record

　　　　　　（3）Two recent photos

本人对贵公司五月二日在《中国日报》上招聘证券经纪人的广告极感兴趣。我认为本人可以填补贵公司其中一个空缺的职位。

我现年 22 岁，女性，即将于 7 月份毕业。我在大学所学专业正是证券交易。近两年来，我为北京商品期货交易所当兼职经纪人，从中获得了一些经纪方面的实际经验。我在学校参加了许多活动，既有学校级的，也有高一级的。我还参加了不少以股票买卖为专题的研讨会和会议。本人精力充沛，而且有良好的人际关系。我之所以提及这些是因为我知道这种工作是要求很严的工作，但是我愿意面对出现在我面前的任何挑战。

贵公司如对我的申请惠予考虑，本人将竭诚工作，以不负贵公司之愿望。期望你们尽早回复。

附件：　　　（1）个人简历

　　　　　　（2）成绩单

　　　　　　（3）两张近照

Exercises

I. Answer the following questions

1. List the five major steps needed to develop a typical e-commerce application.

2. List three basic options for developing an EC Web site.

3. If a company decides to buy or lease an EC application, what the representative selection criteria need to be considered?

4. List six steps Martin et al. identified in selecting a software vendor and a package.

II. Fill in the blanks in each of the following

1. Small storefronts with a few key components can be developed with HTML, Java, or another_____ language. Larger or special EC applications can be developed _____ or_____.

2. The traditional system development life cycle (SDLC) systematically leads developers through six analysis and design stages: problem identification, _____, logical design, _____, implementation, and _____.

3. Projects can be managed with project management software. Best practice management also includes _____ of system performance.

4. Few organizations, especially _____, have the time, _____, or technical expertise required to develop today's complex e-business systems. This means that most EC applications are built with hardware, software, hosting services, and development expertise provided by _____ vendors.

5. The most difficult and crucial task in evaluating a vendor and a packaged system is to determine a _____ for choosing the best vendor and package.

6. Once a short list has been prepared, negotiations can begin with vendors to determine how their packages might be modified to remove any _____ with the company's desired EC application.

7. The contract with the software vendor is very important. Not only does it specify the price of the software, but it also determines the _____ and _____ of support to be provided by the vendor.

8. Both B2C and B2B Web sites require a thorough understanding of the _____ and patterns—the who, what,

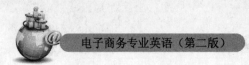
where, when, and how. This can be done by analyzing Web _____.

9. Every time a user accesses a Web server, the server logs the transaction in a special _____.

III. Questions and discussion

1. Why did D-M-E decide to utilize WebSphere for its portal? Explain in detail.

2. How can D-M-E leverage this application with other e-commerce processes?

Chapter 14　Case Study of E-Commerce

互联网为我们提供了一种全新的商务活动方式。本章从不同角度、不同层次的电子商务应用出发，对电子商务的典型案例进行介绍。既阐明了互联网企业如何规划并发展自己的业务，又详解了传统企业如何利用互联网开展在线业务。

通过本章学习，读者应掌握以下内容并能够用英语表达：

● 商业模式的概念、内涵及实现。
● 电子商务网站的功能。
● 电子商务网站一般商务流程。

学习指导

14.1　Amazon.com

It was not a business problem but rather an opportunity that faced entrepreneur Jeff Bezos: He saw the huge potential for retail sales over the Internet and selected books as the most logical product for e-tailing. In July 1995, Bezos started Amazon.com, an e-tailing pioneer, offering books via an electronic catalog from its Web site (amazon.com). Over the years, the company has recognized that it must continually enhance its business models and electronic store by expanding product selection, improving the customer's experience, and adding services and alliances. Amazon.com's challenge was how to compete in selling consumer products online, showing profit and a reasonable rate of return on the huge investment it has made.

14.1.1　Background

Amazon.com was founded by Jeff Bezos, a computer science and electrical engineering graduate from Princeton University. Bezos had moved to Seattle after resigning as the senior vice president at D.E. Shaw, a Wall Street investment bank. He did not know much about the Internet, but, he came across a statistic that the Internet was growing at a rate of 2,300 %, which convinced him that it was a large growth opportunity. Not knowing much more, he plunged into the world of e-commerce with no prior retailing experience.

He located the company in Seattle because the city had a large pool of technical talent and was close to one of the largest book wholesalers, in Roseburg, Oregon, because the company began as a bookseller.

Bezos' first choice for the company name was Cadabra. He quickly dropped this name when a lawyer he contacted mistook it for cadaver. He picked Amazon because it started with the letter A, signified something big, and was easy to spell.

For his contribution, Jeff Bezos was picked as the 1999 Time person of the year at the age of

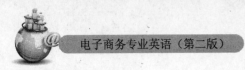

thirty-five. Describing why it chose Bezos, Time magazine said, "Bezos' vision of the online retailing universe was so complete, his Amazon.com site so elegant and appealing that it became from Day One the point of reference for anyone who had anything to sell online."

14.1.2 Vision and Value

Jeff Bezos was one of the few people to understand the special nature of Internet retailing and e-commerce. This is how he compares e-tailing to traditional retailing:

Look at e-retailing. The key trade that we make is that we trade real estate for technology. Real estate is the key cost of physical retailers. That's why there's the old saw: location, location, location. Real estate gets more expensive every year, and technology gets cheaper every year. And it gets cheaper fast.

There were really two elements to his vision:

• He wanted to build the world's most customer-centric company.

• He wanted to establish a place where customers could buy anything.

This is how he characterizes his vision of customer-centrism:

Our goal is to be Earth's most customer-centric company. I will leave it to others to say if we've achieved that. But why? The answer is three things: The first is that customer-centric means figuring out what your customers want by asking them, then figuring out how to give it to them, and then giving it to them. That's the traditional meaning of customer-centric, and we're focused on it. The second is innovating on behalf of customers, figuring out what they don't know they want and giving it to them. The third meaning, unique to the Internet, is the idea of personalization: Redecorating the store for each and every individual customer. If we have 10.7 million customers, as we did at the end of the last quarter, then we should have 10.7 million stores.

The value elements Amazon.com sought to deliver are illustrated in this Bezos quote:

Bill Gates said, "I buy all my books at Amazon.com because I'm busy and it's convenient. They have a big selection, and they've been reliable." Those are three of our four core value propositions: convenience, selection, service. The only one he left out is price: we are the broadest discounters in the world in any product category. But maybe price isn't so important to Bill Gates.

In addition to customer-centricism, Bezos wanted Amazon.com to be the place where you could buy anything and everything online. Although the company started out as the world's biggest bookstore, it aimed eventually to become the world's biggest store. The company has made some progress by expanding into new product categories, such as cookware and tools, and also providing new services such as auctions. However, Bezos has conceded that becoming the place to buy any product is a "multi-decade proposition."

14.1.3 Books—The Entry Point

Bezos had no experience in the book-selling business, but he realized that books had an ideal shipping profile for online sales. He believed that many customers would be willing to buy books without inspecting them in person and that books could be impulse purchase items if properly promoted on a Web site. By accepting orders on its Web site, Bezos believed that Amazon.com could reduce transaction costs in the sale to the customer.

More than 4 million book titles are in print at any one time throughout the world, and more than 1 million of those are in English. However, the largest physical bookstore cannot stock more than 200,000 books and carries even fewer titles because bookstores stock more than one copy of each title. Having a wide selection was important because Bezos believed it would help create a network economic effect. People would visit Amazon.com whenever they wanted to buy a book because it would be the most likely store to have a particular title. After becoming satisfied customers, people would return to Amazon.com to buy more books and would eventually stop looking elsewhere.

The structure of the supply side of the book business was equally important to Amazon.com's success. There were a large number of book publishers, none of which held a dominant position in the book-selling marketplace. Thus, it was unlikely that a single supplier could restrict Bezos' supply of books or enter his market as a competitor.

Bezos encouraged early customers to submit reviews of books, which he posted with the publisher's information about the book and with reviews written by Amazon.com employees. This customer participation served as a substitute for the corner bookshop staff's friendly advice and recommendations. Bezos saw the power of the Internet in reaching small, highly focused market segments, but he realized that his comprehensive bookstore could not be all things to all people. Therefore, he created a sales associate program in which Web sites devoted to a particular topic could provide links to Amazon.com books that related to that topic. In return, Amazon.com remits a percentage of the referred sales to the owner of the referring site.

14.1.4　Moving Beyond Selling Books

Although Bezos' original vision was to create an online bookstore with the world's best selection, Amazon has moved into other product lines where opportunities for network economic effects and transaction cost reductions looked promising. In 1998, Amazon.com began selling music CDs and videotapes. The Web site's software can track a customer's purchases and recommend similar book, CD, or video titles. In fact, the site can recommend related products in a variety of product categories now sold on Amazon.com. These product categories include consumer electronics, computers, toys, clothing, art, hardware, housewares, furniture, and car parts.

By paying attention to every process involved in buying, promoting, selling, and shipping consumer goods, and by working to improve each process continually Bezos and Amazon.com have become one of the first highly visible success stories in electronic commerce. In fact, Amazon.com now generates significant revenue by supplying other sellers of consumer goods with the technology to sell those goods online. One of its first partnerships was with Toys R Us, a company that had experienced difficulties in selling online and making deliveries on time in the 1999 holiday shopping season. Toys R Us signed an agreement with Amazon.com in 2000 that placed Toys R Us products on the Amazon.com Web site. Amazon.com would accept the orders on its Web site and would ship products to customers for Toys R Us in exchange for a percentage of each sale.

In addition to the online sales services Amazon.com provides to Toys R Us, Target, Borders, CDNow, and other large companies, it provides similar services to many smaller companies with its zShops offering. In zShops, small retailers become members of an online shopping mall on Amazon's site.

Toys R Us sells more than $300 million worth of toys each year through the Amazon.com site. Both Toys R Us and Amazon.com benefit from the network economics effect they obtain by having toys available for sale on Amazon.com's well-known electronic commerce site. Many small retailers in the zShops program who sell toys also benefit because shoppers visit the Amazon.com site looking for toys. When a site visitor searches for a toy, the zShops retailers' offerings are presented on the search results page along with results from Toys R Us, Amazon.com, and other companies for which Amazon.com provides online sales services.

14.1.5 Amazon.com Technology

The true core competence of Amazon may be its technology and the web site that manifests it.

First, Amazon took a fundamentally different approach to developing an online store. As described by Salon.com's Scott Rosenberg:

Five Years ago, entrepreneurs thought the way to duplicate the retail experience online was to build virtual replicas of physical stores. The theory was that you had to orient users spatially. Amazon never went down that path. Its founder, Jeff Bezos and his talented crew of site builders seemed to understand from Day 1 that information organized thoughtfully can create its own experience—one entirely different from the familiar store geography of aisles and shelves. They started with a vast but bare database of books in print and kept adding new layers of valuable information to it.

Second, Amazon pioneered new ways to enhance the shopping experience. Here is a partial list of their innovations:

• One-click shopping

Amazon.com recognized that one of the most important ways in which it could increase value was to reduce the transactional burden on customers. If the company could remember all of the relevant information about the customer, the individual could breeze through the ordering process. This also established switching costs, making it irksome to switch to other online stores that may or may not have any given customer's information. In a controversial move, the company also obtained a patent on its one-click shopping system and successfully stalled its usage by its rival—bn.com.

• Product review information

All products on Amazon can be reviewed. Moreover, customers can rate each other's reviews: a rating figure is placed against each review to help customers decide whether to read it.

• Purchase circles

Suppose you are interested in learning about the books being read by your rival firm or scientists at MIT—Amazon provides you a means to do this. In the company words:

We group the items we send to particular zip and postal codes, and the items ordered from each domain name. We then aggregate this anonymous data and apply an algorithm that constructs bestseller lists of items that are more popular with each specific group than with the general population. No personally identifiable information is used to create purchase circle lists.

• Email alerts

Amazon allows consumers to keep tabs on their favorite author or musician. Individuals can enter the name of their favorite author, for example, and when that person's next book comes along, Amazon e-mails the customer with an alert.

• Recommendations

The company uses collaborative filtering and other personalization techniques to recommend books and music to users. The company remembers the name of each customer and the web site greets each individual as he or she logs in. Then, when the user picks a book, the system recommends a few other books that may be of interest, encouraging users to browse and buy more than they had originally intended.

• Wish list

Each individual can create a wish list of items he or she would like to acquire. This list is public so that a friend or acquaintance could order and send you the items you want.

These innovations resulted in Amazon's leadership role.

New Words & Phrases

come across　偶遇，不期而遇	plunge into　投入，跳入
vision　n. 景象	real estate　房地产，不动产
saw　n. 谚语	characterize　vt. 描绘，刻画
figure out　断定，领会到	on behalf of　代表……
reliable　adj. 可靠的，可信赖的	concede　v. 承认，退让
proposition　n. 主张，命题	impulse　n. 刺激，冲动
in print　已出版，在销售中	stock　n. 库存；v. 进货，备有
dominant　adj. 占优势的，支配的	substitute　n. 代用品，替代品
consumer goods　生活消费品	partnership　n. 合伙，伙伴关系
manifest　v. 表明，证明	duplicate　vt. 复制
replica　n. 复制品	geography　n. 布局，地理
irksome　adj. 讨厌的，令人厌烦的	anonymous　adj. 匿名的
algorithm　n. 算法	bestseller　n. 畅销书
keep tab on　记录，监视	

Abbreviations

MIT（Massachusetts Institute of Technology）　（美国）麻省理工学院

Notes

1. He believed that many customers would be willing to buy books without inspecting them in person and that

books could be impulse purchase items if properly promoted on a Web site. 他认为很多顾客并不当面检查就愿意购买图书，并且如果网站促销得当，图书就会成为冲动购买商品。

2. When a site visitor searches for a toy, the zShops retailers' offerings are presented on the search results page along with results from Toys A Us, Amazon.com, and other companies for which Amazon.com provides online sales services. 当网站访问者搜索玩具时，zShops 零售商的产品会同玩具反斗城、亚马逊以及由亚马逊提供网上销售服务的其它公司所销售的玩具一起出现在搜索结果页面。

14.2　Dell

Headquartered in Austin, Texas, Dell had gained a reputation as one of the world's most preferred computer systems companies and a premier provider of products and services that customers worldwide needed to build their information-technology and Internet infrastructures.

14.2.1　The Story of Dell

Dell was founded in 1984 by Michael Dell. In 1983, Michael Dell, an 18 year old freshman at the University of Texas at Austin, spent his evenings and weekends pre-formatting hard disks for IBM-compatible PC upgrades. A year later, he dropped out of college to attend to his burgeoning business, which had grown from nothing to $6 million in 1985 by simply upgrading IBM compatibles for local area businesses. In 1985, Dell shifted his company's focus to assembling its own brand of PCs and the business grew dramatically, with $70 million in sales at the end of 1985. By 1990, sales had grown even further to over $500 million and with it Dell's capabilities as a national supplier to Fortune 500 companies.

Dell's success continued through 1992, until in 1993 it faced an operating loss for the first time in its history, despite a 40% increase in sales. The problems, Dell quickly discovered, stemmed in part from its attempts to sell its products through retail channels. Moreover, quality problems with its laptops had exacerbated Dell's financial woes. While some pundits were questioning Dell's future, the company acted decisively, exiting the retail channel and resolving to re-enter the laptop market only when that product's quality matched or exceeded the quality of the Dell desktop.

By 1996, Dell sales reached $7.8 billion with an operating income of more than $710 million. Dell's climb to market leadership was the result of a persistent focus on delivering the best possible customer experience. Direct selling, from manufacturer to consumer, was a key component of its strategy.

14.2.2　The Dell Direct Model

The Dell Direct Model was a very efficient, "made-to-order", high velocity, low cost distribution system characterized by direct customer relationships, "build-to-order" manufacturing, and products and services targeted at specific market segments.

The traditional value chain in the personal computer industry was characterized as "build-to-stock" PC manufacturers, such as IBM, Compaq, and Hewlett-Packard, designed and built their products with preconfigured options based on market forecasts. Products were first stored in company warehouses and later dispatched to resellers, retailers, and other intermediaries who typically added a 20-30 percent markup before selling to their customers. PC manufacturers controlled the upstream part of the value chain, giving the downstream part to middlemen. Retailers justified their margins by providing several benefits to customers: easily accessed locations, selection across multiple brands, opportunity to see and test products before purchasing, and knowledgeable salespeople who could educate customers about their choices.

Two trends in the early 1980s allowed Michael Dell to radically reengineer the PC industry value chain. First, corporate customers were becoming increasingly sophisticated and therefore did not require intense personal selling by salespeople. By the late 1980s, individuals—especially those buying their second or third PCs—had become savvy and experienced technology users. Second, the different components of a PC—the monitor, keyboard, memory, disk drive, software, and so on—became standard modules, permitting mass customization in PC system configuration.

The Dell Direct Model departed from the industry's historical rules on several fronts: The company outsourced all components but performed assembly. It eliminated retailers and shipped directly from its factories to end customers. It took customized orders for hardware and software. And it designed an integrated supply chain linking Dell's suppliers very closely to its assembly factories and order-intake system.

14.2.3 Dell Goes Online

By the early 1990s Dell had begun experimenting with the Internet in response to customer demand, delivering online technical support and order status information. Michael Dell established a small team of about nine people to explore using the Internet as a means of communicating with customers, delivering information, and selling its products.

As the team investigated the Internet they became increasingly convinced that it was a viable channel for Dell's product. Many at Dell were excited by the online prospects, believing that the Net was a natural extension of Dell's direct business model. Moreover, industry analysts suggested that few PC vendors were as well positioned as Dell to take advantage of the Internet opportunity—unencumbered by an existing distribution channel, Dell could go direct to the customer as usual, but others had to use a different medium to go direct. One analyst remarked, "Dell has been positioned for something like this since its beginning. They can migrate what they do in the real world to the Web easily without upsetting any of these existing sales channels."

In late 1995, the team began designing an online retail store and technical support vehicle for Dell's products. By the end of the first quarter of 1996, the online system began to take shape.

14.2.4 How Dell Fulfills Customer Orders

One of Dell's success factors is its superb logistics and order fulfillment systems. Customer orders, which are received mostly online, are automatically transferred to the production area, where configuration is done to determine which components and parts are needed to create the customized computer that the customer wants. Once configuration is done, the problem becomes how to get all the needed components so that a computer can be ready for shipment the next day. As part of the solution, Dell created a network of dedicated suppliers for just-in-time deliveries, as well as a sophisticated computerized global network of components and parts inventories. The global network is also used for product services.

Let's examine how Dell provides service when a computer that is in the customer's possession needs to be repaired. Dell is trying to achieve for repairs, upgrades, and other services the next-day shipment that it uses for new computers. For repair activities, Dell needs parts and subassemblies to be delivered to hundreds of repair stations, worldwide, from internal warehouses or external vendors. The search for the parts and their delivery must be done very quickly. To facilitate this, Dell is using an online intelligent inventory optimization system from LPA software (xelus.com). The system can reconcile the demand for parts, with the action needed (e.g., repair or upgrade).

The online system generates timely information about demand forecast, the cost of needed inventory, and "days of supply of inventory". It compares actual to forecasted demand. This enables Dell to communicate critical information to external and internal customers, reducing order fulfillment delays.

New Words & Phrases

burgeon　v. 萌芽，（迅速）成长

stem from　源于

pundit　n. 博学的人，权威性的评论者

persistent　adj. 坚持的，持续的

value chain　价值链

margin　n. 利润

sophisticated　adj. 老练的，成熟的

assembly　n. 集合，装配

upset　v. 推翻，倾覆

reconcile　vt. 使和谐，使一致

operating loss　营业损失

exacerbate　vt. 恶化，使加剧

operating income　营业收入[收益]

velocity　n. 速度，流通速度；周转率

dispatch　vt. 派遣，发送

radically　adv. 根本上，以激进的方式

outsource　vt. 外包

unencumbered　adj. 没有阻碍的，不受妨碍的

subassembly　n. 部件，组件

Notes

1. Dell's success continued through 1992, until in 1993 it faced an operating loss for the first time in its history, despite a 40% increase in sales. 戴尔公司的成功持续到1992年，到1993年，尽管公司销售额增长了40%，但却遭遇到了它历史上首次营业损失。

2. The traditional value chain in the personal computer industry was characterized as "build-to-stock" PC manufacturers, such as IBM, Compaq, and Hewlett-Packard, designed and built their products with preconfigured options based on market forecasts. 在个人电脑行业，传统的价值链可以描绘为"生产后再销售"的PC制造商（如IBM、康柏、惠普）基于市场预测设计和生产预先配置选项的产品。

3. Moreover, industry analysts suggested that few PC vendors were as well positioned as Dell to take advantage of the Internet opportunity—unencumbered by an existing distribution channel, Dell could go direct to the

customer as usual, but others had to use a different medium to go direct. 此外，行业分析人士认为很少有 PC 机销售商能有像戴尔公司那样好的定位来利用互联网的机会：不受现有分销渠道的阻碍，戴尔公司像往常一样直接面向消费者，而其他厂商则必须通过不同的方法来进行直销。

14.3　Alibaba

14.3.1　Alibaba Group

Alibaba Group was founded in 1999 by Jack Ma. It reaches Internet users in more than 240 countries and regions, and employs 12,000 people in more than 40 cities in mainland China as well as in Hong Kong, Taiwan, London and Silicon Valley.

Companies in Alibaba Group are:

（1）Alibaba.com

Alibaba.com Limited is the global leader in business-to-business (B2B) e-commerce and the flagship company of Alibaba Group.

Founded in 1999, Alibaba.com makes it easy for millions of buyers and suppliers around the world to do business online through three marketplaces: a global trade marketplace (www.alibaba.com) for importers and exporters, a Chinese marketplace (www.alibaba.com.cn) for domestic trade in China, and, through an associated company, a Japanese marketplace (www.alibaba.co.jp) facilitating trade to and from Japan. Together, its marketplaces form a community of 40 million registered users from more than 240 countries and regions. Headquartered in Hangzhou, Alibaba.com has offices in more than 40 cities across Greater China as well as in Europe and the United States.

（2）Taobao

Launched in 2003, Taobao (www.taobao.com) is the largest Internet retail website in China with more than 75 percent of the Chinese-domestic online consumer market. It provides the most comprehensive product offering ranging from collectibles and hard-to-find items to mainstream retail categories such as consumer electronics, clothing and accessories, sporting goods and household products. It serves nearly 100 million registered users and more than 1.5 million sellers have opened up stores on Taobao. In 2008, Alibaba Group announced it will be investing more than $700 million in Taobao in the next five years. Alimama (www.alimama.com), an online advertising exchange and affiliate network, was merged into Taobao in 2008.

（3）Alipay

Alipay (www.alipay.com) is the leading third-party online payment platform in China. It provides an easy, safe and secure way for millions of Chinese consumers to purchase goods and services on the Internet. With more than 50 percent of the market share, it is the payment service of choice for consumers and merchants alike, and has the largest network of partnerships with banks in China. In 2008 Alipay facilitated nearly $20 billion in online payment volume. By the end of February 2009, it had a registered user base of more than 150 million accounts. Alipay provides an escrow payment service that reduces transaction risk for online consumers. Alipay has significantly accelerated the growth of consumer e-commerce in China.

In August 2007, Alipay launched an online payment solution to help merchants worldwide sell directly to consumers in China. It now cooperates with more than 300 global retail brands and supports transactions in 12 major foreign currencies.

（4）Alisoft

Alisoft (www.alisoft.com) develops, markets and delivers Internet-based business management solutions targeting small businesses across China. Through its Software as a Service (SaaS) model, Alisoft provides small businesses with low-cost, user-friendly enterprise and financial management tools. It commands more than 40 percent of the Chinese SaaS market.

Alisoft was the first in Asia to launch a "software store" platform that integrated advanced Internet, telecommunication and software applications. With support from the fast growing number of Independent Software Vendors (ISVs) in China, its "software store" introduced an online supermarket for software on a pay-as-you-go basis.

（5）Yahoo! Koubei

Yahoo! Koubei operates portals focused on local listing services powered by search, maps and social networking technology. The two websites under Yahoo! Koubei are: China Yahoo! (www.yahoo.com.cn), a leading Chinese-language portal offering search, interactive community and one of the most popular email services in China; and Yahoo! Koubei (www.koubei.com), China's leading classified listing website providing more than 20 million registered users with local information covering more than 2,000 cities across China on topics essential to people's daily lives.

14.3.2　Alibaba Culture & Values

Since Alibaba Group's inception, a strong company culture based on a shared value system has served as the cornerstone of the Group and its subsidiaries. Alibaba Group's business success and rapid growth has been built on the spirit of entrepreneurship, innovation, and an unwavering focus on meeting the needs of our customers.

Alibaba Group has six core values which are an important part of the company's DNA. These six core values are:

• Customer First: The interests of our community of users and paying members must be our first priority.

• Team work: We expect our employees to collaborate as a team. We encourage input from our employees in the decision-making process, and expect every employee to commit to the team's objectives.

• Embrace Change: We operate in a fast-evolving industry. We ask our employees to maintain flexibility, continue to innovate and adapt to new business conditions and practice.

• Integrity: Integrity is at the heart of our business. We expect our employees to uphold the highest standards of integrity and to deliver on their commitments.

• Passion: Our employees are encouraged to act with passion whether it is serving customers or developing new services and products.

• Commitment: Our employees have a dedicated focus and commitment to understanding and delivering on the needs of Chinese and global SMEs.

Strong shared values are essential in building a harmonious community where people feel comfortable working together and in ensuring that decisions and behaviors are aligned with company direction. Alibaba Group has gone the extra mile to make sure that people share the same values. When Alibaba Group hires people, they look for people with the same "smell"—people who are optimistic, happy, team oriented, hard working, and willing to invest their lives to achieve an ideal. When employees join the company, they attend at least 10 days of orientation, focusing primarily on the company's vision, mission, and values. When employees demonstrate behaviors contrary to company core values, they are asked to leave no matter how strong their business results are, or how senior they are. Jack Ma expressed it best when he said, "The value system is very important at Alibaba. People who don't fit into our values cannot survive in the company."

Alibaba Group has grown from 18 founders in Hangzhou, China to thousands of employees around the world. The company strives to provide a community where employees can work closely together in a positive, flexible and results-oriented environment. Strong shared values have enabled Alibaba Group to maintain a common company culture and Ali-community, no matter how large the company grows.

14.3.3 Alibaba.com

Jack Ma, a former English teacher from the eastern Chinese city of Hangzhou, founded Alibaba.com with 17 other founders in 1999 as a trading platform for small and medium manufacturers to sell their wares. Since then Alibaba.com has grown into the premier online marketplace for small and medium-size companies around the world to identify potential trading partners and interact with each other to conduct business online.

Alibaba.com has always concentrated on small and medium-sized businesses. Ma believed that global companies spend most of their efforts on doing business with large companies. He sees China (and the rest of Asia) as having a different economic structure than the United States or Europe, where the economies are dominated by large companies. Ma believes that Alibaba.com's true opportunities lie in connecting SMBs around the world with SMBs in China. He argues that SMBs seldom have any sales channels outside of their own country. To compensate, SMBs must travel extensively to meet suppliers and customers at exhibitions or trade fairs. Ma believes that Alibaba.com offers SMBs a reasonably-priced alternative.

（1）Revenue Model

Alibaba.com had 432,031 paying members as of December 31, 2008, representing a 41% year-on-year increase.

Total revenue for 2008 was RMB3.0 billion, representing a 39% increase from 2007. The year-on-year growth was driven mainly by increases in the number of paying members of its

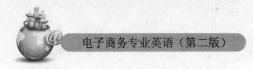

combined marketplaces and sales of value-added services (such as keyword bidding and branded advertisements).

• International Marketplace

Revenue from Alibaba.com's international marketplace was RMB1.9 billion for 2008, an increase of 23% year-on-year, accounting for 64% of total revenue. The growth was primarily due to gains in Gold Supplier members and sales of value-added services.

As of December 31, 2008, Alibaba.com's international marketplace had 43,028 Gold Supplier members, representing a robust increase of 57% year-on-year and 40% quarter-on-quarter. The number of International TrustPass members reached 16,136 as of December 31, 2008, a net increase of 3,984 from 2007.

• China Marketplace

Revenue from Alibaba.com's China marketplace was RMB1.1 billion in 2008, an increase of 78% from 2007, largely due to increases in the number of paying China TrustPass members and sales of value-added services. Alibaba.com's China marketplace accounted for 36% of total revenue in 2008 compared to 28% in 2007.

As of December 31, 2008, Alibaba.com's China marketplace had 372,867 China TrustPass members, a net increase of 106,858 from 2007, or a 40% increase year-on-year. The growth was driven by the overall expansion of China's domestic economy as well as the strong execution of Alibaba.com's sales team.

Alibaba.com, like all portal sites, suffered a setback during the 2001-2002 time period, but its fee-based revenue model allowed it to recover more quickly than portals that were dependent on advertising revenue. The company sees future growth in the continued expansion of trade between Chinese manufacturers and the rest of the world.

（2）Buying on Alibaba.com（www.alibaba.com）

• Product Catalog

Alibaba.com's online product catalog is the largest in the world with products from over 34 different industries. Organized by industry type, the catalog is easy to browse and even easier to search through.

• Company Profiles

Can a supplier handle OEM orders? What's its largest monthly capacity? Find answers to many important questions about a supplier from their company profile. Each profile lists important information regarding their management, R&D, quality control and more, making your search for the right supplier much easier.

• Business Verification

Sourcing online has its risks, although very convenient to use, the internet also makes it easier for individuals to perform fraudulent acts. Alibaba.com protects you against these risks with supplier verification as well as account security measures to keep your information safe. That way, you can enjoy all the benefits of sourcing online.

• Buying Leads

Why bother searching for suppliers when you can have them line up to meet you? As a buyer, you can post buying leads on the website, describing what you're looking for. Suppliers will then contact you based on your specifications. And when you're sourcing multiple products from different categories, buying leads can save you much time and effort.

• Tradeshow Channel

If you visit trade shows to meet new suppliers, Alibaba.com can help point you in the right direction. Not only does Alibaba.com provide you with a comprehensive list of the most important trade shows around the world, it also provides vital information on what each trade show has to offer.

• Communicating with Suppliers

Finally found the right supplier for you? Send an e-mail to the supplier through Alibaba.com instantly! Alibaba.com even make it easy for you to keep in touch with suppliers with its "TradeManager" program, an instant messenger tool that allows you to video conference online, manage trade records and send files of unlimited size to each other.

（3）Selling on Alibaba.com（www.alibaba.com）

• Post Products and Selling Leads

Displaying your product images, specifications and descriptions on Alibaba.com increases your exposure to buyers. On Alibaba.com, free members can display up to 50 products and premium members can display unlimited products.

A selling lead is a trade lead posted by a supplier. It can contain product information, availability and more. Trade leads are sorted according to the date they are posted. This makes for a highly interactive method to sell your products.

• Looking for Buyers

Though most buyers prefer to look for products and suppliers through searches and browsing, almost a third of them would rather publish buying trade leads to let sellers find them. As a seller, you can search the buying trade leads posted by those buyers and send instant quotations.

• Contacting Buyers

Once a buyer sends an inquiry about one of your products or Selling Leads, the inquiry will be sent to your "Message Center" in "My Alibaba".

As a supplier, you can view buying leads posted by buyers and send quotations accordingly by clicking the "Contact Now" button beside each lead. Buyer responses will be sent to your "Message Center" in "My Alibaba."

New Words & Phrases

flagship n. 旗舰，王牌	collectible n. 收藏品
inception n. 开始，开端	cornerstone n. 基石，基础
subsidiary n. 子公司；adj. 辅助的	unwavering adj. 不动摇的，坚定的
integrity n. 正直，诚实	uphold vt. 支持，赞成
harmonious adj. 和谐的	align v. 使密切合作，匹配
fit into 适合	ware n. 商品

trade fair　商业展览会，贸易展销会
trade show　商业展览

fraudulent　adj. 欺诈的，欺骗性的
specification　n. 规格，说明书

Abbreviations

SaaS（Software as a Service）软件服务化
ISVs（Independent Software Vendors）独立软件开发商
SMBs（Small and Medium Businesses）中小企业
SMEs（Small and Medium Enterprises）中小企业
OEM（Original Equipment Manufacturer）贴牌生产

Notes

1. It provides the most comprehensive product offering ranging from collectibles and hard-to-find items to mainstream retail categories such as consumer electronics, clothing and accessories, sporting goods and household products. 它提供了从收藏品、不易找到的商品到主流零售类商品（如消费类电子产品、服装服饰、体育用品和家庭用品）最全面的商品销售。

2. With more than 50 percent of the market share, it is the payment service of choice for consumers and merchants alike, and has the largest network of partnerships with banks in China. 它是个人消费者和商家均可选择的支付服务，目前占有超过50%的市场份额，在中国拥有最广泛的银行合作伙伴关系。

Reading Materials——Ebay: A Business History

Introduction

eBay is a vibrant gathering place where consumers can sell anything to interested buyers. Items sold include Harley Davidsons, cars, antique vases, stamps, coins, dolls, Beanie Babies, jewelry, computers, software, concert tickets, and cameras. The list is endless.

Meg Whitman, the CEO, describes the nature of the company in this Way：

We think of eBay as a global, online trading company. That might sound foreign, but that's because we really did create something entirely new that took unique advantage of the Internet. It connects many-to-many every single day. You can come to eBay to buy or sell practically anything in both the auction format and most recently, with the acquisition of Half.com, in the fixed-price format. Every day thousands and thousands of people come to buy and sell, everything from Beanie Babies to cars to skis.

eBay views itself as an intermediary that helps buyers meet sellers. Unlike the traditional retailer, eBay has created a unique business model. The company makes money by matching buyers with sellers. Sellers ship the items directly to the buyers. As a result, eBay does not have any distribution or fulfillment cost which gives it a tremendous advantage.

There are a multitude of analogies that can be used to describe eBay. One of them is to think of it as a giant "classified advertisement" page. Individuals can advertise an item that they would like to sell for a price and buyers can contact the sellers directly. eBay is also an auction house since the method used to sell goods is an auction.

Buyers bid on items and the highest bidder wins. Some have also described the company as a large swap meet or yard sale where individuals can buy directly from consumers.

Services Offered by eBay

The company started with the basic auction service. It now offers a variety of services:

• Billpoint. One of the big challenges in an online auction environment is to ensure that the sellers are paid for the item that has been auctioned. eBay has created an online bill payment service that facilitates credit card payment between buyers and sellers in collaboration with Wells Fargo Bank. However, buyers are free to use other services such as Paypal.

• Half.com. One of the biggest uses of eBay is to sell previously owned merchandise. However, not all such merchandise needs to be sold in an auction format. Half.com fills this gap by providing previously owned items in a fixed-price format.

• eBay International. eBay has consciously tried to create a global marketplace. Even though users from other countries may bid on US auctions, the legal and financial barriers prevent easy trading. Country-specific sites are seen as the way to overcome this.

• eBay Motors. In addition to selling used cars online, this site features motorcycles, as well as auto parts. The company has created a unique trading environment with services such as financing, inspections, escrow, auto insurance, vehicle shipping, title & registration, and a lemon check.

• eBay Stores. eBay Stores expands the marketplace for sellers by allowing them to create customized shopping destinations to merchandise their items on eBay. For buyers, eBay Stores represents a convenient way to access sellers' goods and services. Buyers who shop at eBay Stores are able to make immediate and multiple-item purchases for fixed-price and auction-style items.

• eBay Professional Services. Professional Services on eBay serves the fast growing and fragmented small business marketplace by providing a destination on eBay to find professionals and freelancers for all kinds of business needs such as web design, accounting, writing, technical support, among others.

• eBay Local Trading. eBay has local sites in 60 markets in the U.S. These sites feature items that are located near them. As a result, buyers pay low shipping rates—especially for difficult-to-ship items such as automobiles, furniture or appliances.

• eBay Premier. This is a specialty site on eBay, which showcases fine art, antiques, fine wines and rare collectibles from leading auction houses and dealers from around the world. Through its "Premier Guarantee" program, all sellers on eBay Premier stand behind and guarantee the authenticity of their items.

• eBay Live Auctions. This interesting feature allows consumers to participate in auctions being conducted by the world's leading auction houses.

Why is eBay Unique?

Even early on, eBay had a completely different view of the world and the Internet and how it applied to retailing. While most companies were interested in opening online stores where they could sell products to consumers, Pierre Omidyar was interested in creating a trading community. As Omidyar said:

The first commercial efforts were from larger companies that were saying, "Gee, we can use the Internet to sell stuff to people". Clearly, if you're coming from a democratic, libertarian point of view, having corporations just cram more products down people's throats doesn't seem like a lot of fun. I really wanted to give the individual the power to be a producer as well.

Meg Whitman, the CEO of eBay, has identified three reasons why eBay was successful. First, she said that in her mind, successful consumer business models will either create an entirely new business that could not have existed without the Web or offer a service that becomes much more efficient with the Web. Of eBay, she said:

We created a business that took unique advantage of the properties of the Net—the Net's ability to connect many to many—allowing a business to be created where there was no land-based analog. If you can't buy your book at Amazon, you can still go down to Barnes & Noble. eBay has no land-based analog—not in one place. It was a business model that was created out of the technology called the Internet. Some of the most successful companies are those that had an entirely new model that could not have existed without the Net. eBay might be one of the only businesses that was created on the Internet.

The second reason identified by Ms. Whitman was the company's successful business model. The idea was not just to create a new concept. But, rather to create a concept that could make money and be profitable.

Finally, the third reason was, in her words, "old-fashioned execution—building a company to last, building cost behind revenues, not ahead of revenues, having a returns-based investment philosophy". She described how the company exerted a strong financial discipline by measuring the return of every dollar spent on marketing and technology. Moreover, eBay never planned to grow for growth's sake. Rather, the goal was always to be profitable.

New Words & Phrases

analogy	n. 类比	authenticity	n. 确实性，真实性
leading	adj. 领导的，最主要的	democratic	adj. 民主的
libertarian	n. 自由的	analog	n. 类似物

广告文体简介

一、产品广告的结构（Elements of product advertisement）

一则广告一般包含如下内容：

（1）标题，用于阐述该产品名称和最显著、最重要的特点，有的还用小标题进一步说明。

（2）产品样本照片或外形图、剖面图。这部分往往与标题相互配合，简短广告常省略此部分。

（3）正文列举其主要品种、规格、性能、用途和特点。

（4）商标、名称、代理机构、经销单位及地点、邮政编码、电话号码、用户电报、电报挂号及联系人等商业信息。

二、广告语言的特点（Characteristics of advertising language）

广告与其他科技文体有很大区别，它的语言不但精练，而且生动、活泼。它广泛采用了形象、拟人、典故、夸张等修辞手法和押韵、叠文、一语双关等文字技巧，以增强广告的渲染力。广告英语具有如下重要特色。

（1）使用不同字体和图形，突出最重要的、最令人感兴趣的信息。这种手段简洁易懂，使人一目了然。如：

（a）Finally, the dBASE, you've been waiting IV.

Get the new dBASE IV, Now for just $ 449

这是一份计算机软件广告。它通过变换字体清晰地告诉用户"大家盼望已久的 dBASE 增强型版本 dBASE IV 终于问世了。该软件目前的售价仅为 449 美元。

（b）Twice the performance at half the cost.

The New Ultra Graphics Accelerator from Metheus

"花一半的钱，却得双倍的性能，何乐而不为！"这是 Methus 公司为其图形加速器所作的广告。

（2）别出心裁，用违反常规的说法，夸大其辞。如：

Are you getting fat & lazy waiting for your plotter?

Don't wait! — Get PLUMP

"绘图仪的速度实在太慢，使人等得又胖又懒，还是买 PLUMP 吧！"这是一家公司为推销其 PLUMP 产品而作的极为夸张的广告。

（3）为使广告通俗易懂，常采用家喻户晓的口语和俗语等非正式文体，使公众感到亲切，便于记忆。如：

Here's proof that something small can be powerful.

这条广告说明了某微型机"体积虽小，但功能强大"。

A whole year without a single bug!

这说明该公司的产品质量过硬，"整整一年没有出一次故障"。

（4）为吸引顾客，使语言生动活泼，常采用形象化、拟人化等手段。例如，有一幅画着驴的广告，上写：

I feel like a donkey! For not buying the "Access" portable computer.

这是 Access 为其便携式计算机做的广告，它给人一种幽默感、新鲜感。

下面是两则广告，读者可从中体会广告文体的特点。

（a）Pentium, P6, P7: 86 Architecture's Attempt to Survive Future

As industry pundits put it, "No computer architecture can survive longer than two decades." Intel Corp, however, introduced Pentium in an attempt to extend the life of the 86 architecture which appears to be in its prime. Pentium achieves a performance comparable to RISC chips. The 86 architecture's survival strategy doesn't stop there. The next 86 family CPU, P6, will have more general-purpose registers, one of the 86 family's sore spots. The P6 will also offer hardware implementation of out-of-order processing, where immediately executable instructions can be carried out regardless of the instruction stream sequence. More pipelines will also be used. The P7 will be the first 64-bit 86 family CPU, maintaining object-code compatibility with the 32-bit 86-family CPUs.

（b）Over l00 MB Removable Drives Fight it Out: Magnetic vs Optical

Storage systems with removable disks and capacities of 100 Mbytes or more are beginning to be mounted in personal computers. Within a few years floppy disks with capacities of over 100 Mbytes and optical disks with capacities of 650 Mbytes are expected to be standard storage devices. There types of high-density floppy disks have appeared in the US and Japan, with the Zip drive from Iomega Corp of the US leading in shipments. The LS-120 from Matsushita Industries, Ltd of Japan and the drive being developed by Mitsumi Electric Co, follow closely in second and third place. In optical disk drives, the CD-R drives are receiving high praise because it allows data to be read on a standard CD-ROM drive

三、常用广告用词（Advertising commentary）

式样齐全 A wide selection of styles   款式入时 Stylish; In up-to-date style

结构合理（结构紧凑）Compact   经久耐用 Durable

安全可靠 Secure , Dependable, Safe   使用方便（携带方便）Handy

性能可靠 Reliable (Satisfactory) performance   造型美观 Sleek (Stylish, Attractive) design

外型美观 Luxuriant finish, Attractive design   款式新颖 styling is in the latest fashion

备有样本、样品，函索即寄 Catalogues and samples sent upon request

品质优良 Good (Best, Top, Superb, High, Reliable) quality

四、经典广告欣赏

1. To me，the past is black and white，but the future is always color.

对我而言，过去平淡无奇；而未来，却是绚烂缤纷。（轩尼诗酒）

2. no business too small, no problem too big.

没有不做的小生意，没有解决不了的大问题。(IBM)

3. let's make things better.

让我们做得更好。（飞利浦电子）

4. Connecting People.(Nokia)

科技以人为本。（诺基亚）

5. Things go better with Coco-Cola.(Coco-Cola)

饮可口可乐，万事如意。（可口可乐）

6. Make yourself heard.(Ericsson)

理解就是沟通（爱立信）

7. Time is what you make of it.(Swatch)

天长地久（斯沃奇手表）

Exercises

I. True or False

1. In July 1995, Bezos started Amazon.com, an e-tailing pioneer, offering books via an electronic catalog from its Web site (amazon.com).

2. Bezos established a place where customers could buy anything.

3. Bezos' original vision was to create an online bookstore with the world's best selection

4. One of Dell's problems is its logistics and order fulfillment systems.

5. Dell's climb to market leadership was the result of a persistent focus on delivering the best possible customer experience.

6. Alimama (www.alimama.com), an online advertising exchange and affiliate network, was merged into Alipay in 2008.

7. Alibaba.com has always concentrated on small and medium-sized businesses.

8. Alibaba.com was dependent on advertising revenue.

II. Fill the blanks

1. Amazon.com obtained a patent on its _____ and successfully stalled its usage by its rival—bn.com.

2. On Amazon, each individual can create a _____ of items he or she would like to acquire.

3. Alibaba.com Limited is the global leader in _____ e-commerce and the flagship company of _____.

4. _____ is the largest Internet retail website in China with more than 75 percent of the Chinese-domestic online consumer market.

5. Alipay (www.alipay.com) is the leading _____ in China.

III. Answer the following questions

1. Why did Bezos choose books as the entry point?

2. What are the two trends in the early 1980s that allowed Michael Dell to radically reengineer the PC industry value chain?

3. List the six core values of Alibaba Group.

IV. Questions and discussion

1. What are the factors that contributed to the success of eBay?

2. Will eBay be limiting itself if it stuck to auctions as the only form of transacting?

3. Is eBay a retailer? Discuss.

V. Almost all car manufacturers allow consumers to configure their car online. Visit a major automaker's Web site and configure a car of your choice. Also visit one electronic intermediary. After you decide what car you want, examine the payment options and figure your monthly payment. Print your results. How does this process compare to visiting an auto dealer? Do you think you found a better price online? Would you consider buying a car this way?

参考文献及网站

[1] 孙建忠，王斌. 电子商务专业英语. 北京：中国水利水电出版社，2004.

[2] 孙建忠，姚卫红，白凤仙编著. 计算机专业英语. 北京：中国水利水电出版社，2005.

[3] Gary P. Schneider. Electronic Commerce, 7th Edition. 北京：机械工业出版社，2006.

[4] Efraim Turban,David King,Jae Lee,Dennis Viehland. Electronic Commerce: A Managerial Perspective 2006,4th Edition. Prentice Hall,2005.

[5] Rafi Mohammed, Robert J. Fisher, Bernard J. Jaworski, Gordon Paddison. Internet Marketing: Building Advantage in a Networked Economy. McGraw Hill, 2002.

[6] Efraim Turban, David King, Judy Lang. Introduction to Electronic Commerce, 2/E. Prentice Hall, 2008.

[7] Jeffrey H. Matsuura. An Overview of Leading Current Legal Issues Affecting. Information Technology Professionals. Information Systems Frontiers, 6:2, 153–160, 2004.

[8] Lei-da Chen, Gordon Skelton. Mobile commerce application development. CyberTech Publishing, 2005.

[9] Sandeep Krishnamurthy. 电子商务管理 课文和案例（英文影印版）. 北京：北京大学出版社，2003.

[10] 哈佛商学院案例精选集. B-to-C 电子商务（英文影印版）. 北京：中国人民大学出版社，2003.

[11] Nagmetov, B.A. Trust, as a main barrier in adoption to B2C E-Commerce. 3rd IEEE/IFIP International Conference in Central Asia on Internet, 2007. Page(s):1-5.

[12] www.amazon.com

[13] www.dell.com

[14] www.alibaba.com

[15] 刘玲，电子商务和电子支付体制，北京大学硕士学位论文，2001.

[16] 中国翻译网，http://www.chinatranslate.net/asp/index.asp

[17] 清华大学学报，http://www.tsinghua.edu.cn/docsn/qhdxxb/myweb/abstract.htm

[18] 才思论文网，http://Thesis.Xiloo.Com